The Dynamics of News

D1528395

This new and highly readable textbook by Richard M. Perloff introduces students to the complex world of contemporary news and its theoretical underpinnings, engaging with debates and ethical quandaries.

The book takes readers on a concept-guided tour of the contours, continuities, and changing features of news. It covers a huge breadth of topics including: the classic theories of what news should do, its colorful history in America and popular myths of news, the overarching forces involved in contemporary news gathering, critical economic determinants of news and social system influences, and innovative trends in the future of journalism. Drawing on scholarship in the fields of journalism studies and sociology of news, Perloff offers readers a critical, in-depth exploration of news filled with relevant examples from newspapers, newscasts, and social media.

Students of journalism, communication, sociology, politics, and related courses, as well as inquisitive scholars, will find this book's intellectual focus enriching, the writing and examples engaging, and the thoroughness of its search of the contemporary media scene invigorating. Boxes summarizing theory and key concepts help students to deepen their understanding of both what news is now and its future.

Richard M. Perloff, Professor of Communication, Political Science, and Psychology at Cleveland State University, is the author of well-regarded scholarly textbooks on political communication and persuasion. Perloff's articles on communication theories, the hostile media effect and third-person-based perceptions of news have appeared in *Communication Theory, Communication Research*, and *Mass Communication and Society*. He was the recipient of the University of Amsterdam School of Communication Research McQuail Award for the Best Article Advancing Communication Theory, 2012–2013. He is the recipient of Ohio journalism awards, including 2018 and 2019 Press Club of Cleveland, Ohio Excellence in Journalism Awards for Best in Ohio Essay Writing.

The Dynamics of News
Journalism in the 21st-Century Media Milieu

Richard M. Perloff

Routledge
Taylor & Francis Group

NEW YORK AND LONDON

First published 2020
by Routledge
52 Vanderbilt Avenue, New York, NY 10017

and by Routledge
2 Park Square, Milton Park, Abingdon, Oxon, OX14 4RN

Routledge is an imprint of the Taylor & Francis Group, an informa business

© 2020 Taylor & Francis

The right of Richard M. Perloff to be identified as author of this
work has been asserted by him in accordance with sections 77
and 78 of the Copyright, Designs and Patents Act 1988.

Library of Congress Cataloging-in-Publication Data
A catalog record for this title has been requested

ISBN: 978-0-815-37788-7 (hbk)
ISBN: 978-0-815-37789-4 (pbk)
ISBN: 978-1-351-23351-4 (ebk)

Typeset in Times New Roman
by Swales & Willis, Exeter, Devon, UK

Printed and bound by CPI Group (UK) Ltd, Croydon, CR0 4YY

Contents

Image Credits

Figures

1.1a Photo by Mario Tama/Getty Images
1.1b Photo by Jim Mone/AP/Shutterstock
1.1c Photo by F42PIX/Shutterstock.com
2.1 Figure courtesy of Pew Research Center: 'How News Happens', 2010
4.1 Image courtesy of Library of Congress (LC-DIG-pga-04906)
4.2 Photo by RHONA WISE/AFP/Getty Images
4.3 Photo by AP/Shutterstock
4.4 Photo by Hulton Archive/Getty Images
5.1 Image courtesy of Library of Congress (LC-DIG-ppmsca-02949)
5.2 Image courtesy of Library of Congress (LC-USZ62-15887)
5.3 Image courtesy of Library of Congress (LC-DIG-pga-02667)
5.4 Photo by Bettmann/Contributor via Getty Images
5.5 Photo by NY Daily News Archive via Getty Images
5.6 (1) Photo by Dimitri Iundt/Corbis/VCG via Getty Images
    (2) Photo by Evan Agostini/Liaison via Getty Images
6.1 Photo by Ilpo Musto/Shutterstock
6.2 Photo by Mostafa Alkharouf/Anadolu Agency/Getty Images
7.1 Copyright Taylor and Francis © 2009. From *Mediating the Message, 3rd Edition* by Pamela J. Shoemaker and Stephen D. Reese, p. 9
7.2 From *2014 Key Findings* report by Lars Willnat & David H. Weaver, 2015 © Lars Willnat. Used with permission
8.1 Copyright Taylor and Francis © 2005. From *News Around the World: Content, Practitioners, and the Public* by Pamela J. Shoemaker and Akiba A. Cohen, p. 9
9.1 CC BY 2.0 image courtesy of Ninian Reid on Flickr:/25034321@N05/33929564373
9.2 *Collapse of the US newspaper industry: Goodwill, leverage and bankruptcy* (© Sage Publications/John Soloski, 2013)

Table

Preface

As usual, you start with T.J.

The Declaration of Independence author – brilliant, eloquent, erudite, though racially prejudiced and incontrovertibly complex (Ellis, 1997) – articulated a guiding mantra for journalism when he famously said, "Were it left to me to decide whether we should have a government without newspapers or newspapers without a government, I should not hesitate a moment to prefer the latter." And while, with most things Jeffersonian, T.J. frequently contradicted the attitudes he espoused, castigating the press while in the Oval Office, his ringing words have served as inspiration for journalists for decades, perhaps centuries, as they have pursued truth against a multitude of odds.

In our own time, journalism is under siege, its time-honored gate-keeping role turned upside down by social media, its economic foundations torn asunder by technological developments, public confidence in its mission in a state of decline, and news credibility under constant attack by politicians the world over. And yet, like a house fortified by structural strengths, it blows this way and that, but remains standing, as conventional news, citizen journalism, and burgeoning online sites offer a wealth of information about the public world; people continue to hunger for news, reading, sharing, and arguing about it over the course of a day; and journalism adapts, fitfully, yet persistently, to the vicissitudes of an unpredictable present. And this is how it must be, for society needs news, an institution that is indispensable for democracy and the articulation, however fraught and imperfect, of truths that government needs to function effectively, and citizens require to be thoughtfully informed about the challenges of public life.

This book is about news and journalism in a milieu much different from any that have preceded it, and, like all previous eras, filled with parallels to the past. It endeavors to illuminate the workings of news, its contemporary contours, blurred boundaries and definitions, as well as epistemological issues in its factual underpinnings, myths about biased content, explanations of its varied determinants, and normative philosophies of what news should be. The book offers ample criticisms of news's many shortcomings, while appreciating foundational virtues that never cease to impress. As one who has worked in journalism, writes for newspapers, but, as a scholar, is committed to unpacking the powerful and articulating complex, intersectional truths, I have sought to write a textbook that displays a commitment to the journalistic mission, but ceaselessly exposes the multifaceted nature and quandaries of news in our contemporary milieu.

Drawing on the vast journalism and academic literature, as well as many journalistic accounts, I have tried to write a book that is both scholarly and readable, analytical, but engaging, a sourcebook for readers who want to understand, appreciate, and critique the bewildering world of news that greets us on paper, the airwaves, and on millions of mobile devices, where the most comprehensive of news stories can adjoin bogus accounts, and the most credible news sites coexist with goofy lists, pictures, and downloads that amuse and stupefy.

The Dynamics of News: Journalism in the 21st-Century Media Milieu is a book about both news and journalism, designed to help students bent on a career in journalism better apprehend the field which they are courageously entering. It is also intended to introduce students, faculty, and other readers to scholarship on journalism – what we know about news, from historical, sociological, political, and critical cultural vantage points. Like my other books, I draw on concepts and research because I believe you cannot understand communication phenomena without them. I enliven the scholarly discussions with a multitude of examples from news and popular culture, shedding light, harnessing humor, raising questions, applying a variety of concepts to today's journalistic domain, in the manner of the fox, who draws on many ideas, rather than the hedgehog who views life through just one coherent philosophical lens (Berlin, 1953).

If students read the book, and come away with new frameworks for apprehending news, as well as more critical knowledge of its shortcomings, gain insight into biases they harbored which they now view in a different light, and close the book, with new questions and perhaps just a little more appreciation for the indisputable importance journalism has for our troubled society, I will have succeeded, at least for a time, until new issues and discontents raise questions that demand attention from scholars, journalists, and critical thinkers alike.

References

Berlin, I. (1953). *The hedgehog and the fox: An essay on Tolstoy's view of history.* London: Weidenfeld & Nicolson.
Ellis, J.J. (1997). *American sphinx: The character of Thomas Jefferson.* New York: Knopf.

Acknowledgments

This is the section where you kindly express gratitude to people who have given of themselves to help you, as you wrote a book, from halting beginnings to clearheaded completion. Without the generous assistance of the staff at the Michael Schwartz Library at Cleveland State University, I would have never gained access to the many books on news. Thank you to Terri Greer, Nedra Haymon, Pat MacIntosh, Vern Morrison, Donna Stewart, and the ever-reliable Patrice Johnson-Brown. For his kind, patient help with my questions and requests, thank you to Dominic Tortelli, and in particular I want to thank Zach Lynn, for his dependable, knowledgeable, and humor-sprinkled library assistance.

Thank you, as always for her work on my books, to Sharon Muskin, whose technical expertise, aesthetic care, and conscientiousness nonpareil are immensely appreciated.

I am grateful to Erica Wetter for her wisdom about books and the writing process, truly an academic writer's editor who appreciates the process of crafting a book, and communicated this artfully to me throughout the book-writing period. Thanks also to Emma Sherriff in Oxford, for her ability to juggle so many aspects of this project thoughtfully and flexibly, as well as for the convivial conversations, and Christina Kowalski in New York, for her reliable, conscientious assistance. I also really appreciate the editorial acumen and meticulous care shown by copy editor Alice Stoakley.

Thanks also to the students I have jovially and dutifully worked with as faculty adviser to the Cleveland State University student newspaper, *The Cauldron*. Their dedication and appreciation of the values of journalism and a free press have emboldened and enriched my work. Thanks to KC Longley, Katie Hobbins, Regan Reeck, Beth Casteel, Adam Schabel, Kourtney Husnick, Anna Toth, Ashley Mott, and Mollee Ryan.

I also appreciate the encouragement from valued, learned administrative leaders at Cleveland State, notably William J. Dube and Robert A. Spademan, and Harlan M. Sands, Cleveland State's energetic president.

I also want to thank faculty colleagues in the Cleveland State School of Communication. Thanks to Gary Pettey, whose questions and insights many years back about systemic foundations of news, like hegemony, introduced me to engaging ideas I might never have probed. Thanks also to Anup Kumar, Rob Whitbred, Leo Jeffres, and Betty Clapp, along with Harlan Spector, for their suggestions and ideas.

Thank you to all the colleagues to whom I sent chapters, completely out of the blue, and who offered comments, encouragement or indirectly conveyed confidence to keep going. Thanks to Dan Berkowitz (particularly, for your early reinforcing comments), Sandrine Boudana, Carl Bybee, Matthew Carlson, Juliette De Maeyer, Shahira Fahmy, Robert Gutsche, Jr., Alfred Hermida, David Mindich, John Nerone, Steve Reese, Sue Robinson, David Ryfe, Adam Schiffer, Pam Shoemaker, Jane Singer, Nikki Usher, Tim Vos, Silvio Waisbord, David Weaver, Lars Willnat, and Barbie Zelizer. Thanks also to Melanie Faizer for her helpful review of a batch of my chapters during the winter months. I want to especially thank Linda Steiner for her encouragement, kindness, and thoughtful suggestions. Thanks are also extended to the anonymous reviewer of the book prospectus, who expressed such confidence in me and suggested that I not hold back on my values and passions about journalism.

Finally, my family: my perspicacious wife, Julie, son, Michael, with his legal acumen and passionate pursuit of justice, and Cathy, boundlessly committed to a career in the field that is the focus of this book; thanks for your support. And, last but not least, my mother; her endlessly skeptical questions about … everything (including, here, the bases by which reporters decide what is accurate and true) helped strengthen the book and fortified me, as the writer.

Richard M. Perloff
Cleveland

Part I
Foundations

1 Prologue

News in a Fragmented Age

A routine day in the verdant, storied city of Greensboro, North Carolina: Rufus Scales, 26, was driving his pickup truck, taking his younger brother, Devin, to a class in haircutting, doing the older brother thing, helping Devin learn the tools of the hairstyling trade. In a heartbeat, life changed, as the unmistakable shriek of a police siren pierced the air and the young men, both Black, stared at the blue light of a police car in their rear-view mirror. Two officers ambled out, pulling them over for minor violations that included expired license plates. What happened next was neither minor nor routine.

Unsure whether to leave the car, Rufus tried to keep his brother from opening the door when a Black officer shot Rufus with a Taser gun, stunning him, temporarily immobilizing him as a White officer lugged him across the road. By the time the incident ended, Rufus had a chipped tooth, a bloody upper lip that required stitches, and four traffic tickets, including assaulting a police officer. Traumatized by the encounter, which occurred back in May 2013, Devin now carries a small video camera and business card embossed with a toll-free phone number for legal assistance wherever he goes. Whenever he sees a police car, he turns away immediately. "Whenever one of them is near, I don't feel comfortable. I don't feel safe," he said.

So began a banner-headlined Sunday *New York Times* story, written in the wake of deaths of unarmed Blacks at the hands of police, deaths that stoked national controversy about police, prejudice, and crime prevention. The *Times* article, featured under the memorable headline, "The Disproportionate Risks of Driving While Black," was written in the classic style of contemporary journalism: dispassionate tone, source attributions, interviews with a variety of victims of police harassment, and comments from both sides in the controversy – police and civil rights leaders, with corroborative findings from both academic research and a *Times* analysis of thousands of traffic stops in Greensboro over a five-year period (LaFraniere & Lehren, 2015).

Combining powerful anecdotes with social-scientific research, reporters Sharon LaFraniere and Andrew W. Lehren came to a hard-hitting conclusion: Greensboro police officers pulled over African American drivers for traffic infractions at a rate that was disproportionate to their share of the city's driving population. They stopped Black drivers more than twice as frequently as their White counterparts, even though they consistently found drugs and guns significantly more often when the motorist was White.

The *Times* story attracted considerable national attention, befitting an investigative article in the nation's venerable elite newspaper. Intriguingly, in a sign-of-the-times development, the article recruited more than 1,000 thoughtful comments from *Times* readers; yet a video that younger brother Devin Scales posted on Facebook a year after the incident, which showed a White police officer cursing at him for no apparent reason while he walked down a residential street (later arresting him), recruiting not 1,000, but 10,000 likes.

More than a year later, another incident of police violence against African Americans occurred, this one in the Midwest, not the South, and it too captured national attention. It was documented not by reporters working for a mainstream media outlet, but by a young woman, in an electrifyingly tense, life-and-death situation, where her boyfriend was shot by a frightened young police officer.

The story, live-streamed on Facebook in July, 2016, began with the image of a Black woman, Diamond Reynolds, sitting in the passenger seat of a car, her anchor-woman-calm voice pleading with her boyfriend to "Stay with me," as she narrated a series of gripping and ultimately tragic events. Viewers watch as Diamond Reynolds speaks to her boyfriend, Philando Castile, collapsed on the driver's seat, blood oozing from a white T-shirt, a police officer aiming a gun through the car window, as Ms. Reynolds's 4-year-old daughter sits in the back seat of the car.

"Please, officer, don't tell me that you just did this to him," she pleads. "You shot four bullets into him, sir. He was just getting his license and registration, sir" (Bosman, 2016). According to Diamond's video, Castile, driving a white Oldsmobile near Minneapolis, was pulled over by police for a broken taillight, informed the officer he had a licensed gun in the car, reached to retrieve his identification, and the police officer fired the shots that killed Castile. Less than a day after the tragic incident, the video had been viewed more than 4 million times on Facebook. It was a powerful visual that related a compelling "story of race and law enforcement in America," playing out "a life-or-death interaction" in real time between a Black woman and a Latino police officer trying mightily to do an impossibly difficult job, but tragically executing his duties with excessive force – or so her video suggested (Poniewozik, 2016). A jury later acquitted the officer, concluding he had reason to fear for his life, although the video told a different story.

And then, a year later, the scourge of racial animus never ending in America, a group of White supremacists violently tangled with protesters in Charlottesville, Virginia in August, 2017, leaving one person dead at the hands of a deranged Supremacist car driver, as the nation wondered how a group of men could be so filled with hate to protest the city's decision to remove a Confederate statue painfully associated with the country's racist past. This time the story was not covered by a mainstream news organization or a pained citizen, but by a courageous reporter from Vice News, an online public affairs channel. The 22-minute video, "Charlottesville: Race and Terror" (which would capture more than 6 million YouTube views), dramatically recreated the chronology of events, beginning with an electrifying frisson of verbal violence, as young Supremacists, carrying placards and torchlights, marched through the University of Virginia inexplicably, but hatefully, chanting, "Jews will not replace us. Whose streets? Our streets! White lives matter."

The video cuts to White supremacist leader Christopher Cantwell, a bald, brawny, unapologetic tribal leader, greeting his troops, asking them where they travelled from to arrive at the rally, and moves to a one-on-one interview between Elle Reeve, a bespectacled young Vice reporter, and Cantwell. Reeve looks beyond exasperated as Cantwell delivers prejudiced epithets, but maintains her composure. The cameras roll as the Charlottesville protest unfolds, counter-protesters challenge the White supremacists, and a fight erupts. Clearly appalled by what she hears, Reeve lets her sources tell the story. Without filtering or amplifying with broader evidence, she shows, not tells, relating footage of interviews and action, climaxing with a Supremacist's car deliberately ramming into counter-protesters and the shocked reaction, the narrative eerily ending as Cantwell, brandishing multiple guns, proudly justifies the car violence against his rivals, calling them "a bunch of stupid animals," proclaiming his desire to build a White ethno-state, as the rapid drumming in the aural background provides a haunting conclusion to the news video.

In providing a heartrending education about the realities of race and police work in America, the media performed a service, illuminating both racial inequities and the challenges police face. Without coverage by media, broadly defined, news about the poisonous problem of racial strife, one of the oldest and most critical issues facing the nation, would go unreported, its import unknown to the public and its leaders. But the three stories – one in *The Times*, harnessing the detached canons of traditional journalism; the Vice story, told via an online news channel, dispassionately narrated, but with a clear political slant; and the third, a citizen's account, viscerally situated in the moment – emotional, immediate, dramatic, with no attempt to get beyond a personal tragedy – illustrate three very different story-telling techniques, differing in form, content, news-gathering strategies, verifiability of the evidence presented, and degree to which personal perspectives richly informed the story. The stories offer a spectacularly contemporary window into the nature of journalism in a time of dizzying change (see Figure 1.1).

On a broader level, underscoring a focus of this book, these media accounts are a continuing, vexing testament to American journalism's

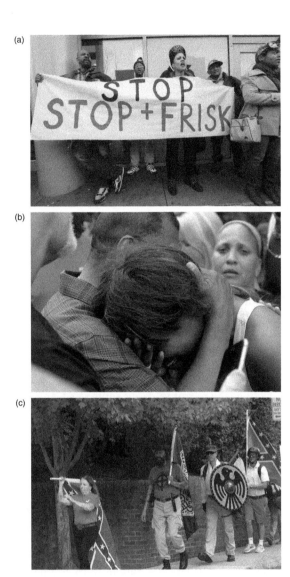

Figure 1.1 In a digital online age, the media describe the scourge of racial prejudice in dramatically different ways. Figure 1.1a depicts a protest against stop and frisk, the focus of a classically in-depth *New York Times* investigation of racial profiling in Greensboro, North Carolina. Figure 1.1b shows Diamond Reynolds, comforted by a local minister. Reynolds live-streamed on Facebook the violent, tragic story of how a Minneapolis officer, fearing for his life, fatally shot her boyfriend as he reached to retrieve his identification. Figure 1.1c depicts demonstrators wielding Confederate flags and the Nazi Party Eagle, the focus of an impassioned Vice News story on a violent Charlottesville, Virginia protest of the removal of a statue of Robert E. Lee. The three stories showcase the strikingly different ways that media narrate, verify, and portray stories about racial issues, underscoring the variegated, complex nature of contemporary news.

struggle to apprehend social problems, in this case the role played by race in America – a journey that has moved from sensationalized newspaper accounts of late 19th century lynchings that blithely assumed Blacks were guilty of heinous, frequently invented crimes (Mindich, 1998; Perloff, 2000; Stabile, 2006) to 1960-style path-breaking coverage that illuminated racial segregation in the South (Roberts & Klibanoff, 2006), through the non-stop, entertainment-glazed television focus on the O.J. Simpson trial in the 1990s that treated Simpson as an archetype, a symbol, and commodity for the expansion of cable news, and, finally, to the multifaceted journalism of today, with its impassioned stories of racial injustice, sometimes marred by insufficient journalistic empathy for marginalized perspectives in minority communities, as well as ethical tensions between reporters' traditional emphasis on detachment and a feeling on the part of communities of color that more active engagement is needed to establish trust (Robinson & Culver, 2019). Even as journalism becomes inseparable from the contemporary digital sphere, it continues to wrestle with time-honored cultural and structural issues in American society, underscoring the inseparability of news, society, power, and culture.

With these examples in mind, this chapter moves to introduce the broad contours of news, offering an overview to the book. The next section describes the overarching reasons why news is important to democratic society, ways news falls short, and the daunting political issues facing news during an era when it is in flux, maligned by political leaders and misunderstood by the public. To underline the importance of news, as well as its illustrious history, a boxed section offers a thumbnail sketch of continuities of news over the centuries that preceded the 21st.

Introducing the Issues

News plays an indispensable role in a democratic society. As the storied architect of the Bill of Rights, James Madison, emphasized, democracy cannot function properly if individuals are ill-informed about government.

"News matters," scholars Graham Meikle and Guy Redden (2011, p. 1) observed. Focusing on a contemporary value of news – public discourse – long associated with political philosopher Jürgen Habermas (1989) and communication scholar James W. Carey (1987), they note:

> It remains the main forum for discussion of issues of public importance. It offers an arena in which journalists and media firms, politicians, other high-status sources of information and audiences come together to inform, persuade, influence, endorse or reject one another in a collaborative process of making meaning from events.

News is important for other reasons. It monitors and describes the world in which we live, explains and interprets complex events, fosters empathy for those marginalized or afflicted by tragedies, and cultivates accountability of leaders to citizens by serving as an autonomous check of power, famously exemplified by newspaper exposés of the Pentagon Papers, Watergate, the Catholic Church sex abuse scandal, and the never-ending cases of powerful men from Hollywood to Congress to blue-collar automobile plants sexually exploiting women. At its best, a Columbia University Journalism School report noted:

> Journalism exposes corruption, draws attention to injustice, holds politicians and businesses accountable for their promises and duties. It informs citizens and consumers, helps organize public opinion, explains complex issues and clarifies essential disagreements.
>
> (Gajda, 2015, p. 226)

Those are the guiding ideals, but it doesn't always work this way. News outlets, particularly at the local level, frequently lack the resources necessary for first-rate investigative reporting, as a result of plummeting newspaper revenues (Hamilton, 2016). The glorious exposés cited above are invariably the exception, as journalists frequently prop up the powers-that-be, their stories cheerleading questionable foreign interventions and, on the local level, giving wholesale support to downtown development projects that rarely come close to fulfilling highfalutin promises (Berkowitz, 2007; Feldstein, 2007; Herman & Chomsky, 2002). Far from illuminating the public sector, news is consumed by the sexy, dramatic, and trivial aspects of politics – lascivious affairs, poll results, idle speculation about the political horse race, endless political celebrity gossip, as television reporters prioritize these stories over deeper coverage of issues that could engage the citizenry (Patterson, 1993). Too many stories, written with an eye to capturing attention on the ubiquitous Internet where so much of the public attention is focused, can take on the trappings of a much-discussed video on the online news site, Buzzfeed, famous for its listicles and cat videos gone viral (Tandoc, 2018).

In April, 2016, two BuzzFeed staffers wrapped a bunch of rubber bands around the center of a huge berry watermelon, causing it to explode. Close to a million people (almost twice the population of Wyoming) viewed the watermelon pop like a detonated balloon, and it attracted more than 10 million Facebook views over the ensuring days. In today's online environment, this was news! Really? asked columnist Jim Rutenberg (2016) in a widely-read article. Increasingly, he observed, social news media feeds feature "zany kitchen experiments, your friend's daughter's bat mitzvah; and that wild video of a train whipping through a ridiculously narrow alleyway in Thailand. If that's the future of news and information," he asked, "what's next for our democracy? President Kardashian?"

People now have endless choices, from the meticulously informative to the weird and deceptive, with the origins of messages sometimes difficult to determine. In an age when traditional journalism coexists with new media outlets of varied credibility, people must "navigate an impossibly chaotic ocean of information," scholar Silvio Waisbord (2013) notes (p. 221).

We live in a journalistically turbulent – and strange – time, a decentralized era of news, where many people get news over their phones, sometimes of unknown provenance and dubious credibility. News can be by shared by a friend via an algorithm that favors edgy, rather than socially significant, content or that emphasizes stories people enjoy, exposing them to stories of little public significance. Rather than receiving an entire newscast or the front page of a newspaper, they get articles in fragmented fashion, although with links that promise detailed knowledge, if individuals are motivated and able to pursue the information. There is an endless supply of information, offering instant updates, giving people an immediacy and breadth inconceivable in eras when established news organizations had total control over what people viewed, and when.

As social media sites have become major vehicles by which people receive news, and key factors in news outlets' profit-making calculus, the news game has changed. As Jill Abramson (2019), former editor of *The New York Times*, observed, discussing changes Facebook produced, news has become

> a game of presenting a version of the day's events that would electrify conversation on the social network … What made a story work was not its scope or substance; as BuzzFeed had all but empirically proven, it was the extent to which the content had the power to make readers *feel* something.
>
> (pp. 279–280)

There is also a new, darker side. Interspersed, interwoven, and inter-mingled with both BuzzFeed-style listicles and serious news analyses are a plethora of extremist, ideological news sites that claim to serve up news, when what they serve up is venom and partisan animus. News, which for most of the 20th century, was an easy commodity to define, is now a more complicated entity, no less important, but frequently blurred, fraught, contested, and even claimed as a marquee, a branding mechanism to build an ideological audience base.

A half-century ago, the American public trusted news. Not so today, surveys tell us. Confidence in journalism has declined dramatically over the years (Lee, 2018; Zelizer, 2017). A Gallup poll revealed that only 20 percent of Americans express a great deal of confidence in television news, placing it behind the criminal justice system and banks, institu-tions that don't inspire a great deal of confidence themselves (Saad, 2018). News is frequently doubted, mistrusted, and reflexively perceived as biased (Fenton, 2019; Jones & Ritter, 2018; Lewis, 2019; Mitchell et al., 2016). And it *is* biased, yet not in the ways people presume. Understanding the nature of news bias, the multifaceted, controversial nature of bias itself, and appreciating areas where news transcends bias to deeply inform the public are issues discussed throughout the book.

The most visible, grandiose accuser of news bias has been the president, Donald Trump, who condemned news in ways no other president has, castigating it hundreds of times as "fake," "fraudulent," and "garbage journalism," going so far as to call journalists "the enemy of the American people," following words up with action by banning a CNN reporter from the White House, an act with little modern precedent (Lee & Quealy, 2018; Shear, 2017; Baker & Peters, 2018, p. A12).

During his first year in office, Trump transmitted about 150 tweets that mentioned "fake news," charging credible news stories were false, typically using the "fake" appellation to derogate news stories he disliked, while making more than 8,700 false or misleading claims over the course of his term (Coll, 2017; Kristof, 2019; Qiu, 2017, 2018; Rutenberg, 2018). The Trump administration is not the first to lambast the news, although its denunciations have been blunter and more resonant with particular political groups than those of previous presidents. Yet its exhortations that mainstream news containing criticism of the White House is fake raises more serious concerns, suggesting to people that nothing is true, all is nihilistic, and news reports that speak truth to power cannot be trusted, inviting the inference that the only views to be trusted are those that come from the president.

Outside the U.S., autocrats in some of the world's most anti-democratic countries – Syria, Venezuela, China, Russia, Saudi Arabia, and Turkey – have castigated the press. They have followed or anticipated Trump's example, using the fake news moniker to attack dissidents or reporters, creating an alternative reality in which "everything was possible" and "nothing was true," as Hannah Arendt (1951) famously observed in a book on the origin of dictatorships. It is all part of a disturbing narrative with anti-democratic overtones that confuses people about the facts, shaking confidence in the capacity of the press to offer an independent check on power (Erlanger, 2017). When political leaders excoriate news in this way, contending that a verifiably factually based claim does not authentically exist, they gaslight political reality, undermining the role of social institutions, such as the media, whose democratic raison d'être is to provide an autonomous check on unbridled coercive power. Indeed, press freedom around the world has plummeted to its lowest point in 13 years in the wake of political threats to reporters in established democracies and crackdowns on news in authoritarian states (Abramowitz, 2017). Authorities' contempt for the press fits into a broader narrative of anti-journalism state violence regularly directed at dissidents, women, and minority reporters, which misunderstands (or fears) the values of an unabashedly free press (Waisbord, 2019).

Political leaders are not the only ones who deliberately misunderstand or simply fail to appreciate the purposes of news. The American public lacks basic understanding. Half do not know what an op ed contribution to the editorial page is. Nearly 1 in 3 do not know the difference between an editorial and a news story, and more than 40 percent do not understand the critical term, "attribution," referring to how reporters explain information obtained from sources, the lifeblood of news (Young, 2018). If people don't appreciate the foundations of news, how can they trust reports that challenge hallowed institutions?

Is news in trouble, in jeopardy – or worse, passé, a victim of political manipulation and increasing public skepticism about once-venerated institutions? During a time when your grandmother's post may adjoin *The New York Times* and people trust readers' frequently opinionated comments more than news stories (von Sikorski & Hänelt, 2016), can a journalism of factual verification survive? Given relentless economic forces, from heartless conglomerate ownership of newspapers to competition from online outlets that has trivialized the quality of news (see BuzzFeed's balloon video), can meaningful journalism endure for more than a decade? Or is this scholarly cynicism misplaced? Viewing the cornucopia of choices more optimistically, are new technologies exerting salutary influences, challenging mainstream journalism, exposing people to more voices that can expand the bandwidth of journalism, enlarging the chorus that partakes in public discourse? Does the future herald democratic changes or darker forces? We don't know all the answers to these questions, but they are bookends that frame contemporary discussion of the dynamics of news.

Shoved by economic forces, pushed by technological changes that undermine its traditional authority as information-providers, and undercut by political leaders on both sides of the spectrum, journalism – its legitimacy, credibility, and raison d'être – is under siege (Bogaerts & Carpentier, 2013; Deuze, 2007; Hanitzsch, 2013). What is happening? What is the essence of journalism today? Is news serving its basic functions, and exactly what are these philosophical tasks? With all the centrifugal forces whipsawing against it, can news survive?

This book addresses these issues, seeking to unpack, understand, and – yes – appreciate news. In an era when the very definitions of news and journalism are up for grabs, the time-honored concept of facts is open to question, and media are manipulated by an ever-diverse group of political actors, it is important to comprehend the nature of news. Calling on diverse academic disciplines, including journalism, sociology, and political science, this book places news under a scholarly microscope (and, when looking at broader contours, "macroscope") in an effort to illuminate its features and performance. It examines the contemporary features of news, positive and negative, functional and dysfunctional, tracing and explaining changes in news, issues that date back to antiquity (see Box 1.1).

By introducing you to major "analytic perspectives and belief systems," I hope, as the venerable scholar Dan Berkowitz (2011) notes, to help you generate "new insights about the cultural meanings of news" (p. xxii). My goal is to help you look at news through a fresher, sharper set of eyes, understanding its limits, appreciating forces impinging on its content, comprehending its complexity, and apprehending its outsized capacity to usher in sweeping social change. Even as journalism bends and contorts to accommodate technological and economic changes that are retrofitting society at a dizzying pace, it remains important, even noble, in its effort to ferret out a first draft of truth, emphasizing at its best, in conventional and citizen journalistic formats, verifiable evidence, a check on abuses of power, a place for debate about ideas, an arena showcasing new ways to apprehend life.

Box 1.1 What's Old About News?

Like so many features of Western civilization, news began with the Greeks – the ancient Greeks of Athens, circa 490 B.C. Legend has it that after Athenians repelled the Persian invasion of their city-state, an intrepid reporter (dubbed a messenger in those days) ran from Marathon (not the race, but the city of yore) to Athens to spread the news. Soon after he told his gleeful fellow citizens, he fell dead from exhaustion. (But let the record show that he was the first to break the story.)

Then came Rome, where Julius Caesar reportedly ordered public posts (the non-digital kind, of course) of daily occurrences in Rome, with postings prominently describing the bloody power struggles that followed Caesar's assassination. More than two centuries later, around the 3rd century, in China, following the invention of paper, the Han dynasty developed an elaborate system of written news (at least as they viewed news back then). The Sung dynasty exploited the elite news outlets some 700 years later, censoring newssheets produced by people outside government. The torturous relations between government and the press were now set in motion. Indeed, the earliest news media systems, launched in China and Korea, were developed to serve elite authorities (Nerone, 2015).

As Mitchell Stephens (2007) notes, in his authoritative account of news history, there are endless examples of news, broadly defined, chronicling events formal, celebrated, and prosaic, that parade across human history. A court poet traveled with the English army in 1352 during a battle of the Hundred Years War (we would call him an embedded reporter today), producing a handwritten description in verse of the English victory. In 1470, the oldest known news-oriented publication, printed on a letter press machine in Italy, described events at a sports tournament, an early example of the celebrated genre we now call sports news.

Moving ahead to the 17th century, an expansive century for news, German newsbooks appeared in 1609. They were hailed as the first newspapers because they were published regularly, had a variety of articles in each issue, and were intended for a broad audience, not just the powerful (as so many of the early news outlets had been), in this way initiating the long, fraught connection between the public and the press.

Soon after the German papers appeared, the first English and French newspapers were published, with one English paper containing the wordy, but informative, name, "The continuation of the weekly newes." News organs focused on lurid events – murders, the execution of a witch, and drowning of drunks in an English river – presaging the journalistic preoccupation with sensationalism. In France, a French gazette reported the trial of Galileo with a pro-Establishment, anti-Galileo bias, calling his ideas "absurd and false" (Stephens, 2007, p. xv). It would not be the last time that news outlets, with their preoccupation with the powers-that-be, got things wrong – but, say this for the new newspapers: their printing presses were rolling.

The rollicking news beat throbbed on in the early 1700s. A leaflet printed by London coffeehouse owners accused newspaper publishers of paying people to snoop around to snag an interview, a forerunner of ethical conundrums to come. In the United States, England's unruly colony, the press, to use the print term that predates news media, played an instrumental role in the American Revolution. Many (though by no means all) colonial scribes penned stories designed more to foment revolution than offer an unbiased view of the early battles in Boston (see Chapter 5). With this auspicious beginning, the press (a term probably derived from the printing press) became a fixture in America, an institution that would shape the definition of problems, relationships between politicians and the electorate, and the illumination of social ills, transforming politics. However, news, as we think of it today in form, content, and economic function, did not emerge until the penny press of the 1830s, and its demeanor and fabric would change over the many decades that followed (Rantanen, 2009; Schudson, 1978; Vos, 2015). (Interestingly, Stephens, in his 2014 book, observes that the term "journalism" was first used to describe newspaper work during this period too. Its meaning changed from "journal-keeping" to "the intercommunication of opinion and intelligence," with "intelligence" a stand-in for news, presaging an intellectual search for facts, a fraught, complex term that would evolve over time as well [p. 31].)

Yet, for all the changes in news and journalism over the years, there are also striking continuities, notably our yearning, hankering, indeed craving for news. Egged on by printed news sheets and the voracious desire to appreciate the world outside their heads – famously dubbed FOMO today – people have always hungered for the latest information – gossip? – about social events. A 16th-century English newsbook reporting on an English military venture declared that its goal was to unabashedly satisfy "the thursty desyer that all our kynde hath to know"; even with those archaic Old English spellings, we feel a kinship with voracious readers of yore.

Convinced that their era was characterized by an unquenchable "thirst after news," as English writer Joseph Addison called it, a 1712 newspaper described "the furious itch of novelty" that afflicted shopkeepers, spending days in coffeehouses to catch the latest juicy news tidbits, while their wives and children languished at home, waiting for their news-obsessed providers to bring home their daily ration of bread (Stephens, 2007, p. 7). The obsession with novelty did not just afflict residents of Western nations. Two centuries later, an anthropologist reported that when the Polynesian residents of the Pacific island of Tikopia met in a village, they would aggressively interview one another to learn what each had recently seen and heard in their small villages. The anthropologist, Raymond Firth, walked from his house in a Tikopian village to a religious temple, and every day the chief of the temple would ask him, "Any news?" (Stephens, 2007, p. 9).

In a city that could not be more different from the villages of Tikopia, the same pattern emerged. In New York, the nation's media capital, newspapers went on strike in 1945, providing early media sociologists with an opportunity to study New Yorkers' reactions. These cosmopolitan city dwellers, no less than their Polynesian counterparts, confessed a feverish thirst for news. Bereft of their newspapers, one lamented feeling "like a fish out of water"; another New Yorker felt "awfully lost," while still another said, "I am suffering! Seriously! I could not sleep. I missed it so" (Berelson, 1949, pp. 125–126). Not so different, right, from how you or your friends might feel after losing your cellphone, finding yourself instantly adrift, isolated, unable to keep in touch with your News Feed, latest tweets, urgent updates, national news, and swirling messages about the world on Facebook and Twitter.

"It is difficult, if not impossible," Stephens (2007) notes,

> to find a society that does not exchange news and that does not build into its rituals and customs means for facilitating that exchange. Indeed, there are many societies in which that exchange seems to consume much of their members' time and attention.
>
> (p. 8)

News has been such a staple of societies that scholars have suggested it performs a basic evolutionary function, helping humans adapt to the social environment. Those who are most adept at appraising their social environment, their knowledge facilitated by news, may be most likely to fend off physical and psychological predators, perhaps increasing their ability to survive and reproduce (Shoemaker & Cohen, 2006). That's surely a time-tested testament to the importance of news!

Roadmap

Throughout this book, we will examine themes in the scholarly study of news – the varied determinants of news; the ways news is shaped by the larger society, yet has served as an agent of change; how news fits into the networked digital sphere, as well as normative perspectives that help us evaluate the multitude of changes in contemporary journalism. The chapters that follow call on the wealth of scholarly perspectives that examine the dynamics of news: journalistic, historical, sociological, philosophical, and cultural (Zelizer, 2009). They combine research in journalism studies, a field within the broader communication discipline (Carlson et al., 2018; Peters & Carlson, 2019), scholarship in other social science disciplines, and the cornucopia of analyses, features and investigative news stories that are regularly published in burgeoning, if frequently controversial, online news outlets.

The first section of the book, initiated by this chapter, sets the stage, introducing issues that course through the text. Chapter 2 discusses the main characteristics of today's news and their implications. The third chapter defines key terms – news and journalism – delineating their essential aspects. Chapter 4, adopting a philosophical approach, presents major theories of what news should be, examining their implications, good, bad, and a combination of the two, for the digital informational sphere. Chapter 5 presents a concept-focused overview of the history of news, offering a bridge from the journalistic past to present, exploring continuities and contrasts.

Part 2 examines what makes news tick – its determinants and implications for democratic society. Chapter 6 inaugurates the section, debunking a popular misconception of news and discussing the complex, messy, ever-controversial area of facts. Chapter 7, introducing Pamela J. Shoemaker and Stephen D. Reese's (2014) landmark gatekeeping model, initiates a rich discussion of news determinants, examining individual factors, and explaining and debunking the oh-so-popular (but oh-so-oversimplified) myth of liberal news bias. Chapter 8 focuses on the critical facets of news values; the central role that everyday journalistic routines, adapted to conventional and social media, play in news; and the key influences of sources ("who says it") on news, with their implications for the exercise of power.

Chapter 9 turns to the influences of larger organizational and economic factors, delving into news organizational biases, the role of economic forces, why news organizations are struggling financially, and consequences for local news. Chapter 10 examines the larger social system, focusing on the controversial roles played by ideology in news, whether news props up the status quo or serves as an agent of change, and how it all works in an era of WikiLeaks, exposés of global surveillance, and #MeToo. In many ways this is a key chapter of the book because it examines the role journalism plays in the larger social system and confronts head-on the question of whether news props up the powers that be or acts as an influence of change. Chapter 11, an epilogue, takes stock, noting continuities and changes, and providing a hard-edge, optimistic perspective on the future course of journalism in the 21st century.

The book's focus is American news. This is not the only national context in which news is produced – far from it, in a global time – but it allows for an in-depth, rather than superficial, account of determinants of news. However, I do call on examples from news in other countries, as well as academic research on journalism penned by scholars from across the world.

Conclusions

The chapter began with telling examples of news of the time-honored scourge of race in America. I described three very different examples of how racial issues are covered, showcasing how they highlight the changing mien of journalism in a bedazzling online age.

News, perhaps all the more today, plays an indispensable role in a democratic society. As democratic theorists have long emphasized, news ideally ensures the citizenry is properly informed, affirms the centrality of free speech, provides a forum for discussion of public issues, and, through the power of investigative journalism, illuminates the problems that afflict us.

A constancy of human society, news is nearly as old as civilization itself, dating back to the Greeks, Julius Caesar's public postings in Rome, and China's Han Dynasty in the 3rd century B.C., following the invention of paper. Over the tumultuous centuries, the news beat throbbed on, as news publications, and later full-fledged newspapers, emerged, chronicling events from sports to wars, inflaming authorities, and satisfying a quintessentially human thirst for the latest stirring, spectacular summary of occurrences in one's own corner of the sky. Of course, news changed dramatically in form, content, functions, economics, and impact over the centuries, morphing, little by little, beginning in the 19th century, into the dramatic narrative style that characterizes conventional news today.

We are in the throes of a transformative period today, as journalism struggles with existential questions that strike at the heart of its mission. What forces are whipsawing journalism in the tumultuous era of online news? How have they changed news and what implications do they foretell? The next chapter focuses on these questions, shedding light on how an ancient cultural form, news, adapts, withers, and transforms itself in ways both impressive and disturbing.

References

Abramowitz, M.J. (2017). Hobbling a champion of global press freedom. *Freedom of the press 2017: Press freedom's dark horizon*. Freedom House. Online: https://freedomhouse.org/report/freedom-press/freedom-press-2017. (Accessed: November 7, 2018).

Abramson, J. (2019). *Merchants of truth: The business of news and the fight for facts*. New York: Simon & Schuster.

Arendt, H. (1951). *The origins of totalitarianism*. New York: Harcourt, Brace.

Baker, P., & Peters, J.W. (2018, October 26). Call for unity quickly fades into acrimony. *The New York Times*, A1, A12.

Berelson, B. (1949). What "missing the newspaper" means. In P.F. Lazarasfeld & F.N. Stanton (Eds.), *Communications research, 1948–1949* (pp. 111–129). New York: Harper.

Berkowitz, D. (2007). Professional views, community news: Investigative reporting in small US dailies. *Journalism, 8*, 551–558.

Berkowitz, D. (2011). Introduction: From sociological roots to cultural perspectives. In D.A. Berkowitz (Ed.), *Cultural meanings of news: A text-reader* (pp. xi–xxii). Thousand Oaks, CA: Sage.

Bogaerts, J., & Carpentier, N. (2013). The postmodern challenge to journalism: Strategies for constructing a trustworthy identity. In C. Peters & M. Broersma (Eds.), *Rethinking journalism: Trust and participation in a transformed news landscape* (pp. 60–71). New York: Routledge.

Bosman, J. (2016, July 7). After poised live-streaming, tears and fury find Diamond Reynolds. *The New York Times*. Online: http://www.nytimes.com/

2016/07/08/us/after-poised-live-streaming-tears-and-fury-find-diamond-rey nolds.html. (Accessed: February 16, 2019).

Carey, J.W. (1987). The press and public discourse. *Center Magazine, 20* (2), 4–32.

Carlson, M., Robinson, S., Lewis, S.C., & Berkowitz, D.A. (2018). Journalism studies and its core commitments: The making of a communication field. *Journal of Communication, 68*, 6–25.

Coll, S. (2017, December 11) Faking it. *The New Yorker*, 21–22.

Deuze, M. (2007). *Media work*. Cambridge, UK: Polity Press.

Erlanger, S. (2017, December 13). Globe's autocrats echo Trump's "fake news" cry. *The New York Times*, A1, A12.

Feldstein, M. (2007). Dummies and ventriloquists: Models of how sources set the Investigative agenda. *Journalism, 8*, 499–509.

Fenton, N. (2019). (Dis)trust. *Journalism, 20*, 36–39.

Gajda, A. (2015). *The First Amendment bubble: How privacy and paparazzi threaten a free press*. Cambridge, MA: Harvard University Press.

Habermas, J. (1989). *The structural transformation of the public sphere: An inquiry into a category of bourgeois society*. Cambridge, MA: The MIT Press.

Hamilton, J.T. (2016). *Democracy's detectives: The economics of investigative journalism*. Cambridge, MA: Harvard University Press.

Hanitzsch, T. (2013). Journalism participative media and trust in a comparative context. In C. Peters & M. Broersma (Eds.), *Rethinking journalism: Trust and participation in a transformed news landscape* (pp. 200–209). New York: Routledge.

Herman, E.S., & Chomsky, N. (2002). *Manufacturing consent: The political economy of the mass media*. New York: Pantheon.

Jones, J.M., & Ritter, Z. (2018, January 17). Americans see more news bias; most can't name neutral source. Online: http://news.gallup.com/poll/225755/ameri cans-news-bias-name-neutral-source. (Accessed: May 23, 2018).

Kristof, N. (2019, February 28). "A racist … a con man … a cheat." *The New York Times*, A27.

LaFraniere, S., & Lehren, A.W. (2015, October 28). The disproportionate risk of driving while Black. *The New York Times*, 1, 18, 19.

Lee, J.C., & Quealy, K. (2018, January 30). All the people, places and things Donald Trump has insulted on Twitter since being elected president of the United States. *The New York Times*, A14–115.

Lee, T.-T. (2018). Virtual theme collection: "Trust and credibility in news media". *Journalism & Mass Communication Quarterly, 95*, 23–27.

Lewis, S.C. (2019). Lack of trust in the news media, institutional weakness, and relational journalism as a potential way forward. *Journalism, 20*, 44–47.

Meikle, G., & Redden, G. (2011). Introduction: transformation and continuity. In G. Meikle & G. Redden (Eds.), *News online: Transformations and continuities* (pp. 1–19). New York: Palgrave Macmillan.

Mindich, D.T.Z. (1998). *Just the facts: How "objectivity" came to define American journalism*. New York: New York University Press.

Mitchell, A., Shearer, E., Gottfried, J., & Barthel, M. (2016, July 7). *The modern news consumer: News attitudes and practices in the digital era*. Pew Research Center (Journalism & Media). Online: www.journalism.org/2016/07/07/the-modern-news-consumer/. (Accessed: February 18, 2019).

Nerone, J.C. (2015). *The media and public life: A history*. Malden, MA: Polity Press.

Patterson, T.E. (1993). *Out of order*. New York: Knopf.

Perloff, R.M. (2000). The press and lynchings of African Americans. *Journal of Black Studies, 30*, 315–330.

Peters, C., & Carlson, M. (2019). Conceptualizing change in journalism studies: Why change at all? *Journalism, 20*, 637-641.

Poniewozik, J. (2016, July 7). A killing. A pointed gun. And two Black lives, witnessing. *The New York Times*. Online: www.nytimes.com/2016/07/08/us/phi lando-castile-facebook-police-shooting-minnesota.html?_r=0. (Accessed: June 1, 2017).

Qiu, L. (2017, December 30). Much that wasn't true in a 30-minute interview. *The New York Times*, A16.

Qiu, L. (2018, December 31). Deciphering the patterns in Trump's lies. *The New York Times*, A14.

Rantanen, T. (2009). *When news was new*. Malden, MA: Wiley-Blackwell.

Roberts, G., & Klibanoff, H. (2006). *The race beat: The press, the civil rights struggle, and the awakening of a nation*. New York: Knopf.

Robinson, S., & Culver, K.B. (2019). When White reporters cover race: News media, objectivity and community (dis)trust. *Journalism, 20*, 375–391.

Rutenberg, J. (2016, April 17). For news outlets squeezed from the middle, it's bend or bust. *The New York Times*. Online: www.nytimes.com/2016/04/18/business/ media/for-news-outlets-squeezed-from-the-middle-its-bend-or-bust.html. (Accessed: June 3, 2017).

Rutenberg, J. (2018, October 29). Chipping away at the "enemy". *The New York Times*, B1, B4.

Saad, L. (2018, June 28). Military, small business, police still stir most confidence. *Gallup*. Online: https://news.gallup.com/poll/236243/military-small-business-police. (Accessed: September 23, 2018).

Schudson, M. (1978). *Discovering the news: A social history of American newspapers*. New York: Basic Books.

Shear, M.D. (2017, July 2). Trump tweet attacks states' refusal to give data to voter fraud panel. *The New York Times*, 18.

Shoemaker, P.J., & Cohen, A.A. (2006). *News around the world: Content, practitioners and the public*. New York: Routledge.

Shoemaker, P.J., & Reese, S.D. (2014). *Mediating the message in the 21st century: A media sociology perspective* (3rd ed). New York: Routledge.

Stabile, C.A. (2006). *White victims, Black villains: Gender, race and crime news in US culture*. New York: Routledge.

Stephens, M. (2007). *A history of news* (3rd ed.). New York: Oxford University Press.

Stephens, M. (2014). *Beyond news: The future of journalism*. New York: Columbia University Press.

Tandoc, Jr., E.C. (2018). Five ways BuzzFeed is preserving (or transforming) the journalistic field. *Journalism, 19*, 200–216.

von Sikorski, C., & Hänelt, M. (2016). Scandal 2.0: How valenced reader comments affect recipients' perception of scandalized individuals and the journalistic quality of online news. *Journalism & Mass Communication Quarterly, 93*, 551–571.

Vos, T.P. (2015). Revisiting gatekeeping theory during a time of transition. In T. P. Vos & F. Heinderyckx (Eds.), *Gatekeeping in transition* (pp. 3–24). New York: Routledge.

Waisbord, S. (2013). *Rethinking professionalism: Journalism and news in global perspective.* Cambridge, UK: Polity Press.

Waisbord, S. (2019). The vulnerabilities of journalism. *Journalism, 20*, 210–213.

Young, E. (2018, June). Americans and the news media: What they do – and don't – understand about each other. *The Media Insight Project.* Online: mediainsight.org/PDFs/Journalism 2018/Americans_News_Media__Report__2018. (Accessed: December 6, 2018).

Zelizer, B. (2009). Journalism and the academy. In K. Wahl-Jorgensen & T. Hanitzsch (Eds.), *The handbook of journalism studies* (pp. 29–41). Thousand Oaks, CA: Sage.

Zelizer, B. (2017). *What journalism could be.* Cambridge, UK: Polity Press.

2 News and Journalism in the 21st-Century Milieu

Once upon a time, newspapers, radio, and television delivered the news. People became accustomed to getting a newspaper on their doorstep, savoring "the thrill of the first hit of newsprint in the morning, with its slightly acrid odor and its ironclad association with the first cup of coffee" (Sante, 2019, p. 2). Readers knew that the most important stories were on page 1 and gleaned from the size of the headline which ones were most significant. Features had italicized headlines, and stories below the fold were less consequential.

Radio broadcasts, then 15-minute television newscasts, and later half-hour TV newscasts attracted huge, devoted audiences, as people huddled next to their radio set, and later stretched out on a living room couch to watch the latest news of the world, dismal and grim as it frequently was. Radio and TV news placed their most important items first, delivering them with urgency. Network television news interspersed the serious with the frivolous and heartrending, closing with a sober, frequently self-important sign-off, typified by CBS anchor Walter Cronkite's "And that's the way it is."

These quaint days of legacy news preeminence are long over. The online world has knocked journalism off its pedestal, undercutting its authority as informational gatekeeper, in the process creating new platforms and diverse pathways to truth, as well as searing falsehoods. News still matters, a centerpiece of democratic society, but is different today. But how? What characterizes news today? What are its main features, as well as core conundrums? This chapter examines these questions, focusing on four characteristics of contemporary news that have emerged as a result of transformative technological and economic changes of recent years (see Table 2.1).

Journalism and News in a Dazzlingly Digital Era

1. **The contemporary news architecture is multifaceted and multitudinous, characterized by instantaneity and depth, but also fragmented, filled with information of questionable veracity**

Table 2.1 Four Characteristics of Contemporary News

Four Characteristics of Contemporary News
1. News architecture is multifaceted, non-linear, fragmented, a study in contrasts, from incredible informational depth to searing falsehoods.
2. Conventional news, still important, no longer is the preeminent gatekeeper. It is enmeshed in a networked online sphere, surrounded and sometimes overwhelmed by disparate social media platforms, which have changed the way news is received and processed.
3. Citizen journalism has broadened journalism, raising new issues, bringing new voices into the conversation.
4. News, once easy to categorize, is complex and nuanced, as journalistic categories bend, blend, and blur.

Changes in the Form of News

Nineteen-sixties-style news, with its banner headlines shouted out by news vendors on city streets and conveyed with almighty importance by imperturbable television anchors, may have seemed veridical, a "high-modern" reflection of reality (Hallin, 1994). But it was far from objective, steeped, as it was, in mid-20th-century journalistic routines and subtle ideological biases. Yet it had a certain linear order, coherent sense of place, and clearly-demarcated agenda, with TV viewers attributing more importance to lead stories than those appearing later in the newscast (Iyengar & Kinder, 1987). The form and content of contemporary news today is jarringly different from these decades of yore (Barnhurst & Nerone, 2001). There can be a seemingly endless number of stories to click on, parading down a phone, with no particular rhyme or reason or appealing aesthetic architecture. Stories or pictures can appear one after the other, with news gathered by very different platforms that vary in their approaches to news and journalistic integrity.

Importantly, the stories are not necessarily viewed in the same modality they were prepared on. In the old days, stories dug up by reporters from *The New York Times* or your local newspaper appeared on the pages of *The Times* or your home-town daily. Similarly, CBS investigative programs that its legendary reporters uncovered appeared exclusively on CBS News. Nowadays, you might get updates from *The Times* on your phone, or watch breaking CBS or CNN news on Twitter. The common channel that carries news (of varying quality and sometimes ideological complexions) is the Internet or social media, and the mode of reception (the mobile phone) is the same, an equalizer of sorts that compresses stories into the same electronic and experiential space. In the past, an individual's relationship was with the news outlet that reported the story. Nowadays, in varying degrees, the reader's or viewer's connection with the news outlet that did the reporting is severed, as the relationship is with the social network that distributed the story (Hermida, 2016), raising journalistic, economic, and relational issues.

These changes in news reception have been gradual, but they are staggering. Two-thirds of American adults receive their news at least occasionally on social media sites, and 93 percent of American adults obtain some news online (Digital News Fact Sheet, 2018; Matsa & Shearer, 2018). Facebook is particularly popular, with many Americans obtaining news from recommendations via online friends (Grieco, 2017; Hermida, 2012).

When people hear this, they sometimes infer that conventional, mainstream, or legacy news, as it is called, is dead, supplanted by online and social media. But this is a misconception. Even today, half of Americans often get their news from television, about a fourth from radio, and close to a fifth from print newspapers (Gottfried & Shearer, 2017). Television remains Americans' preferred platform for receiving news (Mitchell, 2018). What's more, those who get news from social media aren't reading stories written by reporters who work for Mark Zuckerberg at Facebook, Jack Dorsey at Twitter, or Sundar Pichai, CEO of Google. The social media platforms that disseminate the news are not the ones who gather and report it. People who receive news updates on Facebook or Twitter frequently read stories gathered by journalists at conventional, mainstream news organizations that are disseminated by Facebook and Twitter. News aggregation services like Google and Yahoo News select and organize articles from mainstream news outlets, based on somewhat abstruse formulas, sometimes displaying them in long lists of headlines (Choi & Kim, 2017; Wakabayashi, 2017). As Figure 2.1 shows, the news content that you see on your phone has been gathered and produced by mainstream news outlets. However, the decisions on what and how to display it are made by online platforms, typically by algorithms, a procedure discussed later in the chapter.

It is frequently assumed that news that appears on mobile devices is gathered by social media networks or digital platforms. A study of a week's worth of major news in Baltimore showed that it is typically gathered by conventional news organizations, chiefly print, attesting to newspaper reporters' continued role in reporting and writing news. What has changed is how news is distributed, monetized, and experienced, which has important consequences for journalism (see How News Happens, 2010).

These changes in distribution significantly affected news outlets. As the Internet and then social media became a major modality that delivered news, the economics and experience of news changed. Young people, attuned to online information, deserted conventional news platforms for the more edgy and interactive Internet. News outlets, chiefly newspapers, once the recipients of lucrative advertising accounts, found themselves out of the loop, as Google, Facebook, Twitter, and other platforms became the middlemen that interceded between consumers

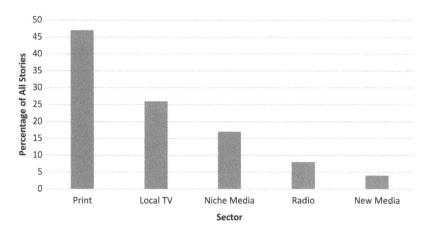

Figure 2.1 Where news comes from

and news outlets. Classified advertising, then display ads increasingly migrated to the Internet, decimating the economic model that financed newspapers. This shrunk the newspaper market, reduced the number of newspapers, and produced huge layoffs, diminishing the quantity and quality of news. In so doing, it reduced the breadth of political knowledge that could be acquired by print readers, undercutting journalism's ability to monitor the political environment and hold leaders' feet to the fire, particularly on the local level where many print newspapers have gone out of business.

The effects have been experiential, as well as well as existential. For years and decades, even centuries, the newspaper literally bundled different sections together at a printing plant. However, as Carr (2008) notes:

> When a newspaper moves online, the bundle falls apart. Readers don't flip through a mix of stories, advertisements, and other bits of content. They go directly to a particular story that interests them, often ignoring everything else. In many cases, they bypass the newspaper's "front page" altogether, using search engines, feed readers, or headline aggregators like Google News, Digg, and Daylife to leap directly to an individual story. They may not even be aware of which newspaper's site they've arrived at. Each story becomes a separate product standing naked in the marketplace. It lives or dies on its own economic merits.
>
> (pp. 153–154)

Consider the case of sports news. *The Athletic*, a sports website and app, features up-to-date coverage of local sports in at least 15 cities (Draper,

2017). *The Bleacher Report* app offers the latest sports news, embedded videos of game-changing moments, trending stories, and lots of comments. Sports fanatics no longer have to buy the print bundle or view the newspaper website to read about their favorite teams. They just look for stories that interest them and click. The old bundlers no longer structure the way people search for news; instead, people look for individual stories themselves, curating search engines and social media (Pearson & Kosicki, 2017).

You could even say, in a broader sense, that Google, Facebook and Amazon have become the bundlers of news, packaging a staggering diversity of media content they do not themselves generate, creating a new architecture from these diverse constituents (Foer, 2017; Herrman, 2017). While old-time newspaper reporters bemoan the changes, younger consumers appreciate the benefits. Online formats have virtues, offering readers a wealth of information that surpasses what they could get on the front and then the jump page, where the story was briefly continued, or in a 2-minute segment on the evening news. Articles can be longer and thoughtful, with links to other reports, amplified by interactive storytelling.

People have many more choices than they did in decades past (Ryfe, 2012a). Readers and viewers now select stories, even voting on Reddit as to which posts should appear on the website's front page. It is, to some degree, a transfer of agenda-setting from big media to individuals, one that empowers ordinary people, an empowerment long overdue. However, the reduction of journalistic gatekeeping power, as discussed in the next section, can put people at the mercy of the Wild, Wild Web. Users may believe information that appears on fake or extremist news sites that are dressed up to seem credible, in this way spreading false information. Nearly a fourth of Americans trust Info-Wars, a conspiracy site that peddles false information. Just 12 percent more trust Politico, a highly reputable news site (Benton, 2018).

News is thus part of what is popularly called the **networked public sphere**, an ecosystem of "multidirectional connections" and interconnected platforms that expand the range of participatory discourse (Benkler, 2006, p. 212). There are multiple delivers of information, spanning mainstream news outlets in the U.S., bloggers in Egypt, and citizen journalists in South Korea that all partake in a networked global space. This wide-open domain exposes people to news, a multitude of citizen voices, connections, real and perceived, to the powers that be, and a host of ideologically passionate websites (Russell, 2016). In the new geographic space of journalism, the contemporary "interactive sphere" of news, conventional news has lost its place at the top of the pyramid (Heinrich, 2011). As media scholar Silvio Waisbord (2017) pointedly observes:

Journalism is no longer the pre-eminent, all-dominant purveyor of news and information, sitting atop news systems as it has for the past two centuries. It now competes with other forces – from citizens to organizations routinely engaged in producing and disseminating news and information. Its traditional wares are no longer the exclusive property of one single institution. News, opinions, data, information, headlines, updates and conversation are everywhere. Journalism's once unique output is now the air in today's digital life suff used with news and information. Consequently, journalism does not toil in barren, information-poor landscapes, but is nestled within multilayered and dynamic networks of communication.

(p. 207)

Besides conventional news, there are blogs that provide long-overdue access to citizens and thoughtful activists, who serve as "watchdogs of the watchdogs," countless online discussion boards, and a multitude of invigorating citizen journalism sites (Matheson, 2009; Robinson, 2006; Singer, 2005, 2013; Vos, Craft, & Ashley, 2012, p. 857; Wall, 2005). Exposure to these sites can deepen knowledge, offering exposure to perspectives that few would receive during the three-broadcast-networks-bestrode-the-world days of the 1960s.

Yet this assumes that people trek outside their online comfort zones to read perspectives with which they disagree. Algorithms and the time-honored psychological tendency to gravitate to supportive information pushes against these treks (Miller, 2014). There is another an even darker side, the multitude of popular, politically extreme platforms that conflate fact with ideological opinions and publish falsehoods galore, in these ways weaponizing digital information. These sites have raised significant concerns, dampening the heady enthusiasm that greeted the dawning of online journalism and the prospect of enhanced public participation in news that would nourish the civic spirit (see Boxes 2.1 and 2.2).

Box 2.1 Disseminating Falsehoods

Fake news has become a catch-all phrase that encompasses a host of different memes and meanings. **Fake news** can be defined as false information, frequently dressed up with the accoutrements of mainstream reporting, that is deliberately introduced into the media ecosystem, with the intent of deceiving news consumers

During the 2016 election, Russian operatives created thousands of fake Facebook and Twitter accounts that posted numerous messages – some undoubtedly disguised as news stories, disseminated via automated bots – that sought to sow division and undermine support for Hillary Clinton, a nemesis of the Russian government because she criticized Russian policies as Secretary of State. Russian cyber-experts devised false websites that credibly, playfully offered links to so called news (Shane, 2017). During the 2016 election campaign Russian agents posted more than 130,000 incendiary messages on Twitter and about 80,000 divisive communications on Facebook that were shared and followed by other users, reaching as many as 126 million people on Facebook (Isaac & Wakabayashi, 2017). What's more, fraudulent Russian news posts reached some 20 million Instagram users and 1.4 million people on Twitter, with some messages deliberately targeting African Americans in an effort to suppress Democratic voter turnout (Goldberg, 2018; Shane & Frenkel, 2018).

It wasn't just Russia – and indeed the degree of Russian involvement remains a matter of debate (Boyd-Barrett, 2019) – that has perpetrated fake news. A venomous far-right political group, determined to pin the 2017 Las Vegas massacre on liberal Democrats, circulated a false report that the shooter was reportedly a Trump-hating liberal who liked MSNBC host Rachel Maddow (Roose, 2017a). Extremist groups posted false news after other shootings in the U.S. as well. In the Southeast Asian country of Myanmar, extremist groups targeted the Muslim minority with fabricated news posts, and in India fake news posted on WhatsApp about child kidnappings went viral, possibly provoking revengeful beatings (Goel & Raj, 2018; Roose, 2017b).

How serious and pervasive is fake news? Although the effects may seem immense, a scholarly analysis suggests caution. Extensive research shows that people may presume that new media genres, from comic books to video games to fake news, have strong effects on others, while presuming they themselves are uninfluenced (Perloff, 2009). Just because the sites are out there doesn't mean most people frequent or believe them. Of the many provocative videos Russian agents posted to YouTube during the 2016 campaign, most had low view counts and relatively few views, the posts representing a miniscule fraction of the billions of posts viewed on Facebook over the campaign period (Carey, 2018; Isaac & Wakabayashi, 2017). The audience for fake news is small, tiny in relation to the audience for mainstream news. On the other hand, there is a vulnerable public out there – those deeply skeptical about American politics, on the fringes of public opinion, and prone to conspiracy theories. Fake news reports, confirming these Americans' deep fears and biases, can go viral, reinforcing, priming, and influencing these individuals' political prejudices.

Far-reaching technological advances in image synthesis, which combines artificial intelligence and computer graphics, has troubling implications. Research scientists created a video in which former President Obama seems to be mouthing words – "President Trump is a total and complete dipshit" – spoken by someone else. If circulated by strident Obama opponents and falsely labeled as a news report, the video could inflame Trump supporters. "Now that everything can be faked, how we will know what's real?," a journalist asked (Rothman, 2018, p. 34.) The question points up the importance of helping citizens develop mental detectors to discriminate between blatant falsehoods and probable truths.

Box 2.2 Unmasking Fake News

In the seemingly infinite potpourri of information that streams across phones, laptops, and television, it can be difficult to evaluate the truthfulness of information and hard to know whether a news site offers legitimate, incomplete, or fallacious information.

Some of you may have a good idea about what constitutes good journalism, while others may be confused by the patina of truthfulness that so many news sites purport to offer. In any case, it is instructive to gain insights on how to spot fake news. Here are a handful of suggestions.

- *If it sounds questionable, it probably is.* Headlines on fake news sites can attract attention, inviting attention from the curious or bored. Consider these headlines: "World's First Head Transplant a Success After Nineteen Hour Operation"; "Man Arrested for Having Sex with a Pig at Walmart"; and "Central Colombia Woman Grows Potato in Vagina in Ill-Advised Contraception Attempt." Okay, few of us would believe those are true! But consider these: "Pope Francis Shocks World, Endorses Donald Trump for President, Releases Statement"; or "Saudi Arabia has funded 20% of Hillary's Presidential Campaign, Saudi Crown Prince Claims." Reading quickly and hurriedly, one might accept those as true. But think about it. A pope endorsing a U.S. presidential candidate, particularly one who married three times; really? Saudi Arabia ponying up money for a U.S presidential candidate? Upon more thoughtful analysis – even just a little – the stories are preposterous.
- *If the story is possible, but intuitively implausible, consider the probability that it is fake.* For example, a story purporting that a CIA agent confessed to killing Marilyn Monroe or claiming that the Federal Drug Administration approved the sale of tranquilizer guns for use on children do not pass the smell test. A rule of thumb to invoke is: Be aware that fake news

stories are planted on social media and YouTube. Read stories a little more carefully, with this in mind.

- *Be attuned to incredulous stories that appeal to your biases.* If you don't like Hillary Clinton, you might entertain the possibility that a headline claiming Yoko Ono confessed she once had an intimate partnering with Hillary Clinton is true. You might believe that Hillary Clinton is on crack cocaine. If you don't like Donald Trump, you might buy into a story, such as one that described how an elementary school boy was suspended from school for saying he didn't like the president. Upon closer consideration, it becomes clear stories like these are forgeries.
- *Be on the lookout for cues suggesting falsehood.* If there are spelling errors, the story is nothing more than a headline, and there is no author or the author is anonymous, the story is suspect. If the grammar is weird, then the story might very well be fake. The Russian trolls who posted false messages designed to cripple Hillary Clinton's presidential campaign wrote that "actually we are open for your thoughts and offers" and used unusual verbal constructions.
- *Check that the story has come from a reliable site.* These include *The New York Times, The Washington Post*, NBC, CNN, Fox, the BBC, or a blog you trust. If it comes from a Facebook page or is shared by a friend and has an unusual address, be suspicious. Just because a story has been shared a lot does not make it true.
- *Make sure the story cites sources from government, business, politics, or activist circles.* The more the story quotes sources from these arenas, cites sources you have heard of, names well-known companies or groups (as opposed to fictitious ones), and quotes sources from both ends of the political spectrum, the more likely the story is to be journalistically sound. (Of course, quoting official sources exclusively can be a sign of faulty reporting, that reporters have bought into the government version of events; see Chapter 8.)
- *If the story seems unusual, check to see if other sites offer confirmatory evidence.* If it's a big story, all the news outlets will be there in force to cover it. If not, a headline shouting that a 75-year-old woman was thrown out of McDonald's for breast-feeding her 45-year-old son is what it seems – totally bogus.
- *Check Facebook's fact checks.* Facebook, faced with mounting criticism of its unwitting dissemination of fake news in the 2016 presidential campaign, now flags stories believed to be false, showing fact checks along with a fake news story in an

individual's news feed, counteracting the faux information (Carey, 2018).

- *Most importantly, check the online reliability of the site.* Beginning in 2018, veteran journalist Steven Brill and colleagues developed NewsGuard, a systematic system to evaluate the credibility of some 7,500 news and informational websites that accounts for about 98 percent of the news articles read online in the U.S. A series of nutrition labels for news, NewsGuard addresses fake news by providing a reliability rating of each news site: green signifying basically trustworthy, accurate and accountable; yellow for requiring reader caution; and red for intentionally deceptive, purveying fake news. (See also Haigh, Haigh, & Kozak, 2018 for another interesting technique to counter fake news reports.)

2. Social Media and the Internet Have Usurped the News Media's Exclusive Gatekeeping Role

Let's begin again with the way it used to be, the ways old movies retold the myth of glorious newspapers that, as people used to pun, were black and white, but read all over. The newsrooms all had a police radio that would shrilly blast out an emergency – robbery of a department store, murder on the subway, an explosion downtown – and reporters would rush to the event, cover the story (and loving the adrenalin rush of being there, those high-octane moments), dictate paragraphs (or grafs, as they called them, in the abbreviated slang); these would be typed up and converted into a news story that would splash across the front page, appear on the television evening news, or be narrated with immediacy on radio. In more formal settings, at a frenzied press conference, the governor or president would announce a new policy – say, calling up Army or National Guard troops for a military venture. Reporters would take notes and photographs, and their stories would reach the public through the evening news. The trajectory was frequently the same: Events occurred, key leaders relayed them, and the news was the middleman or mediator that transmitted information, melded into news, to the mass citizenry. In early studies of political communication, this was called the two-step flow (Katz & Lazarsfeld, 1955).

How convenient, quaint, and strangely simplistic, you may think. For more than a century, the news media controlled the informational gates, determining, through a multitude of criteria both conventional and controversial, the information that diffused to leaders, activists, opinion leaders, and the general public. Scholars invoked the concept of gatekeeping to explain the process, defining **gatekeeping** as "the process of culling and crafting countless bits of information into the limited number of messages that reach people each day," noting "it is the center of the media's role in modern public life" (Shoemaker & Vos, 2009, p. 1). Through gatekeeping, the news media, broadly defined, control the flow of messages in society, making complex judgments about what is transmitted, what is suppressed, and how the messages that reach millions of readers are crafted (Bro & Wallberg, 2015; Coddington & Holton, 2014).

From a democratic perspective, gatekeeping is important because it determines the flow of information – "the fuel of democracy," the foundational bricks and mortar necessary for communication in any democratic society (Berkman & Kitch, 1986). Citizens cannot reasonably participate in democracy, and leaders cannot govern, in the absence of reliable information. Information is also a source of power, the power to frame situations in ways that challenge – or prop up – an inequitable status quo.

In the old days, news editors would select newsworthy information from wire services, with their clickety-click teletype machines, determining which stories would get into the next day's newspaper or broadcast news (Bleske, 1991; White, 1950). It was a linear, top-down process, never without political or organizational considerations, but was performed by mainstream media. They were the top dogs, the ones who decided what people – from rich to poor, along with political leaders, influential citizens, and ordinary voters – read and viewed. While a host of journalistic, as well as political, even ideological, factors, determined which information media selected and how journalists framed it in particular stories, the process was entirely within the purview of journalists, the messages taking on a uniformity and patina of objectivity in the early "Gee whiz" days of 1960s live television. The legendary television journalist, Walter Cronkite, was himself a cultural authority, inextricably linked with the tragic and euphoric events of the 1960s, whose closing line "And that's the way it is" signified truth on both a literal and deeper spiritual level (Carlson, 2012). News, as NBC anchor David Brinkley, pithily put it, "is what I say it is" (Davis, 2018, p. 1). In sum, during the heyday of modern journalism, in the late 20th century, journalists were the key informational gatekeepers, cementing a century-long process in which reporters evolved as the arbiters of news judgment and newsworthiness (Vos & Finneman, 2017).

To be sure, political elites, powerful institutions, and the social system as a whole critically influenced the decisions that news media gatekeepers made about which information to pass on and how to package it into news stories (Gitlin, 1980; Hallin, 1986). But the media were in the metaphorical middle, passing on, selecting, and modifying information delivered from elected officials to the citizenry, as Figure 2.2 shows. Political elites and change agents – activist leaders and grassroots protesters – depended on the media to circulate their messages to the mass public.

OLDER MODEL OF GATEKEEPING MODELS

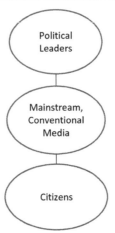

Figure 2.2 The older classic model of gatekeeping, with news media as the key, sole informational mediator

This has changed today, with the advent of community news sites, ideological platforms and social networking sites. "There has never been a time in which more news is produced than today," David M. Ryfe (2019) notes, "yet not since the 19th century has so little of it been produced by journalists" (p. 206). News written by journalists stands side-by-side with information or news gathered by other groups, which vary in their integrity, authenticity and commitment to long-standing journalistic standards.

To be sure, conventional, mainstream news organizations – newspapers, television, online news outlets – are still important gatekeepers, particularly when the news concerns foreign threats, like North Korea; complex political issues, like the Trump campaign's alleged election campaign collusion with Russia, where reporters have special knowledge and access to powerful insiders; and problems exposed by mainstream news exposés, like sexual exploitation across different occupational contexts. But issues discussed on community blogs, ideological outlets, and social media can take on a life of their own, eliding mainstream media, or working in concert with social media, to influence public opinion, in ways that can be both salutary and problematic.

The proliferation of social networking sites has enabled people to digitally connect inexpensively, communicate easily across national borders, and share information with millions across the globe, resulting in "a larger, more dispersed, and more complex network of civic information" than existed when three broadcast networks bestrode the journalistic universe

(Nadler, 2016, p. 125; Tufekci, 2017). The guiding metaphor may no longer be "All the news that's fit to print," the iconic epigram on the first page of *The New York Times*, but "All the news that's fit to share" (Hermida, 2016). Readers share a link to *New York Times* stories every four seconds, and do the same for countless other news. Links, conveyed through social media, can have positive, as well as troubling, consequences.

Let's look at how this works in two situations. The first showcases the ways ideological sites can shape the flow of information for sympathetic users, and the second focuses on the ways social media, alone and in combination with mainstream media, have altered the gatekeeping process.

Gatekeeping Today

Ideological Platforms

The advent of online platforms like Breitbart News for right-wing conservatives changed the gatekeeping equation by allowing media and political opinion leaders to communicate directly with followers, diffusing slanted information. These platforms allow citizens to get information directly, frequently inaccurately, without the mediation of conventional media. To be clear, mainstream or conventional media include national newspapers and magazines, radio and television networks (CBS, NBC, and ABC), local newspapers and television stations, and cable networks, like CNN, MSNBC, and Fox; the latter two skew to the left and right respectively. Online platforms vary greatly from Salon on the left and National Review on the right, which have opinionated, but thoughtful articles, to the variety of ideological, extremist websites, such as the right-wing Breitbart and conspiracy theory-focused Infowars.

Increasingly, online outlets with ideological, not journalistic agendas, can push information out into mainstream and social media, as occurred in 2019 when an obscure right-wing news outlet, Big League Politics, discovered, then published a picture of people dressed in Blackface and Ku Klux Klan garb that appeared on the page of Virginia Democratic Governor Ralph Northam's medical school yearbook of 35 years ago. The picture exploded onto mainstream media, causing volcanic controversy in Democratic Party circles.

When ideological outlets communicate information factually, transparently convey opinions, or present thoughtful articles, the information can exert salutary effects. But that's not the norm for the most extreme outlets. On many occasions, some of these new online gatekeepers distort information, presenting falsehoods and exaggerations, in line with their biases. Although both sides do this, the conservative media system has tighter connections among its leaders, followers, and media outlets, and has been more successful commercially than its liberal counterparts (Entman &

Usher, 2018). During the white-hot 2016 presidential campaign, Breitbart recruited more traffic than CNN.com (Entman & Usher, 2018).

Increasingly, online platforms can present skewed information, and falsehoods are exchanged between ideological and social media with such velocity and perceived credibility that conventional media are unable to staunch the damage. This happened with predictable tenacity back in 2018, when conservative online outlets presented vociferously false information about a caravan of Honduran migrants journeying via Mexico toward the U.S. President Trump may have instigated the process by falsely tweeting there were "criminals and unknown Middle Easterners" on the caravan, and the Breitbart outlet, undoubtedly energized by Trump's comment, falsely stated that the migrants had diseases "that could pose a threat to public health" (Peters, 2018, p. A15). A similar tweet was shared on Twitter and posted on a conspiracy theory site, while Fox News broadcast misleading information, suggesting that the caravan was a haven for terrorists, also untrue (Baker & Qiu, 2018; Roose, 2018).

As Figure 2.3 shows, the new gatekeeping works with information traded back and forth in a feedback loop between ideological online outlets and social media, like Twitter and Facebook. The distorted

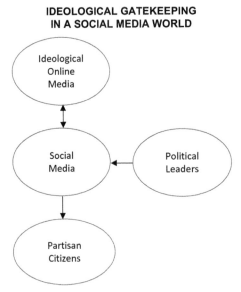

**IDEOLOGICAL GATEKEEPING
IN A SOCIAL MEDIA WORLD**

Figure 2.3 Ideological media outlets, frequently reflecting extremist views, can disseminate information through social media and vice versa. Like-minded political leaders offer their viewpoints through social media as well, with mainstream media out of the loop, depriving citizens of accurate information.

information then gets reinforced by like-minded political leaders, reaching citizens who share this partisan perspective. National newspapers like *The New York Times* can debunk this false information, noting that the caravan was not a haven for terrorists, criminals, or unknown Middle Easterners, but their corrections may never reach strong partisans, who live in an on-line echo chamber and distrust newspapers like *The Times*, vehemently believing they trend to the left (see Chapter 7). As a result of exposure to a stream of false, prejudicial information, staunchly partisan individuals can develop more extreme attitudes, hardening prejudices.

Social Media Interfaces

In other, less ideological arenas, conventional, mainstream news, works in concert with social media to influence attitudes of a broader cross-section of the public. *The New Yorker*'s and *New York Times*'s blockbuster exposés of sexual abuses by Harvey Weinstein – and later, other powerful men in the media and entertainment worlds – unleashed a firestorm of tweets and outrage from women, who had themselves experienced abuse, resulting in the emergence of the symbolic, online #MeToo movement (e.g., Kantor & Twohey, 2017).

In the wake of the news exposés, social media became a primary vehicle for women to share stories of sexual harassment, in turn building social support via the hashtag #MeToo. The hashtag was accessed more than 500,000 times on Twitter and 12 million times on Facebook within the first 24 hours and employed in millions of posts in the weeks to come, as it diffused globally, even getting translated into French as "out your pig" (Bennett, 2017; Renkl, 2017). News coverage launched a social media explosion where women shared horrific experiences of sexual abuse via social networks, and the immense outpouring of tweets and posts on social media propelled news to cover the problem (see Figure 2.4). Social media, alone and in combination with mainstream news, exerted palpable effects on citizens, leading about 70 percent of Americans to believe the online movement created a public opinion climate in which sexual offenders will be held accountable (Smith, 2018).

With more than 2 billion active Facebook users and 3 million people conducting Google searches each day, we no longer have a mass media world where there were "a few centralized choke points with just a few editors in charge" (Tufekci, 2017, p. 29). Instead, there are a multiplicity of gatekeepers. "Search engines are news gatekeepers in their own right," Tim P. Vos (2015) aptly notes (p. 12). Google chooses and organizes stories from conventional news outlets, showing them in long, unappealing headline lists. Newspapers, television, and online Web pages are still gatekeepers, but their dissemination routes have changed. Before the advent of social media, news outlets recruited readers through their online home pages or search engines. But with the exponential growth

SOCIAL MEDIA AND MAINSTREAM MEDIA
GATEEPING IN A SOCIAL MEDIA WORLD

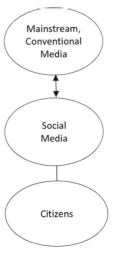

Figure 2.4 Contemporary gatekeeping can flow from mainstream media to social
media, or social media to mainstream media, adding a layer of complexity and citizen participation not available in earlier eras.

of Facebook and smartphones, readers live on Facebook, and the social
networking site has become an intermediary between online news outlets
and their audience, a go-to place where many people get news (Herrman,
2016; Valenzuela, Piña, & Ramírez, 2017).

   You see this clearly in news about celebrities, that august caste created
and magnified by news, and who are adulated by consumers of magazines that splash them on their covers, including *People, Time, and
Vanity Fair.* In the old days, news helped construct celebrities, giving
these media personae "relatively durable fame," such that their "private
and off-screen life attract as much attention as their professional work
does" (Steiner, 2019, p. 304). Newspapers, magazines, and TV were the
only go-to outlet to which celebrities and their agents could turn gain
access to the larger celebrity-consumed culture. Reporters interviewed
John Lennon about the Beatles break-up; Tupac Shakur spoke with
a reporter from jail, and Courtney Love conducted an in-depth interview
after the suicide of her husband, the rocker Kurt Cobain. The news
media were the big dogs, the sole gatekeepers through which celebrities
had to communicate if they wanted to feed their public images.

   Alas, in the spinning hurricane of mediated change, social media have
cast celebrity journalism aside, offering ways for celebrity musicians to
circumvent media and speak directly to fans. Several years back the late

rapper XXXTentacion responded to charges of sexual assault, not by talking with reporters, by via his Instagram Story, and Logan Paul, a YouTube star, apologized for filming a dead body on his customary platform (Caramanica, 2018). Mainstream media picked up these stories, but the arrow went from social media to mainstream media, and then diffused to the culture at large.

Celebrities usurp journalists' role even in mainstream outlets, as when actor Sean Penn interviewed the violent, legendary Mexican drug lord famously known as El Chapo for *Rolling Stone*, controversially agreeing to submit the story to the drug kingpin for pre-publication approval. More prosaically, in the entertainment world, actress Jennifer Lawrence, rather than a feature writer, interviewed Emma Stone for an article in *Elle*. The intimacy of celebrity-to-fan communication has replaced the older tradition, whereby reporters provided a space in which thoughtful, critical questions could be asked that probed the inner workings of the celebrity's psyche. Of course, this lament, typically offered by mainstream journalists, ignores the many times when questions were sycophantic, fawning, and designed to lure fans to buy the magazine.

In short, gatekeeping still exists, but is vastly different today – less top-down, more decentralized, and less linear – as mainstream news sites adjoin search engines and other networked platforms that vary in their credibility, all diffusing information simultaneously in the dizzying net-worked communication domain. "We have gone from 'one medium, one gatekeeper' to ... multiple autonomous gatekeeping processes," scholar François Heinderyckx (2015) notes (p. 255).

Jeff Bezos, Amazon's founder and chief executive, said he looked forward to the "elimination of gatekeepers everywhere" (Herrman, 2017, p. 13). This has not happened. His company, Google, Facebook, and other tech giants are now the new gatekeepers. The new gatekeepers have rules of their own, ingenious, intriguing, but not without flaws. They do exponentially more than distribute conventional news, but are media platforms, with new metrics and rules. The keys, of course, are, **algorithms**, problem-solving formulas or computerized criteria employed to determine which information people see, and the prioritization this information receives. Indeed, Facebook's business model, providing mar-keters with users' private data, which marketers harness to promote products, services, and candidates, has led to exploitation of private information for commercial gain. Far from being neutral, the new social media have their own biases, shortcomings, and strengths. Face-book's algorithms do not prioritize information that serves journalistic values or normative functions, but "the posts that spur the most com-ments, clicks, and controversy, creating a feedback loop in which buzzy topics generate yet more buzz" (Marantz, 2018, p. 20; Herrman, 2018).

Its algorithms promote posts that elicit the most engagement from users, favoring content that kindles negative emotions like fear and anger, and can even prime group social identities, as when posts activate a feeling that partisans' religious or political group is superior to those of their antagonists (Fisher & Taub, 2018a, 2018b). As the rock group, The Who, famously crowed, "Meet the new boss, same as the old boss."

These social media and technology companies – their existential identity unclear (is Facebook a media company, publisher, or communications utility with responsibilities to the public?) – are certainly gatekeepers, and they are uprooting the rules in innovative, unpredictable, increasingly disturbing ways. As people increasingly get news from a mixture of platforms and mobile devices, which place a premium on affect and sociality, rather than factual evidence, yet intersect with conventional sites that emphasize factual claims, a new ecosystem has developed, with multiple gatekeepers, overlapping spaces, and a myriad of yardsticks to adjudicate truth (Hermida, 2019).

3. Citizen journalism has entered the fray, broadening journalism and raising new questions

On November 22, 1963, Abraham Zapruder, a Russian-born clothing manufacturer who had moved from New York to Dallas and loved taking home movies of his family, took his trusty Bell and Howell 8 millimeter camera to film President John F. Kennedy's visit to Dallas. Zapruder loved JFK and must have relished the opportunity to film Kennedy in his hometown. After a few practice shots, Zapruder let his camera roll, filming the president after his dark black Lincoln Continental convertible glided past the adoring crowds and crossed into Dealey Plaza. Then came the instant the world changed, the sudden, sickening moment when Kennedy slumped into his wife's arms. Zapruder captured the assassination live, with the rough, grainy texture of the Bell and Howell cameras of the era, 26 seconds and 486 frames. Over the course of the ensuing decades, the film became a touchstone of controversy and an indelible piece of American pop culture (Zapruder, 2016).

Zapruder was one of the first citizen journalists, on hand to record history on the spot. Although one might trace citizen journalism to the colonial press, these newspaper scribes were reporters with an attitude, writers with a mission: furthering the nascent American Revolution. They weren't journalists as we define the term (see Chapter 3). By contrast, Zapruder, a veritable photojournalist, used the technology of his era to provide a visual rendition of history. Of course, if Zapruder were filming – rather, videotaping – an assassination today, his smartphone video would instantly be on YouTube and social media, eliding conventional media, part of an endless debate, as would another famous pre-Internet act of citizen journalism, George Holliday's video, filmed from his balcony on March 3, 1991, of four Los Angeles Police

Department officers viciously beating an African American, Rodney King, when he was pulled over for speeding by the LAPD.

Citizen journalism may date back decades, but it is vastly more pervasive, multifaceted, and impactful in our era. As the term suggests, citizen journalism assumes that journalism does not belong exclusively to conventionally trained reporters, but to citizens – ordinary, often committed, individuals who harness digital technologies to enrich, empower, and inform the public (Hartley, 2008). Citizen journalists are an incredibly diverse lot and the term "citizen journalism" encompasses an array of journalistic acts that vary in level of commitment, expertise, and depth of reporting.

You can view posts and tweets transmitted during terrorist incidents as rudimentary citizen journalistic acts. Eyewitness accounts and photographs posted on alternative news sites like Slashdot.org during 9/11 provided "clarity and accuracy" for millions of Americans, offering "a first-person news network, a collective form of collaborative news gathering" with grassroots and alternative perspectives conventional news did not carry (Allan, 2011, pp. 176–177). At other terrorist events – the 2005 London bombings, 2015 Paris attacks, 2017 Manchester, UK, bombings after an Ariana Grande concert, and a 2017 Texas Baptist Church shooting – first-hand reports, mobile telephone images, video clips, and tweets, some with high-quality videos, beat established journalists to the punch, sometimes providing the grist for reporters' stories (Allan & Thorsen, 2009). These posts were without question news (Meikle & Redden, 2011).

More substantial citizen journalism has emerged on the local level. Activist citizens with a strong attitude, passion for democracy, and technical expertise have fortified the declining local journalism scene with online websites, where citizens have performed a variety of roles: fact-checking news articles, aggregating information, sharing photos, and blogging about city council meetings (Allan, 2013; Allan & Thorsen, 2009). They have produced up-to-the-minute, sometimes hard-hitting, blog posts about issues local news couldn't or didn't cover, spanning fires, oil spills, and, most graphically a Steubenville, Ohio rape that blew open a story conventional news ignored (see Chapter 8).

So, what exactly is citizen journalism? Jay Rosen, an early proponent, proposed a broad, democratizing definition, arguing eloquently that "when the **people** formerly known as the audience employ the press tools they have in their possession to inform one another, *that's* citizen journalism" (Rosen, 2008). His definition nicely calls attention to ways that journalism has broadened to include citizen participation, but it is glib and diffuse. Is anyone who uses a cell phone to tweet on social media a citizen journalist? Is any sharing of a message with press tools (which means what exactly?) journalism?

Other scholars argue that citizen journalism involves "contribution to discussion in the public sphere, whether in the form of simple information, synthesis, reporting, or opinion," with individuals partaking more broadly in a conversation about democratic society (Nah et al., 2015, p. 400). Citizen journalism encompasses prosaic comments that people post online after a snowstorm, community event, or election, some of which are recruited by local television stations not to expand the institution of citizen journalism, but to help these news outlets broaden their audience and increase revenues (Min, 2016; Singer, 2013). Yet citizen journalism also refers to content that is hosted by outlets outside the terrain of conventional journalism, such as alternative local websites and digital platforms.

Thus, it is helpful to distinguish between *citizen journalistic acts*, like pictures after a snowstorm or tweets about a terrorist tragedy that people quickly post online on local TV websites or Facebook, and *committed citizen journalism* written by activist citizens – some with a journalism background, others critical of traditional journalism, and still others infused by commitment to community. This includes reporting on community issues that criticizes and deepens conventional press coverage, published on bona fide citizen journalism websites and other digital platforms. This committed citizen journalism is usually distinct from the domain of conventional, professional journalism (Singer, 2005), presenting challenges, broadening the journalistic boundary, and frequently impelled by a different ethos, one that emphasizes participation rather than detached observation, focusing on community enhancement rather than a standard objective journalistic orientation that stands outside the community, peering in (Hanitzsch, 2007). In contrast to the more disengaged, thematic, third-person journalistic narratives about crisis events, citizen journalists can also provide more conversational, personalized and experiential, if sometimes less reliable, perspectives (Robinson, 2009).

Citizen journalists have transformed the practice of journalism and raised existential questions for the profession. By posting information immediately, they can scoop conventional reporters, undercutting one of the classic roles of the journalist: breaking the story first, before all competitors. By providing content in outlets that are outside the traditional purview of journalism, but reach people on the web, citizen journalists have simultaneously challenged and broadened journalism. By raising factual questions about reporters' stories, forcing journalists to revise their first drafts of history, they have undermined mainstream reporters' authoritative gatekeeper roles. And by suggesting there is more to journalism than "who, what, when and where," but also "us" (the community), they have amplified journalistic commitment to the larger public good.

Over the past several decades, as citizen journalism has grown by leaps and bounds, its long-time proponents have celebrated the strengths of this participatory, grassroots approach, famously expressed by Clay Shirky in his 2008 book, *Here comes everybody*. For many years, established journalists cried foul, regarding citizen journalists as amateurs, noting they had not acquired the tools of the journalistic trade, with their interspersing opinions throughout their stories, and failing to adequately verify information before they published it (Allan, 2010; Hermida, 2015; Kovach & Rosenstiel, 2014; Meraz & Papacharissi, 2016). Some journalism scholars have derided these claims, calling them efforts at turf protection, an attempt of the so-called professionals to maintain their authority in the wake of challenges from dedicated citizens, an effort to ensure that the hallowed community of established journalists can preserve its authority to relay the news (Blaagaard, 2013; Eldridge, 2014; McNair, 2011; Zelizer, 1993; see also Berkowitz, 2000; Steiner et al., 2013).

In recent years, the two sides – conventional and citizen journalists – have reconciled many of their differences. In an era when citizens are the first to tweet news about natural disasters and (in more committed instances) cover issues cash-strapped newspapers no longer examine, it is difficult to say that citizen journalism is not bona fide journalism, albeit with a different orientation (Deuze, 2009). The White House has issued press releases to bloggers, and at least a third of Americans read blogs (Robinson & DeShano, 2011).

When local television stations depends on citizen journalism posts to engage viewers, there is an economic incentive for professional journalists to accept comments from citizens, even if they range from the helpful to the goofy. Increasingly, news organizations have partnered with bloggers, respecting their expertise, accepting their information, even hiring them in newsrooms (Robinson & DeShano, 2011). More committed citizen journalism outlets complement traditional news with in-depth reporting conventional outlets don't always provide, offering a grassroots storytelling ethos (Bruns, 2008; Papacharissi, 2015).

Examples are plentiful. Back in 2004, in the early hours of a Saturday morning, a fire ravaged a historic building in a small town in Vermont. The local newspaper had stopped publishing for the day, and the burden to cover the story fell on local citizens, who readily harnessed digital technology to post stories, photographs, and information on how to help people who had been injured or dislocated. Citizen posts served a long-established journalistic function. "For many people, it was the only place to find any news throughout the day," observed the co-creator of a local news site (Walker, 2004). In New York City, homegrown digital news sites like Bklyner exposed neighborhood problems, like a 27,000 gallon oil spill in Brooklyn that authorities had not revealed, motivating a city council member to introduce a bill that required agencies to immediately inform city officials of pollution risks (Newman, 2017). The big city New York press covered the story after the website broke the news.

Citizen journalism is not without faults. While some grassroots sites supplement conventional news coverage, others provide little in-depth analysis of public issues or permit the use of fake screen names, which can free respondents from norms of civility (Grubisich, 2005; see also Cooper, 2019). In some cases, citizen sites and blogs can reaffirm, rather than question, community values, failing to provide the necessary investigative exposés that local newspapers, at their best, provide. What's more, political blogs have traditionally failed to reflect demographic diversity, with many reproducing the affluent, White American hierarchy (Hindman, 2009; Robinson, 2017), although that may be changing, in light of social empowerment unleashed by #BlackLivesMatter and the #MeToo symbolic movement. Still, inequities remain. Poorer neighborhoods can lack needed citizen reporting outlets because residents lack the resources and skills to develop hyperlocal sites (García De Torres & Hermida, 2017; Williams & Harte, 2016).

With its array of shortcomings and strengths, citizen journalism is experiencing growing pains even as it provides a useful complement to mainstream media gatekeeping. It represents an important development in the history of the journalistic craft, raising existential issues for the larger journalism field. Conventional journalists lament that the decline of conventional objective journalism has meant that we are "losing the news," threatening the bulwark of democracy (Jones, 2009). But journalism scholars, like Ryfe (2010), noting that journalism has long promoted the status quo, are more bullish about a future filled with more voices, more tenacious gatekeepers, and robust citizen journalism.

4. The lines have blurred and boundaries among journalistic categories are harder to draw

During the tempestuous 2008 Democratic presidential campaign, Mayhill Fowler, an aspiring, not-yet-famous 60-something, former stay-at-home mom, was one of many unpaid reporters working with BuzzFeed's experiment in campaign citizen journalism when she happened on the story of her life. While listening to candidate Barack Obama speak at a San Francisco fundraiser, she recorded him commit a memorable gaffe, as he insensitively disparaged the "bitter" small-town Americans who "cling to guns or religion or antipathy to people who aren't like them." Obama's clumsy comment on the eve of the April Pennsylvania primary rocked the campaign, contributing to his loss in the Keystone State primary. Ordinarily, a newspaper or television journalist would have broken the story, but this time an amateur BuzzFeed reporter snagged it, raising intriguing questions. Was Fowler a journalist? Had she engaged in journalism? What is the relationship between journalism and news (Carlson, 2015)? More generally, how do we demarcate the professional boundaries of journalism in an era of YouTube videos, citizen tweets, fake news, and a clamorous public sphere in which news co-exists with a multitude of public posts?

One of the characteristics of our age is the ways journalism concepts that were once clear and obvious are no longer, and overlap in complex, freighted ways (Carlson & Lewis, 2015). Journalism scholars have described this quandary as one of overlapping boundaries, characterized by ways that diverse participants struggle for symbolic control over the content of journalism (Jenkins & Tandoc, 2017). Journalism is increasingly a field where a host of participants and gatekeepers struggle for control (Bourdieu, 1995).

Fifty years ago, it was easy to describe journalism. (Yes, here we go again!) There were just mainstream newspapers, magazines, old-fashioned AM radio, local TV news, and the ubiquitous NBC, CBS, and ABC. That was it! Nowadays, by way of review, in an era of multiple platforms, print newspapers, online conventional news sites, mainstream news transmitted via Facebook, ideological outlets that conflate facts and news, thoughtful citizen journalism blogs, emotive tweets sent hurriedly during crises, countless retweets, and comments about news stories that take on a patina of credibility, it is hard to know just what constitutes news, let alone journalism. Differentiating between journalists and non-journalists, tweets and news, news and information, as well as news and advertising is vexing and fraught, far more than in years past (Carlson, 2017). As Matt Carlson and Dan Berkowitz (2014) helpfully point out, journalism should best be viewed as in flux, in a state of change, and engaged in an "ongoing definitional struggle in the face of the changing conditions of news" (p. 391).

A major focus is control. Who controls the border? Who influences the journalism field? Who determines what a journalist is and what constitutes journalism? Trying to offer theoretical clarity, Carlson (2015) points out that boundaries can be demarcated in three different ways: by *protection of autonomy; expulsion*; and *expansion*.

As an example of the first, autonomy protection, mainstream journalists long excluded citizen reporters from their august domain, ensuring their own autonomy, protecting the journalistic turf, and exerting control by labeling citizen reporters' work as insufficiently factual.

Second, mainstream journalists sought to symbolically expel outside participants who engaged in unacceptable, "non-journalistic" practices, typified by the "vulture-like" paparazzi photographers who swooped down on public figures, aggressively interfering with their privacy. Reporters, earnestly but in ways designed to protect their profession, denigrated the paparazzi who descended on celebrities (tragically in the case of Princess Diana) while celebrating the superiority of "serious" reporters who supposedly covered news rather than creating it themselves (Berkowitz, 2000). (In Diana's case, the paparazzi, or freelance photographers who aggressively pursue celebrities, gave chase to her in

Paris, perhaps contributing to her death in a car crash. In the tragic aftermath of her death, mainstream reporters were at pains to differentiate their more "serious and ethical" profession from the tawdry celebrity-chasing paparazzi.) Yet in a variety of sensational cases – the O.J. Simpson trial, and feeding frenzy coverage of the presidential sexual scandals from Clinton to Trump – mainstream journalists could borrow or cite stories from the tabloid *National Enquirer*, while symbolically maintaining their superiority, demeaning the *Enquirer*, labeling it a "pariah publication" (Goldstein, 2007, p. 113).

Decades later, in our age of digital crossovers, journalists are frequently engaged in expansion, the third category that embraces boundary-crossing and extends recognition to once-off limits participants and practices. Mainstream journalists are now more likely to acknowledge that they too descend on celebrity politicians, stalking politicians suspected of having an affair, sometimes becoming part of the story themselves. In a similar fashion, reporters who years ago might have turned their nose down on a tweet as an all-too-brief opinionated expression, unabashedly tweet observations, as well as personal opinions, today. And, as discussed in the previous section, the exclusion of citizen reporters as interlopers not engaged in "serious journalism" has given way to more journalistic acceptance of citizen reporters as storytellers and "fact custodians," as Robinson (2015) nicely puts it.

When conventional and citizen reporters call on each other's work, and citizen reporters' links, stories, and comments digitally adjoin mainstream reporters' articles, we have reached a point where borders porously and seamlessly cross. The public space of journalism has expanded to include new actors and perspectives outside conventional journalism. Conflict, a mainstay of journalistic reportage, continues, with proponents of citizen journalism and more traditional defenders of conventional mainstream journalism viewing boundary-crossing through different lenses.

Proponents of citizen journalism praise the critical comments that appear alongside traditional news stories as usefully questioning journalists' interpretations, while defenders of conventional journalism worry that readers' comments can have distorting effects. Research shows that readers may downgrade the credibility of a news article that appears alongside comments, perhaps placing more trust in factually inaccurate comments from fellow readers than the more factually correct standard news story (see Sikorski & Hänelt, 2016). If this happens, the new border-crossing journalism can unwittingly magnify misperceptions of public issues, the opposite of the informational, monitorial goal of journalism (see Chapter 4).

Figure 2.5 illustrates this, displaying a variety of contemporary boundary crossings or overlapping arenas: (1) citizen journalism intersecting with conventional media when mainstream news draws on citizen news

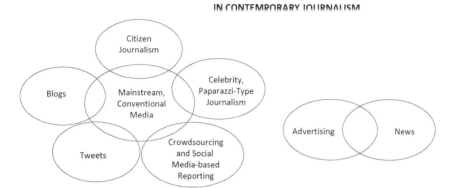

Figure 2.5 Contemporary news is characterized by crossing of boundaries and blurred lines, muddying the journalistic waters, making clear delineations difficult, and showcasing the hybrid, networked public domain in which news controversially appears.

sites or bloggers' exposeé; (2) connections between the supposedly outside-journalism paparazzi and news that mimics its techniques; (3) tweets that once were outside mainstream journalism's purview, but now are regularly posted by reporters; and (4) print reporters regularly monitoring social media, employing crowdsourcing techniques and mining tweets, to write up stories for publication. In addition, as noted above, when news stories elicit a torrent of comments online, the comments can blend with the actual news in readers' minds, so that readers may trust the comments more than the actual news (Gajda, 2015; Sikorski & Hänelt, 2016), raising questions about whether this contaminates or enriches journalism.

Add to this a final disturbing boundary-crossing, increasing blurred lines between advertising and news (Li, 2019). Truth be told, the lines between commercial marketing and journalism have never been sacrosanct, but most news outlets adhered, as much as possible, to a formal wall between the editorial and business sides. But digital sites, desperate for revenues in the volatile online market, changed the equation. Buzz-Feed has showcased sponsored posts, in which companies pay for posts to promote products, as well as native advertising, paid ads that resemble the form and style of the platform on which they appear. The content resemblance deceptively suggests the articles are news stories when they actually function as advertisements.

For example, a news site might run a story about jokes only fans of the shooter video game, "Call of Duty," will appreciate, which publicizes "Call of Duty" games. Vice News developed branded content for big advertisers, sometimes killing news stories that placed the advertisers in a negative light (Abramson, 2019; Lee, 2019; Thompson, 2019). These advertised posts shade into news, making it difficult to tell the difference, again deceptively giving the advertised posts journalistic panache. Even major news organizations, like *The New York Times*, trying to survive in the volatile new media environment, have at times relaxed the barrier between news and business, using metric charts that suggested editors push stories based on their online traffic. To journalism purists, this raises questions about how economic exigencies are chipping away at the core values that underpin news.

It's all interesting, complicated and disturbing, filled with gray areas, and cautionary tales for the future. As a result of these inroads and blurred boundaries, journalism may be losing its integrity as a distinct social domain. Ryfe (2012b) observes:

> As the field weakens, and its boundaries become porous and permeable, professional journalists are no longer able to keep others out. Journalism becomes something like a natural act, to borrow from scholar Jay Rosen, that anyone can do. And as new players enter the field, it becomes increasingly difficult for journalists to set the terms of what counts as good or credible journalism.
>
> (p. 201)

The stretching, buckling, and expanding of journalism is full of negative and positive aspects, the evaluation depending on your criteria and philosophical standards. Journalistic authority, once a sanctified given, is constantly a matter of negotiation and social construction (Robinson, 2017). Mainstream media sometimes sets the agenda of important issues; in other cases, agendas are set by blogs, social media, and political websites. In some cases, the expansion of voices is salutary, in other cases, when the impetus comes from ideological sites, polarizing.

And yet, the fact that journalism is broader, more diverse, and permeable does not mean that it will disintegrate. Journalism will become more variegated and more multifaceted, with a wider range of meanings. But it will not become less important to democratic society.

Conclusions

This chapter described four characteristics of contemporary news, showcasing the transformative changes that have convulsed the news industry over the past decades. In the new online environment, the architecture of news is multifaceted, fragmented, and interactive, a far cry from the historic past when newspapers bundled stories into a diverse, but coherent, whole.

People now receive news in fragmented form, reading or viewing news from this outlet or that on their phones – an endless potpourri of information, the provenance of which can be unknown, unclear, or manipulated by foreign operatives. Conventional media – newspapers, local television, and national TV networks – still gather stories and deliver them in older formats, notably television, Americans' favored platform for receiving news, However, on the Internet conventional outlets appear cheek to jowl with online news platforms, as well as innumerable blogs, weaponized ideological sites (which frame facts so they fit a particular political perspective), fake news that appears on faux Facebook pages, and a host of posts from like-minded others that reinforce, rather than challenge, preexisting views. It is all part of what is called a networked public sphere that provides people with more depth, diversity, and opportunities for interaction than was possible in the analogue days of print and television glory. However, the difficulty of deciphering fact from falsehood on ideologically weaponized sites has dashed some of the initial optimism that greeted the online news environment.

Once the sole gatekeepers, who sifted through the vast plenitude of information to decide what both leaders and citizens read, mainstream news is now one among many gatekeepers, one of a variety of platforms that determine the information people literally have at their fingertips. The news media, or press as it was called in its years past, is still important, particularly when news concerns foreign threats and national issues, where mainstream reporters have unique access to the powers-that-be. But unlike earlier times, where mainstream news played a preeminent role in communication among political leaders, activists, entertainment celebrities, and ordinary people, nowadays leaders, activist groups, and celebs can elide conventional media, reducing the gatekeeping authority of news.

Power abhors a vacuum, and the new gatekeepers – search engines and social media platforms – employ complex algorithms, rarely transparent, to determine the content and ordering of information people receive. But algorithms are computerized formulas that were not designed with news in mind and are imperfectly matched to the world of journalistic gatekeeping. Alas, we are now fully immersed in a hybrid environment, where online media sites of varied commitment to journalism and social networking platforms play important roles in determining the news of politics and society people read. The irony is breathtaking: The innovative inventors of social networking sites dreamed of a "here-comes-everybody" (Shirky, 2008) ecosphere devoid of gatekeepers. Instead, Facebook, Twitter, Google and other sites are the new gatekeepers, devising rules for what we see on the overcrowded powerlines that contain news.

There are many benefits in having a variety of gatekeepers to choose from, including those that offer grassroots citizen perspectives. The many links contained in articles can put us in touch with information we would have never seen in earlier times. But the lack of transparency of algorithms, coupled with their tendency to favor information that resonates with preexisting preferences, raises questions about how effectively and comprehensively news is fulfilling its democratic functions.

A primarily positive change that has altered the way journalists approach their jobs and the way the public receives news is the advent of citizen journalism. Citizen journalists, who do not work for established journalistic organizations, call on digital technologies, expertise in community issues, and passion for the community collective to display a multitude of articles that once would have been the province of conventional news work. More broadly, from coverage of city council meetings, on the local level, to tweets about terrorist incidents, on the international stage, citizens have changed the nature of journalistic news by scooping journalists, challenging the factuality of their accounts, and offering up a participatory ethos congenial with the best of the networked online sphere.

Citizen journalism is not without problems, as citizen reporters can make mistakes and transmit stories that have not been adequately verified, in this way undercutting one of the cornerstones of journalism, the emphasis on factual verification. Citizen journalism is also a multifaceted term encompassing so many different attributes – from a worried warning about a hurricane to a deeply-reported citizen blog about an urban problem – that it can be cumbersome conceptually. But there is no doubt that citizen reporting and event eyewitnessing have influenced the ways news is gathered and received, expanding its range, offering access to a larger range of news producers, but also raising ethical questions when it comes to accuracy and authenticity of information.

Ours is a world of blurred lines and boundary-crossing, where citizen journalism intersects with time-honored gathering of news; once-shunned journalistic practices are embraced by journalists; and advertising can mask as news. It is all more complicated, variegated, and so much less governed by a singular journalistic authority that one can hanker for the old days, forgetting that they had such serious shortcomings that critics once longed for an era of decentralized news outlets that seemed so promising and pristine. Be careful what you wish for!

References

Abramson, J. (2019). *Merchants of truth: The business of news and the fight for facts.* New York: Simon & Schuster.
Allan, S. (2010). Journalism without professional journalists? In L. Steiner & C. Christians (Eds.), *Key concepts in critical cultural studies* (pp. 145–157). Urbana, IL: University of Illinois Press.

Allan, S. (2011). Reweaving the Internet: Online news of September 11. In B. Zelizer & S. Allan (Eds.), *Journalism after September 11* (2nd ed., pp. 169–190). New York: Routledge.

Allan, S. (2013). *Citizen witnessing: Revisioning journalism in times of crisis.* Cambridge, UK: Polity Press.

Allan, S., & Thorsen, E. (Eds.). (2009) *Citizen journalism: Global perspectives.* New York: Peter Lang.

Baker, P., & Qiu, L. (2018, November 1). Along campaign trail, a litany of untruths. *The New York Times*, A14.

Barnhurst, K.G., & Nerone, J. (2001). *The form of news: A history.* New York: Guilford Press.

Benkler, Y. (2006). *The wealth of networks: How social production transforms markets and freedom.* New Haven, CT: Yale University Press.

Bennett, J. (2017, November 7). How Weinstein scandal became the final straw. *The New York Times*, A1, A17.

Benton, J. (2018, October 5). Here's how much Americans trust 38 major news organizations (hint: not all that much!). *Nieman Lab.* Online: www.niemanlab.org/2018/10/here's-how-much-americans-trust-38-major. (Accessed: November 9, 2018).

Berkman, R., & Kitch, L.W. (1986). *Politics in the media age.* New York: McGraw-Hill.

Berkowitz, D. (2000). Doing double duty: Paradigm repair and the Princess Diana what-a-story. *Journalism, 1*, 125–143.

Blaagaard, B.B. (2013). Shifting boundaries: Objectivity, citizen journalism and tomorrow's journalists. *Journalism, 14*, 1076–1090.

Bleske, G.L. (1991). Ms. Gates takes over: An updated version of a 1949 case study. *Newspaper Research Journal, 12*, 88–97.

Bourdieu, P. (1995). The political field, the social science field and the journalistic field. In R. Benson & E. Neveu (Eds.), *Bourdieu and the journalistic field* (pp. 29–47). Cambridge, UK: Polity Press.

Boyd-Barrett, O. (2019). Fake news and "russiagate" discourses: Propaganda in the post-truth era. *Journalism, 20*, 87–91.

Bro, P., & Wallberg, F. (2015). Gatekeeping in a digital era: Principles, practices and technological platforms. *Journalism Practice, 9*, 92–105.

Bruns, A. (2008). *Blogs, Wikipedia, Second Life, and beyond: From production to produsage.* New York: Peter Lang.

Caramanica, J. (2018, September 20). The celebrity profile: Endangered species. *The New York Times*, C2.

Carey, B. (2018, January 2). Sizing up the impact of fake news. *The New York Times*, D5.

Carlson, M. (2012). Rethinking journalistic authority: Walter Cronkite and ritual in television news. *Journalism Studies, 13*, 483–498.

Carlson, M. (2015). Introduction: The many boundaries of journalism. In M. Carlson & S.C. Lewis (Eds.), *Boundaries of journalism: Professionalism, practices and participation* (pp. 1–18). New York: Routledge.

Carlson, M. (2017). Establishing the boundaries of journalism's public mandate. In C. Peters & M. Broersma (Eds.), *Rethinking journalism again: Societal role and public relevance in a digital age* (pp. 49–63). New York: Routledge.

Carlson, M., & Berkowitz, D. (2014). "The emperor lost his clothes": Rupert Murdoch, *News of the World* and journalistic boundary work in the UK and USA. *Journalism, 15*, 389–406.

Carlson, M., & Lewis, S.C. (Eds.). (2015) *Boundaries of journalism: Professionalism, practices and participation.* New York: Routledge.

Carr, N. (2008). *The big switch: Rewiring the world, from Edison to Google.* New York: W.W. Norton.

Choi, S., & Kim, J. (2017). Online news flow: Temporal/spatial exploitation and credibility. *Journalism, 18*, 1184–1205.

Coddington, M., & Holton, A.E. (2014). When the gates swing open: Examining network gatekeeping in a social media setting. *Mass Communication and Society, 17*, 236–257.

Cooper, G. (2019). Why livestreaming symbolises journalism's current challenges. *Journalism, 20*, 167–172.

Davis, D. (2018). Introduction. In D. Davis & J. Mazzolini (Eds.), *Plain Dealing: Cleveland journalists tell their stories* (pp. 1–6). Cleveland, OH: MSL Academic Endeavors (Cleveland State University).

Deuze, M. (2009). Journalism, citizenship, and digital culture. In Z. Papacharissi (Ed.), *Journalism and citizenship: New agendas in communication* (pp. 15–28). New York: Routledge.

Digital News Fact Sheet. (2018, June 6). *Pew Research Center (Journalism & Media)*. Online: www.journalism.org/fact-sheet/digital-news/. (Accessed: January 20, 2019).

Draper, K., (2017, October 24). They're out to kill every paper's sports section. *The New York Times*, B7, B11.

Eldridge II., S.A. (2014). Boundary maintenance and interloper media reaction: Differentiating between journalism's discursive enforcement processes. *Journalism Studies, 15*, 1–16.

Entman, R.M., & Usher, N. (2018). Framing in a fractured democracy: Impacts of digital technology on ideology, power and cascading network activation. *Journal of Communication, 68*, 298–308.

Fisher, M., & Taub, A. (2018a, April 23). Tracing Facebook's harms in Sri Lanka. *The New York Times*, A2.

Fisher, M., & Taub, A. (2018b, April 26). Does Facebook just harbor extremists? Or does it create them? *The New York Times*, A11.

Foer, F. (2017). *World without mind: The existential threat of Big Tech.* New York: Penguin Press.

Gajda, A. (2015). *The First Amendment bubble: How privacy and paparazzi threaten a free press.* Cambridge, MA: Harvard University Press.

García De Torres, E., & Hermida, A. (2017). The social reporter in action. *Journalism Practice, 11*, 177–194.

Gitlin, T. (1980). *The whole world is watching: Mass media in the making & unmaking of the new left.* Berkeley, CA: University of California Press.

Goel, V., & Raj, S. (2018, July 21). How WhatsApp leads mobs to kill in India. *The New York Times*, B4.

Goldberg, M. (2018, December 18). Yes, trolls helped elect Trump. *The New York Times*, A23.

Goldstein, T. (2007). *Journalism and truth: Strange bedfellows.* Evanston, IL: Northwestern University Press.

Gottfried, J., & Shearer, E. (2017, September 7). *Americans' online news use is closing in on TV news use.* Pew Research Center (Fact Tank: News in the numbers). Online: www.pewresearch.org/fact tank/2017/09/07/americans online-news. (Accessed: November 9, 2018).

Grieco, E. (2017, November 2). More Americans are tuning to multiple social media sites for news. *Pew Research Center: Fact Tank, News in the numbers.* Online: www.pewresearch.org/fact-tank/2017/11/02/more-americans-are-turning-to-multiple-social-media-sites-for-news/. (Accessed: November 9, 2017).

Grubisich, T. (2005, October 5). Grassroots journalism: Actual content vs. shining ideal. *Online Journalism Review.* Online: www.ojr.og/p051006/. (Accessed: October 21, 2017).

Haigh, M., Haigh, T., & Kozak, N.I. (2018). Stopping fake news. *Journalism Studies, 19,* 2062–2087.

Hallin, D.C. (1986). *The "uncensored war": The media and Vietnam.* New York: Oxford University Press.

Hallin, D.C. (1994). *We keep America on top of the world: Television journalism and the public sphere.* New York: Routledge.

Hanitzsch, T. (2007). Deconstructing journalism culture: Toward a universal theory. *Communication Theory, 17,* 367–385.

Hartley, J. (2008). Journalism as a human right: The cultural approach to Journalism. In M. Löffelholz & D. Weaver (Eds.), *Global journalism research: Theories, methods, findings, future* (pp. 39–51). Malden, MA: Blackwell.

Heinderyckx, F. (2015). Gatekeeping theory redux. In T.P. Vos & F. Heinderyckx (Eds.), *Gatekeeping in transition* (pp. 253–267). New York: Routledge.

Heinrich, A. (2011). *Network journalism: Journalistic practice in interactive spheres.* New York: Routledge.

Hermida, A. (2012). Social journalism: Exploring how social media is shaping journalism. In E. Siapera & A. Veglis (Eds.), *The handbook of global online journalism* (pp. 309–328). Malden, MA: Wiley-Blackwell.

Hermida, A. (2015). Nothing but the truth: Redrafting the journalistic boundary of verification. In M. Carlson & S.C. Lewis (Eds.), *Boundaries of journalism: Professionalism, practices and participation* (pp. 37–50). New York: Routledge.

Hermida, A. (2016). Social media and the news. In T. Witschge, C.W. Anderson, D. Domingo & A. Hermida (Eds.), *The Sage handbook of digital journalism* (pp. 81–94). Thousand Oaks, CA: Sage.

Hermida, A. (2019). The existential predicament when journalism moves beyond journalism. *Journalism, 20,* 177–180.

Herrman, J. (2016, August 24). Inside Facebook's (totally insane, unintentionally gigantic, hyperpartisan) political-media machine. *The New York Times Magazine.* Online: www.nytimes.com/2016/08/28/magazine/inside-facebooks-totally-insane-unintentionally-gigantic. (Accessed: October 17, 2017).

Herrman, J. (2017, October 8). Trust bust. *The New York Times Book Review,* 13.

Herrman, J. (2018, April 15). When the social bubble bursts. The New York Times Magazine, 12, 14–15.

Hindman, M. (2009). *The myth of digital democracy.* Princeton, NJ: Princeton University Press.

How news happens: A study of the news ecosystem of one American city. (2010, January 11). *Pew Research Center: Journalism & Media.* Online: www.journalism.org/2010/01/11/how-news-happens/. (Accessed: October 12, 2018).

Isaac, M., & Wakabayashi, D. (2017, October 31). Broad reach of campaign by Russians is disclosed. *The New York Times*, B1, B3.

Iyengar, S., & Kinder, D.R. (1987). *News that matters: Television and American opinion.* Chicago, IL: University of Chicago Press.

Jenkins, J., & Tandoc, Jr., E.C., (2017). The power of the cover: Symbolic contests around the Boston bombing suspect's *Rolling Stone* cover. *Journalism, 18*, 281–297.

Jones, A.S. (2009). *Losing the news: The future of the news that feeds democracy.* New York: Oxford University Press.

Kantor, J., & Twohey, M. (2017, October 5). Harvey Weinstein paid off sexual harassment accusers for decades. *The New York Times*. Online: https://www.nytimes.com/2017/10/05/us/harvey-weinstein-harassment-allegations.html. (Accessed: August 5, 2019).

Katz, E., & Lazarsfeld, P.F. (1955). *Personal influence: The part played by people in the flow of mass communication.* Glencoe, IL: Free Press of Glencoe.

Kovach, B., & Rosenstiel, T. (2014). *The elements of journalism (3rd edition).* New York: Three Rivers Press.

Lee, E. (2019, February 5). Digital media hit a rut. What's next? *The New York Times*, B1, B4.

Li, Y. (2019). Contest over authority: Navigating native advertising's impacts on journalistic authority. *Journalism Studies, 20*, 523–541.

Marantz, A. (2018, April 16). About Facebook. *The New Yorker*, 19–20.

Matheson, D. (2009). What the blogger knows. In Z. Papacharissi (Ed.), *Journalism and citizenship: New agendas in communication* (pp. 151–165). New York: Routledge.

Matsa, K.E., & Shearer, E. (2018, September 10). *News use across social media platforms 2018.* Pew Research Center (Journalism & Media). Online: www.journalism.org/2018/09/10/news-use-across-social-media-platforms. (Accessed: November 9, 2018).

McNair, B. (2011). Managing the online news revolution: The UK experience. In G. Meikle & G. Redden (Eds.), *News online: Transformations and continuities* (pp. 38–52). New York: Palgrave Macmillan.

Meikle, G., & Redden, G. (2011). Introduction: Transformation and continuity. In G. Meikle & G. Redden (Eds.), *News online: Transformations and continuities* (pp. 1–19). New York: Palgrave Macmillan.

Meraz, S., & Papacharissi, Z. (2016). Networked framing and gatekeeping. In T. Witschge, C.W. Anderson, D. Domingo & A. Hermida (Eds.), *The Sage handbook of digital journalism* (pp. 95–112). Thousand Oaks, CA: Sage.

Miller, C.C. (2014, August 26). How social media silences debate. *The New York Times*. Online: www.nytimes.com/2014/08/27/upshot/how-social-Media-silences. (Accessed: November 3, 2018).

Min, S.-J. (2016). Conversation through journalism: Searching for organizing principles of public and citizen journalism. *Journalism: Theory, Practice and Criticism, 17*, 567–582.

Mitchell, A. (2018, December 3). Americans still prefer watching to reading the news – and mostly still through television. *Pew Research Center: Journalism & Media.* Online: www.journalism.org/2018/12/03/americans-still-prefer-watching-to-reading-the-news. (Accessed: January 23, 2019).

Nadler, A.M. (2016). *Making the news popular: Mobilizing U.S. news audiences.* Urbana, IL: University of Illinois Press.

Nah, S., Yamamoto, M., Chung, D.S., & Zuercher, R. (2015). Modeling the adoption and use of citizen journalism by online newspapers. *Journalism & Mass Communication Quarterly*, 92, 399–120.

Newman, A. (2017, November 6). Neighborhood news websites hoping to fill a digital void. *The New York Times*, A16.

Papacharissi, Z. (2015). *Affective publics: Sentiment, technology, and politics.* New York: Oxford University Press.

Pearson, G.D.H., & Kosicki, G.M. (2017). How way-finding is challenging gate-keeping in the digital age. *Journalism Studies*, 18, 1087–1105.

Perloff, R.M. (2009). Mass media, social perception, and the third-person effect. In J. Bryant & M.B. Oliver (Eds.), *Media effects: Advances in theory and research* (3rd ed., pp. 252–268). New York: Routledge.

Peters, J.W. (2018, October 30). Caravan rhetoric intersects with deadly hatred. *The New York Times*, A1, A15.

Renkl, M. (2017, October 20). The raw power of #MeToo. *The New York Times*, A25.

Robinson, S. (2006). The mission of the j-blog: Recapturing journalistic authority online. *Journalism*, 7, 65–83.

Robinson, S. (2009). A chronicle of chaos: Tracking the news story of Hurricane Katrina from *The Times-Picayune* to its website. *Journalism*, 10, 431–450.

Robinson, S. (2015). Redrawing borders from within: Commenting on news stories as boundary work. In M. Carlson & S.C. Lewis (Eds.), *Boundaries of journalism: Professionalism, practices and participation* (pp. 152–168). New York: Routledge.

Robinson, S. (2017). Check out this blog: Researching power and privilege in emergent journalistic authorities. In P.J. Boczkowski & C.W. Anderson (Eds.), *Remaking the news: Essays on the future of journalism scholarship in the digital age* (pp. 217–233). Cambridge, MA: The MIT Press.

Robinson, S., & DeShano, C. (2011). "Anyone can know": Citizen journalism and the interpretive community of the mainstream press. *Journalism*, 12, 963–982.

Roose, K. (2017a, October 3). Capitalizing on a mass killing to spread fake news online. *The New York Times*, A19.

Roose, K. (2017b, October 30), Furor abroad is far darker for Facebook. *The New York Times*, B1, B7.

Roose, K. (2018, October 25). Appearances can be deceiving: How images are misrepresented. *The New York Times*, A8.

Rosen, J. (2008, July 14). A most useful definition of citizen journalism. *Pressthink.* Online: archive.pressthink.org/2008/07/14/a_most_useful_d.html. (Accessed: October 20, 2017).

Rothman, J. (2018, November 12). Afterimage. *The New Yorker*, 34–36, 38, 40–44.

Russell, A. (2016). Networked journalism. In T. Witschge, C.W. Anderson, D. Domingo, & A. Hermida (Eds.), *The Sage handbook of digital journalism* (pp. 149–163). Thousand Oaks, CA: Sage.

Ryfe, D.M. (2010). Book reviews. (Review of Alex S. Jones, *Losing the news: The future of the news that feeds democracy.*) *Journalism*, 11, 375–377.

Ryfe, D.M. (2012a). *Can journalism survive? An inside look at American newsrooms.* Cambridge, UK: Polity Press.

Ryfe, D.M. (2012b). Why objectivity is impossible in networked journalism and what this means for the future of news. In B. St. John, III & K.A. Johnson

(Eds.), *News with a view: Essays on the eclipse of objectivity in modern journalism* (pp. 189–204). Jefferson, NC: McFarland.

Ryfe, D.M. (2019). The ontology of journalism. *Journalism, 20*, 206–209.

Sante, L. (2019, March 24). An introduction. *The New York Times* (Special section, The Daily Miracle), 2.

Shane, S. (2017, September 8). To sway vote, Russia used army of fake Americans. *The New York Times*, A1, A10-A11.

Shane, S., & Frenkel, S. (2018, December 18). Russian election effort focused on influencing African-American vote. *The New York Times*, A1, A14.

Shirky, C. (2008). *Here comes everybody*. New York: Penguin Press.

Shoemaker, P.J., & Vos, T.P. (2009). *Gatekeeping theory*. New York: Routledge.

Sikorski, C., & Hänelt, M. (2016). Scandal 2.0: How valenced reader comments affect recipients' perception of scandalized individuals and the journalistic quality of online news. *Journalism & Mass Communication Quarterly, 93*, 551–571.

Singer, J.B. (2005). The political j-blogger: "Normalizing" a new media form to fit old norms and practices. *Journalism, 5*, 173–198.

Singer, J.B. (2013). Networked news work. In B. Brennen (Ed.), *Assessing evidence in a postmodern world* (pp. 137–150). Milwaukee, WI: Marquette University Press.

Smith, T. (2018, October 31). On #MeToo, Americans more divided by party than gender. *NPR*. Online: www.npr.org/2018/10/31. (Accessed: October 31, 2018).

Steiner, L. (2019). Scandal and celebrity. In H. Tumber & S. Waisbord (Eds.), *Routledge companion to media & scandal* (pp. 304-314). New York: Routledge.

Steiner, L., Guo, J., McCaffrey, R., & Hills, P. (2013). *The Wire* and repair of the journalistic paradigm. *Journalism, 14*, 703–720.

Thompson, N. (2019, February 3). Journalism's stormy seas. *The New York Times Book Review*, 11.

Tufekci, Z. (2017). *Twitter and tear gas: The power and fragility of networked protest*. New Haven, CT: Yale University Press.

Valenzuela, S., Piña, M., & Ramírez, J. (2017). Behavioral effects of framing on social media users: How conflict, economic, human interest, and morality frames drive news sharing. *Journal of Communication, 67*, 803–826.

Vos, T.P. (2015). Revisiting gatekeeping theory during a time of transition. In T.P. Vos & F. Heinderyckx (Eds.), *Gatekeeping in transition* (pp. 3–24). New York: Routledge.

Vos, T.P., Craft, S., & Ashley, S. (2012). New media, old criticism: Bloggers' press criticism and the journalistic field. *Journalism, 13*, 850–868.

Vos, T.P., & Finneman, T. (2017). The early historical construction of journalism's gatekeeping role. *Journalism, 18*, 265–280.

Waisbord, S. (2017). Afterword: Crisis? What crisis? In C. Peters & M. Broersma (Eds.), *Rethinking journalism again: Societal role and public relevance in a digital age* (pp. 205–215). New York: Routledge.

Wakabayashi, D. (2017, September 27). Google as traffic cop. *The New York Times*, B1, B3.

Walker, L. (2004, December 9). On local sites, everyone's a journalist. *The Washington Post*. Online: www.washingtonpost.com/wp-dyn/articles/A46519-2004Dec8.html. (Accessed: October 20, 2017).

Wall, M. (2005). "Blogs of war": Weblogs as news. *Journalism, 6*, 153–172.

White, D.M. (1950). The "Gate Keeper": A case study in the selection of news. *Journalism Quarterly*, 27, 383–390.

Williams, A., & Harte, D. (2016). In Hyperlocal news. T. Witschge, C. W. Anderson, D. Domingo & A. Hermida (Eds.), *The Sage handbook of digital journalism* (pp. 280–293). Thousand Oaks, CA: Sage.

Zapruder, A. (2016). *Twenty-six seconds: A personal history of the Zapruder film.* New York: Twelve.

Zelizer, B. (1993). Journalists as interpretive communities. *Critical Studies in Mass Communication*, *10*, 219–237.

3   Defining News and Journalism

Some years back, a New York City woman, Ivanna (no, not that Ivana, President Trump's first wife!) lost her phone in a New York taxi, and was understandably beside herself. She was getting married soon and the phone contained valuable information about her wedding, like the guest list. Would she ever find her phone? Was the phone forever lost?

She feared it was. She bought a new phone, but soon, she and a friend, Evan, came across some disturbing information – photographs that a girl from Queens had taken of herself that had been transferred to Ivanna's new phone. The young woman had Ivanna's phone! Over the next several weeks, a drama ensued that involved the woman who took Ivanna's phone from the taxi and her friends. It piqued Evan, propelling him to engage in a mad online search for the phone, eliciting threats, provoking racial animus, and engaging thousands of New Yorkers who followed the story of the missing phone on early social media sites, ultimately transforming the story into news (Shirky, 2008). The online conflagration, described later in the chapter, complete with an unexpected surprise ending, provides insights into the meaning and definition of news.

This chapter focuses on definitions – the challenges of defining terms in an area of blurred boundaries, but also the importance of articulating clear definitions of foundational concepts. As intriguing as it is to describe porous, overlapping boundaries in contemporary news, it is also important to gain closure. Definitions are indispensable to scholars. They may seem boring, but they aren't, because when you define something, you are penetrating its essence, plumbing its depth, pinpointing what is unique about your concept, and delineating how it differs from other ideas. You are like a geologist classifying rocks or a geneticist staking out the genes in the human genome, except you are studying the messy, political, symbolic world, trying to define the terminology underlying the journalistic project, the chronicling of daily events, illumination of societal problems, the first rough draft of social history. The definitions of journalism and news in this chapter, based on careful review of scholarly articles, organize and set the stage for the chapters that follow.

Journalism

Definitions of journalism abound, emphasizing that journalism involves credible information "that is tested, investigated, sorted, checked again (and) analyzed," as well as "a set of transparent, independent procedures" designed to verify and report "truthful information of consequence to citizens in a democracy" (see Craft & Davis, 2016, p. 58; Stephens, 2014, p. xxiii). Journalism has been viewed as a business, an institution, set of practices, a profession (this is controversial) – and, more deeply, an interpretive community that emphasizes certain rituals, ideological beliefs, and consensual ways of framing complex phenomena (Borden, 2007; Deuze, 2005, 2011; Hallin & Mancini, 2004; Hanitzsch, 2009; Josephi, 2009; Zelizer, 1993, 2004, 2005).

Truth be told, journalism is a capacious, large domain with an array of features and functions that complexly differ, as a function of a nation's economic, political and historical foundations. One can't define journalism so narrowly that it excludes citizens, who have expanded the journalistic realm, even if tweets transmitted during crises are so short and emotive that they push the definitional envelope. By the same token, we can't define journalism so broadly that it includes every social post that broaches political or personal issues, or fake news pages developed by foreign governments and ideological groups that deliberately distort information with an eye toward political control.

It would be incorrect to define journalism as the collection of accurate, truthful information because news does not always get the truth right. Historically, journalism has never been predicated on truth, or legions of yellow, sensationalizing reporters of the 19th century and tabloid journalists of the 20th would never have made the grade. And even if elite journalists like to draw boundaries between this seedier reporting and their more informative work (Carlson & Berkowitz, 2014), hyped-up, exaggerated, specious reporting has a long, if problematic, tradition in journalism.

Journalism is not simply the aggregation of content. It is not a product, but a process, "a way to search for truth" and "a conversation, not a lecture" (Tucher, 1994, p. 208). Pulling these different perspectives together, I offer an integrative definition of journalism. **Journalism** is defined as:

> a craft collectively devoted to truthfully assembling, reporting, and verifying information, based on particular criteria, transforming the accumulated information into news of matters of public importance, while, at the same time, illuminating social problems, articulating opinions about topics of public interest, and engaging richly with the community.

The definition emphasizes that journalism is a broad-based domain that includes conventional newspapers and television, online news outlets, citizen journalism sites, and a range of controversial online platforms. Just because a particular entity falls under the broad umbrella of journalism does not mean it offers up cogent or high-quality journalism. Journalism can be magnificent or mediocre, its stories stupendous or silly.

The definition stresses that journalism has different facets. First, it is *a craft*, an occupation that requires analytical and interpersonal skills. Is it also a profession? Scholars have long debated this. Because a profession involves licensing requirements (think of medicine or the law) and journalism, as practiced by people freely and in very different ways, eschews this, it is difficult to call journalism a profession in the technical sense (Bromley, 2019; Waisbord, 2013). However, journalists maintain professional norms and ethics. Splitting the difference between calling journalism a profession and just an ordinary trade, it seems fair to say that journalism is clearly a craft – an occupation requiring numerous skills that are underpinned by standards and values.

Second, journalism involves *truthfully assembling, reporting, and verifying information about issues of the day.* No one is objective, and truth is elusive. But journalism involves a conscientious attempt to assemble and report information as truthfully as possible, vetting and verifying the information. Verification has long been the gold standard of journalism, underscoring the importance of holding off publishing information that has not been checked, using rigorous criteria to ensure that information included in stories is as truthful as humanly possible. Of course, today, those rules are almost quaint.

Verification is under siege in the wake of pressure to be first to break a crisis news story online and the proliferation of impulsive online tweets that can bear a loose relationship with the facts. As Alfred Hermida (2015) aptly noted, "the role of the journalist as bearing witness to the news is usurped when the public itself takes on the role of documenting events" (p. 40). There is great variability in the degree to which journalistic outlets, including citizen sites, rigorously verify information. And there is no doubt that in an era of multiple gatekeepers, journalism is less the final, definitive word about what is true than a process by which truth claims are adjudicated by journalistic professionals and citizens, communicating in an all-too-public arena (Hermida, 2012).

Yet truth – verifying facts, "getting it right" – still remains a fundamental purpose of journalism, whether by conventional reporting, citizen journalism, or hybrid combinations – because you can't have an informed citizenry if information on which news is based (and citizens' judgments are formed) is unreliable, suspect, and even outright false.

Let's move to the third, related attribute of journalism: *the use of particular criteria that govern the truthful assembling, reporting, and verification of information.* Journalists have many ways to verify facts and assess their accuracy, making certain that the story satisfies rules of journalistic evidence, and deciding just how to handle information that varies along the continuum of credibility. Like social scientists, journalists apply canons of measurement. These include assessing the reliability of sources (i.e., individuals with information) who talk to reporters, such as the consistency with which they have been correct in the past, as well as the likely validity of the information, based on whether the same facts have been provided by different sources (the more sources, the more confidence one has in informational accuracy); the probability that the source actually had access to the facts she is providing; and even whether a source is providing information that, were it revealed, would prove damaging to the source, a long-established indicator of credibility as it attests to the degree to which the source is willing to go to speak the truth. In addition, journalists can cross-check information provided by sources or obtained first-hand against public records, legal documents, databases, social media profiles, and facial recognition software.

Criteria for verifying truth claims differ, depending on whether the journalist works for a top-notch newspaper, local TV news station, online news outlet, or citizen journalism site. There has been debate about the criteria citizen journalists use, with advocates of traditional journalism questioning the rigor with which some citizen bloggers check their facts. Bloggers, for their part, have responded that they have their own procedures to gather news that emphasize transparency, links, interviews with different sources, and community perspectives, all of which constitute distinctive "ways of knowing" that differ from the way "the press has traditionally practiced, negotiated and shared news stories," as Sue Robinson and Cathy DeShano (2011, p. 963) note. Increasingly, there is respect for multiple ways of knowing and different ways of verifying information employed by conventional and citizen journalists. Although conventional and citizen journalists can differ in their criteria for verifying the truthfulness of claims, there is consensus that more inclusive criteria are more useful, showcased in the broad view of a journalist, defined by two legal scholars as an individual involved in investigative reporting, gathering news, and intent on disseminating news to the public (Pember & Calvert, 2008, p. 383).

This brings us to a fourth attribute of journalism: *transforming information into news of matters of public importance.* Information is not the same as news. News is constructed from information. As noted in Chapter 6, there is a seemingly infinite amount of information available online and in everyday life, but only a small portion becomes news. Deciding what's news, as Gans (2004) famously put it, is a matter of controversy, debate, finely-honed professional judgment, and a host of factors that are the stuff of this book. There are many determinants of news operating on different levels, but at the very least news involves sculpting information into a narrative of matters in the public domain.

The final attribute of journalism extends beyond gathering and produ-cing news that monitors the social environment. Journalism also involves broader aspects: *illuminating social problems, articulating opinions about public issues, and engaging richly with the broader community.* News analyses and features shed light on moral wrongs and societal imperfec-tions. Journalists also articulate opinions, in editorials and ideological web sites, about politics and society. At their best these opinions are thoughtfully elaborated in essays and blogs, and at their worst are full of vitriol. One could say that only thoughtful opinions constitute journal-ism, but that forces us into making value judgments about just what constitutes a thoughtful opinion. (Good luck with that!) Such judgments would be impossible to adjudicate, require a contestable perspective outside journalism and would be inconsistent with history; newspapers have always expressed opinions that were both insightful and short-sighted. Yet these papers have long been regarded as part of the press, even if one could find some of their views wanting or untenable in hindsight. Lastly, scholars emphasize that journalism performs a broader role, enriching and provoking the community of citizens, striving, through language and ideas, to constitute the citizenry that is the historical centerpiece of democratic societies (Nord, 2001).

News

Okay, so what's news? I don't mean this in the quizzical way that question is asked, but more conceptually. Historically, news refers to the recent, the new, the breaking event (Fuller, 1996; Stephens, 2007), even if in centuries past it could take weeks or more for an event to become widely known. Does that mean that everything that happened recently to a friend, described narcissistically on Facebook, is news? Is a hot YouTube video news? An oh-so-cute video of a verbally loquacious child trying to convince his father to let him eat a cupcake, a baby biting an older child's finger, or the BuzzFeed video of the bizarre balloon burst? No – and this is because news does not involve recent events that happened in private or are devoid of consequences to the citizenry, real or imagined. News centers on the public – on events, issues, people, places, and ideas that bear broadly on society as a whole. Let's return to the quirky, true story described earlier in the chapter, based on Clay Shirky's (2008) rendition, to appreciate this more fully.

Sashsa, Sidekick, and News

As you recall, back in 2006, a New York City woman, Ivanna, misplaced her phone in a New York City taxi and was desperate to locate it. It was a year before the iPhone had been invented, and Ivanna owned an expensive multifunction phone called a Sidekick that had a keyboard, screen, and camera. The phone contained lots of information about her forthcoming wedding, like the guest list and catering company. When Ivanna noticed the phone was missing, she undoubtedly was very upset.

A few days later, concluding the phone was lost, she bought a new Sidekick. It turned out that the phone company had stored copies of Ivanna's information, like the guest list for her wedding, on the company's server and shifted it to her new phone. Soon after shelling out several hundred dollars for the new phone, she and her friend Evan, a computer nerd (this will become relevant shortly), happened on some alarming information. They spotted photographs that a girl from Queens named Sasha had snapped of her friends and herself. The photos taken on Ivanna's old phone had been automatically transferred to her new phone. Sasha had taken Ivanna's phone!

With Sasha's picture and email address now available, Evan emailed Sasha, explained their predicament, and asked her to return the phone. Sasha responded that her brother, Luis, found the phone in the taxi, gave it to her, but she was not stupid enough to return a phone under these shady circumstances. Sasha, who is Hispanic, added a racial dimension when she noted that Evan's "White ass" did not deserve getting the phone back, perhaps inferring Evan and Ivanna's race from photographs that appeared on the phone. The conflagration continued. Sasha said she and her boyfriend would meet Evan to return the phone, giving her home address. Evan, nervous about scheduling a meeting both because Sasha threatened to hit Evan with the phone and because he thought the address was fake (it was), opted not to meet the two. Instead, he went public with the story, initiating its transformation into news.

He explained what happened and uploaded Sasha's photos to his personal website, titling the new webpage "StolenSidekick." Evan's friends spread it around the Internet, prompting a discovery (this was 2006) that a page on the social networking site, MySpace, contained photos of Sasha. Evan, whose determination to get the phone back combined a friend's devotion with apparent vengeance, updated his page a few times, triggering an email from Luis, Sasha's brother, who claimed to be a member of the military police (whatever that meant). Luis told Evan to quit bugging Sasha, or violence might ensue. Disturbing as all this was, in the larger public scheme of things, the case remained one of those all-too-familiar stories of several people arguing over a phone one of them had pilfered.

Then something significant happened. The whole weird affair made it onto Digg, an early social networking site that recruited millions of readers, many of whom, at the rate of 10 emails per minute, responded sympathetically to Evan, even volunteering their help. Encouraged by the response, but seemingly on an adrenalin-infused mission, Evan continued his updates. Other posts followed, producing additional MySpace profiles of the now-famous Sasha, her boyfriend, and brother, prompting one reader to figure out Sasha's last name and address, even driving by her house and posting a video on the Internet.

Thousands of people followed the trials and tribulations of the stolen phone, with some asking about Sasha's moral values, raising questions about their own motives. Was this curiosity, empathy with the victim of a theft they too had experienced, or were there racial aspects? As the saga continued, Sasha's friends kept in touch with Evan, posting different stories about where the phone actually was. Sasha's brother, Luis, said they planned to sue for harassment. The police got wind of the story, initially explaining how one could file a claim with the NYPD, and later becoming more aggressively involved when they arrested Sasha, a 16-year-old from Queens, perhaps in response to pressure from the online crowds sympathetic to Evan. The police recovered the Sidekick phone and returned it to Ivanna. In the end, a happy ending: the police released Sasha because Evan and Ivanna chose not to press charges; Ivanna's wedding, undoubtedly more gratifying because of the phone snafu, proceeded smoothly; and Evan, inspired by his ability to solicit interest on the web, began getting work as a freelance public relations consultant. (Only in New York, right!)

It is striking that a rather ordinary conflict among a group of private individuals in the big city became news, transformed from a private con-flagration to an Internet saga to a news story covered in mainstream media. A key reason the story became news is it spilled into the **public** domain, first with a prominent posting on Digg, then because it spurred reader interest (for a host of sociological and psychological reasons) morphing into a topic of considerable concern and online attention, with Evan, Ivanna, Sasha, and Luis actors in a riveting crime drama with moral overtones.

News centrally involves issues of public concern, highlighting journal-ism's foundational roots in the public sphere. In one sense it has always been this way. In 1836, when legendary newspaper editor James Gordon Bennett prowled about a crime scene, in search of a story, a police officer allowed him to do so, pronouncing that "he is an editor – he is on public duty" (Tucher, 1994, p. 25). Or, as Carey (2007) noted, from a scholarly perspective: "Journalism transfers a private habit onto the community" (p. 8).

The story about Sasha also points up another aspect of journalism – how a story was *constructed* or stitched together from the bits of disparate information gleaned from Sasha, Ivanna, Evan, Luis, reactions on Digg, and the police arrest. And this is a key characteristic of news. News does not exist out there, as a facticity in the external world. Journalists may know it when they see it, but news is also a social construct, harnessed by reporters as they cognitively organize disparate events into a coherent whole, based on established, if changing, rules of reporting. Drawing on these lines of thinking, I define news as **a narrative account of new or recent matters of public interest**.

Let's unpack the definition. First, news offers a narrative, an explanatory account connecting different events and unifying them under the rubric of a coherent framework. It is frequently dramatized, revolves around conflict (Bantz, 1997), and, as will be discussed in later chapters, does not reflect, but helps construct, social reality.

Second, news involves novel, new, or recent events. This classic aspect of news dates to antiquity. After a certain amount of time has passed, a story is no longer news. It may be important and socially significant, but it is not news.

Third, the "public" in "public interest" is the larger populace or community that extends beyond the cocoon of an individual or family. "Public" is a complex, fluid term, but necessarily involves real or constructed issues that bear on the citizenry, society, institutional roles performed, and identities displayed in formal and informal social settings. News necessarily transcends private matters, though public and private can intersect, as when politicians' sexual infidelities are news because they presumably – there is debate about this – bear on the political leader's capacity to credibly hold office or raise questions about the politician's integrity. Posts about your friends' love lives, breakups, athletic achievements, and goofy exploits may be news to you, but they don't qualify as news, in the journalistic sense, until they bear on the public domain, as illustrated by the story about Sasha and the Sidekick.

Some scholars argue that for public information to qualify as news, it must be checked and scrutinized by established journalists, based on conventional journalistic criteria. But this is a circular definition that places definitional power in the hands of mainstream journalists: News is only news if it appears in, say, *The New York Times* or Fox, begging the question of why editors decided it was fit to print as news to begin with. Information about public issues can fit under the rubric of news if it appears in a Facebook post, even if this does not satisfy traditional journalistic gatekeeping rules that evolved over the course of the 20th century (Kumar, 2009). One does not want exclude the multitude of relevant public narratives of recent events that appear on social media that were not are not distilled by traditional reporters. It is more parsimonious and accurate to define news as a narrative account of an issue of public interest, while recognizing these narratives do not always rise to the level of journalism.

Increasingly, in an age of nonstop online editing, news no longer takes on the trappings of a finished product that appears on a newsstand or on a flat-screen TV authoritatively located in the family living room. Instead, it has the accoutrements of a just-completed draft that may be modified over the course of a day, with the news-editing processes less opaque and more conspicuous to the audience than in earlier eras (Karlsson, 2011). Certain attributes of news, like drama and novelty, stand the test of time, but the form and style in which news is presented can change with the times. Table 3.1 summarizes the main characteristics of the concepts of journalism and news.

Journalism and News

Journalism involves gathering information and the construction of a narrative called news. But is all news journalism? In the old days, even if the answer begged the question, one could at least put forth an argument that that news was by definition journalism because the only people gathering up information and transforming it into news were journalists. It's different today. There are loads of articles purporting to be news on the Internet that run the gamut from thoughtful to the fictitious; some are heavily tinged by the ideological perspective of the author, others are frenzied tweets, and the writers can be mainstream reporters, citizen journalists, ideological activists, trolls, or ordinary individuals punching out a piece.

Should we decouple news and journalism? C.W. Anderson, Michael Schudson, and Leonard Downie, Jr. (2016) pointedly assert that "news is not necessarily journalism, in which newsworthy information and content is gathered, filtered, evaluated, edited, and presented in credible and engaging forms" (p. 60). They are correct. Journalistic news writing presumes a methodology, commitment to verification of facts, and invocation of specific criteria for determining which information merits inclusion in a story about public issues. Journalism, as Nerone (2012) notes, "defines the appropriate practices and values of news professionals, news media, and news systems" (p. 447; see Glasser, Varma, & Zou, 2019).

In the online digital milieu, people can capture a novel public moment, a terrorist incident, a devastating storm, and communicate this worldwide. One would be hard-pressed **not** to call these news, based

Table 3.1 Definitions

Key Aspects of Journalism
1. Craft dedicated to truthful reporting and verifying information
2. Calls on systematic criteria to report and verify information
3. Transforms information into news, based on diverse, time-honored procedures
4. Sheds light on social problems, with perspectives and opinions, and engages with the broader community.
Key Aspects of News
• Narrative account
• Involves a new phenomenon
• Bears on matters of public interest.

on the definition. But are they journalism? Not necessarily. Diamond Reynolds' impassioned narration of the incident where a police officer shot her boyfriend was certainly news, satisfying criteria of newsworthiness, like novelty, and congealing with the notion that news involves sharing matters of public interest with a wider audience (Shoemaker & Cohen, 2006; Stephens, 2007). However, Reynolds was not concerned with reporting or verifying her information; nor did she invoke specific criteria to assess the accuracy and validity of what she reported, which is fundamental to the practice of journalism.

In a similar fashion, a video posted to Twitter in April, 2018 of police arresting two African American men without cause in a Philadelphia Starbucks was viewed more than 10 million times online, prompting outrage and illustrating racial prejudice in action (Dias, Eligon, & Oppel, 2018). The video was unquestionably news – a narrative of a recent, highly public event, a somewhat novel incident even in the tortured history of American race relations, and one that touched on broad public values. It was unquestionably a cause for serious concern, perhaps even protest, but did not meet the canons of journalism. The video accurately conveyed the information; three police officers arrested two Black men, placing them in handcuffs, even after they calmly responded to the officers' questions. (The arrests followed a Starbucks manager's call to the police when the two men, waiting for a business associate to join them, had not ordered anything.) The video did not cover all angles (for example, that of the Starbucks employee or police), was not concerned with truthful assemblage or verification of information, and did not take into account criteria that would determine the validity and accuracy of the information transmitted.

It is a difficult task, defining journalistic concepts in a blurred, boundary-crossing online world. The Starbucks example clearly blurs the lines, as a television crew could take a similar video, and, with an audio track accompanying the visual, could be considered news. Presumably, TV journalists would make sure the video offered an accurate rendition of events, qualify information of questionable import, and supply a narrative that took contextual issues into account. However, network news regularly shows videos shot at scenes of accidents that can raise questions about accuracy and validity.

It seems strange – and out of sync with a century of professional journalism tradition – to label as *news* a tweet of a shooting or a passerby's video about a hurricane, which have not gone through the rigors of journalistic editing. Are these really *news*, one asks? In today's world, one is hard-pressed to call them anything else. To define as news only that which conventional journalists gather is to offer a circular definition, one that makes news the exclusive province of old-style institutions and overlooks the fact that narrative stories about public issues posted by ordinary people online can contain as much news as did short snippets from network anchors that interrupted regularly-scheduled programs to describe an emergency of national import. To refuse to call these tweets or posts news has little face validity, as it denies that they are as authentic or immediate as 8-millimeter film photojournalists shot at scenes of tragedies and disasters decades ago. Thus, *a story can be news, but not be regarded as an instance of journalism because it has not met the canons of journalistic verification, however diverse they may be.* But precisely because news can be conveyed by individuals who are not associated with – or certified by – traditional journalism means that the former's errors and biases, as well as authenticity and immediacy, are also an issue, as has occurred when online reports misidentified the culprits in tragic shootings.

Online news sites also differ in the degree to which they verify public affairs information and the quality of journalism they provide. Certain so-called news sites that promote themselves as purveying news or journalism provide neither. For example, Infowars is an uber–right-wing, conspiracy theory site that posts fake news and false reports, exemplified by its outrageous claim that the 2012 Sandy Hook Elementary School shooting was a government hoax (Williamson, 2018). Infowars makes no claim to be anything other than a right-wing information-pedaling website. It makes little pretense of presenting or verifying consensually truthful information, and its opinions hardly illuminate social or political issues. You could call Infowars journalism, but it would be like calling a quack with a fake medical degree a doctor.

Complicating matters, *The National Inquirer* is a time-honored, frequently disreputable supermarket tabloid that shows how difficult it can be to make clean distinctions in the current milieu. *The Inquirer*'s publisher, David Pecker, a friend of President Trump, reportedly paid hush money to keep stories of Trump's affairs out of public view. He later may have blackmailed Amazon president Jeff Bezos, who bought *The Washington Post*, a newspaper that has offered journalistically solid, and appropriately critical, coverage of Trump, threatening to publish lewd text messages that Bezos and a lover exchanged unless Bezos stopped an investigation of how *The Inquirer* obtained the messages. (Bezos believed *The Inquirer*'s motives were abjectly political.)

For its part, *The Inquirer* has published flagrantly biased, false stories, but has also scored significant scoops, such as stories that revealed that long-married, 2008 presidential candidate John Edwards had an extramarital affair on the campaign trail with a filmmaker, who later gave birth to a daughter. (You can't make this stuff up, and if you could, it would pale compared to what actually happens!). Does *The National Inquirer* do journalism? Yes, as this one-off example illustrates, and more generally, it engages in journalism, at least as practiced by the sleazy tabloids that have been hawked on the street (and now online) for more than a century. *The Inquirer* shows how uneasy and difficult it is to clearly define terms in an era when news blurs traditional lines and is the province of so many different reporters and posters.

Conclusions

Ours is a world of boundary-crossing, where citizen journalism intersects with time-honored gathering of news, once-shunned journalistic practices are embraced by journalists, and the boundary between fact and opinion can be more difficult for readers to discern. News and journalism are important concepts in a democratic society, but more difficult to define today than in decades past. In the end, we need definitions to clearly demarcate our concepts and make distinctions between related terms.

Journalism is usefully defined as a craft dedicated to truthfully assembling, reporting, and verifying information, based on specific criteria, transforming information into a news narrative, while articulating opinions and engaging richly with the community. Journalism is capacious, encompassing citizen reporting, mainstream news, and a multitude of online outlets.

For its part, news is a narrative constructed from recent information on matters of public interest. News can fall into the category of journalism, but does not always, raising questions about the accuracy and validity of what passes for news in the dazzling, but fractious, online milieu. And news is nothing if not in flux, fraught with negative aspects, like strikingly sensational coverage of local crimes, as well as stunningly positive features, spanning immersive storytelling and captivating multi-media narratives (Usher, 2016).

So too with journalism. It is multifaceted, rich, flawed, and always changing. But at its best it has tremendous value. As the revolutionary political activist Thomas Paine is rumored to have claimed more than two centuries ago, journalism helps us "see with other eyes, hear with other ears, and think with other thoughts than those we formerly used" (Zelizer, 2017, p. 32). It remains as true then – during an era when journalism, as practiced today, did not exist – as now. In an era of fake news, when artifice, artificial intelligence-based, and troll-distributed stories can mask as news, and when news is slanted to target a marketing niche, trite as it may sound, but important as it is to state, journalism matters.

References

Anderson, C.W., Downie, Jr., L., & Schudson, M. (2016). *The news media: What everyone needs to know*. New York: Oxford University Press.

Bantz, C.R. (1997). News organizations: Conflict as a crafted cultural norm. In D. Berkowitz (Ed.), *Social meanings of news* (pp. 123–137). Thousand Oaks, CA: Sage.

Borden, S.L. (2007). *Journalism as practice: MacIntyre, virtue ethics and the press*. Aldershot, UK: Ashgate.

Bromley, M. (2019). "Who are those guys?" The challenge of journalists' identity. *Journalism, 20*, 13–16.

Carey, J.W. (2007). A short history of journalism for journalists: A proposal and essay. *The Harvard International Journal of Press/Politics, 12*, 3–16.

Carlson, M., & Berkowitz, D. (2014). "The emperor lost his clothes": Rupert Murdoch, *News of the World* and journalistic boundary work in the UK and USA. *Journalism, 15*, 389–406.

Craft, S., & Davis, C.N. (2016). *Principles of American journalism: An introduction* (2nd ed.). New York: Routledge.

Deuze, M. (2005). What is journalism? Professional identity and ideology of journalists reconsidered. *Journalism: Theory, Practice and Criticism, 6*, 442–464.

Deuze, M. (2011). What is journalism? Professional identity and ideology of journalists reconsidered. In D.A. Berkowitz (Ed.), *Cultural meanings of news: A text-reader* (pp. 17–32). Thousand Oaks, CA: Sage.

Dias, E., Eligon, J., & Oppel, Jr., R.A. (2018, April 18). Outrage for some, for others it's just everyday life. *The New York Times*, A11.

Fuller, J. (1996). *News values: Ideas for an information age*. Chicago, IL: University of Chicago Press.

Gans, H.J. (2004). *Deciding what's news: A study of CBS evening news, NBC nightly news, Newsweek and Time* (25th anniversary edition). Evanston, IL: Northwestern University Press.

Glasser, T.L., Varma, A., & Zou, S. (2019). Native advertising and the cultivation of counterfeit news. *Journalism, 20*, 150–153.

Hallin, D.C., & Mancini, P. (2004). *Comparing media systems: Three models of media and politics*. New York: Cambridge University Press.

Hanitzsch, T. (2009). Comparative journalism studies. In K. Wahl-Jorgensen & T. Hanitzsch (Eds.), *The handbook of journalism studies* (pp. 413–427). Thousand Oaks, CA: Sage.

Hermida, A. (2012). Tweets and truth. *Journalism Practice, 6*, 659–668.

Hermida, A. (2015). Nothing but the truth: Redrafting the journalistic boundary of verification. In M. Carlson & S.C. Lewis (Eds.), *Boundaries of journalism: Professionalism, practices and participation* (pp. 37–50). New York: Routledge.

Josephi, B. (2009). Journalism education. In K. Wahl-Jorgensen & T. Hanitzsch (Eds.), *The handbook of journalism studies* (pp. 42–56). Thousand Oaks, CA: Sage.

Karlsson, M. (2011). The immediacy of online news, the visibility of journalistic processes and a restructuring of journalistic authority. *Journalism, 12*, 279–295.

Kumar, A. (2009). Looking back and looking ahead: Journalistic rules, social control, social change and relative autonomy. *Journal of Media Sociology, 1*, 135–159.

Nerone, J. (2012). The historical roots of the normative model of journalism. *Journalism, 14*, 446–458.

Nord, D.P. (2001). *Communities of journalism: A history of American newspapers and their readers*. Urbana, IL and Chicago, IL: University of Illinois Press.

Pember, D.R., & Calvert, C. (2008). *Mass media law (2009–2010 edition)*. New York: McGraw-Hill.

Robinson, S., & DeShano, C. (2011). "Anyone can know": Citizen journalism and the interpretive community of the mainstream press. *Journalism, 12*, 963–982.

Shirky, C. (2008). *Here comes everybody: The power of organizing without organizations.* New York: Penguin Press.

Shoemaker, P.J., & Cohen, A.A. (2006). *News around the world: Content, practitioners and the public.* New York: Routledge.

Stephens, M. (2007). *A history of news* (3rd ed.). New York: Oxford University Press.

Stephens, M. (2014). *Beyond news: The future of journalism.* New York: Columbia University Press.

Tucher, A. (1994). *Froth & scum: Truth, beauty, goodness, and the ax murder in America's first mass medium.* Chapel Hill, NC: University of North Carolina Press.

Usher, N. (2016). *Interactive journalism: Hackers, data, and code.* Urbana, IL: University of Illinois Press.

Waisbord, S. (2013). *Reinventing professionalism: Journalism and news in global perspective.* Cambridge, UK: Polity Press.

Williamson, E. (2018, May 24). Sandy Hook suits target fabulist and online "post-truth" culture. *The New York Times*, A1, A16.

Zelizer, B. (1993). Journalists as interpretive communities. *Critical Studies in Mass Communication, 10*, 219–237.

Zelizer, B. (2004). *Taking journalism seriously: News and the academy.* Thousand Oaks, CA: Sage.

Zelizer, B. (2005). Definitions of journalism. In G. Overholser & K.H. Jamieson (Eds.), *The press* (pp. 66–80). New York: Oxford University Press.

Zelizer, B. (2017). *What journalism could be.* Cambridge, UK: Polity Press.

4   What Should News Do?
Ideals and Complicating Realities

It is a cottage industry, a favorite pastime, a delightful ritual, the journalistic equivalent of Harry Potter's game of Quidditch, a rough semi-contact sport in which media aficionados and ordinary gamers enthusiastically engage, sometimes as soon as the object – the news article, commentary, or opinionated post – appears on screen. Typically the verbal jousting is ferocious as commenters unceremoniously denounce news they dislike; other times, remarks can be humdrum or hackneyed, and on other less frequent occasions, observations are civil, even thoughtful. Commentary is almost never absent – and that is as it should be. In a democracy, criticism of the press is unquestionably a citizen's right. Harboring an opinion about the nature of news, given its ubiquity, is almost a requirement for participating in democratic debate.

Okay, we get that. The more difficult issue – and for us, the important one – is articulating the criteria by which we evaluate the news media in a networked public era. For this we turn to venerable **normative theories**, or prescriptive constellations of concepts of what news ought to do in society. Normative philosophical theories set forth ideas of what the news should do to best serve democratic – or, more broadly, sociopolitical – ends. There are no perfect theories; each has limits and deficiencies, but taken together, theories offer insights on what the news should do, of particular interest today when the news is in flux, its facts open to question, and its authority fragmented among different gatekeepers.

Journalism scholars have written astutely about these issues, beginning with Fred S. Siebert, Theodore Peterson, and Wilbur Schramm's (1956) classic book, *Four theories of the press*. Taking a broad view of the burgeoning mass media, Siebert, Peterson, and Schramm examined news through the lenses of four philosophical perspectives: libertarian, social responsibility and, writing in the thicket of the Cold War, the Soviet communist, and authoritarian frameworks. In its heyday, *Four theories* was quite the book – read by journalism students, aspiring scholars, and professors in the new field of mass communication; to its credit, it was the first major academic attempt to offer a sweeping panorama of different media systems. Over the years, as scholars developed a more critical and globalized view of news, they developed a more complex view of this elegant little book, appreciating its strengths, yet lamenting its cultural and philosophical shortcomings (Berry et al., 1995; Christians et al., 2009; Merrill, 2002; Merrill & Lowenstein, 1979; Nerone, 2002, 2004; Wasserman & de Beer, 2009).

Although the book broke normative ground, it reflected the Cold War political environment, implicitly and ethnocentrically favoring the libertarian approach and adopting a pejorative attitude toward so-called authoritarian media. It neatly divvied up the world of media systems into just four, neglecting Asian, African, and Latin American frameworks, while emphasizing the Soviet Communist system that would cease to exist with the demise of the Soviet Union in 1991 (although many of its coercive aspects remain in Russia today). The book used "theory" loosely – neither in the descriptive scientific sense, nor the more normative political philosophical perspective. Siebert and his colleagues' book tended to oversimply matters, neglecting overlaps among theories, the role played by economic and cultural factors, and ways power is wielded in the private business sector (Berry et al., 1995; Hallin & Mancini, 2004). And yet, despite its shortcomings, proponents and critics alike admire the authors' pioneering determination to explore big issues and examine the all-important question of what news should do.

Emboldened by early and contemporary journalism scholars' conceptual work on normative issues, we now have a better handle on how to approach the daunting assumptions that underlie people's everyday criticisms of media, as well as more fundamental questions that strike at the heart of public life. How can news advance democracy? Which model of news best serves democratic society? How do philosophical, political, and media concepts shed light on these issues? Culling through this work in search of clear introductory perspectives on these complex ideas, I suggest there are three broad traditions that address the role news should play in society: libertarian theory; the social responsibility perspective, with its varied roles, from watchdog to civic democratic deliberation; and the collaborative approach, controversially and complexly, focusing on accommodating government (see Table 4.1). In each case, the discussion that follows outlines the gleaming ideas that characterize the particular perspective, followed by a critical examination of more complicating realities. The discussion draws on journalism scholarship by Clifford G. Christians and his colleagues (2009), interesting new work on journalism roles by Thomas Hanitzsch and Tim Vos (2017, 2018), and contemporary research on news.

The chapter begins with the libertarian approach to news, examining its foundations and conundrums. The next section describes social responsibility perspectives, a broad category that includes informational monitoring; interpretation; social empathy (Schudson, 2008a), along with ritualistic nation-healing; the investigative watchdog function; and facilitation of democratic

Table 4.1 Key Normative Perspectives on News

I. Libertarian Theory: Focus on liberty. Shortcoming: Total liberty may be problematic when extremist groups propagate falsehoods and hate.

II. Social Responsibility Theory

A. Informational monitoring: Focus on news surveillance of social environment. Shortcomings: Monitorial news can neglect or obfuscate problems.
B. Interpretation: Focus on analysis of underpinnings of issues. Shortcomings: In today's news, there is much superficial analysis revolving around strategic aspects of politics rather than deep examination of social issues.
C. Emotional roles of social empathy and ritualistic healing: Focus on news promotion of emotional understanding and healing on the macro scale. Shortcomings: Stories can neglect marginalized victims; the need to unify the community can obscure telling unpleasant truths.
D. Investigative watchdog: Focus on exposure of moral misconduct and systemic abuse. Shortcomings: Can compromise personal privacy and national security, also raising questions of whether the ends (publication of the exposé) justify the means (intrusion into a source's private life).
E. Facilitating democratic dialogue: Focus on news encouraging citizen involvement and community enhancement. Shortcomings: It is increasingly difficult to foster deliberative dialogue in the acrimonious online milieu.

III. Collaborative Approach: Focus on working and collaborating with government policymakers. Shortcomings: At its worst, it encourages censorship and violation of press freedoms.

---

dialogue. The final portion examines the collaborative approach, a decidedly different perspective on news with intriguing complexities, as well as red flags for democracy.

Libertarian Theory

This is the classic, liberty-loving, marketplace-of-ideas-embracing, unabashedly optimistic view of the press. It is old, hallowed, almost ancient, yet as relevant and controversial today as it was when the poet John Milton articulated its principles in a 1644 essay containing an eloquent argument against the British monarchy's pre-publication policy of licensing and censoring books. Incensed by censorship of his storied work, Milton argued that people should have unlimited access to others' ideas, noting that truth would emerge and survive in a "free and open encounter" (Siebert, Peterson, & Schramm, 1956, p. 44; see Figure 4.1). But there was more to it than just abstract philosophy. There was a personal angle, and it involved Milton's marriage, a jilted poet, and emotional turmoil.

Around 1642, Milton's wife, Mary Powell, who was 17, half Milton's age, left him after only a few weeks of marriage. She returned to her parents and stayed at home for several years, until she and Milton reconciled, at least for a time. While she was at home with her parents, Milton pushed for divorce,

Figure 4.1 John Milton, the celebrated English poet, who wrote "Areopagitica," a pamphlet extolling freedom of the press, a classic statement of the libertarian philosophy. Few may realize that the pamphlet had personal roots in Milton's objection to government's blocking his publication of a treatise affirming divorce (his own).

arguing philosophically (and insensitively because his wife was young and could not easily challenge his view, particularly then) that marriage was intended to represent a spiritual bond between a man and woman, and emotional incompatibility constituted legitimate grounds for divorce (Standage, 2013). He articulated his arguments for divorce in a pamphlet, only to discover that he could not receive a license to publish it. Denounced in Parliament and branded a radical who favored polygamy, Milton went to the heart of the matter, focusing less on the personal than the political.

He lambasted the licensing rules in a pamphlet, using the term, "Areopagitica," based on a Greek reference to a call for political reform by a well-known Athenian orator (or perhaps to a Biblical sermon against ignorance). With stirring arguments, Milton argued that since people are imperfect, prone to mistakes, no one could perfectly determine what was acceptable to print. Let truth and falsehood grapple, he said, famously observing that "who ever knew Truth put to the worse, in a free and open encounter?" (Standage, 2013, p. 99). It would be best, he wrote, to let every opinion be printed, exposing readers to a diversity of views. Better, he said, to allow truth and falsehood to tussle, recognizing that truth should overcome falsehood when they encounter each other in an open, freewheeling debate, even if that debate might bring up personal issues involved in marriage and divorce. (Milton may have been a difficult husband. He married three times, undoubtedly unusual for his times. He also championed the radical concept of divorce. We remember him for the strength of his arguments, not his emotional sensitivity.)

The backstory of Milton's personal life should not divert attention from the power of his principles. In fact, Milton was not a free speech zealot who believed in the untrammeled flow of news as an end itself; he believed the goal of free expression was to locate the divine value of truth, which he viewed as God's word. To Milton, free expression was linked with spiritual, not commercial, aspirations (Berry et al., 1995). And yet, even if he was not the ideal secular messenger for unbridled free speech, his difficult-to-pronounce "Areopagitica" stood the test of time, finding its impassioned way into the writings of Jefferson, Thomas Paine, and the great English philosopher, John Stuart Mill.

What came to be known as the libertarian theory of the news media, arguably the most famous and discussed normative theory, emphasizes **first**, that people have a natural, inalienable right of freedom of speech and press, embracing the principle that "all with something to say (should) be free to express themselves" (Siebert, Peterson, & Schramm, 1956, p. 45). **Second**, the theory reminds us this is a negative freedom – a freedom *from* restriction by government. The state does not have "the right to restrict that which it considered false and unsound" (Siebert et al., 1956 p. 31.) **Third**, libertarianism stipulates that individuals should be allowed to advocate for their own viewpoint, so long as they give others the identical right. **Fourth**, the theory includes a prescriptive pathway for truth, arguing that an open, self-correcting competition of ideas in the open marketplace provides the best way to ensure that truth, rather than falsehoods, will emerge (see Nerone, 2017, for an interesting historical perspective on the storied marketplace). **Finally**, libertarianism – for all but the most absolutist libertarians, beginning with the august framers of the American Bill of Rights (Levy, 1985) – allows for a handful of exceptions, where free expression can be abridged, the rare circumstances depending upon the nature of the times.

Libertarian theory recognizes that in the multiplicity of political voices, some opinions will lack cogency, and some information will be false. Rather than license (as it did in Milton's day) or ban scandalous or false information, government (libertarian theory argues) should be prohibited from restricting the press, trusting that the public can ferret through the cacophony of information, determine what is true, reject the specious argument, and embrace the most cogent, well-reasoned arguments. In his famous defense of this intellectual liberty, John Stuart Mill passionately argued:

If all mankind minus one, were of one opinion, and only one person were of the contrary opinion, mankind would be no more justified in silencing that one person, than he, if he had the power, would be justified in silencing mankind ... But the peculiar evil of silencing the expression of an opinion is, that it is robbing the human race; posterity as well as the existing generation; those who dissent from the opinion, still more than those who hold it ... If the opinion is right, they are deprived of the opportunity of exchanging error for truth; if wrong, they lose, what is almost as great a benefit, the clearer perception and livelier impression of truth, produced by its collision with error.

(Mill, 1859/2009, p. 20)

It is beautiful, eloquent prose, but invites a series of questions, not least the relevance of this idealistic posture for our chaotic, global age of non-stop, privacy-invading searing speech, sometimes infused with troubling falsehoods. The next section takes up the ways that two consequences of libertarianism not imagined by its 19th century advocates – invasion of privacy and digital falsehoods – complicate the normative playing field.

Complications

Privacy concerns

The libertarian approach embraces the publication, televising, streaming, and blogging of views across the political spectrum – a full spectrum of views, from liberal and extreme radical left to classically conservative and ultra-right; from the eloquent and nuanced to the simplistic and conspiratorial. Nonjudgmental in its orientation, it embraces screaming, factually dubious headlines in *The National Enquirer* about the love lives of celebrities: Jennifer Aniston, Brad and Angelina (no last names needed), as well as the uninterrupted feeding of British readers' voracious appetite for tabloid gossip, including libertarian-stoked news about a crime story that would even shock American newspapers.

The British paper, *News of the World* (actually its name), exploiting reader interest in the whereabouts of a missing 13-year-old girl, Milly Dowler, paid a private investigator to illegally hack into the girl's voicemail, listening in as her parents and friends left voice messages that begged Milly to get back to them, only to discover later that her daughter had been abducted and murdered. Simply to increase readership and beat the competition, *News of the World* hacked into the phone of a murdered schoolgirl, in a brazen act of journalism. It was all part of a long tradition of press invasion of privacy that called to mind the paparazzi's trailing of Princess Diana in 1997 that led to her death in a car crash, confirming that, as one British editor observed, "you don't get to be the editor of [a British tabloid newspaper] without being a fairly despicable human being" (Davies, 2014). Public revulsion with blatant invasions of privacy in the Dowler case, coupled with losses in advertising, led to the demise of the newspaper in 2011, though British tabloids, newspapers with smaller pages, lots of photos and sensational headlines, continue to rock the UK.

The same, centuries-old libertarian spirit that, for better or worse, animates sensational stories in the tabloid press burns fiercely on hundreds of websites, famously including the once-powerful Gawker, which coordinated public sightings of celebrities in its Gawker Stalker feature and followed its libertine sensibilities to the climax (in, as it turned out, the sexual sense of the word) when it ran a videotape of world-famous, celebrity wrestler Hulk Hogan having apparently consensual sex with the wife of his best friend that not surprisingly attracted more than five million views. In a truth-is-stranger-than pornographic fiction story, Hogan successfully sued in an invasion-of-privacy lawsuit, bankrupting the new media company, raising intriguing questions about whether the courts would apply stricter legal criteria to Internet websites than they would to newspapers that have been largely immune from lawsuits for running similarly risqué stories (Toobin, 2016; see also Gajda, 2015).

In all these cases, libertarianism celebrates the public's right to know – or, more exactly, the press's right to profit from that so-called right. In so doing it can run roughshod on a right to privacy, or an individual's right to keep information about the self outside the public domain. In the case of celebrities, from Brad Pitt to Hulk Hogan, their privacy may be ethically nullified by their frequent desire to exploit their private lives for fame. From a legal perspective, the Supreme Court has ruled that there must be a higher standard for public officials – and frequently public figures – to prove they were defamed by statements appearing in the press than for private citizens in order to ensure there can be uninhibited critical debate on issues of the day. In any case, tabloid and sensational websites exploit libertarianism for greedy, entertainment-driven purposes never intended or imagined by libertarian theory's august proponents.

Digital Falsehoods

Libertarian theorists have long prized a vigorous exchange of ideas in the political marketplace, never wanting to silence the expression of incorrect opinions, or those based on faulty facts. Mill famously argued that even when opinions are untrue, the collision of truth with error helps to clarify the perception of truth, sharpening its luster, accentuating in the minds of observers the reasons why it is true. The First Amendment, which derived from libertarian principles, says that Congress cannot abridge freedom of speech, though some false speech, like defamation, is not constitutionally protected.

This brings us to an interesting, treacherous intersection between libertarian theory and the new media ecosystem. As you know and recall from Chapter 2, fake news developed by extremist political groups and Russian operatives engulfed the Internet and Americans' Facebook pages, featuring automated Twitter accounts that spewed out false reports, cresting during the 2016 presidential election, but continuing as fake news reports swirled after gun violence in the United States and in the wake of searing national controversies. In one of many examples, an extremist group, Right Wing News, posted fake news about Christine Blasey Ford when she accused Justice Brett Kavanaugh of sexual assault, falsely claiming her lawyers had been bribed by Democrats, and disseminating the falsehoods widely (Frenkel, 2018).

Social media companies, which distribute news, are caught in between virtuous libertarian values and the cacophonous viral sphere that bears no resemblance to the print pamphlets of Milton's time. From a libertarian perspective, leaders at tech companies like Google and Facebook long embraced "lofty goals of unfettered speech," arguing that companies should not be "in the business of censoring what its users have to say" (Isaac, 2017, p. B3). But this assumes that Mill's precept remains true: when error collides with truth – fake news is corrected by accurate accounts – people exchange error for truth, acknowledge the news account they once believed is fraudulent, or emerge with a deeper appreciation of what is true about the issue.

Yet in the unfettered, no-holds-barred digital universe, extremist groups deliberately diffuse false information, a malicious phenomenon that was uncommon, or certainly less pervasive, in Mill's 19th century. What's more, individuals with strong – to say nothing of extreme – positions on issues tend to selectively expose themselves to information that reinforces their viewpoint, tuning into sites that embrace their perspective, algorithmically gaining exposure primarily to supportive content (Stroud, 2014). Thus, they may see only fake reports and never encounter facts that prove the falsehoods wrong. What's more, there is a large body of psychological research indicating that even when people encounter evidence from the other side, or facts that prove the fake news incorrect, they stubbornly adhere to their original view, denying the falsehoods are false (e.g., Nyhan & Reifler, 2010, 2015). In today's world, error may never collide with truth and if it does, can emerge unscathed.

Unbridled libertarianism has consequences that could not have been anticipated by its eloquent, ideal proponents. In the limitless digital domain, it stokes anger and hate. More than 11,000 hateful posts appear on Instagram, falsely, viciously claiming Jews instigated the September 11 attacks (Frenkel, Isaac, & Conger, 2018). Cesar Sayoc, the accused mail bomber who sent pipe bombs in 2018 to notable critics of President Trump, and CNN, posted conspiracy theory links about illegal immigration on Twitter. Robert Bowers, accused of murdering 11 members of a Jewish synagogue the same year, posted anti-Semitic material on Gab, a website that has attracted extremists, including neo-Nazis and White nationalists who were banned from participating in other social media sites (Roose, 2018). Outside the U.S., fabricated news posts targeting a Muslim minority in Myanmar and that alleged a gang kidnapped children in India seemed to have provoked violence, perhaps fueled by villagers' belief the report must be true because it appeared on social media (Goel & Raj, 2018; Roose, 2017a).

While conventional news also contains inaccurate information that can have behavioral consequences, its insistence on verification tamps down the publication of outrageously fallacious reports that can stir the violent cauldron.

As much as one can appreciate the principle that "more speech is always better," legal scholar Tim Wu (2017) cautions, "no defensible free-speech tradition … treats foreign propaganda campaigns as legitimate debate or thinks that social-media bots ought to enjoy constitutional protection" (p. A19). To be fair, libertarians would reply that propaganda is a freighted construct and can be in the eye of the beholder. If sites begin banning speech that offends one side, they could soon do the same for posts on the other, raising the specter of censorship.

This raises intriguing questions about how to apply laudable principles of libertarian theory that were developed to describe an era dominated by print, a homogeneous public, and optimistic assumptions about human nature to our age, when bots, foreign power-instigated fake news, and polarization-stoked selective perceptions did not exist. For their part, social media's liberty-loving executives have come to realize this. Twitter has taken steps to prevent its trending topic pages from promoting fake news. Cloudflare, a popular content-delivery network, made a judgment call expelling a neo-Nazi site from the public web (Streitfeld, 2017), a distinctly non-libertarian decision reflecting a darkening of expectations about the once-vaunted public sphere.

Facebook has tried to thread the needle, striving to avoid outright censorship, changing its policies in recent years, allowing posts with disturbing falsehoods, but pushing them down in individuals' news feeds, unless they constitute hate speech or are likely to incite violence, in which case Facebook would likely remove the posts (Manjoo, 2018). Struggling with the impossible task of deciding which messages from its two billion users should be removed, allowed, or pushed down and just what constitutes hate speech, Facebook has developed a hodgepodge of rules, barring some extremist provocateurs from the platform (Isaac & Roose, 2019), blocking hate groups in some countries, but not others, allowing some extremist speech, but censoring other incendiary messages (Fisher, 2018).

If Facebook were merely "the modern public square," analogous to the Speaker's Corner in the northeast corner of Hyde Park in London, where speakers can talk about any issue in whatever way they want, with only benign consequences, banning speech would be unconscionable on libertarian grounds. But Facebook reaches two hundred million users each month, three-fifths of the U.S. population, and its messages exert palpable consequences. And Facebook defies easy categorization. It is a gatekeeper, a publisher, and a media company, with responsibilities. Yet, frustratingly, libertarian theory eschews responsibilities; let a thousand flowers bloom, it proclaims; liberty is sacrosanct.

In a nation, America, "forged from raucous speech," how do you reconcile liberty with responsibility, freedom with cognizance of consequences (Coll, 2018, p. 14)? Where do you draw the line? How can the valorous principles of libertarianism, penned more than six centuries ago, be intelligently applied to an era in which unrestrained speech causes harm?

Social Responsibility Perspective

Libertarian theory is like the highflying adolescent, who soars above the stifling conventions of the status quo, emboldened by her freedom, liberated by the belief that she has the right to chart out new paths by saying whatever comes to mind, convinced that new ideas are urgently needed, oblivious to harmful consequences these ideas may cause. Social responsibility is the mature, ever-cautious adult parent (cue your mother's voice), who, distancing herself from her freewheeling past, recognizes that actions have consequences and, in a messed-up society filled with social problems, people can't do whatever they want. They have (ahem) responsibilities to make things better for society, or at least not make them worse.

This simple metaphor provides an introduction to the multifaceted social responsibility concept of the news media. Let's turn the clock back to see how it developed. Over the course of the 20th century, technological changes increased the speed and impact of media, *Mad Men*-era advertising branding of cigarettes and headache remedies became inescapable, the imitative effects of television violence raised social concerns, the ability of news to bring home visceral images of war and urban unrest unnerved the public, and new awareness of racism placed pressure on society's messengers to do more than mirror the status quo. If this was the new normal, classic libertarian philosophy seemed quaintly out of place, a reflection of what ailed us not a recipe for improvement. Enter social responsibility theory, to some degree borne in the early 20th century with newsmagazine exposés that called attention to widespread injustice, and formalized in the mid-20th century with a 1947 report of the Hutchins Commission on Freedom and the Press. The Commission emphasized that the press (to use the term that preceded the broader media construct) should provide "a truthful, comprehensive, and intelligent account of the day's events," as well as clarification of the values and goals of society. In response to libertarian proponents, who boldly argued that the news media are private enterprises that owe nothing at all to the public, social responsibility theory countered that the press is not an independent island with no moorings to the larger society in which it existed, but instead plays a critical information role in society, and therefore is ethically required to harness journalism as a force for social good, however vague that term may be.

Much has been written in the social responsibility vein over the years, from sociological accounts that articulate the functions media serve (e.g., Wright, 1960, 1986) to journalistic essays articulating core duties news owes to the larger society (Kovach & Rosenstiel, 2014). Journalism scholars Hanitzsch and Vos (2017, 2018), working within a broad social responsibility framework, have emphasized the roles news plays in society, calling attention to its complexity, fraught cultural meanings, and different dimensions. Articulating roles that journalists play in Western and non-Western countries, they propose broad categories consisting of informational, analytical, watchdog, radical advocacy, developmental-educative (promoting social change), and partnering in various ways with government. Calling on this, and Christians et al.'s (2009) philosophical framework, I identify five broad social responsibilities, roles, or functions news should perform: (1) informational monitoring; (2) interpretation; (3) social empathy and unifying rituals; (4) investigative watchdog, and (5) facilitation of democratic dialogue. Each of these is discussed below, followed by a description of complicating factors that muddy the idealistic waters in intriguing ways.

Informational Monitoring

Perched above the fray of everyday events in government, the journalistic equivalent of a drone or satellite, the news **monitors** the information environment, describing key events and policies in the vast public sphere that extends beyond our personal, private lives. Monitoring incorporates a wealth of roles, including warning citizens of threats and dangers, including natural disasters, global warming, health crises, domestic perils, and political calamities; offering up-to-the-minute (or up-to-the-second in the case of tweets) notification of momentous and significant events; providing live coverage of important announcements by public officials, as well as criticism from opposing voices; and setting a public agenda on key issues facing the community by deciding which issues are of greatest consequence to the citizenry. As Kovach and Rosenstiel (2014) note, monitoring cuts to the core of journalism by providing citizens with the information, facts, and ideas that they require to be "free and self-governing" participants in democracy (p. 17).

Complications

Simple and uncontroversial as informational monitoring sounds, it is fraught with difficulties. News can appraise people of dangers and tragedies, as in the affecting 24/7 coverage that followed the September 11 attacks. However, such coverage can be problematic if it parrots the government line or frames issues in "good versus evil" ways, as some 9/11 coverage did (McChesney, 2011; Reese & Lewis, 2009). News can fail to monitor the environment, missing or playing down big stories, from the AIDS crisis in the 1980s to the 2008 financial melt-down, a case where "the watchdog didn't bark," as journalist Dean Starkman (2014) observed (see Chapter 10).

There are other shortcomings in monitorial or surveillance journalism, not least the failure to communicate problems clearly. News report are frequently full of jargon. For example, in news about the 2008 global financial crisis, articles referred to "asset bubbles," "credit default swaps," "collateralized mortgage obligations," or even the more commonly used, but infrequently explained, "hedge fund." It is easier to write stories with jargon-y terms that allow reporters to meet a deadline than to explain what these ideas mean. But this does not fulfill the function of adequately, clearly monitoring the social environment so citizens are informed and appraised.

Sometimes surveillance news is silly and ratings-driven. Reporters covering Hurricane Irma in Florida stood smack dab in the middle of the hurricane to get good visuals (you have seen these types of daredevil poses). But when people can get information about the storm through tweets, critics questioned the necessity – and wisdom – of reporters placing themselves in harm's way while urging viewers to stay at home, noting it could encourage some viewers to engage in risky behavior, braving the cold to imitate the famous anchor (Deb, 2017).

Good journalism needs to monitor the environment, but today it must do more. The classic informational monitoring function has changed in an age when social media provide instantaneous reports of a terrorist incident, natural disaster, or bombshell political announcement. There is considerable inaccuracy, some deliberately manufactured, in socially mediated instantaneous information, typified by the irresponsible sensationalist, who falsely claimed on YouTube that the mass shooter at a Texas church was a Muslim Bernie Sanders supporter (Roose, 2017b). Thus, journalism is increasingly important in providing the role of *authenticator*, publishing vetted information, helping citizens intelligently sort through different assertions, so they "know which of the facts they may have encountered they should believe and which to discount" (Kovach & Rosenstiel, 2014, p. 27).

You can go even further, emphasizing the role authentication and verification plays in a democracy. Citizens cannot make competent judgments about policies and leaders if they lack accurate knowledge about public issues. Consider that in January, 2019 President Trump appealed to the American public to support building a border wall arguing that the "big, beautiful wall," as he liked to put it, was needed to stem the flow of migrants and terrorists streaming across the southwest border. Some

Americans, moved by Trump's speech, might accept his factual statements because of the credibility they attach to the office. But news articles fact-checked the claims, pointing out his statements were overstated, exaggerated, or flat-out false (Baker, 2019; Schmitt, Sanger, & Thrush, 2019). Absent news media monitoring of a president's exaggerated claims – and Trump was hardly the first to engage in factual hyperbole; Obama did it too – citizens might readily accept statements that, while shrouded in patriotism, oversimplify complex problems.

Interpretation

A second social responsibility role the news performs is **interpretation**, making sense of the unfathomably complex public world. Interpretation involves offering a keen analysis of problems, intelligent efforts to lay out the array of causes, perhaps isolating the most important, suggesting potential consequences of policy options, assessing their relative merits, and discussing ins and outs of the political underpinnings and ramifications of policies. Interpretive journalism, as Salgado and Strömbäck (2012) note, "aims to find out the truth behind the verifiable facts," with an emphasis on "journalistic explanations, evaluations, contextualizations, or speculations going beyond verifiable facts or statements by sources" (p. 154). Interpretive news evolved from the "who-what-when-where" style of journalism. Fueled by social and economic factors, it increased dramatically over the past half-century, offering more of the "why," as well as probing macro factors that shape events (Barnhurst & Mutz, 1997). The availability of relevant social science data and stronger academic background of journalists have also expanded news emphasizing context and interpretations of complex events (Fink & Schudson, 2014). You can find interpretive stories all over the news, particularly when Congress plans sweeping overhauls in policies that affect the American public.

For example, in 2017 when the Republican leadership proposed major tax changes, interpretive news stories sought to broaden understanding of the merits of the bill by noting that cuts in taxes reflected a conservative philosophy that prioritized major tax cuts for corporations, assuming that tax cuts would produce economic growth, boosting wages and creating jobs (Tankersley, 2017). In one analysis, reporters, quoting different sources and citing evidence, concluded that the tax plan, subsequently signed into law, would have far-reaching consequences on American life, increasing inequality by cutting back safety nets, while reducing taxes on the wealthy, guided by the view that savings would trickle down to the middle class (Goodman & Cohen, 2017). An interpretive story a year after Trump's tax cut sought to measure its effects, concluding that, as Republicans argued, some corporations added workers; however, other companies cut employees, while enjoying big profits (Tankersley, 2018). Articles also deconstructed meanings of the abstruse catch-phrase, "Medicare for all," examining how a proposed change could change health care (Sanger-Katz, 2019).

Some years back, *The New York Times* became so convinced that interpretation was an important component of journalism that it initiated a regular feature appropriately titled, "The Interpreter." Articles probed a wealth of topics, asking – and trying to answer – questions we all are curious about, with evidence and a wealth of thoughtful perspectives. Topics included how prejudiced Facebook posts can incite violence, why America experiences so many deadly mass shootings, and the meanings of the controversial phrase, "Radical Islam." Other deeply reported interpretive stories explore the ways social class or race influence jobs, lifestyle, and mental health in a society that proclaims itself to be a champion of egalitarianism.

In an online era when people don't need news to provide instant information, news excels by adding value – interpretation, thought, and context – to the mind-numbing multitude of events that bombard people every day (Jarvis, 2011). At least that is the hope.

Complications

The quality of interpretive news varies greatly. Some stories, like those above, call on social science evidence, viewpoints from across the political spectrum, and analysis of the merits of different explanations of complex events. Other interpretative news can be superficial, backed up by flimsy evidence, or sources biased toward one side of the issue. Still other interpretive new endlessly focuses around reporters' explanations of the horse race or the game of politics, neglecting more substantive issues (Patterson, 1993). During a presidential election year, cable news viewers are treated to mind-numbing speculation by a panel of journalistic pundits about what a candidate's primary election victory means for the rest of the nomination process. After the election, the same or similar panel will drone on for several hours a night about, say, what Trump's latest tweet means or how it will play, or the legal and political implications of a trivial development in the scandal of Russia's involvement in the 2016 election. While this news can be fun to watch and is the equivalent of high-caloric potato chips for news junkies, it elides the major issues facing the country, with an interpretive focus on the trivia of politics.

At their best, interpretive news stories shed light on the underpinnings of social issues. They are especially thought-provoking when focused on the waterfront of perspectives that ask "how" and "why," harnessing the multitude of frameworks and links available in online news (Delli Carpini, 2017). The best scholars of interpretive news argue that news should present a diversity of perspectives, not just the usual left versus right, but shades of gray, encompassing frameworks from leaders, political groups, social movements, dissidents, and marginalized groups, amplified by comments from citizen journalists, with their distinctive viewpoints (Beattie & Milojevich, 2017; Gans, 2004; Porto, 2007; Waisbord, 2017).

By presenting these diverse viewpoints in news, journalists can expose people to perspectives they don't usually encounter, enriching the quality of public conversations. To be sure, it gets complicated in white-hot areas of controversy, like coverage of the Middle East, when facts themselves are open to question, labels ("militants" versus "terrorists") reflect different ideological frameworks, and choice of historical explanations of fractious events hinge on which side (Israel or the Palestinian) reporters turn to for information (see Chapter 6). In cases like these, no matter what reporters do, they will be accused of bias. Nonetheless, an emphasis on interpretation argues for bringing a variety of perspectives to the story, trying to adjudicate them, based on multiple sources, while also applying evidence to sort out the merits of different claims.

Unfortunately, in a world where news is a stunningly competitive commodity and owners are trimming their staffs to bare bones levels, interpretation is a luxury that few news outlets are willing to offer. Its paucity reduces the degree to which the public and its leaders can consider multifaceted approaches to problems, including those with which they disagree. The lack of interpretive journalism encourages Twitter-style politics, with its focus on simplicity and raw emotion.

Emotional Functions: Social Empathy and Ritualistic Nation-Healing

Social Empathy

> She wakes to the sound of breathing. The smaller children lie tangled besides her, their chests rising and falling under winter coats and wool blankets. A few feet away, their mother and father sleep near the mop bucket they use as a toilet. Two other children share a mattress by the rotting wall where the mice live, opposite the baby, whose crib is warmed by a hair dryer perched on a milk crate.

So begins Andrea Elliott's (2013) affecting series on Dasani – the feisty 11-year-old girl who society has pushed callously to the margins, the child of Brooklyn whose ramshackle reality, a decrepit homeless shelter, closes in on her buoyant walk every day, who lives amid filth, vomit, feces, and fears of sexual predation, but refuses to let her situation define her, singing "Black is beautiful, Black is me." Elliott tells Dasani's story, opening readers' eyes to the destitute world in which she lives, contrasting it with the sharp, shapely spires of the opulent New York about which politicians boast, taking us, day by day, through a grueling tour of her chaotic young life, the mouse-infested surroundings in which she tends daily to her younger siblings' needs, her heart-pounding first day at a new school, where her uncanny intelligence attracts notice, and her body resonates to the dance class that lifts her spirits. We learn how the city has failed children like Dasani, neglecting to clean up decrepit, crack pipe-filled conditions in her shelter, and come to appreciate how conditions at home lead to deteriorating grades at school. Yet through it all, the feisty 4-foot-8 girl with delicate features refuses to let her tribulations define her, as she moves excitedly with her family to an apartment with hardwood floors, resiliently resolved to study, seize the opportunity, and triumph.

Dasani's story is one many reporters relate with compassion, transporting readers to different realities they would not otherwise encounter, in this way helping readers develop social empathy for people and situations far different from their own. Those realities, described so powerfully by journalists, include the struggles of Shannon Mulcahy, who toiled for years in an Indianapolis steel plant, trying to help her daughter fulfill her college dreams, only to find she was a casualty of the global manufacturing crisis, as the factory moved her job to Mexico (Stockman, 2017). They encompass the very different dreams of hockey player Derek Boogaard, who set his sights on becoming a hockey enforcer, the noble savage of hockey, and succeeded, until he experienced the ravages of hundreds of concussions, leading to a tragic accidental drug overdose at the age of 28 (Branch, 2011).

In these articles reporters shine a light on the intersection of societal conditions – homelessness, decline of manufacturing, hockey's insensitivity to its players – and the ways particular people cope, shine, or fail. News paints pictures of the calamitous effects of hurricanes, tragedies that befall people caught in the web of gun violence, and struggles of immigrants, minorities, disabled individuals, and children felled by disease, in these ways transporting readers to contexts they might never experience directly, building social empathy, understanding of life's afflictions, and a deeper appreciation of the dignified ways human beings cope, struggle, but also fall victim to distresses beyond their control. More optimistically, by narrating stories of how people have overcome struggles to chart innovative paths, social empathy-based news can suggest new pathways, identities, and existential directions for young people beginning life's journey.

Ritualistic Healing

On a broader, macro level, news sustains another emotional function – fulfilling social rituals, cementing society, and building a sense of solidarity through coverage of spectacular, celebratory, but also, tragic events. News does not only monitor and interpret; it conveys shared values that stitch society together during crisis moments, fortifying society's social sphere (Hess & Gutsche, 2018; Matthews, 2016). This is a different way of looking at news, focusing less on its literal content than the broader meanings it conveys and ways it helps society, in the mode of a therapist, to collectively cope with unexpected events, frequently tragedies.

Dispensing with routine coverage in cases of terrorist bombings, natural disasters, and celebrity deaths, journalists cast aside their traditional focus on information, neutrality, and back-and-forth renditions of both sides. Instead, they let national values shine through their reports, showcasing a message of solidarity, reassurance, and national unity (Schudson, 2011). After the World Trade Center attacks, and continuing for months, *The New York Times* offered moving, magnificently crafted "Portraits of Grief" that captured the particular vitality that made each individual who died singular and unique. During national tragedies, news serves as a symbolic outlet to convey national grief, facilitating healing; at the same time, news expresses collective outrage at the act, emphasizing connections that bind together citizens of a nation (Berkowitz, 2017). As Matthews (2016) noted, the news offers a sense of "'we-ness' as it progresses to *cauterize* and move beyond the social wound inflicted by the terrorist incident" (p. 175; see Elliott, 1980).

After gun massacres – Pittsburgh, Parkland, Florida, Las Vegas, Orlando, Newtown, the list is endless – news offers symbolic support, turning to grieving relatives to offer memorable portraits of the victims' lives, sometimes emphasizing how they epitomized the best of their country, in this way making the story of one nation, people, and shared humanity rather than meaningless gun shots that rain down on victims (see Figure 4.2) Like terrorism, news of gun violence vilifies the perpetrators of these heinous acts, calling on classic symbols of evil to sharpen the contrast between the murderous actions of one person and the broader values the victims represented, as well as the heroes who put their lives in harm's way to rescue others (Berkowitz, 2010). Through its moving stories of victims' lives, the news helps people vicariously mourn the dead, making individual deaths universal (Kitch & Hume, 2008; Morse, 2017).

News also performs ritualistic functions in the case of deaths of celebrities, a type of "commemorative journalism" where reporters function as "mourners and healers," helping people deal with a huge symbolic loss (Kitch, 2000, pp. 171, 178). Commemorative news about the deaths of celebrities – Elvis Presley, John Lennon, Princess Diana, Kurt Cobain, Michael Jackson, Robin Williams, and Prince – take on iconic proportions, with a uniformity of narratives, despite differences among the celebrities and ways they died. The media take on the dramaturgical role of spiritual healers, helping people move from the societal rupture the death produces to acceptance of death and a collective affirmation to move on. The celebrity is mythically celebrated

Figure 4.2 News serves a ritualistic function in cases of national tragedies, such as the mass shooting at Marjory Stoneman Douglas High School in Parkland, Florida, where 17 people were killed in February 2018. By showing a picture like this, news puts aside the usual routine coverage, offering symbolic support for victims, depicting collective outrage at the act, and embracing calls for unity.

as "one of us," sometimes a symbolic hero for one generation, but of overweening cultural importance. The media help people cope with a symbolic loss, doing so "through the same forum in which they came to 'know' the celebrity in life – the news media, which take on the role of national healers" (p. 189).

Complications

Both social empathy, on the individual level, and unifying ritualistic healing, on the societal level, fulfill emotional functions. In some ways they showcase the media at their best. And yet, critical questions must be asked to deepen our understanding of even these salutary aspects of media.

Critics emphasize that reporters must decide who is deserving of empathy, and their decision reflects values, even stereotypes. A multitude of stories in 2017 related sexual abuse by men in power, laudably offering social empathy to victims, who, in the main, were well-to-do actresses and members of the media elite. However, one critic noted, "There are still huge swaths of women – the poor, the queer, the undocumented – who can't count on the security that feminism has conferred on its wealthier, whiter adherents, or trust that their victimization would even become news"

Tolentino (2017, p. 16). As positive as empathy-building and ritualistic stories are, they frequently foster social empathy and affirm rituals for established, mainstream groups.

While ritualistic news dispenses with routine journalism's emphasis on giving both sides, focusing on healing the nation's wounds, there are prominent exceptions. When government fails, or is widely perceived as not doing enough to mitigate the disaster, news takes on a populist quality, offering sympathy to the victims, and shoving the problem back in government's face, accusing authorities of forsaking its citizens (Durham, 2008). This occurred dramatically in the case of Hurricane Katrina, where the federal government failed to respond effectively, bodies piled up in the streets, the president was charged with racial insensitivity to the city's Black residents, and violence flared.

Increasingly, as partisan divisions shape responses to national problems, news of national disasters has been sullied by partisan discord. Traditional unifying stories were in ample supply after Hurricanes Harvey and Maria devastated Houston and Puerto Rico respectively. However, in Puerto Rico's case, they were marred by controversy, as the San Juan mayor criticized the Trump administration, Trump fired back at the mayor, and both leaders politicized the issue.

On a broader level, the strength of ritualistic news is its greatest weakness. Reporting can favor jingoistic, overly-patriotic coverage that ignores dissent or alternative perspectives on the disaster that run counter to national norms and myths (Waisbord, 2011). The responsibility of news to offer reassurance clashes with "the training of professional journalists to use skepticism in the service of accuracy" (Aufderheide, 2002, p. 10). Yet this criticism itself raises questions. Isn't an important role of the nation's news system to mend wounds and bind a nation during national crises? Doesn't journalism owe this to the government, which protects its security and guarantees reporters First Amendment freedoms? Isn't one of the social responsibilities of the press to calm the frayed nerves of the country and provide citizens with a sense of unity and purpose? On the other hand, news has an obligation to tell the truth, covering shortcomings in government's unity frames, revealing the marginalized groups not embraced by the warm blanket of rhetorical unity. Balancing the need to inform with the need to reassure is important, pointing up complications in the commonly accepted ritualistic function of news.

Commemorative news of celebrities' deaths highlights the contradictory roles celebrities play in modern society. They bring great joy to people and can be symbolic sources of solace and psychological inspiration. But their all-encompassing coverage in the news displaces the importance of other lives and accomplishments, minimizing, on a broad social level and sometimes more personal dimension, the significance of so many ordinary and extraordinary people, who don't happen to be celebrities.

On the other hand, the lamentation that news overplays celebrities' deaths neglects that celebrity deaths affect individuals more deeply than those of their less famous compatriots. As vessels communicating broad cultural aspirations, celebrity deaths tear at a thread in the nation's mythical fabric. And yet, as society becomes more fragmented and national news is displaced by niche social media emphasizing celebrities in a particular arena of society, one wonders whether news of deaths of global celebrities will occupy the role it has in the past. As celebrities become increasingly rooted in a particular generation, ethnic group, specific demographic, or online community, the mourning and healing news performed may gravitate to social media, with its more participatory, edgy, and variable rituals.

Watchdog Journalism: Investigative News

This is the gold standard of journalism – the richly reported investigative news stories that expose corruption, out legions of powerful male sexual abusers, illuminate business wrongdoing, and shine a light, lit by the power of evidence and whistleblowers' testimony, on the ways ordinary people have been wronged by the system.

Like dogs watching over their keepers, ensuring their safety, watchdog journalists stand sentinel over authorities, holding them accountable for the powers they wield. Watchdog journalism dates back to muckraking, a Progressive era term invoked to describe reporters who metaphorically raked up the muck of society by exposing its corrupt underbelly. From early 20th-century investigations of political corruption and cruelties of monopoly capitalism through Watergate to exposés of sexual abuse today, journalists have distinguished themselves by shining a light on problems that would not have been revealed had it not been for their courageous efforts. Here are a handful of classic investigative news accomplishments:

- Neil Sheehan's 1971 Pentagon Papers series in *The New York Times* exposed years of presidential deception about the Vietnam War, including White House planning military escalation long before revealing this information to the public or Congress. The Johnson Administration engaged in brutal, intensified bombing of North Vietnam, despite evidence it was not working. The Pentagon Papers – so named because they involved a Defense Department study of U.S. involvement in Vietnam and were leaked by a Pentagon official, Daniel Ellsberg, who worked on the study – documented the ways presidents from Truman to Johnson embroiled the U.S. in a land war in Asia, without coming clean with the public.

- A year later came Watergate, precipitated by the Nixon Administration's overblown concerns about the Pentagon Papers and news leaks to reporters. Two *Washington Post* cub reporters, Bob Woodward and Carl Bernstein, in path-breaking coverage conspicuously absent in the rest of the media, connected a burglary of the Democratic National Headquarters at the Washington, D.C. Watergate Hotel to the 1972 Nixon reelection campaign; campaign pay-offs of Watergate burglars; and, based on tips from a key inside source, dubbed Deep Throat (based on a double entendre on the pornographic movie of the era), a massive political sabotage campaign aimed to reelect Nixon in 1972. Reporting by *The Post* and other media led to Senate televised hearings on Watergate, producing a bombshell of political developments, culminating in proof Nixon orchestrated the cover-up and his resignation from the presidency on August 9, 1974.
- Focusing on abuses and injustices on the local level, as well as Washington, D.C., reporters drawn to journalism by the exemplary work of Sheehan, Woodward, Bernstein, and their contemporaries produced a legion of outstanding Pulitzer Prize-winning investigative exposés. Among them: documentation that a convicted man was innocent of murder (*The Philadelphia Inquirer*); wrongful seizure by a sheriff's drug unit of millions of dollars from drivers (*The Orlando Sentinel*); unlawful and unethical fertility procedures at a major university research hospital (*The Orange County Register*); and ways that opioids inundated poor West Virginia communities that have the highest rates of overdose death in the U.S. (*Charleston Gazette-Mail*); famously. Add to this exposés documenting scores of sexual abuse by priests (*The Boston Globe*) that was the basis of the award-winning film, "Spotlight"; revelations in the Harrisburg *Patriot-News* that assistant football coach Jerry Sandusky had sexually assaulted young boys amid university inaction; and, of course, Pulitzer Prize-winning investigations by *The New York Times* and *The New Yorker* on wanton sexual abuse in the corridors of Hollywood.

At their courageous, stirring best, investigative journalists perform the moral excavations democracy requires. They "investigate and open channels of communication … excavate documents, chase down sources and sort out systems," are truly "democracy's detectives" (Hamilton, 2016, p. 63). As scholars James S. Ettema and Theodore L. Glasser (1998) note, "investigative reporting engages our conscience by inviting us to identify with the plight of the less fortunate … [promising] forms of public deliberation in which the powerless are empowered to speak" (pp. 197, 200). The best investigative stories bring public attention to systemic abuse that has gone unnoticed or been intentionally covered up, require action from public officials accountable for these crimes, and create an emotional linkage among those who have suffered moral wrongs, concerned activists, and citizens, who may become politically engaged to demand change directly or through institutional mechanisms.

Complications

Perhaps more than other journalistic functions, the investigative watch-dog role raises moral dilemmas. Reporters must weigh the public benefits that come from exposing wrongdoing with harm that disclosures of government secrets cause to national security or that revelations of sexual misconduct, from abuse to infidelities, cause to families of perpetrators or victims. The utilitarian calculus frequently favors the investigative journalist, given the scope of wrongdoing and harm to the fabric of a community. However, sensationalized local TV news investigations that expose a local business executive for a modest moral misdemeanor, fail to look at the larger systemic context, and are hyped to increase ratings can lack ethical justification (Feldstein, 2007).

Exposés of political misconduct usually advance the public interest, but tawdry examinations of a particular politician's sexual impropriety raise questions. Reporters have done considerable soul-searching about the journalistic merits of *The Miami Herald*'s now-classic exposé of Senator Gary Hart's liaison with a model in 1987, as Hart pursued a promising campaign for the 1988 presidential nomination (Bai, 2014). (The two appeared in a titillating pose on a boat actually called "Monkey Business"; truth remains stranger than fiction in the political arena!). *Miami Herald* reporters staked out Hart's Washington, D. C. home to see if the married Colorado senator was having an affair with a blonde woman in her late 20s. When a *Herald* reporter spotted Hart and the woman together near his townhouse on two occasions, they confronted Hart, who denied he had sex with the woman (Donna Rice, a model and aspiring actress). Reasoning that the suspicious liaisons undermined Hart's denials that he was involved in an extramarital relationship, the reporters published a story stating that Hart had spent Friday night and Saturday with the woman, suggesting the titillating trifecta of adultery, power, and politics. Faced with a media scandal, Hart withdrew from the race.

Although some reporters have persuasively defended the stories as bona fide news, relevant to voters contemplating their choice for president, critics have argued that there was no compelling evidence, other than innuendo and hearsay, that Hart was involved in a sexual relationship. Moreover, the stories focused not on a politician's public behavior or policies, but his private life, of questionable, if any, relevance to his presidential candidacy. On the other hand, one can defend the Hart exposés on journalistic grounds, noting that they pointed to Hart's hypocrisy and lack of candor, a relevant issue for voters to consider. In any case, there is little doubt that the stories blurred – indeed, eviscerated – the boundaries between news and celebrity-driven entertainment, shoving political journalism into the sleazy sex-driven domain of entertainment reporting, setting the stage for non-stop coverage of Bill Clinton's sexual liaisons.

Exposés in the Digital World

No discussion of investigative reporting would be complete without discussing their digital extensions, as seen in the cases of WikiLeaks and Edward Snowden.

WikiLeaks is the controversial international online non-profit organization dedicated to transparency that reveals secret information and classified government documents. The group's name reflects its original focus on collaborative editing by all users, coupled with its determination to publish leaks of secret government information in the service of the public's right to know. The "wiki" denotes a website that permits collaborative editing, perhaps less valid today than when it began (Karhula, 2011). The leaks it embraces have spread like wildfire, raising many ethical questions.

Over the past two decades, WikiLeaks released a treasure trove of classified government documents. For example, in 2010, it released material documenting that hundreds of civilians were killed in Afghanistan by U.S. and allied troops over the course of the long war. In 2017, the organization revealed electronic surveillance strategies the CIA uses to break into computers and smartphones, circumventing encryption protections. Famously and controversially, during the 2016 election, WikiLeaks posted thousands of hacked emails from the Democratic National Committee that intelligence experts believe were provided by the Russian government to derail Hillary Clinton's presidential campaign. This suggested that WikiLeaks may have been acting as a virtual conduit for Russian agents, raising questions about the integrity of an organization many freedom of information advocates had long respected (Schmidt & Fandos, 2017).

WikiLeaks shows how the watchdog function has changed and become more complicated in a digital world. Daniel Ellsberg leaked the Pentagon Papers documents to leading newspapers, and, as mainstream gatekeepers, they disseminated this to the public. WikiLeaks is a public website that has published posts on political and diplomatic issues from non-journalists with access to classified or confidential documents. However, WikiLeaks also has disseminated documents via the news media, using the news to spread information, as when it collaborated in 2010 with leading newspapers, sharing documents with *The New York Times*, a British newspaper, the *Guardian*, and a German newspaper, *Der Spiegel*.

WikiLeaks prominently illustrates boundary-blurring changes in gatekeeping, discussed in Chapter 2. It is not a conventional for-profit news outlet, housed in a city in a particular country, which employs conventional investigative reporters. Instead, it is an elusive non-profit organization that transcends national borders, which acquires classified documents through sometimes-suspicious digital leaks.

Although WikiLeaks has engaged in bona fide investigative journalism, some news organizations have sought to protect their turf, distancing themselves from WikiLeaks by defining WikiLeaks as an interloper, outside the boundaries of conventional, professional journalism (Carlson, 2015; Coddington, 2012; Eldridge, 2014). But this turf protection elides the ways that WikiLeaks, working in a digital era where leaking can occur seamlessly by transmitting an email across national borders from one part of the world to another, has forced a rethinking of the major paradigm of news gathering in journalism (Kumar, 2013).

Is WikiLeaks a journalistic organization? On one level, one would be hard-pressed to call it anything other than a news organization. It does "what traditional news organizations, like *The New York Times*, do every day: seek out and publish information that officials would prefer to be kept secret, including classified national security matters," one experienced investigative reporter notes (Savage, 2018, p. A16). On the other hand, WikiLeaks lacks the professionalism of traditional news organizations, failing to protect the identity of its secret informants, in some cases circulating conspiracy theories, and in the Hillary Clinton case, arguably undermining democracy by colluding with a foreign adversary of the United States, releasing emails the foreign government (Russia) pilfered from Democratic Party officials to influence the outcome of a presidential election (Jamieson, 2018).

All this has raised normative questions. One view is that WikiLeaks is an avant-garde organization dedicated to the transparency of documents governments hide, unnecessarily deemed classified, and that citizens have a right to see. The other view is that WikiLeaks is irresponsible, releasing documents that place diplomats' lives at risk and disrespecting governments' need to classify documents in a dangerous world, as well as private citizens' right to maintain secrets (Allan, 2013). Others counter that there is little functional difference between WikiLeaks' publication of classified documents and investigative newspaper stories that print classified information without gaining official permission. However, conventional journalists tend to be more careful about publishing information that can reveal the identity of government sources, recognizing that these sources are the lifeblood of the journalistic craft (see Chapter 8).

What's more, WikiLeaks' mass revelations have extended to hundreds of private citizens, individuals whose personal information was, for some reason, included in the organization's massive data dumps. It posted the financial records of ordinary people, named adolescent rape victims, and published egregiously personal information, including the specifics of a male partner's infertility, and the partners of women with sexual transmitted diseases, including HIV (Satter & Michael, 2016). And, of course, its release of hacked emails from the Democratic National Committee that seemed to have been provided by the Russian government have raised questions about its ethics. To be sure, WikiLeaks has its ardent defenders, delighting in an organization that is dedicated to the transparency of information they believe citizens ought to know, unencumbered by norms to protect the government of the country in which the medium is housed. However, some advocates have begun to take a dimmer view in light of the organization's recent activities, noting that journalism involves careful verification of facts, not simply dumping information, a distinction that becomes particularly acute when the dumped documents, stolen from a political party's national headquarters by a foreign adversary, favor one candidate over another in a democratic election (Sullivan & LaFraniere, 2019).

The debate over WikiLeaks has additional implications for journalism more generally. If one views WikiLeaks as a legitimate media organization, just one with different (albeit unsavory) practices and tailored to fit the digital age, it deserves First Amendment protection. One legal expert acknowledged that he felt "personal disgust" for WikiLeaks' founder, "a narcissistic egomaniac with an apparent personal grudge against the intelligence apparatuses of the Western democracies" (Moss, 2018; see Figure 4.3). Taking a broad view of the First Amendment, Moss added that "if Assange can be prosecuted merely for publishing leaked classified documents, every single media outlet is at risk of prosecution for doing the exact same thing." Assange's fierce critics would disagree, arguing that WikiLeaks is hardly a bona fide news organization, which adheres to journalistic practices, broadly defined, but is instead an extralegal group willing to break laws and cavort with authoritarian governments to accomplish anarchistic goals.

Yet even editors who have sparred with Assange, like former *New York Times* editor Bill Keller, are uncomfortable with legal actions that would prosecute Assange for engaging in what investigative reporters do every day. Indeed, during the 2016 campaign, news organizations published WikiLeaks' revelations freely, while seemingly maintaining an above-the-battle detachment that distanced them from tough ethical decisions for which they were also responsible. Once again, distinctions are difficult, and boundaries blur as debate rages on where to draw the line on watchdog journalism in a digital age. Increasingly, though, WikiLeaks' ends-justify-the-means philosophy raises ethical red flags, suggesting lines may have been crossed in the group's admirable, but zealous, desire to reveal political secrets.

Similar, though not identical, investigative reporting-type issues emerged in the wake of Edward J. Snowden, the former CIA computer technician, who leaked as many as 200,000 highly classified U.S. government documents to the media in 2013. Concerned about the expansion – in his view, metastasizing – of a global surveillance state secretly, unethically

Figure 4.3 Julian Assange, the controversial founder of WikiLeaks, which has taken investigative news to the digital sphere, with release of classified documents, including hacked Democratic National Committee emails. Is Assange a new type of investigative reporter or a rogue actor who comports with authoritarian regimes and breaks laws with impunity? First Amendment advocates deplore his personal values, but see broad similarities between WikiLeaks and investigative news teams, even as questions about the group's disruption of the 2016 election continue to concern proponents of electoral democracy.

spying on its citizens, Snowden leaked the information to documentary filmmaker Laura Poitras and Glenn Greenwald, a reporter for the British newspaper, the *Guardian*, who he viewed as sympathetic to his cause. His revelations were nothing short of gargantuan, calling attention to a *Minority Report*-like surveillance state, in which massive data about citizens are obtained after suspects have been targeted, but "*before* determining the full range of their actual and potential uses," with personal data identified to forecast when suspicious activities may occur (Lyon, 2015, p. 77).

As with WikiLeaks, the leaked information was digitized, but Snowden worked more closely and cooperatively with the news media, in the manner of Daniel Ellsberg, who broke the Pentagon Papers story in 1971 and praised Snowden's actions. While Ellsberg approached a prestigious established newspaper, *The New York Times*, Snowden sought out fringe, but respected, journalists of a similar liberal ideological bent, showcasing the power of gatekeepers with a political attitude.

News was the conduit for this information, breaking a story of massive importance, calling attention to its continued importance while raising contemporary questions about the proper balance between libertarian publication of information and journalistic responsibility to protect national security, as well as defense secrets. Increasingly in a digital age, investigative reporting blurs boundaries and raises questions, but there is little doubt that it fulfills critical democratic functions (Rosenzewig, McNulty, & Shearer, 2014). When it ferrets out moral wrongdoing, it is journalism at its best, a "public good" (Hamilton, 2016).

Facilitating Democratic Dialogue: Improving the Public Sphere

The news media's responsibility to generate democratic dialogue – and facilitate a robust public life among citizens – could not be more different from the watchdog function, with its focus on challenging the powers-that-be and speaking truth to power. The investigative news watchdog role is about power and its abuses; the role of facilitating dialogue is about acceptance of different views and encouraging cooperative openness to diverse viewpoints. Investigative news, the heart of the watchdog role, focuses on the powerful, but the news media's role in the public sphere is to revitalize the citizenry, emphasizing the "interconnections of citizenship, media, and democracy" (Bybee, 1999, p. 30). In performing the role of watchdog – as well as other roles discussed above – journalists stand, to some degree, above the fray, surveying, interpreting, arousing empathy, and ferreting out problems with public life. The democratic dialogue perspective views journalists as participants, as well as observers, who help the public partake more actively to solve the problems that afflict their communities. As discussed later in the chapter, contemporary scholars have adapted this notion to the present milieu, emphasizing ways journalists can produce publicly "empowering constructive news coverage" that explores dilemmas positively, seeking remedies, and, in some contexts, acting more as a rescue dog than a watchdog (Bro, 2019; Hermans & Gyldensted, 2019, p. 540).

This broad approach dates back to the philosopher John Dewey (1927), who wrote in the early decades of the 20th century. In contrast to his contemporary, journalist Walter Lippmann, who was skeptical of the public's ability to understand the increasing complexity of the world, Dewey had more faith in the public's capability to partake in public decisions (Allan, 2010; though see Schudson, 2019). He had a more expansive, publicly focused view of journalists, arguing that their job was to encourage citizens to participate in public dialogue. For Dewey, conversation – talk – was of key importance in democracy; it was the path by which people arrived at truth and built a robust public life (Hermida et al., 2011; Schudson, 2008b; see Figure 4.4).

Since Dewey, a multitude of scholars, most famously the philosopher Jürgen Habermas (1989), have emphasized the importance of a vital public

Figure 4.4 John Dewey, the American philosopher whose books of the early decades of the 20th century emphasized the role that public conversation played in democracy, laid the groundwork for the notion that journalism should engage and invigorate the public sphere.

sphere where citizens can broadly debate and participate in public issues. Lamenting the superficial, "this side versus that side," strategic game focus of political news coverage, they yearned for a revamped media presence, where news helps revitalize a fragmented (increasingly polarized), politically inert public life.

Out of these concerns a revamped, Dewey-esque news model emphasizing participatory journalism emerged some years back, with a focus on **public journalism**, as the movement of the 1990s came to be known. Unlike libertarianism, public journalism does not focus on the *rights* of the individual, but on ways news can contribute to the larger social *good* (Berry et al., 1995; Christians et al., 2009). In contrast to libertarianism and much of social responsibility theory, public – or its close compatriot, civic – journalism takes a communitarian approach that emphasizes the ways journalism can build communities, collective structures, and invigorate the cynical, politically fractionated state of civic life in America (Nip, 2008; Nord, 2001).

Disdaining news that talks at individuals rather than with them, public journalism spearheaded projects that involved citizens centrally in the creation and development of news (see Black, 1997; Haas & Steiner, 2001; Kaplan, 2002; Nerone, 2015; Rosen, 1999). Emphasizing the need to revitalize the metaphorical public space in which citizens live, public journalism views news outlets as "conversational commons": a public space for the deliberation of issues of importance to the social fabric of the community, one that stimulates problem-solving and new solutions to time-honored problems (Anderson, Dardenne, & Killenberg, 1994; Howley, 2003, p. 276; Nip, 2008).

The *Akron Beacon Journal* received a Pulitzer Prize for public service in 1994 for its year-long "A Question of Color" articles that sought to improve racial relations in a city with severe racial chasms. Supplementing news articles on racial disparities in housing and employment, the newspaper partnered with more than 100 civic groups, encouraged cross-racial communication and listening, created a reader-generated community agenda, and formed an organization dedicated to racial sensitivity. In the digital era, citizen journalism sites that probe public problems, engaging community members and prodding political leaders into action, exemplify public journalism.

Complications

When public journalism emerged in the 1990s, it was praised as a way to revitalize an ailing public sphere, in which elite politicians and journalists spoke louder and more often that the citizenry. Its emphasis on civic virtue struck many as just the right medicine for a journalism that had lost its way, stuck, as it seemed to be, in an obsession with politics-as-theater and the presidential election-as-sporting event. The emphasis on the public offered a new way of thinking about how news should cover politics, race, and a panoply of community problems. Some valuable news projects emerged.

At the same time, some journalists argued that it was not their job to improve the public sphere – vague as that term sometimes seemed to be – but to report as objectively as they could about problems facing the community. That was exactly the problem, public journalism advocates noted, pointing out that journalism's emphasis on objectivity blinded them to the role they ought to play in fostering democratic values and building a stronger democracy. Proponents of public journalism offered a useful corrective, noting that reporters too often presumed that the agenda of important problems they carried in their heads was the same as what the public believed. Ask and listen to voters, public journalism advocates stressed.

By the same token, critics of public journalism aptly pointed out that sometimes voters don't know or are confused about what the key problems are, and their job as reporters is to illuminate those issues in their reporting. Too often, critics of public journalism noted, public journalism had an "evangelistic fervor" that blinded them to shortcomings in their vision for a community and ways that particular community leaders could hijack public journalism stories for their own political ends (Steele, 2002).

As scholars explored the foundations and potential of public journalism, they recognized the issues underpinning the movement were more complex than originally assumed. As Tanni Haas and Linda Steiner (2001) noted, in a perceptive essay, calling on Fraser's (1990) work, public journalism frequently neglects the fact that there are different *publics* – community groups – that have divergent perspectives of community problems, their perceptions complemented by ways that citizens' race, gender, and class interact to influence perceptions of community issues. Applying this analysis to the "Question of Color" campaign, Haas and Steiner lamented that the *Beacon Journal* assumed that more communication would produce agreement on solutions, in this way neglecting the deep-seated racial gulf in perceptions and experiences that led Blacks and Whites to disagree on almost every community issue at the get-go. In Haas and Steiner's view, the newspaper could have harnessed these differences in perceptions, asking participants to reflect on how their *different* understandings of racial prejudice influenced their attitudes toward community problems and possible solutions. They could have encouraged residents to consider how the intersection of race, class, and gender affected their perceptions of racial inequality, even sponsoring constructive debates between residents and policymakers to help turn questions of color into answers about how the community could collectively correct fundamental inequities, like in schooling and property tax funding.

While acknowledging the contributions that public journalism projects have provided communities, economically-oriented scholars have pointed to their limits, noting that, in a capitalist society, they are constrained by market forces, and public journalism may not recruit readers (Howley, 2003; Kurpius, 2003). On the other hand, top-notch public, civic-minded journalism series like the *Beacon Journal*'s touched a chord in community members, stimulating engagement.

Over the past couple of decades, public journalism projects have faded, a casualty of economic downturns in the newspaper business, and conventional editors' cynical calculations that public journalism experiments won't improve circulation. In addition, social media, and the many networks people develop to discuss social and community problems online, took the wind out of the sails of public journalism. When social media and websites encourage dialogue about community issues, why do you need civic projects arbitrarily sponsored by news outlets? However, some of this heady enthusiasm has been dashed by the development of homogeneous online communities that post false information and are more interested in acrimony than advancing dialogue.

Undaunted by these criticisms, citizen journalism advocates have launched innovative projects that involve citizens in the gathering and development of news. These include a Connecticut newspaper's newsroom cafeteria, where community members offer contributions to local news over caffeine (Ferrucci, 2015; Usher, 2016; see also Wenzel et al., 2018), and a host of projects initiated by Hearken, a Chicago startup that helps journalists partner with citizens in covering community issues. In this vein, as part of its "Hey Area" storytelling project, San Francisco's public radio station, KALW, invited listeners to share questions they hoped the station could explore. This prompted Elizabeth Marlow, a nurse practitioner, concerned about providing health care resources for homeless individuals in the wake of the city's homeless crisis some years back, to ask where people living in tents along the city's Division Street were from, hoping something could be done to help. Her query prompted an answer on the station's Crosscurrents daily news show that explained that about 70 percent of San Francisco's homeless population became homeless as a result of the 2008 financial crisis, in turn providing Marlow and other listeners with insights about the underpinnings of a homeless problem the city needed to address (Jolly, 2016).

Promising as this is, there remain questions about whether such projects, which have been popular on public radio stations, reach a larger audience beyond the well-educated who listen to these shows, along with concerns about whether this earnest programming produces both the dialogue and policy reforms public journalism advocates emphasize.

While questions remain, contemporary scholars, convinced that journalism must change to move society forward, have adapted, enlarged, and adjusted the older public and civic journalism approaches, incorporating them in a broader focus on constructive journalism. Applying positive psychology ideas to the news project, scholars have argued that journalists should try to move society forward by emphasizing carrots, as well as sticks, viewing problems from different perspectives, and seeking remedies to social ills (Bro, 2019; Gyldensted, 2015; Haagerup, 2014; Mast, Coesemans, & Temmerman, 2019). Constructive journalists add a "what now?" query to the time-honored who-what-where-when-why questions, focusing on providing context, including diverse voices and perspectives to news gathering, and empowering the public (Hermans & Gyldensted, 2019).

This represents an innovative, positive direction, but it too raises questions. What is the unique essence of the constructive journalism concept that separates it from previous approaches that emphasize civic solutions, interpretive stories, and multiple frameworks in news-gathering? How can journalism emphasize these ideas, while not losing sight of the deeper social problems that news seeks to illuminate? How can journalism adapt its norms to emphasize solutions without surrendering its emphasis on verification or lending itself to accusations of bias?

Collaborative Approach

This final normative approach is the toughest one for journalism students to wrap their heads around. At first blush it seems to affirm everything they oppose. Far from emphasizing that news should publish information no holds barred, or that it has certain social responsibilities to citizens, the collaborative approach emphasizes that news ought to work with, even serve, government, collaborating with leaders to convey information and developing stories that improve the functioning of society. It turns out that it's not all bad. There are contexts in which you can make a strong argument that news should work with government to further worthy societal goals. The question of when news should work with government and when it should defy government raises normative issues that are further complicated by their interactions with the structures and values of different nations' media systems (Hallin & Mancini, 2004). Indeed, collaboration between the press and government can take different forms. It can be coercive, forced on the press (this is the one that first comes to mind and is usually the most disconcerting). Collaboration can also serve instrumental goals, offering benefits to both journalists and government, or even be freely viewed as the most proper course by reporters.

Complications

Scholars coined the term "development journalism" to describe news media practices that help newly formed nations grow, fortify their institutions, and harness communications for the greater good of society. Thus, journalists committed to the growth of Singapore viewed themselves "not as critics but as partners of the state" working toward the joint goal of nation-building (Christians et al., p. 205). Collaborative journalists in other nations put their patriotic identity before their professional role as reporters. "I am first of all an Israeli, then an officer in the reserves, and only after that a journalist and an editor," an Israeli editor observed (Christians et al., p. 209). The idea that national duty comes before journalistic interests is one that many Americans, some journalists, and conservative commentators would endorse. Conservative critics rebuke reporters for running critical stories about the U.S. military during war-time, arguing that reporters have a duty to support the government that sustains them. They question the merits of WikiLeaks and Snowden's exposés that put secret projects – and diplomats whose names have not been redacted – at risk. Naturally, many reporters, operating from libertarian and watchdog perspectives, disagree.

It turns out that the bright line that supposedly separates news media from the state is blurrier than frequently assumed. The press confers with government on a host of issues, including national security, kidnapping of journalists, hostage seizures, and joint agenda-building collaborations between policymakers and reporters (Protess et al., 1991). Reporters can be more likely to don the collaborative hat in particular contexts, such as when their country's national security is under siege and in small towns where journalists view it as their job to advance the community's interests (see Chapter 9). Elite journalists have long had direct, close relationships with political leaders, spanning Walter Lippmann's speech-writing for Woodrow Wilson, George F. Will's coaching Ronald Reagan in a presidential debate, and Sean Hannity's speaking at a rally on behalf of President Trump. What's more, radical critics argue that, more generally, American news frequently affirms national values and offers the government patriotic pro-war coverage, although there is considerable debate about this, as Chapter 10 discusses.

And yet there are clearly cases where journalistic collaboration with – and acquiescence to – government crosses democratic lines, chiefly in cases of government censorship and intimidation of journalists.

The evidence is striking and the examples chilling. Across the world, just 13 percent of the world's population revels in the fruits of a free press. Fewer than one in seven people reside in countries "where coverage of political news is robust, the safety of journalists is guaranteed, state intrusion in media affairs is minimal, and the press is not subject to onerous legal or economic pressures" (Dunham, 2017). For example, after an abortive coup attempt in Turkey back in 2016, the Turkish president, Recep Tayyip Erdogan, intensified his intimidation of the press, throwing 173 journalists in prison and closing the country's only Kurdish-language newspaper, as well as 10 TV channels that broadcast at least partly in Kurdish (Kingsley, 2017), exacerbating Turkey's long-time prejudice against the Turkish minority.

In Vladimir Putin's Russia, the government has secured near-complete control of the domestic press and conducts disinformation campaigns in the Ukraine, propounding false, pro-Russia narratives. More darkly, courageous reporters are routinely and frequently murdered when they expose unpleasant truths about the government, leading to widespread suspicion that Russian authorities are behind the killings. Poland has assumed greater control over government-controlled broadcast outlets, passing a law that lets the Polish government hire and fire directors of the state news media (Specia, 2017). China, ever-sensitive to the Internet's potential to fuel dissent, has denied access to news websites, blocked Facebook apps for years, banned Twitter, and partly sealed off the WhatsApp messaging app, preventing users from sharing videos and text messages (Mozur, 2017a, 2017b; Mozur, 2019).

Not to be outdone, Mexico cynically uses the power of the purse to stifle free expression and block the flow of critical news. The government doles out millions of dollars a year to preferred news outlets, demanding news organizations provide positive press before formally agreeing to an advertising contract. Mexico officials regularly suppress investigative stories. And, in Saudi Arabia, in a case that captured the world's attention, a dissident Saudi journalist, Jamal Khashoggi, was murdered in 2018, apparently by the Saudi government.

News is covered in these non-democratic countries and journalists collaborate with government, but not always willingly. This is not a journalism founded on freedom of expression and journalistic autonomy.

The United States is not exempt from government controls. There are historical examples of government censorship of the news, such as during World War I, when Congress passed a Sedition Act that banned statements criticizing the U.S. government, giving the Wilson administration license to censor German newspapers and arrest more than 2,000 Americans. Since then, illustrating that truth is the first casualty of war, the U.S. government deceived the public about the scope of Vietnam military escalation, spread false information about Iraqi president Saddam Hussein in the 1991 Persian Gulf War, and, in the run-up to the 2003 Iraq war, made the case that Iraq had weapons of mass destruction, which turned out to be palpably false (see Chapters 8 and 10).

During our own time, President Donald Trump (like presidents who preceded him) has regularly denounced news he does not like, going so far as to call it fake news, prompting autocratic leaders across the world to use the phrase to discredit their critics in the press (Erlanger, 2017). He has lambasted journalists who do not support his policies, calling them "enemies of the people," and banned a feisty CNN reporter from the White House. (The White House backed down, restoring the reporter's press credentials after a judge ordered that his press pass must be reinstated.) The press, for its part, has fought back, as hundreds of newspapers wrote editorials in defense of press freedom some years back, emphasizing that a free press is not the enemy of the people but a way to sustain a democracy in which citizens must be informed to challenge the state.

Conclusions

This chapter grappled with the big normative questions – the "should" issues that underpin the role of news in democratic society. The normative approach to news owes much to the pioneering work of Siebert, Schramm, and Peterson, though their book is not without its ethnocentric and ideological biases

The first view, the time-honored libertarian perspective, emphasizes citizens' right to freedom of expression, prohibition on government regulation of free press, and the notion that the open competition of ideas provides the best way for truth to emerge from falsehood. Long celebrated as the purist's view of news in a democratic society, libertarian theory continues to offer helpful prescriptions for the press in modern times. However, it also has darker, problematic aspects.

Sensational reporting, including hacking into a murder victim's email that is conducted not for grand philosophical motives, but to increase publishers' profits, raises ethical questions about the virtues of unbridled libertarianism. Libertarian theory's time-worn affirmation that even false information should be printed, presuming that truth will win out, is complicated by the pervasive impact that fake news can exert, as well as the possibility that algorithms delivering people politically congenial information can reduce the chances they will be exposed to truthful information from the other side. Unabridged libertarianism can also stoke anger and hate on social media posts, raising questions about how to apply laudable principles of a theory penned centuries before digital diffusion, and where to draw the line between liberty and social control.

In contrast to libertarianism, the more diffuse social responsibility perspective ticks off a number of roles news should perform. Its assumption is the non-controversial, but instructive, notion that, in view of its power and pervasiveness, news has responsibilities to society. The first responsibility, informational monitoring, presumes that news should survey dangers in the social environment, providing citizens with facts they need to be self-governing participants in society, an assumption that clashes with libertarian theory's indifference to the provision of consensually validated facts. The practice of monitorial reporting has imperfections, such as failure to adequately cover stories that threaten the status quo (though this is unusual in current times) and jargon-y news items that monitor the environment using words few can understand. Nonetheless, in the no-holds-barred, authentication-free social media, surveillance reporting that is carefully vetted fulfills societal responsibilities.

A second social responsibility is interpretation, helping make sense of the crazy-quilt world, a function that evolved as magazines, then television, could cover breaking events, undermining newspapers. Carefully reported interpretive stories that offer multiple perspectives are a gleaming virtue of news, but they can be a rarity, given journalists' routine preference for simple stories about the strategic game, economic cutbacks, and reporters' concern that if they present one side, they will be viewed as biased. The best scholars of interpretive news emphasize that journalists enhance the public's understanding of issues by exploring underlying "how" and "why" issues from different viewpoints.

A third role articulated by social responsibility advocates fulfills emotional functions, via stories that offer social empathy on an individual level and perform ritualistic healing on a macro level. Journalists have provided deep, compassionate articles about people marginalized by society, enhancing readers' empathy with different populations and their understanding of social problems. On a broader level, news fulfills social rituals, building solidarity through coverage of celebrity deaths and national traumas. Complications emerge in the inevitable decision of who is most deserving of empathy, and why.

The fourth socially responsible role, the gold standard of journalism, is investigative journalism, fulfilling a watchdog function. At their best, journalists are the detectives of democracy, spotlighting wrongdoing, misconduct, and systemic breakdowns in need of urgent reform. As beneficial as these stories are, they involve ethical trade-offs when exposés needlessly invade personal privacy, causing individual harm or destroying the careers of promising political figures, whose sexual infidelities may not bear on the public interest. Deciding when these infidelities are worthy of coverage is a news judgment, which frequently involves the question of whether the sexual impropriety touches on broader public or legal issues.

In the digital era, WikiLeaks, the controversial (courageous or reckless, and probably both, depending on one's perspective) international online organization has taken investigatory stories to new extremes, with release of documents on topics spanning civilian deaths by U.S. forces in Afghanistan to the posting of thousands of hacked Democratic National Committee emails in 2016, apparently furnished by Russian cyber spies. Debate rages as to whether WikiLeaks is a bona fide news organization or rogue outlet thwarting ethical and democratic norms. It is an interesting discussion that once again illustrates boundary-blurring in journalism. Many experts, even those who cringe at Julian Assange's personal values, see broad similarities between his mission and those of conventional investigative reporters, as well as threats if he is prosecuted for doing what traditional reporters do in their line of work.

A fourth social responsibility function is facilitation of democratic dialogue, in the service of improving deliberative, thoughtful reasoning about public issues. With its emphasis on citizen engagement, Deweyesque emphasis on conversation, and ameliorating community ills, the democratic dialogue function owes much to the public journalism movement of the 1990s. It has produced some stellar newspaper series illuminating the dynamics of political debate and racial conflict, while missing opportunities to explore solutions to problems these articles identified. In today's online milieu, where acrimonious platforms can polarize public discussion, citizen news sites have offered an opportunity to reinvent public journalism, although questions remain about their impact and reach, particularly in poorer communities. In recent years, scholars have expanded the deliberative democratic perspective, incorporating its tenets in a broader constructive journalism framework. Constructive journalism promises to take news-gathering in more forward-thinking, solutions-oriented directions. It will have to grapple with pinpointing the quintessential aspects of the constructive journalism construct, as well as making certain that its positive features do not devolve into oversimplified remedies with insufficient emphasis on the verification foundations of journalism.

Finally, the collaborative perspective takes a different tack, with its emphasis on how news can assist, even serve, government by collaborating with leaders to solve political problems. Although popular myth holds that reporters never collaborate with government leaders, the truth is more nuanced. Even in the U.S., with its long history of press freedom, the news media have acquiesced to, or allowed themselves to be subtly manipulated by, government. However, in its extreme (though not uncommon, in today's world) practice, press collaboration with government – frequently by authoritarian leaders – has led to censorship, killing of journalists, and squelching investigative stories that speak truth to coercive power.

To be sure, the news makes mistakes and when it is unfair to political leaders, it deserves criticism. And though it monitors, interprets, investigates, and facilitates dialogue, news has significant flaws and limitations, the focus of subsequent chapters in this book. And yet it is important, I think, to remember, with all the nuance and valued complexity, that, in an age of subtle and not-so-subtle censorship of news, economic cutbacks, and political attacks, journalism – celebrated by a variety of normative theories of press and democracy – plays a central role in protecting a critical citizenry, offering fact-based reporting that restrains power-hungry leaders, and preserves checks and balances in democratic government. "Whatever its faults," scholar Stephen D. Reese (2018) notes, "the press matters greatly as defense against repressive power." A vibrant press serves as an institutional safeguard against authoritarian tendencies. It provides society with a precious intellectual, emotional, and critical resource, what Kreiss (2016, p. 62) calls "institutionally organized civic skepticism," or, in Ernest Hemingway's famous words, "a built-in bullshit detector."

References

Allan, S. (2010). Journalism and its publics: The Lippmann-Dewey debate. In S. Allan (Ed.), *The Routledge companion to news and journalism* (pp. 60–70). New York: Routledge.

Allan, S. (2013). Journalism as interpretive performance: The case of WikiLeaks. In C. Peters & M. Broersma (Eds.), *Rethinking journalism: Trust and participation in a transformed news landscape* (pp. 144–159). New York: Routledge.

Anderson, R., Dardenne, R., & Killenberg, G. (1994). *The conversation of journalism: Communication, community, and news.* Westport, CT: Praeger.

Aufderheide, P. (2002). All-too-reality TV: Challenges for television journalists after September 11. *Journalism, 3,* 7–14.

Bai, M. (2014). *All the truth is out: The week politics went tabloid.* New York: Knopf.

Baker, P. (2019, January 9). Trump appeals directly to U.S. for border wall. *The New York Times,* A1, A13.

Barnhurst, K.G., & Mutz, D. (1997). American journalism and the decline in event-centered reporting. *Journal of Communication, 47,* 27–53.

Beattie, P., & Milojevich, J. (2017). A test of the "news diversity" standard: Single frames, multiple frames, and values regarding the Ukraine conflict. *The International Journal of Press/Politics, 22,* 3–22.

Berkowitz, D. (2010). The ironic hero of Virginia Tech: Healing trauma through mythical narrative and collective memory. *Journalism, 11*, 643–659.

Berkowitz, D. (2017). Solidarity through the visual: Healing images in the Brussels terrorism attacks. *Mass Communication & Society, 20*, 740–762.

Berry, W.E., Braman, S., Christians, C., Guback, T.G., Helle, S.J., Liebovich, L.W., Nerone, J.C., & Rotzoll, K.B. (Ed., J.C. Nerone) (1995). *Last rights: Revisiting four theories of the press.* Urbana, IL: University of Illinois Press.

Black, J. (Ed.). (1997). *Mixed news: The public/civic/communitarian journalism debate.* Mahwah, NJ: Erlbaum Associates.

Branch, J. (2011, December 3). Derek Boogaard: A boy learns to brawl. *The New York Times.* Online: www.nytimes.com/2011/12/04/sports/hockey/derek-boogaard-a-boy-learns-to-brawl.html?pagewanted%3Dall. (Accessed: November 22, 2017).

Bro, P. (2019). Constructive journalism: Proponents, precedents, and principles. *Journalism, 20*, 504–519.

Bybee, C. (1999). Can democracy survive in the post-factual age?: A return to the Lippmann-Dewey debate about the politics of news. *Journalism and Communication Monographs, 1*, 28–66.

Carlson, M. (2015). Introduction: The many boundaries of journalism. In M. Carlson & S.C. Lewis (Eds.), *Boundaries of journalism: Professionalism, practices, and participation* (pp. 1–18). New York: Routledge.

Christians, C.G., Glasser, T.L., McQuail, D., Nordenstreng, K., & White, R.A. (2009). *Normative theories of the media: Journalism in democratic societies.* Urbana, IL: University of Illinois Press.

Coddington, M. (2012). Defending a paradigm by patrolling a boundary: Two global newspapers' approach to WikiLeaks. *Journalism & Mass Communication Quarterly, 89*, 377–396.

Coll, S. (2018, August 20). The digital public square. *The New Yorker*, 13–14.

Davies, N. (2014). *Hack attack: The inside story of how the truth caught up with Rupert Murdoch.* New York: Faber and Faber.

Deb, S. (2017, September 11). As winds rise, so does debate over derring-do of TV storm reporters. *The New York Times*, A16.

Delli Carpini, M.X. (2017). Postscript: The who, what, when, where, why, and how of journalism and journalism studies. In P.J. Boczkowski & C.W. Anderson (Eds.), *Remaking the news: Essays on the future of journalism scholarship in the digital age* (pp. 273–287). Cambridge, MA: The MIT Press.

Dewey, J. (1927). *The public and its problems.* New York: Holt.

Dunham, J. (2017). Press freedom's dark horizon. *Freedom of the Press 2017.* Online: https://freedomhouse.org/report/freedom-press/freedom-press-2017. (Accessed: July 7, 2017).

Durham, F. (2008). Media ritual in catastrophic time: The populist turn in television coverage of Hurricane Katrina. *Journalism, 9*, 95–116.

Eldridge, II, S.A. (2014). Boundary maintenance and interloper media reaction: Differentiating between journalism's discursive enforcement processes. *Journalism Studies, 15*, 1–16.

Elliott, A. (2013, December 9). Invisible child. *The New York Times.* www.nytimes.com/projects/2013/invisible-child/#/?chapt=1. (Accessed: November 21, 2017).

Elliott, P. (1980). Press performance as political ritual. In H. Christian (Ed.), *The sociology of journalism and the press* (Sociological Review Monograph No. 29, pp. 141–177). Keele, UK: University of Keele.

Erlanger, S. (2017, December 13). Globe's autocrats echo Trump's "fake news" cry. *The New York Times*, A1, A12.

Ettema, J.S., & Glasser, T.L. (1998). *Custodians of conscience: Investigative journalism and public virtue*. New York: Columbia University Press.

Feldstein, M. (2007). Dummies and ventriloquists: Models of how sources set the investigative agenda. *Journalism*, *8*, 499–509.

Ferrucci, P. (2015). Public journalism no more: The digitally native news nonprofit and public service journalism. *Journalism*, *16*, 904–919.

Fink, K., & Schudson, M. (2014). The rise of contextual journalism, 1950s to 2000s. *Journalism*, *15*, 3–20.

Fisher, M. (2018, December 28). How Facebook controls what world can say. *The New York Times*, A1, A8.

Fraser, N. (1990). Rethinking the public sphere: A contribution to the critique of actually existing democracy. *Social Text*, *25/26*, 56–80.

Frenkel, S. (2018, October 12). Made in U.S.: Untruths infest social media. *The New York Times*, A1, A12.

Frenkel, S., Isaac, M., & Conger, K. (2018, October 29). On Instagram, 11,696 examples of how hate thrives on social media. *The New York Times*. Online: www.nytimes.com/2018/10/29/technology/hate-on-social-media.   (Accessed: November 26, 2018).

Gajda, A. (2015). *The First Amendment bubble: How privacy and paparazzi threaten a free press*. Cambridge, MA: Harvard University Press.

Gans, H.J. (2004). *Deciding what's news: A study of CBS evening news, NBC nightly news, Newsweek and Time* (25th anniversary edition). Evanston, IL: Northwestern University Press.

Goel, V., & Raj, S. (2018, July 21). How WhatsApp leads mobs to kill in India. *The New York Times*, B4.

Goodman, P.S., & Cohen, P. (2017, November 30). G.O.P. tax plan could reshape life in the U.S. *The New York Times*, A1, A20.

Gyldensted, C. (2015). *From mirrors to movers: Five elements of positive psychology in constructive journalism*. Charleston, SC: Group Publishing.

Haagerup, U. (2014). *Constructive news: How to save the media and democracy with journalism of tomorrow*. New York: InnoVatio Publishing.

Haas, T., & Steiner, L. (2001). Public journalism as a journalism of publics: Implications of the Habermas-Fraser debate for public journalism. *Journalism: Theory, Practice & Criticism*, *2*, 123–147.

Habermas, J. (1989). *The structural transformation of the public sphere: An inquiry into a category of bourgeois society*. Cambridge, MA: The MIT Press.

Hallin, D.C., & Mancini, P. (2004). *Comparing media systems: Three models of media and politics*. New York: Cambridge University Press.

Hamilton, J.T. (2016). *Democracy's detectives: The economics of investigative journalism*. Cambridge, MA: Harvard University Press.

Hanitzsch, T., & Vos, P. (2017). Journalistic roles and the struggle over institutional identity: The discursive constitution of journalism. *Communication Theory*, *27*, 115–135.

Hanitzsch, T., & Vos, T.P. (2018). Journalism beyond democracy: A new look into journalistic roles in political and everyday life. *Journalism, 19*, 146–164.

Hermans, L., & Gyldensted, C. (2019). Elements of constructive journalism: Characteristics, practical application and audience valuation. *Journalism, 20*, 535–551.

Hermida, A., Domingo, D., Heinonen, A., Paulussen, S., Quandt, T., Reich, Z., Singer, J.B., & Vujnovic, M. (2011). The active recipient: Participatory journalism through the lens of the Dewey-Lippmann debate. *International Symposium on Online Journalism, 1*, 129–152.

Hess, K., & Gutsche, Jr., R.E. (2018). Journalism and the "social sphere": Reclaiming a foundational concept for beyond politics and the public sphere. *Journalism Studies, 19*, 483–498.

Howley, K. (2003). A poverty of voices: Street papers as communicative democracy. *Journalism, 4*, 273–292.

Isaac, M. (2017, October 28). Tussle within Facebook focuses on how to address misleading material. *The New York Times*, B3.

Isaac, M., & Roose, K. (2019, May 3). Facebooks bars 7 fiery voices, mostly rightist. The New York Times, A1, A17.

Jamieson, K.H. (2018). *Cyberwar: How Russian hackers and trolls helped elect a president*. New York: Oxford University Press.

Jarvis, J. (2011, June 26). Digital first: What it means for journalism. *Guardian*. Online: www.theguardian.com/media/2011/jun/26/digital-first-what. (Accessed: October 10, 2018).

Jolly, J. (2016, August 22). Platform aimed at audience interaction generates story ideas, goodwill. *Columbia Journalism Review*. Online: www.cjr.org/the_profile/hearken_hey_area_homeless_san_francisco_audience.php (Accessed: December 1, 2018).

Kaplan, R.L. (2002). *Politics and the American press: The rise of objectivity, 1865–1920*. Cambridge, UK: Cambridge University Press.

Karhula, P. (2011, January 19). *What is the effect of WikiLeaks for freedom of information?* Online: www.ifla.org/files/assets/faife/publications/spotlights/wiki leaks-karhula.pdf. (Accessed: February 27, 2019).

Kingsley, P. (2017, June 29). Kurdish culture under siege as Turkey broadens its purge. *The New York Times*, A1, A10.

Kitch, C. (2000). "A news of feeling as well as fact": Mourning and memorial in American newsmagazines. *Journalism, 1*, 171–195.

Kitch, C., & Hume, J. (2008). *Journalism in a culture of grief*. New York: Routledge.

Kovach, B., & Rosenstiel, T. (2014). *The elements of journalism: What newspeople should know and the public should expect* (3rd ed.). New York: Three Rivers Press.

Kreiss, D. (2016). Beyond administrative journalism: Civic skepticism and the crisis in journalism. In J. Alexander, E. Breese, & M. Luengo (Eds.), *The crisis of journalism reconsidered: Democratic culture, professional codes, digital future* (pp. 59–76). New York: Cambridge University Press.

Kumar, A. (2013). *News epistemology, radical journalism, and disruption of paradigm in WikiLeaks phenomenon*. Paper presented to the International Communication Association, London.

Kurpius, D.D. (2003). Bucking a trend in local television news: Combating market-driven journalism. *Journalism, 4*, 76–94.

Levy, L.W. (1985). *Emergence of a free press*. New York: Oxford University Press.

Lyon, D. (2015). *Surveillance after Snowden*. Cambridge, UK: Polity Press.

Manjoo, F. (2018, July 20). Once-nimble Facebook trips over calls to control content. *The New York Times*, A1, A11.

Mast, J., Coesemans, R., & Temmerman, M. (2019). Constructive journalism: Concepts, practices, and discourses. *Journalism, 20*, 492–503.

Matthews, J. (2016). Media performance in the aftermath of terror: Reporting templates, political ritual and the UK press coverage of the London bombings, 2005. *Journalism, 17*, 173–189.

McChesney, R.W. (2011). September 11 and the structural limitations of US journalism. In B. Zelizer & S. Allan (Eds.), *Journalism after September 11* (2nd ed., pp. 104–112). New York: Routledge.

Merrill, J.C. (2002). The four theories of the press four and a half decades later: A retrospective. *Journalism Studies, 3*, 133–134.

Merrill, J.C., & Lowenstein, R.L. (1979). *Media, messages, and men: New perspectives in communication* (2nd ed.). New York: Longman.

Mill, J.S. (1859/2009). *On liberty and other essays*. New York: Kaplan Publishing.

Moss, B.P. (2018, November 19). Julian Assange isn't worth it. *The Atlantic*. Online: www.theatlantic.com/ideas/archive/2018/11/prosecuting. (Accessed: December 1, 2018).

Morse, T. (2017). The mourning news: Reporting violent death in a global age. New York: Peter Lang.

Mozur, P. (2017a, July 19). Fortifying its "great firewall," China blocks WhatsApp services. *The New York Times*, B1, B2.

Mozur, P. (2017b, August 12). Facebook uses a stealth app to enter China. *The New York Times*, A1, A7.

Mozur, P. (2019, January 11). He was chained to a chair in China. What was his offense? Posting on Twitter. *The New York Times*, A1, A7.

Nerone, J. (2004). Four theories of the press in hindsight: Reflections on a popular model. In M. Semati (Ed.), *New frontiers in international communication theory* (pp. 21–32). Lanham, MD: Rowman & Littlefield.

Nerone, J.C. (2002). The four theories of the press four and a half decades later: A retrospective. *Journalism Studies, 3*, 134–136.

Nerone, J.C. (2015). *The media and public life: A history*. Malden, MA: Polity Press.

Nerone, J.C. (2017). Review of free speech and unfree news: The paradox of freedom of speech in America. *International Journal of Press/Politics, 22*, 406–408.

Nip, J.Y.M. (2008). The last days of civic journalism: The case of the *Savannah Morning News*. *Journalism Practice, 2*, 179–196.

Nord, D.P. (2001). *Communities of journalism: A history of American newspapers and their readers*. Urbana, IL: University of Illinois Press.

Nyhan, B., & Reifler, J. (2010). When corrections fail: The persistence of political misperceptions. *Political Behavior, 32*, 303–330.

Nyhan, B., & Reifler, J. (2015). Does correcting myths about the flu vaccine work? An experimental evaluation of the effects of corrective information. *Vaccine, 33*, 459–464.

Patterson, T.E. (1993). *Out of order*. New York: Knopf.

Porto, M.P. (2007). Frame diversity and citizen competence: Towards a critical approach to news quality. *Critical Studies in Mass Communication, 24*, 303–321.

Protess, D.L., Cook, F.L., Doppelt, J.C., Ettema, J.S., Gordon, M.T., Leff, D.R., & Miller, P. (1991). *The journalism of outrage: Investigative reporting and agenda building in America*. New York: Guilford Press.

Reese, S.D. (2018). *Does the institutional press still matter? Exploring the hybrid infrastructure in the new media eco-system.* Paper presented to the International Communication Association, Prague, May, 2018.

Reese, S.D., & Lewis, S.C. (2009). Framing the war on terror: The internalization of policy in the US press. *Journalism, 10,* 777–797.

Roose, K. (2017a, October 30). Furor abroad is far darker for Facebook. *The New York Times,* B1, B7.

Roose, K. (2017b, November 8). YouTube's rapid response partisans game the news of tragedy. *The New York Times.* Online: www.nytimes.com/2017/11/08/business/youtube-rapid-response-partisans.html. (Accessed: November 17, 2017).

Roose, K. (2018, October 29). Social site let suspect's hate spill unbridled. *The New York Times,* A1, A14.

Rosen, J. (1999). The action of the idea: Public journalism in built form. In T. L. Glasser (Ed.), *The idea of public journalism* (pp. 21–48). New York: Guilford Press.

Rosenzweig, P., McNulty, T.J., & Shearer, E. (Eds.). (2014). *Whistleblowers, leaks, and the media: The First Amendment and national security.* Chicago, IL: American Bar Association.

Salgado, S., & Strömbäck, J. (2012). Interpretive journalism: A review of concepts, operationalizations and key findings. *Journalism, 13,* 144–161.

Sanger-Kaztz, M. (2019, February 28). "Medicare for all," and the original. *The New York Times,* A21.

Satter, R., & Michael, M. (2016, August 23). *Private lives are exposed as Wiki-Leaks spills its secrets.* Associated Press. Online: https://apnews.com/b70da83fd111496dbdf015acbb7987fb/private-lives-are-exposed-wikileaks-spills-its-secrets. (Accessed: December 2, 2019).

Savage, C. (2018, November 17). The complaint is murky, but the risks to press freedom are clearer. *The New York Times,* A16.

Schmidt, M.S., & Fandos, N. (2017, November 14). Trump Jr. confirms WikiLeaks exchanges. *The New York Times,* A19.

Schmitt, E., Sanger, D.E., & Thrush, G. (2019, January 9). Experts reject claims by Trump that terrorists are menacing border. *The New York Times,* A13.

Schudson, M. (2008a). *Why democracies need an unlovable press.* Cambridge UK: Polity Press.

Schudson, M. (2008b). The "Lippmann-Dewey debate" and the invention of Walter Lippmann as an anti-democrat 1986–1996. *International Journal of Communication, 2,* 1031–1042.

Schudson, M. (2011). What's unusual about covering politics as usual. In B. Zelizer & S. Allan (Eds.), *Journalism after September 11* (2nd ed., pp. 44–54). New York: Routledge.

Schudson, M. (2019). Where we are and whither we are tending. *Journalism, 20,* 77–79.

Siebert, F.S., Peterson, T., & Schramm, W. (1956). *Four theories of the press: The authoritarian, libertarian, social responsibility, and Soviet communist concepts of what the press should be and do.* Urbana, IL: University of Illinois Press.

Specia, M. (2017). Called beacon of freedom, Poland has its detractors. *The New York Times,* A10.

Standage, T. (2013). *Writing on the wall: Social media – The first 2,000 years.* New York: Bloomsbury.

Starkman, D. (2014). *The watchdog that didn't bark: The financial crisis and the disappearance of investigative reporting.* New York: Columbia University Press.

Steele, B. (2002, August 25). *The ethics of civic journalism: Independence as the guide.* Online: www.poynter.org/news/ethics-civic-journalism-independence-guide. (Accessed: December 6, 2017).

Stockman, F. (2017, October 15). Work freed her. Then it moved to Mexico. *The New York Times,* 1, 18–21.

Streitfeld, D. (2017, October 12). Tech giants, once seen as saviors, are now viewed as threats. *The New York Times.* Online: www.nytimes.com/2017/10/12/technology/tech-giants-threat.html. (Accessed: November 17, 2017).

Stroud, N.J. (2014). Selective exposure theories. In K. Kenski & K.H. Jamieson (Eds.), *The Oxford handbook of political communication.* New York: Oxford University Press. Retrieved from www.oxfordhandbooks.com.

Sullivan, E., & LaFraniere, S. (2019, January 26). Here is what we learned from the special counsel's indictment. *The New York Times,* A14.

Tankersley, J. (2017, November 17). Party's priority: Comfort for corporations. *The New York Times,* A1, A14.

Tankersley, J. (2018, December 28). Trump's tax cut, one year later. *The New York Times,* B1, B3.

Tolentino, J. (2017, October 30). Comment: Limits of power, *The New Yorker,* 15–16.

Toobin, J. (2016, December 19 & 26). Gawker's demise and the Trump-era threat to the First Amendment. *The New Yorker.* Online: www.newyorker.com/magazine/2016/12/19/gawkers-demise-and-the-trump-era-threat-to-the-first-amendment. (Accessed: July 1, 2017).

Usher, N. (2016). *Interactive journalism: Hackers, data, and code.* Urbana, IL: University of Illinois Press.

Waisbord, S. (2011). Journalism, risk, and patriotism. In B. Zelizer & S. Allan (Eds.), *Journalism after September 11* (2nd ed., pp. 273–291). New York: Routledge.

Waisbord, S. (2017). Afterword: Crisis? What crisis? In C. Peters & M. Broersma (Eds.), *Rethinking journalism again: Societal role and public relevance in a digital age* (pp. 205–215). New York: Routledge.

Wasserman, H., & de Beer, A.S. (2009). Towards de-westernizing journalism studies. In K. Wahl-Jorgensen & T. Hanitzsch (Eds.), *The handbook of journalism studies* (pp. 428–438). Thousand Oaks, CA: Sage.

Wenzel, A., Gerson, D., Moreno, E., Son, M., & Morrison Hawkins, B. (2018). Engaging stigmatized communities through solutions journalism: Residents of South Los Angeles respond. *Journalism, 19,* 649–667.

Wright, C.R. (1960). Functional analysis and mass communications. *Public Opinion Quarterly, 24,* 605–620.

Wright, C.R. (1986). *Mass communication: A sociological perspective.* New York: Random House.

Wu, T. (2017, October 28). Did Twitter kill the First Amendment? *The New York Times,* A19.

5 The Rich, Colorful History of American Journalism
Overview and Perspectives

"Sooner or later, everything old is new again," a character in a Stephen King (2005) novel quipped, suggesting that old ideas are eventually reborn, experienced as new in the historical present. "Life," King opined, "is like a wheel. Sooner or later, it always comes around to where you started again." So it is with news, where current memes, like fake news, bias, and sensationalism, can be traced to long-ago eras in American journalism. Fake news that emerged during the 2016 Russian hacking scandal? Seen that in 1837. What of people calling out Fox or MSNC for flagrant bias? Try the *really* politically biased newspapers of the early 19th century. Frustrated with local television news's focus on crime? Oh, please, that's nothing, compared to how the penny press mercilessly hyped the murder of New York prostitute Helen Jewett (Cohen, 1998).

Although some of us find history boring, or decry "history as bunk," as a character in Huxley's *Brave New World* exclaimed, it is quite the contrary – vital, insightful, full of life and verve. How could it be otherwise? After all, it is describing human beings in all their glory, optimism, and innovative accomplishments, as well as their hatefulness and prejudice. It is humbling and insight-producing to invoke journalism history as a backdrop to contemporary news. Humbling because it reminds us that the problems of today can also be located in the past; what seems troubling or utterly distinctive in today's journalism has been seen before. And a historical backdrop generates insights, as it clarifies what is different about today's news, suggesting cultural, economic, and technological explanations for characteristics of news that have parallels in the historical past, but are temporally distinctive as well.

Consider social media. In one sense, as Standage (2013) observes, social media "has been around for centuries" (p. 250). Today's Facebook-transmitted blogs are the radical pamphlets of yore, and social networks are the digital equivalent of the old coffeehouses where people used to discuss news and opinions. In more tangible ways, though, social media is revolutionary, changing the way news is distributed, shared, gatekept, experienced, trusted, filtered, and processed.

This chapter presents an overview of news and journalism history emphasizing concepts and themes that course through the varied streams of journalism scholarship. The scope and breadth of journalism history scholarship is too extensive to permit a full discussion here, and such a discussion would extend beyond the purview of this book. However, the history of news is too important – "longer, larger, more various, more beautiful, and more terrible" than commonly assumed, to paraphrase James Baldwin (Gilliard, 2017) – to be ignored and cast aside in a book devoted to the dynamics of contemporary news. This chapter provides a broad introduction to news history in America, enriched by the fascinating, thoughtful scholarship in journalism history (Brennen & Hardt, 2011; Carey, 2007; Hardt, 1995; Mindich, 1998; Nerone, 2015; Schudson & Tifft, 2005; Sloan, 1991, 2005).

The discussion begins with the radical press of the Revolutionary War period, moves to the partisan newspapers of the early and mid-19th century, discusses the development of the mass, commercial press, along with the frequently debated issue of the development of the objectivity norm, marches into the 20th century with a description of the economic and political heights that journalism reached, along with its cozying up to powerful Washington, D.C. elites. The chapter describes the adversarial press of the 1970s, the fusion of news and entertainment in the late 20th century, and the economic factors that traumatized newspapers and changed contemporary news.

Throughout the chapter, you will note some intriguing constancies in news over the years, but will also be struck by the changes: in form (for example, differences between the gray, story-cluttered non-bylined, non-illustrated look of early 1800s newspapers and today's news), and, even more importantly, changes in narrative format, bias, ideological diversity, and reader participation in storytelling (Barnhurst & Nerone, 2001). We begin with a front-row seat at the Revolution.

The Radical Press of the American Revolution

In the beginning, it was boring. Very boring, at least by today's standards. Colonial newspapers were originally weekly make-shift periodicals – 4-page publications designed to promote the shops of printers who produced them. In some cases, they were just 1-page pamphlets focused on a particular issue, with a mundane appearance and dull content that included local ads, as well as economic information lifted from the more established newspapers of London (Barnhurst & Nerone, 2001; Schudson & Tifft, 2005; Sloan, 1991). Politics or controversies that occurred in the 13 burgeoning colonies rarely appeared in the news. Then came rumblings of revolution. And things changed forever.

Some of the first reverberations of the transformative changes in newspapers came in the print shops, no longer places of political quiescence, but suddenly "hives of political activity," as opinions for and against revolution pulsated, centering around words expressed in print (Schudson & Tifft, 2005, p. 19). Printers became the focus of attention, famously including John Peter Zenger (the name is almost melodious and suggestive of legend), who was accused of libel in 1734 for printing criticism of a British colonial governor. Zenger was later exonerated on the grounds that one cannot be found guilty for publishing an article if it is true, a principle that laid the groundwork for the storied First Amendment, even as printers continued to be threatened for questioning the powers-that-be, a constant in journalism history if we consider imprisonment of reporters in autocratic countries today (Nerone, 2015).

Some 40 years later these tensions boiled over as the first battle of the American Revolution in Lexington, Massachusetts raged. Newspapers covered the story, but not in the way it would be covered today. This was not bland, neutral, "objective" journalism that gave a nod to both the Brits and the colonists, offering both sides of the story, concluding that the sources of the violence could not be confirmed. Not by a long shot (and there were plenty of those fired too!). Here is how the *Massachusetts Spy* described the iconic first battle of the revolution:

> AMERICANS! Forever bear in mind, the BATTLE OF LEXING-TON! – where British Troops, unmolested and unprovoked, wantonly and in a most cruel manner fired upon and killed a number of our countrymen, then robbed them of their provisions, ransacked, plundered and burnt their houses! Nor could the tears of defenceless women, some of whom were in the pains of childbirth, the cries of helpless babes, nor the prayers of old age, confined to beds of sickness, appease their thirst for blood! – or divert them from their DESIGN of MURDER and ROBBERY!
>
> (Burns, 2006, p. 189; see Figure 5.1)

This is not news in the sense we use it today, as the modern concept of news had not been invented yet. There were no reporters, directed by an editor to pursue a story (Ryfe, 2017). The earliest journalists (if we use the term as employed in the 18th century) were not news-gatherers, but "controversialists" – rhetorically garrulous ideological proponents (Nerone, 2015, p. 42). Their stories, such as the *Massachusetts Spy* account above, hew much closer to radical journalism, which emphasizes that the purpose of journalism is to question, even undermine the structure of society, particularly a problematic status quo. The so-called news of the incendiary colonial press even had the trappings of propaganda, ironic since we think of early news as a harbinger of American patriotism, highlighting the values built into these storied terms.

It is instructive to observe that patriot Samuel Adams pressed much further than the scribe who penned the Lexington battle story above,

Figure 5.1 The revolutionary colonial newspapers offered up a highly biased, ideologically flavored version of events, resembling underground newspapers of the 1960s and virulent websites of today more than dispassionate news organizations. Embracing a radical theory of news, anti-British newspapers like the *Massachusetts Spy* frequently displayed the symbol of a snake sundered into eight pieces to symbolize the separation of the colonies from Britain, along with the slogan, "Join or Die!"

inventing facts (oh yes, fake news) and creating what we would now call media events, as a member of the partisan Sons of Liberty revolutionary movement. During the fall of 1773 he planned the Boston Tea Party. As Eric Burns writes in a book colorfully titled *Infamous Scribblers*, Adams and his compatriots plotted in the newspaper's back room, hatching plans for the Tea Party.

> On the night in question, in the same back room, they darkened their faces, disguised themselves as Mohawk Indians, and set out for the harbor. After the raid, it is possible that some of them returned to the *Gazette*'s backroom for a cheerful postmortem. The Boston Tea Party was at least as much the newspaper's as it was the town's.
>
> (Burns, 2006, p. 159)

During the era of the colonial press, there was no such thing as objectivity. Some newspapers remained loyal to the British Crown; they appealed, not always truthfully, to the minority of Americans who subscribed to the British cause (Emery, Emery, & Roberts, 2000). On the other end of the continuum were the radical newspapers dedicated to instigating revolution. Patriotic promulgators of colonial newspapers, like Sam Adams of the *Boston Gazette* and Isaiah Thomas, proprietor of the aptly titled *Massachusetts Spy* (which on its front page blared the clarion call of the rebellion: Americans! – Liberty or Death! – Join or Die!), can be viewed as out-and-out persuaders, ideologues whose hearts burned with the zeal of moral righteousness. Neutral, fact-bound, dispassionate observers they were not. They were the Breitbart News, on the right, or the Move on.org, on the left, flamethrowers of their times. Facts were secondary; it was the transmission of rebellious opinions that counted most.

The press seems to have played an important part in the revolution, though their motives and impact (creating, or reinforcing preexisting revolutionary sentiments?) remain in doubt. We can't know for sure, but it is plausible to believe that news cultivated the idea of rebellion, helped set an agenda of violently overthrowing British rule, and mobilized colonists, particularly when papers published the stirring Declaration of Independence in 1776 (Burns, 2006). Pro-revolutionary colonial newspapers may have united the colonies around a common cause, performing new journalistic functions, perhaps even building a nascent, national public sphere. At the same time the early papers helped cultivate a radical norm of citizen involvement that placed "popular consent at the root of political authority," arguably accentuating the importance of freedom of the press, as John Nerone (2015, p. 48) insightfully notes (see also Burns, 2006; Copeland, 2006; Sloan, 2008; Stephens, 2007). But there was moral nuance in this early exercise of American journalism.

As noted above, some scribes, impelled by the political passion of youth, were all too eager to compromise the truth – lie – in the service of what they viewed as noble ends. They grossly exaggerated events, claiming, in one case, that British soldiers physically attacked merchants, possibly with bayonets, and sexually assaulted women. Sometimes their claims were true, while in other instances they were demonstrably false. One historian notes that Adams "employed slanderous lies, unvarnished propaganda, and rabble-rousing rhetoric" (Burns, p. 169).

It is strange to view some of the earliest newspapers as rabble-rousers, given contemporary journalism's tepid reactions to radical change, its tendency to nervously balance one side against the other, and even demonize groups that oppose a U.S. president. To be sure, there were limits: A number of newspapers did not take on a radical role, and more widespread acceptance of press freedom did not emerge until after the Revolution, with the repeal of the repressive Sedition Act of 1798 (Sloan,

1991). But the new political press exerted transformative effects. Newspapers evolved from dull four-page periodicals that reprinted obscure
speeches to a provocative theater of arguments and ideological deliberation, perhaps inventing the public sphere where ideas are debated in full
public view, helping set the stage for profound developments in the years
to come (Barnhurst & Nerone, 2001).

The Partisan (Very Biased) Press of the 19th Century: Dark Clouds and Optimistic Tremors

America's early newspapers were not pretty. They weren't even cute. They
were full of rancor, arguments, vitriol, and cantankerous ideological bile.
Like the colonial press, they were a far cry from the high-and-mighty-
sounding objective journalism of the 20th century, but not too distant
from the acrimonious posts and argumentative websites of today. What do
you expect? They began in earnest in the passionate period of the 1790s,
when the country had just emerged from heady days of revolution and the
creation of a Constitution. The burgeoning newspapers – 100 by 1790 and
twice as many by 1800 – reflected and refracted the tenor of the post-
revolutionary times, as the well-educated, ideologically-motivated elites
harnessed the new medium of the political press to work through some
of the growing pains that ailed – and, in the case of slavery, cursed – the
new nation.

   After a series of newspaper denunciations, including the colorful
Aurora's labeling him "old, bald, blind, querulous, toothless, crippled"
(Burns, 2006, p. 354), President John Adams had enough of nefarious
newspaper negativity. He supported Congressional passage of the infamous Sedition Act in 1798, which criminalized the publication of "false,
scandalous and malicious writing against the government of the United
States," with the intent to defame the U.S. government or incite rebellion. Adams, the once-zealous opponent of authoritarian government as
a colonial rebel, sang another tune as president, jailing 25 opposing
editors and political communicators under the Sedition Act until the
new president, Adams' political opponent Thomas Jefferson, allowed the
acts to expire, delivering a unity-inspiring inaugural that only temporarily silenced the partisan newspaper wars of the early 1800s.

   Although debate and fierce opposition to the Sedition Act helped
derail the law, eventually ushering in the modern freedom of the press,
it is worth remembering that even Jefferson had his biases. The oppositional Federalist newspapers had so debased the press, he declared, that
"the people have learnt that nothing in a newspaper is to be believed"
(Sloan, 2005, p. 119).

   And yet beneath the clouds lurked a more optimistic horizon. The early
decades of the 19th century were a heady time in American politics,
propelling the development of the press and political parties. Newspapers

were in the thick of it, a phenomenon that captivated the French philosopher Alexis de Tocqueville's attention. De Tocqueville, remarking that "there is scarcely a hamlet that has not its newspaper" argued that newspapers' vitality represented the fundamental spirit of democracy, one that enabled communication among strangers across the new nation, an ennobling statement until one recognizes that this excluded slaves and women (Bulla & Sachsman, 2013, p. xvii).

This formative period in U.S. press history was a time of intense partisanship. "Editors frowned on impartiality," Sloan observed (2005, p. 75). Each political group had its own press organ. Hamilton's Federalists had their newspaper; Jefferson's opposing Democrat-Republicans had theirs, and they verbally dueled, with their polemical pens. Not content to depend on ideological appeals, partisans of both sides resorted to unadulterated personal attacks (Perloff, 1999). In the 1800 election, Jefferson's supporters smeared Adams, charging he plotted to create a political dynasty with his sons. Federalist editors called Jefferson a traitor and atheist and accused him of raping a slave (an allegation that historians now believe to be true, in the case of Sally Hemings). Verbal denunciations of government policies did not stem from an adversarial relationship between newspapers and government, an idea that came much later; instead newspapers allied with political factions out of power attacked the group that controlled the White House. Editors believe that *partiality* was an instrument of editorial integrity (Sloan, 2005).

Disheartened by editors' scurrilous attacks on opponents, journalism historians have referred to this period in American history as the dark age of American journalism (Mott, 1962). While there is reason to lament the vitriolic barbs newspaper editors exchanged, it is also important to recognize that this criticism served a broader function for the burgeoning political system. It offered a mechanism by which ideologues of different stripes could communicate their positions, candidates could vent political attacks, and political parties could gain legitimacy, emerging as a more democratic institution than the elite factions that preceded them. Behind the partisan strife, the new nation was feeling its way, as parties began forming and people harnessed established outlets to express their intensely political strivings (Perloff, 1999). And in the 1820s, as the Jacksonian era approached, the relationship between press and politics was about to get much more intense and interconnected.

Press, Political Parties, and Broader Political Issues

It was a heady time in American politics – the development of press and political parties, and newspapers were at the center of the action. With the population increasing and property requirements for voting eliminated, such that that all adult White males could vote, the stage was set for increased political participation, though once again the abhorrent stains on democracy remained as Blacks and women were fundamentally denied voting rights. During an age in which political leaders were discouraged from campaigning for office (it was deemed unfashionably political), and there was no Twitter to upend the press, the single most important linkage between political parties and voters was the unabashedly partisan newspaper, scholar Gerald M. Baldasty (2011) observed. The number of newspapers grew rapidly during the first decades of the 19th century, with 1,200 newspapers by 1833. The partisan press provided political parties a way to organize grassroots support for their candidates.

Let's be clear: The parties weren't just incidentally connected with newspapers. They funded them, providing subsidies that gave them their daily bread. It would be as if the Democratic Party funded MSNBC or left-leaning websites, and the Republican Party bankrolled Fox News. During this 19th-century era of staunch newspaper partisanship, your local newspaper editor was a card-carrying member of the political party (for example Jacksonian Democrat Amos Kendall was editor of Kentucky's *Argus of Western America*, and Whig proponent Thurlow Reed edited the Whig Party's *Albany Evening Journal*). Far from observers, editors served as delegates at their political party's convention. The symbiosis among politics, parties, and newspapers was thick and heavy. Parties fired disloyal editors. Government printing contracts flowed to papers that supported the president, notably the patronizer-in-chief, Andrew Jackson. Presidents could appoint leading editors to government positions, as Jackson did, appointing Kendall auditor of the U.S. Treasury.

Long before Stephen Bannon left his job as executive chair of the ultra-conservative Breitbart News to become chief White House strategist, Kendall and other editors – more than 50 during Jackson's years as president – received plum administration jobs, but apparently donned two hats, government administrator and newspaper editor. It was a win-win for all concerned: newspapers got needed cash to run the presses, the White House garnered experienced political hands, and political parties gained a mouthpiece to mobilize their voters.

For their part, editors, partisan party members that they were, viewed their readers not as part of an audience – for that concept awaited a more capitalistic press – nor as citizens, as one might fondly hope, but as voters, who could be wooed by the press, whose job was to mobilize reader-voters. Editors were opinionated advocates. One Jacksonian editor in upstate New York remarked that the thing we "abhor and detest" most is "a neutral paper" that pretends to be all things to all people (Baldasty, 2011, p. 280). Of course a century-and-a-half later, this was precisely the goal of the then-profitable mass media, aggressively courting viewers through homogenized, ever-so-careful news coverage.

Dissident Voices

And yet through it all, dissent burst through newspaper pages. The technology of the times – newspaper printing presses – allowed for dissident voices to intrude into the public sphere, even if they remained on the periphery. The storied abolitionists, Frederick Douglass and William Lloyd Garrison, bravely founded papers – *North Star* and the *Liberator* – that articulated and disseminated "the moral indictment of slavery" that in turn helped raise "the consciousness of the nation on the issue of slavery" (Mindich, 2000; Streitmatter, 2016, pp. 25, 29; see Figure 5.2). Sadly, or perhaps inevitably given the tendency of news to raise the ire of those targeted by critical stories, these radical newspapers sparked violent reactions from readers committed to the racist power structure. Rioters attacked pro-abolitionist newspapers. Proslavery mobs famously attacked the presses of Reverend Elijah Lovejoy's abolitionist Missouri newspaper four times, dumping his first printing press into the Mississippi River, destroying the second and third presses that he or supporters purchased, finally torching his building and shooting him dead. Violence against the press has a long history in America, as John C. Nerone (1994) observed, a reflection of the nation's violent undertones and willingness to destroy people, property, and an oppositional press in the service of an ideological cause.

The radical advocate's pen continued to wage battles against the more numerous, powerful cudgels of the established partisan media, as well as the swords wielded by mobs tethered to mainstream definitions of the status quo and willing to brandish them to stifle social change. Notably, much later in the 19th century, the women's suffrage movement, supported by 80 newspapers and periodicals, spread the egalitarian perspective of women's rights, sometimes going so far as to advocate for prostitutes and changes in marriage and divorce laws (Chambers, Steiner, & Fleming, 2004; Steiner, 1992), while at the same time building ties among activist women across the country, presaging the similar influences, albeit more quickly, more potently, and via the century's ubiquitous social media, exerted by the #MeToo anti-sexual abuse movement of 2017 and 2018.

Importantly, during the latter decades of the 19th century, the Establishment press disparaged the Women's Rights Movement, portraying feminist leader Elizabeth Cady Stanton as pompous and overweight, calling members of the Women's Rights Movement "mummified and fossilated females, void of domestic duties, habits and natural affections" (Streitmatter, 2016, p. 40).

Verbal and physical violence directed against proponents of dissident newspapers was a pervasive aspect of 19th-century America. And yet, undaunted, dissidents harnessed newspapers to carve out their own public space, as the suffragist editors began to "form their own sisterhood" and

Figure 5.2 Newspapers offered a pathway for change to bubble up to the surface. The storied abolitionist Frederick Douglass courageously founded a newspaper, appropriately called *North Star*, that helped raise national awareness about the scourge of slavery. Was the abolitionist's pen mightier than the sword of a prejudiced nation? No, in the short run, as evidenced by the years of violence – some against the abolitionist press – that preceded the Civil War, but in the longer run, the press offered an avenue for change, instigated by eloquent, innovative journalists, so ahead of their time.

articulate innovative "intellectually plausible models of womanhood," as Linda Steiner (1993, pp. 68, 70) notes. These dissident outlets represented newspapers at their best, helping journalism forge a new public space, one containing alternative voices that harnessed the sociological apparatus of the press to propel social change (Marzolf, 1977).

Alternative newspapers, by mobilizing supporters and forcing new ideas into public view, helped push, inch by column inch, needed political transformations. Alas, these innovations, repeated with new media of different forms and contents over the centuries, would wax and wane, showing that dissidents' battle for public opinion was never easy, not always successful, and inevitably involved confrontation with more established institutional voices and a conventional press that, in the main, was "tolerant, but only on its own terms" (Nerone, 2015, p. 79). The tension between alternative press challenges and news media protection of the status quo is one of the continuities in American journalism history.

Important changes were also afoot during the first decades of the 19th century. An innovative, colorful news outlet was poised to challenge the dominance of partisan newspapers. Although partisan papers continued in varied forms until later in the century, their exclusive hold on the audience was broken by a newspaper that took them by surprise, in the process ushering forth a new journalistic commodity.

This Just In: News is Invented, Journalism Emerges, and a Commercial Press in America, Warts and All, is Launched

The Colorful, Controversial Penny Press

James Gordon Bennett could hardly contain himself. He admired the corpse, even scrutinized it, taken aback by the young woman's "perfect figure – the exquisite limbs – the fine face – the full arms – the beautiful bust" (Cohen, 1998, p. 15). Somehow, he managed to ignore the incisions that defaced the dead woman's abdomen and chest and the autopsy slits down the middle of her bust that bloodied her body. No, the enterprising Scottish-born editor of *The New York Herald* saw what he wanted to see, and what he wanted to view was a beautiful young woman, slashed and killed by a murderer, a wanton act that he described vividly and graphically, with one motive towering above the rest: to sell papers.

Bennett wrote his story, the murder of a young New York City woman, Helen Jewett, and it bodaciously appeared in print on April 12, 1836, helping to unleash a fury of interest in the complex story of the murder of Jewett, a youthful writer and prostitute, and the trial of her alleged – and, in the view of experts, actual – murderer, an abusive clerk, Richard Robinson, with whom she was tragically smitten. *The Herald* and *The New York Sun* leapt at the opportunity to burnish their newly-minted credentials as one of the new papers *selling for just a penny*, kindling public interest in this unusual story, a mixture of sex and murder that editors, with a wink and nod, apologized for covering because it was so sordid, self-servingly justifying their coverage only because it satisfied a "public excitement" (Cohen, 1998, p. 24). They pedaled the story, offering different theories of who did it (Robinson, said *The Sun*; not so, claimed *The Herald*), in both cases with preciously little factual evidence, "making up their stories as they went along" (Tucher, 1994, pp. 40–41).

Although pamphlets had covered crime since the 1770s, New York's older 6-cent daily newspapers focused on political news, with a partisan (sometimes boring) bent, reprinting politicians' speeches and publishing legal notices (Cohen, 1998). But the Jewett story, coming at a time of frenzied competition among the new papers that were hawked on the streets for a penny (and offering the penny press a chance to grab readers from the more sedate 6-centers), was too good an opportunity to pass up. Add to that that it luridly involved "a prostitute, murdered with a hatchet in her brothel bed" (Cohen, 1998, p. 25) – and the stage was set for coverage that transformed the murder of Helen Jewett from a local matter to a national sensation, a story with not just legs, but wings (more on that below), that lifted the penny press from neophyte to journalistic innovation.

The penny press, as it came to be known, exerted seismic effects on news definition, content, form, and economics. Not only did the new 1-cent newspapers undercut the competition in terms of price, but they created a new economic model, recruiting money not from political parties, government, or subscriptions, but from advertisers, who must have quickly noticed that stories like these were wildly popular with readers (Wilson & Gutierrez, 1995, pp. 39–40). The penny papers, in a sense, created the modern concept of news, as papers ceased to be "views" papers and more "news" papers (Folkerts, Teeter, & Caudill, 2009, p. 110). For the first time "news became the mainstay of the daily paper," journalism historian Michael Schudson (1978, p. 23) observed in a pioneering book on the subject. Newspaper stories focused increasingly on local, rather than distant, national events, as reporting, presaging the form it takes today, took shape.

When the partisan newspapers were the only papers in town, few newspapers hired reporters, and reporting – finding, chasing after, discovering that elusive, but all-important, attribute of "news" – did not exist. With the penny press, reporting, as we know it today, began. Editors assigned reporters to cover events, broadening the concept of news, or, more grandly, inventing a new concept of news. Editors promised that the newspaper would provide "ALL THE NEWS OF THE DAY," as Benjamin Day wrote, announcing his *New York Sun* in September, 1833. News took on a new form, with the nascent pursuit of a narrative writing style, as well as a new sense of purpose and function (Folkerts, Teeter, & Caudill, 2009). News became the centerpiece of newspapers, the chief engine by which editors could make a profit, and in the 1830s they began to realize they could attract readers by hook and in some cases, by crook.

In what may be the first – and certainly most historically famous – example of fake news, *New York Sun* reporter Richard Adams Locke revealed to his incredulous readers that a well-respected South African astronomer had in his possession a high-powered telescope that offered glimpses of the moon. Naturally, there was more. He described breathtaking revelations of the moon's terrain, with trees resembling palms and firs, and animals that looked like zebras wandering about the luxuriant lunar surface. Then came the big reveal, in the final installments: An ingenious race of winged creatures (cleverly dubbed Vespertilio-homo), who resembled human beings, "averaged four feet in height, were covered, except on the face, with short and glossy copper-colored hair," and could fly, residing on the moon in temples they imaginatively constructed (Perloff, 2017; Sloan, 2005; Young, 2017, p. 16; see Figure 5.3).

Figure 5.3 In an astounding, very early example of fake news, *The New York Sun* ran stories that described spectacular revelations of the lunar surface, followed by vivid descriptions of an ingenious race of strange, winged creatures who resembled human beings and resided on the moon in temples they created. The newspaper falsely attributed the pictures, such as the one above, to a famous astronomer, who was said to have seen the winged creatures from his South African observatory! New Yorkers could not get their hands on the moon hoax stories fast enough, in one of the most brazen, but not atypical, schemes of penny press publishers to sell newspapers. Despite, or perhaps because of, such stories, the penny press helped invent and sculpt the concept of news, always changing, always controversial, no matter what era it appears.

New Yorkers could not get their hands on the stories fast enough. "It was all anyone could talk about," Young (2017) notes. The stories, cleverly calling on the trappings of authority of the time, jelled with cultural beliefs of the era (Black, 2013; Copeland, 2007). Other newspapers copied the stories, and *The Sun* watched as its circulation climbed, never acknowledging the moon hoax stories were a fabrication, a hoax, but a gift that, when it came to circulation, just kept on giving (Sloan, 2005).

Sociology of the Penny Press

The penny press transformed newspapers, although there is debate among scholars as how just how revolutionary the metamorphosis was (Nerone, 1987). The penny papers made newspapers available to the mass public, differentiated news from editorials, and unveiled new technologies like the telegraph (and carrier-pigeon), as well as new funding mechanisms, chiefly advertising. The penny press helped transform news from opinion-focused to fact-driven stories, though they were frequently far from accurate, and the conventions for determining facts were enormously different than in our era. There was a moral element too: A murder trial that a 6-penny paper deemed too offensive to cover was juicy, seductive grist for front-page penny press stories (Schudson, 1978).

The penny press likely had wide-ranging social effects. The papers engaged a vast new social group (many working in skilled trades) that transcended the rich, literate elites who read the 18th and early 19th-century papers (Schiller, 1987). An increasingly populous, diverse (within the range of one skin color) and occupationally varied American middle-class society saw its needs and interests reflected in the penny press. The new 1-cent papers, the antecedents of the nation's commercial press, "first put newspapers in the hands of the mass public on a regular basis," perhaps cultivating and symbolically enfranchising the new middle-class society (Hallin, 1994, p. 23).

Like the tabloid magazines and television programs of the 1990s that thrived on crime and salacious stories (for example, the O.J. Simpson murder and the exploits of Olympic skater Tonya Harding), the pennies, as David T.Z. Mindich (1998) memorably calls them, exploited ordinary Americans' interest in crime and sensationalism to cultivate new audiences and achieve outsized financial success for their owners. For the many reasons people follow crime-related stories – boredom, curiosity, *schadenfreude*, or pleasure derived from the misfortunes of the more fortunate – the penny newspapers caught on. They recruited new audiences and enlarged the financial base of urban newspapers, helping newspapers emerge as a "ubiquitous institution in American society" (Sloan, 2005, p. 141). Schudson (1978) has gone further, famously arguing that the penny newspapers built democratic market society, offering new egalitarian opportunities, perhaps even advancing political democracy in the new nation.

Other historians have taken issue with this rosy view, noting that the news was not inherently democratic and did not necessarily cause citizens to partake more actively in government (Nerone, 1987; Schiller, 1981). Nerone (1987), noting that the penny press has been richly mythologized, has questioned whether the 1-cent newspapers exerted the transformative effects frequently attributed to them. He, along with other scholars, has argued that the penny papers were not as sensational or scandalous as commonly believed. Their innovations were not the only cause of increased advertising during this period, and they weren't the most broadly circulated newspapers at mid century (Schudson & Tifft, 2005). All true, and the revisionism has provided a more nuanced, less romanticized view of the penny press. Yet we should not minimize the 1-cent papers' impact on the craft of journalism. They helped changed the way stories were written, the manner in which editors and readers conceived of their roles, and the economic foundation of newspapers. They yanked newspapers from their political – and political party – foundation. And while we can't say for sure, it is plausible to argue that the penny papers helped bring ordinary people into society by providing them with a symbolic connection to power, influence, and social intrigue. What's more, although, in a generic sense, news has always been with us, as discussed in Chapter 1, news, as we know it, was invented during the penny press era, with its narrative style and information-gathering foundations, even as these changed over the ensuing years.

As important as 1-penny papers were, they must be understood as operating in a larger context, an expanding, but deeply prejudiced American society (Nerone, 1987). America was, after all, a racist and sexist place in which only White men could partake in public – and many private – activities. The penny press reflected this, perpetrating countless stereotypes of women, Blacks, Native Americans and foreigners (Shaw, 1987). In particular, newspapers disturbingly suggested that city streets were inappropriate places for morally upright white women, who could be viewed as responsible for their victimization by men. The press also portrayed Black men as posing a threat that White ethnic immigrants did not (Stabile, 2005). And while the penny press may have democratized the mass market, bringing in masses of consumer readers who searched for advertised products in stores in the burgeoning public streets, the penny papers were capitalistic institutions that placed economic control of newspapers in owners' hands, allowing them to profit off of increasing circulation. The papers appealed to middle-class readers, but hardly increased their political power, as parties, controlled by frequently corrupt party bosses, ruled the roost.

In the final analysis, the penny newspapers' record was a mixed bag. They probably helped build a stalwart White middle class that served as a bulwark against the wealthy land-owning elites. The penny papers provided a common focus for conversations among the strangers increasingly encountering one another in the expanding cities of the 1800s – a symbolic meeting ground for the public sphere that was fervently developing during this period (Carey, 2007). By enlarging the symbolic reach of a newspaper so that it focused on the public, rather than specialized elites, the penny press helped pave the way for new-media functions, such as the watchdog and facilitative roles discussed in Chapter 4 that have advanced social justice. And yet, once again (in a sadly broken record), the papers' contributions were morally attenuated by their exclusion of people of color, and implicit placement of minorities outside the cultural mainstream, an aspect of journalism history that journalism historians have traditionally ignored (Byfield, 2014; see Mindich, 2000 for a thoughtful account).

As you have noticed, the penny press – because of its novel, spectacular content and sociological impact – has generated a great deal of interest from scholars. But it was not the final chapter in the 19th-century history of the press, not by a long shot.

Growth and Sensationalism in the 19th Century

Over the course of the 19th century, newspapers underwent sweeping changes, with beneficial, problematic, and surprising consequences. As the population grew, fueled by European immigration, public life in cities became ever-richer, literacy rates grew, and printing technologies increased the size of the press run. As a consequence, newspapers proliferated. There were 1,200 newspapers in 1833, compared to 4,500 in 1870 and approximately 12,000 in 1890; the number of readers surged, reaching 15 million in 1900 (Bulla & Sachsman, 2013). News changed over the course of the late 1800s, focusing more on events than opinions, and increasingly centered on dramatic, sensational topics, as entrepreneurial reporters aggressively pursued hot news items, now packaging them into a story that was merchandized and marketed (Dicken-Garcia, 1989, 2011; Sloan, 2005). As financial imperatives shaped news organizations, news became a capitalist commodity bundled to recruit readers (Baldasty, 1993; Dicken-Garcia, 2011; Solomon, 1995).

The old coexisted with the new. While commercialism and advertising were fast becoming critical foundations of the press, partisanship was not dead. Although newspapers focused less on electoral politics, party affiliations remained an important component of newspaper branding until the end of the 19th century (Nerone, 2018). The nation's most partisan papers continued to maintain a biased political party slant, though this began to decline late in the century as advertising emerged as a major source of funding and editors became wary of overly partisan content that might turn off advertisers. During this period, readership grew and news organizations became among the largest business operations in the country (Dicken-Garcia, 1989; Schudson & Tifft, 2005; Solomon, 1995).

Newspapers also took on a distinctive editorial stance, challenging corrupt party bosses with investigations and cartoons, though, as would be true with Watergate a century later, only a handful of newspapers took on the corrupt political machines in their news or editorial pages (Sloan, 2005). But investigative stories, a new concept in American journalism, captivated public attention as investigative writers (Ida Wells Barnett, later

Lincoln Steffens, Ray Stannard Baker, and Ida Tarbell) exposed racial prejudice, government corruption, corporate greed, and social injustice, reflecting and extending the progressive ethos of the times, offering a grand lesson in civics. The press encouraged Americans "to raise their voices against illegitimate power," while also increasing disenchantment with the inevitable limits of political reform (Leonard, 1986, p. 193).

At their best, the investigative news stories of the late 19th century helped transform journalism. They interposed the reporter as a new centerpiece in the public sphere, a mediator between citizens and government, the self-anointed representative of the public, one whose work could produce significant political change (Nerone, 2015).

But there was a new kid (literally and metaphorically) on the journalistic block. He was the celebrated yellow kid, the bane or boon of burgeoning American journalism, depending on your perspective. This grinning, toothless kid with pointy ears, arms extended, and sporting a yellow ballooning nightshirt was the hit of new color comics, later inspiring the immortal idiom, "yellow journalism." Yellow journalism embodied the late–19th-century explosion of grisly crime stories, bizarre, flamboyantly-described events, and large-headlined, generously illustrated, anonymously sourced (not always truthful, but always shocking) stories ginned up to generate readership and win artificially created newspaper wars. Yellow journalism, with its rich use of adjectival modifiers ("barbarous," "disgusting," and "frightful") and tantalizing, graphic headlines ("BOY BRAINS A MAN"; "HACKED TO PIECES") in its stories of homicides, scandals, sex, and calamitous disasters, torqued up the tone and volume of stories of misfortune the penny press had popularized, appealing to mass audiences with a sensational style that transcended the orientation of mid-century newspapers (see Dicken-Garcia, 2011, p. 253).

Yellow journalism, of course, has become the stuff of myth, spawning grandiose, but historically inaccurate, notions, the most famous being that *New York Journal* publisher William Randolph Hearst's telegram cable "You furnish the pictures, and I'll furnish the war" incited the Spanish-American war. The statement is of dubious veracity, as is the *Journal*'s claim that the Spanish deliberately bombed or torpedoed a U.S. battleship, the *Maine*, in Cuba's Havana Harbor in February, 1898 (see Figure 5.4). Subsequent investigations have cast doubt on the popular belief that Spain exploded the *Maine*, suggesting the explosion spontaneously occurred inside the battleship. While the newspaper probably helped set the agenda and galvanized patriotic sentiments, there are strong historical reasons to doubt that the *Journal* pushed the U.S. into war (Campbell, 2013).

The yellow journalism stories of the late 19th century are fun to read, but the journalistic issues are more serious and intellectually intriguing. Yellow journalism is strong in sensationalism and weak in factual accuracy. To the

863,956
WORLDS CIRCULATED YESTERDAY

The

"Circulation Books Open to All."

World. 863,956

"Circulation Books Open to All." WORLDS CIRCULATED YESTERDAY

Department of State,

VOL. XXXVIII, NO. 13,448

NEW YORK, THURSDAY, FEBRUARY 17, 1898.

PRICE ONE CENT

MAINE EXPLOSION CAUSED BY BOMB OR TORPEDO?

Capt. Sigsbee and Consul-General Lee Are in Doubt---The World Has Sent a Special Tug, With Submarine Divers, to Havana to Find Out---Lee Asks for an Immediate Court of Inquiry---Capt. Sigsbee's Suspicions.

CAPT. SIGSBEE, IN A SUPPRESSED DESPATCH TO THE STATE DEPARTMENT, SAYS THE ACCIDENT WAS MADE POSSIBLE BY AN ENEMY.

Dr. E. C. Pendleton, Just Arrived from Havana, Says He Overheard Talk There of a Plot to Blow Up the Ship---Capt Zalinski, the Dynamite Expert, and Other Experts Report to The World that the Wreck Was Not Accidental---Washington Officials Ready for Vigorous Action if Spanish Responsibility Can Be Shown---Divers to Be Sent Down to Make Careful Examinations.

The New York World a day after

who had been Populists and those who became Progressives — clamored for the United States to rescue the Cuban people from the Spanish malefactors.

President William McKinley and the conservative Republican leaders in Congress reluctantly gave way before this pressure. Senator Henry Cabot Lodge warned McKinley, "If the war in Cuba drags on through the summer with nothing done we [the Republican party] shall go down in the greatest defeat ever known."

Already, in November 1897, Spain, at the urging of President McKinley, had granted

Figure 5.4 The yellow journalism of the late 19th century cultivated an engaged readership by covering, hyping, and frequently sensationalizing all manner of shocking events, from crimes to calamitous disasters to the famous sinking of the American battleship, the USS *Maine*, in Havana Harbor in Cuba. Although the New York press claimed Spain had deliberately destroyed the ship, later investigations indicate this was jingoistic hype, not based on fact, designed to sell newspapers. A salutary, if unexpected, effect of yellow journalism is that it strengthened the power of the press, enabling it to (sometimes) serve as a brake on political power.

extent that journalism is a process that strives for truth, yellow journalism is a blot on the record. What's more, for all the emphasis on scandals, journalism of the 1890s steadfastly avoided serious controversies for fear this would alienate readers (Dicken-Garcia, 1989). As always, there is a silver lining. Over the long haul, late–19th-century newspapers' construction of crime, scandals, and political skullduggery probably helped cultivate a public less tied to political parties, more concerned with abuses of the public trust, and increasingly, if fitfully, focused on larger social problems beyond private pursuits (Schudson & Tifft, 2005). And, building on press reportage of earlier decades, the period produced the craft, occupation, profession, or process – choose your term – we now call journalism.

Advent of Journalism and that Wonderful, Fraught, Journalistic "God-Term" of Objectivity

During the late 19th century, journalistic culture began to solidify. No longer propagandistic scribes, partisan ideologues, or writers chasing after stories delivered by carrier-pigeon, reporters began, gradually of course, to view themselves in a more unitary, quasi-professional fashion – as journalists, with their own legends and heroes, gathering places and watering holes, and professional norms. With the establishment of press associations like the Associated Press, growing acceptance of interviewing as a news-gathering technique, and politics based less in loyalty to fervently partisan newspapers than in progressive education based on information, the stage was set for the development of journalism as an occupational culture and professional community (Schudson & Tifft, 2005; Vos & Finneman, 2017). In addition, as newspaper ownership became more consolidated during the early 20th century and publishers increasingly targeted an undifferentiated mass audience, publishing barons came to favor professional norms in journalism that produced middle-of-the-road homogenized stories designed to resonate with the great mass of readers (Nadler, 2016).

There is debate about just when professional journalistic norms gained currency. Journalism historians have long speculated about when objectivity – the core value that has become the centerpiece of the journalistic creed; its holy grail, "God-term," and normative mainstay – formally emerged. If you have written news stories, read about reporting, or aspire to become a professional journalist, you have heard the term, along with the controversies about the inevitable psychological limits of objectivity.

While recognizing that no one can be perfectly objective, the objectivity norm emphasizes the virtues in trying to detach oneself from personal biases and producing stories that are factually based, nonpartisan and fair to all sides (Kaplan, 2002; Knowlton, 2005; Mindich, 1998). Far from a simple notion, objectivity, with its storied history in journalism, is a rich, multifaceted idea, a river with many tributaries (Maras, 2013, p. 56), defined differently by different scholars, its meaning changing over the 19th and 20th centuries. Although objectivity is enshrined in journalism now, it was not always this way, and sharply contrasts richly with newspapers' early partisan, subjective style. Perhaps for this reason, as well as the fact that news, as we will see, strays far from the objective ideal, the concept has intrigued scholars, for whom the study of objectivity's origins has become a cottage academic pursuit.

In rudimentary form, objectivity dates back to the 19th century – perhaps as early as the 1830s (Schiller, 1981) – but, as an occupational and intellectual ethos, it was taking shape by the late 19th century, with the diffusion of scientific theories of human behavior. Economically focused scholars have stressed that as news became a mass commodity, fueled by steam-driven rotary presses that facilitated large-scale printing, newspapers could quickly reach a burgeoning urban audience (Hamilton & Tworek, 2017). Eager to attract advertisers, who increasingly wanted a homogenized product that would not offend different groups, news adopted a blander, neutral approach to issues (though, not as Mindich, 1998, documents, with respect to lynching, which fell outside the norms of civilized press discourse). Interesting as this is, the economic view fails to explain the adoption of the broader objectivity ethos, which has its roots in cultural and political changes.

The movement toward journalistic objectivity began in earnest in the late 1800s, as the intellectual zeitgeist moved from unbridled partisanship to a more rationalistic emphasis on impartiality and disinterested political decision-making (Kaplan, 2010). Journalists began to identify with the trappings of science and Progressive-era reform, particularly its optimistic emphasis on facts, education, and knowledge-based expertise, famously articulated by Lippmann (1922). By the first decades of the 20th century, objectivity had come into its own as a professional value, but was more – an internalized sociological norm, "a moral code ... asserted in the textbooks used in journalism schools [and] in codes of ethics of professional associations" (Jirik, 2012; Schudson, 2001, p. 163).

Even if objectivity was a burgeoning belief system, it did not guarantee that the news took on the trappings of fairness, impartiality, and factual analysis. Yellow journalism hyped, sometimes distorted, the story; articles about gender conformed to stereotypes of the times; and in the case of the lynching epidemic of the late 19th century, the coverage was either offensive, describing public lynchings in grisly terms to sell papers, or racist, presuming the guilt of an accused African American, calling him a "desperado," a "brute" or a "ravisher," and describing lynch mobs with sympathetic language (Perloff, 2000, p. 321). (Even newspapers, like *The New York Times*, which denounced lynching on its editorial pages, described lynchings in a matter-of-fact tone that elided their moral horror, or provided a false balance, covering a lynching, while presuming Blacks were guilty when the facts argued otherwise; see Mindich, 1998.)

Thus, the growing objectivity norm could fail to elucidate the truth. And yet as the 20th century dawned, it was undoubtedly seen as an improvement on partisan biases of yore. Emboldened by their belief in the power of facts, empowered by a moral conviction that objective journalism offered a path to truth, tickled by the prestige accorded to prominent reporters, and swayed by the increasing economic power news outlets wielded, journalists felt their work was of central importance to 20th-century society. We now move to the new century, dominated by an expanding mass media.

The High-Modern Period of Powerful News and Its Inevitable Decline

The Ubiquitous, Authoritative News Media

Early in the century, the newspaper was king (Sloan, 2005). Newspapers could be counted on to relay the stories of the day, offering a bipolar vista on events both glorious – Charles Lindbergh's first nonstop solo transatlantic airplane flight in 1927 ("Lindbergh Does It!", *The New York Times* headline proclaimed) – and devastating: the 1932 abduction and murder of Lindbergh's 19-month-old son, called "the greatest story since the Resurrection," at least until the 1995 O.J. Simpson trial (Sloan, 2005, p. 289). Many cities had not one but several competing daily newspapers, and the number of daily papers increased five-fold from 1860 to 1920. Evening papers, geared to working-class readers, proliferated, and sensational tabloid newspapers that extended 19th-century yellow journalism with a colorful Roaring 20s jazz-age ambience became a major presence on city streets. Schools of journalism opened up, and the objectivity ethos became widely accepted, offering the news a kind of secular religious underpinning for an increasingly routinized style of reporting different events.

News was increasingly big business and lucrative. From 1900 to 1945, the number of cities with monopoly controlled newspapers ballooned, from about 400 in 1900 to close to 1,300 in 1945 (Sloan, 2005). Twentieth-century capitalism came to newspapers, and they – rather, their owners – prospered, while at the same time providing staffers with a reliably middle-class living that eludes many reporters in the current digitally driven milieu. Newsmagazines, chiefly *Time* (named because the word became an early 20th-century advertising meme), became wildly popular, as well as synonymous with American values and shortcomings, like promoting U.S. ventures abroad, narrated in the magazine's famously terse, colorful, clichéd, style. Its interpretations of national events, relayed in *Time* in the century famously dubbed "the American century" by its progenitor, Henry Luce, frequently veered closer to patriotic, pro-Americana accounts than dissenting frames (Baughman, 1987). Guided by newsmagazines like *Time*, the burgeoning press began to view itself as the "official interpreter and purveyor of government publicity," celebrating the "embrace of power with its often corresponding access to insider knowledge" (Kaplan, 2002, p. 193).

Complementing the print media were the broadcast media, initially radio, used masterfully in the 1930s by President Franklin Delano Roosevelt in his evocative "Fireside chats," and increasingly a source of information for Americans during the Depression and World War II. FDR recognized the power of the new broadcast medium, as well as the older, still influential, print medium. Roosevelt, master manipulator that he was, concocted new ways to manage news coverage, providing background facts to reporters that could not be attributed directly to the president; giving off-the-record information so long as it was kept confidential (FDR's term "off-the-record" became so famous it was parodied in a 1937 Broadway musical); holding nearly 1,000 news conferences, reflecting positively on FDR; and helping reporters frame stories about the complexities of the innovative New Deal, but also planting questions at press conferences and banning African American reporters from attending news conferences until 1944 (Perloff, 1998; Steele, 1985; Warren, 1991).

Reporters, awed by their access to power, enthralled by their ability to convey information to masses of citizens, were cowed by powerful elites during the 1940 and 1950s. In the classic case, Wisconsin Senator Joseph McCarthy manufactured a story, exploiting Cold War fear of Communism, repeatedly and falsely claiming the U.S. State Department was filled with Communists, suggesting that a particular government staffer was a known communist when the charge was entirely false. Many reporters deferred to McCarthy because he was a U.S. senator or they were fearful of writing anything that offended the demagogic senator (Rovere, 1959). Driven by competitive zeal, reporters wrote story after story, filling news pages with what really was false news.

McCarthy, attuned to reporter routines, seized on reporters' deference to political authorities, turning the vaunted objectivity on its head, showing it was a sham, a shill to the powerful. But journalism and the new television medium surprised its most cynical practitioners by coming to the rescue, undoing what it had fashioned, unmasking McCarthy for the demagogue he was. Fabled, undaunted television reporter Edward R. Murrow took to the airwaves in 1954 to point out McCarthy's contradictions and falsehoods; this was followed by six weeks of television hearings that revealed to the nation McCarthy's bullying behavior and indecency. This had substantial impact on the press, public opinion, and corridors of Congress, leading to McCarthy's downfall, showcasing the modern mechanisms by which the news media could build up, then afflict the powerful.

As racial protests heated up during the deeply prejudiced 1950s and 60s, the news found a powerful new voice, one predicated not on editorial condemnations of racism (for these were few and far between), but on the capacity of television news, as well as a new generation of journalists, to shine the light of truth on racial discrimination (Roberts & Klibanoff, 2006). The Black press played a critical role, covering racial issues long before the White press, in some cases graphically (Tillet, 2018). In the wake of the vicious murder of 14-year-old Emmett Till by White vigilantes in Mississippi in 1955, *Jet Magazine* published pictures of Emmett's open-casket funeral, bravely arranged by his mother so the world could see "her son's tortured body; his facial features crushed and unrecognizable" (Perloff, 2015, p. E8). The visuals shocked many Americans, and the televised civil rights protests that followed gradually changed public attitudes. It was not an easy fight, and the news media, as is standard given its fraught role in the power structure of society, were reluctant to investigate the discriminatory strictures of American life. But changing norms and the capacity of the news to shine a live light on brutal events slowly, complexly blazed a path in which institutional reforms of racial discrimination could occur.

Television news (its immediacy in our age so much besides the digital point; breaking news alerts experienced today as more media hype; on-the-spot feeds passé in a lightning-fast social media time) was hot stuff in the 1960s. By the early 60s, television had diffused widely and its moving images were viewed for more than four hours daily in the typical American household (Zelizer, 1992). Live coverage was breathtakingly exciting, suggesting (incorrectly, as scholars painstakingly documented) that what TV covered was equivalent to what complexly occurred on the scene, intimating that its reality was Reality itself (see Lang & Lang, 1953, for a classic study).

The Kennedy assassination encapsulated television's role, in which news – and TV reportage in particular – became THE voice that brought the assassination and its terrible aftermath to the public. Television's unprecedented live coverage of the grieving Kennedy family and nation, funeral procession, and murder of Lee Harvey Oswald put TV news front and center in a way print media, even in the rip-roaring days of yellow journalism, never had been. As Barbie Zelizer (1992) perceptively showed, televised coverage of the assassination validated journalistic authority, enabling TV journalism to serve as the teller – the narrator – of a national story, legitimizing "televised journalism as a mediator of national public experience" (p. 4). It was all conveyed through journalism's routines, its largely accurate, but trite, phrases (as in its description of the assassination as "the day the world changed"), and ability to make the Kennedy assassination "a semisacred space" (Zelizer, 1992, pp. 18, 184). (See Figure 5.5.)

Figure 5.5 The assassination of John F. Kennedy in 1963, a transformative
moment in American and journalism history, placed television in the
center of the nation's public culture. TV news became the primary
teller, interpreter, and narrator of national stories, validating journalistic authority, helping make JFK's assassination a sacred part of
secular public space and a centerpiece in journalists' interpretive
history.

Television journalism, now afforded social legitimacy by elites and
citizens to tell the nation's story, as if there was just one version of an
event to tell, became inseparable from the Kennedy assassination in its
aftermath, as well as in the many interpretive iterations that were to

come. It truly was the beginning of "the high modernism of American journalism" (Hallin, 1994, p. 172), a period when journalistic authority reigned supreme. As time wore on, the Kennedy assassination, like Water gate a decade later, slipped into the mythology of journalism, a meta-narrative that journalists, as part of a larger collegial community, viewed through the lens of a common interpretive framework (Zelizer, 1993).

During the 1960s and 70s, as the nation was convulsed by wars, crises, mass protests, and calamitous political events, journalism struggled, like other social institutions, oscillating between propping up the powers-that-be in reporting on the Vietnam War and student protests (Gitlin, 1980; Hallin, 1986) and coverage that framed these issues in terms of dissent and social change (Streitmatter, 2016). It is a constant dialectic in journalism, a necessary, but tension-filled dynamic of news, one that we will intriguingly examine in Chapter 10.

The Press Changes (Again): Adversarial News, Entertainment, and the Economic Imperative

The origins of much of the style and content of contemporary news can be traced to innovative developments in the 1960s and 70s. The looser, more personalized, creative, infinitely less stodgy style of newswriting today has some of its origins in the ways narrative opened up in freer, magazine-style, first-person accounts of writers Tom Wolfe, Norman Mailer, and Gail Sheehy, as well as increases in "how" and "why"-based critical interpretive reporting (Barnhurst & Mutz, 1997). Modern adversarial journalism, in which journalists aggressively confront public authorities, no longer willing to accept their versions of truth as factually true, had roots in journalists' dissatisfaction with their acquiescence to deceptive Vietnam pronouncements of President Lyndon Johnson, as well as subservience to President Kennedy, including press reluctance to reveal Kennedy's sexual affairs. Journalists' subsequent acknowledgment of their failures became part of a new narrative of journalism.

Investigative journalism, described in the previous chapter, accomplished big things in the 1970s. The Pentagon Papers and Watergate were colossal exposes that revealed corruption and systemic deceptions in government, informing public opinion and leading to major policy changes and, in the case of Watergate (complexly through different institutional processes), the resignation of a president.

After Watergate and the popular mythology that surrounded it, every reporter, it seemed, wanted to be the next Woodward or Bernstein who ensnared a corrupt political leader. This orientation yielded journalistic benefits, producing a long-overdue skepticism of official pronouncements. However, it also proved dysfunctional, leading reporters to presume that *all* political decisions are based in canny electoral gamesmanship, thereby minimizing the more salutary reality, that political leaders also base their actions on heart-felt ideologies and an enlightened commitment to public service (Cappella & Jamieson, 1997; Patterson, 1993). In some cases, the latter-day Watergate mentality produced a "Gotcha" orientation that led journalists to stake out candidates suspected of engaging in sexual improprieties, even if the sexual indelicacy (while unquestionably inconsistent with the candidate's statements) was relatively minor (Bai, 2014).

In the 1980s, adversarial journalism, where reporters saw themselves as aggressive combatants of political leaders, became less pronounced as Ronald Reagan rewrote the rules of presidential communication. During his first term as president, Reagan displayed a mastery of the new art of televisual storytelling, news management, and spinning (a word that became fashionable in the Reagan 80s). His aides became modern Svengalis, capable of reframing events so they made the president look good on the evening news, although, scholars have pointed out, his news-making success also had roots in reporters' media-centric *perception* that "a man with Reagan's evident personal charm on the television screen has practically irresistible power to shape public opinion" (Schudson, 1995, p. 137). Convinced that Reagan was an overpowering televisual force, dubbing him "the great communicator," reporters created the myth of the invincible Ronald Reagan, contributing to Reagan's political success.

Even as presidential political communication captured journalists' interest, economic constraints exerted significant influences on the news during the 1980s and 90s. Faced with threats from television and changing cultural norms, the number of U.S. newspapers sharply declined. Competition between newspapers in the same city, which could force newspapers to offer different political perspectives and innovate to recruit an audience (both positive outcomes), dropped enormously. Increasingly, large news and business conglomerates, called newspaper chains, gobbled up independent dailies, reducing the proportion of independent newspapers from about 68 percent in 1960 to just 30 percent by the late 1980s. And as the 2000s dawned, newspaper ownership was concentrated in fewer hands, as the overwhelming majority of newspapers were owned by seven large chains (Schudson & Tifft, 2005; Sloan, 2005). With these corporations focused relentlessly on the economic bottom line, corporate goals often supplanted journalistic values, as investigative stories and regular beat coverage of City Hall played second fiddle to marketing research-driven stories that brought in readers (and later clicks), with European or Australian news magnates coordinating news from afar.

During the late 20th century, economic factors also exerted hard-hitting effects on the once-unassailable television news, as the audience for broadcast television network news dropped in the wake of technological changes, such as the ability of local news stations to cover national events via satellite dishes and the emergence of cable news, chiefly CNN. The nation's first 24-hour cable news network experienced a ratings bonanza with on-the-spot coverage of the 1991 U.S. Persian Gulf War to oust Iraqi forces from Kuwait. It was the first time American viewers witnessed the onset of a war and major battles live on their small television screens. The live footage of computer-guided smart bomb attacks on their targets, raising journalistic questions about whether the news exaggerated the accuracy of the missile attacks, offered a one-sided view of the war (Bennett & Paletz, 1994; see Chapter 10). The coverage, along with live CNN reports of terrorist incidents, put Cable News Network on the map, offering a model for how television could cover international events in a way that guaranteed audience ratings.

At the same time, television news found it could entice millions of viewers with stories of novel human drama, a tried-and-true news formula for more than a century, now amplified by the confluence of glitzy technology, compelling visual footage, and live, on-air discussions of the media drama, now a self-reflective, narcissistic part of the story. Broadcast networks and CNN lavished round-the-clock coverage on a gripping, made-for-TV ordeal, the 58-hour rescue in October, 1987 of an 18-month-old baby, Jessica McClure, who fell into a well in her aunt's backyard. Five years later, in May 1992 a crime drama that, in a sense, reversed the roles in the Helen Jewett case blanketed the airwaves (Tucher, 1994). Cameras fixated on the story of 16-year-old Amy Fisher, who was sexually involved with a 36-year-old Long Island automobile repair shop owner, Joey Buttafuco and, in a fit of rage, shot his wife in the face, earning her the appellation, the "Long Island Lolita."

Two years later, the news could not get enough of the women's sports crime story of the decade, the attack and media frenzy that followed an attack spearheaded by the ex-husband of U.S. figure skating Olympian, Tonya Harding, on fellow Olympics star, Nancy Kerrigan in January 1994, with its criminal aspects and machinations of glamor and social class. And, then six months later, the crime-of-the-century story, now having supplanted the kidnapping of Lindbergh's son, took center stage, as the news transformed the trial of O.J. Simpson, charged with murdering his wife and a friend, into a morality play of more than 2,000 hours of live TV, with multiple layers. The story convulsed the nation and divided the races, its effects refracted and distorted through the news's celebrity, drama-consumed mirror (Sloan, 2005; see Figure 5.6). In all these cases, TV news, desperate for ratings, succumbed to the growing tabloidization pressures (Bird, 2000). More broadly, the way news framed these sensational events transformed the narrative and experience of the events, both at the time they happened and later, demonstrating the ways journalism influences society's collective memory of issues of public importance long after they occur (Zelizer & Tenenboim-Weinblatt, 2014).

Figure 5.6 As news faced increasing competitive pressures amid a fragmented audience, it turned back to its sensational roots in the 1990s, hyping crime stories that conveyed rich cultural narratives. These included the media extravaganza that followed an assault in January, 1994 by the ex-husband of U.S. figure skating Olympian, Tonya Harding (above picture, left), on fellow Olympics star Nancy Kerrigan (above picture, right) with its criminal facets and social class overtones; and the iconic O.J. Simpson story (see picture above) that transformed a tragic murder into a national entertainment extravaganza.

Increasingly, as the media-rich century ended, visual storytelling became the mantra of news, marking an evolution from its more linear architecture of the 1800s. The television newsmagazine *60 Minutes* created a narrative structure to relate a story, one that emphasized "a whodunit" detective formula, introducing the reporter-as-detective, reconstructing the so-called crime scene, confronting "a villain, an unwitting representative of an evil institution, or a bewildered witness or bystander" (Campbell, 1991, p. 50). *60 Minutes* reporters, frequently dressed like a movie detective in a trench coat, staked out businesses of ill repute, confronting "shady characters" in stories "almost too hot to handle," as they hyped them, pitting themselves as Humphrey Bogart-like gumshoes investigating unscrupulous land deals, deception in the food franchising industry, as well as that old stand-by, organized crime (Campbell, 1987, p. 328).

The frequently imitated *60 Minutes* formula depicted the television journalist as sometimes blue-jean clad, working-class-style hero, this time with video montage and television showmanship front and center, the story typically concluding with a satisfying ending as the reporter revealed the wrongdoing and resolved the crime. To its credit, the dramatic formula employed by *60 Minutes* exposed moral transgressions, yet more frequently and deeply offered affirmation of American values, chiefly that "individuals through adherence to Middle American values can triumph over institutions that deviate from central social norms"

(Campbell, 1987, p. 347). In this sense, news performed a ritualistic function, offering weekly affirmation of inspiring, individual-centered American norms.

The drive to capture a larger economic share of the American television audience took on a new hue in the late 1990s and early 2000s, as cable networks developed a distinctive branding strategy, focusing on celebrity anchors, not-to-be-missed on-the-spot disaster coverage, and poll-driven election news, with all the exciting bells and whistles of election night prognostications and vibrant, if trivial, disagreements among guests hand-picked to guarantee an exciting show. A key player was Fox News, which, as Nadler (2016) observed, brashly "introduced the strategy of building a partisan brand and targeting a conservative niche" (p. 111). It marked a return to the 19th-century partisan journalism, in one broad sense, but the economic base and funding mechanisms were very different. From a broader perspective, cable news at Fox and the liberal MSNBC – anticipating the fragmentation of media audiences today – took a more selective, niche-oriented branding strategy, one aimed at dividing the citizenry, rather than developing (albeit inoffensive homogeneous) pro-gramming aimed at reaching the population as a whole (Nadler, 2016). It also rearranged the relationship between expertise and truth, with the consistently entertaining and conservative *O'Reilly Factor* on Fox confer-ring expertise on people who liked to scream at each other, distorting facts in what would later become an Internet free-for-all of facts, falsehoods, and distortion of truths (Rosenfeld, 2019).

Macro Changes and Continuities

On the macroeconomic front, news had become a hot and increasingly economic commodity, and one that played out in the larger nexus of politics and media regulation. In 1985, the pro-business, anti-big-government Reagan administration had relaxed restrictions, such as on the number of stations television and radio conglomerates could own, and media mergers proliferated during the late 20th century as ABC merged with Capital Cities Communications and General Electric bought the RCA Corporation, with the powerful NBC network; subse-quently, AOL and Time Warner joined forces. Several years into the new century, in 2004, five global companies owned the majority of broadcast stations, motion picture studios, magazines, and newspapers in the U.S., and the Internet was increasingly dominated by multinational compa-nies, like Google and Time Warner (Bagdikian, 2004). Monopoly capit-alism's 150-year courtship of news media culminated in a fractious marriage between profit-making and news, one that raised questions for democracy (McChesney, 1999).

The trends continued into the second decade of the century. Charter Communications acquired Time Warner Cable for $57 billion, Verizon purchased AOL for $4 billion, and, on the social media front, Facebook bought WhatsApp for $19 billion. For its part, the Federal Communications Commission, during the pro-free enterprise Trump administration, relaxed rules preventing media mergers, enabling a handful of billion-dollar companies to gain monopoly ownership of different media in a particular media market (Fung, 2017).

The emergence of the Internet and proliferating social media have transformed the economic foundation of news, decimating newspapers, and vastly changing the format and content of news, as discussed in Chapter 2. The era of mass communication, where mass media exclusively determined gatekeeping, had come to a close. But news still mattered, influencing political agendas, with conventional news organizations continuing to supply content widely distributed on social media.

Continuities and contrast are striking. In one sense, like old media, social media works through a centralized organization – for example, Facebook and Twitter (though message transmission occurs through users, as well as journalistic gatekeepers) – and depends on advertising for the bulk of its profit (Standage, 2013). However, social media accords more freedom to its users to choose the news they find most palatable, and, of course, the distribution and economic models of social media are vastly different than those of the conventional press Welcome to 21st-century news – still here, still vital, broadened and more inclusive, transformed by 21st-century technology and economics, but with a lot of that old 19th-century partisan edge.

Conclusions

History is replete with changes and continuities. The continuity that jumps out at you, in light of the loud, inescapable diatribe about bias in contemporary news, is that bias is not new, did not originate with epithets about "the liberal media" or lamentations about Fox News, but dates back to the earliest, most strident newspapers of the 18th and 19th centuries. In an era when bias is frequently lamented, it is instructive to note that the storied colonial newspapers stories of the American Revolution were rife with bias, exemplifying a radical normative theory of journalism. (It is hard to escape the irony that conservatives, who appropriately revel in the best of American history yet are quick to jump on instances of perceived liberal bias, would have to acknowledge that the early American newspapers they embrace were filled with precisely that attribute – bias – they find so objectionable in media today.) And yet, given the striking economic and political changes in journalism over the past three centuries, the bias of yore is not the same as today in form or content. The pro-Revolutionary colonial press wrote stories in a different form, and guided by a different approach to news, than the party-focused partisan press of the early 1800s, and its political bias differed from that of sensational journalism, mid-20th-century journalism, and narratives of today.

News bias – that ever-controversial, ever-relevant whipping boy, the ouroboros of journalism, in that it never disappears, but endlessly re-creates itself to fit the current milieu – is largely a 20th- and 21st-century construct. The partisan editors of the Jacksonian era would not have charged their counterparts with bias any more than they would have accused Old Hickory of prejudice toward Native Americans. It was just the nature of things: newspapers adopted the views of their partisan editors. Perceptions of bias would await the high-modern era of (supposedly) objective journalism, where bias was viewed as a departure from the romanticized ideal.

And yet, the ideologically driven news of the pro-Revolutionary colonial press was not without virtue. In addition to staking out a radical approach to news that emphasized that news (though not the way we use the term now) was an instrument to uproot the status quo, the early newspapers created innovative methods by which the press could serve as an instrument of popular citizen consent, linking the press with the larger democratic project. The passionate partisan press was inextricably bound with political parties, a source of interest and irony for a Founding Generation that sometimes viewed parties as overly political entities and other times harnessed them for their own partisan ends. This was truly a partisan press, in which parties did not just suggest stories, but funded newspapers, editors looked askance at impartiality, and smeared the opposition party. Behind the partisan strife, a new country was finding its way, using press outlets to articulate political goals and priorities. Only a portion of the country, of course, was working out these macro objectives. Mainstream politics and press were closed to people of color and women.

If there was a small silver lining to newspaper developments – and it was very small – it was that oppressed groups – first Blacks, then women in larger numbers in the late 19th century – used alternative newspapers to cultivate, disseminate, and amplify dissident voices. Unfortunately, their alternative views could be greeted with verbal and physical violence, as established groups (White men of varied European ethnicities) held back nothing, destroying dissident newspapers and killing their courageous proprietors, an early indication of the degree to which opponents would seek to silence the political press. Over the long haul, the dissident voices would gain the upper hand, but it would be a long and bloody fight.

Into the press fray next marched, with outsize enthusiasm and greed, the penny press, newspapers that undercut the competition and hawked crime news for a penny, creating a new economic model for the growing urban newspapers in America. Even more importantly, the penny newspapers helped create the modern concept of news, placing newspapers in the hands of White working-class readers, symbolically enfranchising a new middle-class society in America. Filled with crime news designed for the first time to aggressively sell papers, along with faux stories on a moon hoax that predated Russian-inspired fake news by almost two centuries, newspapers exerted wide-ranging social effects. The nature of these influences has long intrigued scholars, who have debated the scope and positivity of the penny press's impact.

Over the course of the rough-hewn century, innovations continued apace. Newspapers expanded in length, reach, and subscriptions. The partisan newspapers slowly died out, first complemented, then replaced by a splashier, ambitious press that aimed high in its investigative muckraking and broad in yellow journalistic undertakings. The sensational press was filled with graphic stories, high in shock value, sometimes low in accuracy, but, over the long haul, it built a venerable news media that cultivated a public less tied to political parties and increasingly focused on a growing sense of journalistic professionalism.

The professionalism term is fraught, widely debated by scholars. Scholars have examined the degree to which journalism is a profession, with professional standards, as opposed to a trade. Articles have noted that there are no certification or licensing requirements to practice journalism, in comparison to professions like law, while also noting journalism has long-standing professional norms. There are different views of professionalism, as well as different journalistic values and roles across different nations (see Boczkowski & Mitchelstein, 2017; Bromley, 2019; Craft, 2017; Reese, 2001; Vos, 2019; Waisbord, 2013; Weaver & Willnat, 2012). For all the debate, there is broad agreement that a diffuse, if not formal, professional orientation took hold in the early 20th century, powered by a growing objectivity ethos. The objectivity norm developed for a host of reasons – economic, cultural, and intellectual – and its promise, as well as frequent failure to be realized in practice, has intrigued and informed scholars.

The 20th century was the century of American media, to paraphrase *Time* publisher Henry Luce, who spoke of the American century and whose magazine epitomized its shortcomings and strengths. An increasingly profitable print media industry was now joined by radio and television, whose fears of impact spawned a government agency (Federal Communications Commission), to regulate it, a recognition that news had formally emerged as an institution in American society, hardly recognizable from the unappealing 4-page sheets of the colonial era. Presidents and politicians learned that the ability to manipulate, even manage, news could enhance their power, and also that journalists could be cowed by their intimidations, as Senator Joseph McCarthy powerfully demonstrated. But journalism – the term was now a part of formal discourse, having evolved to include the conventions of reporting that gradually emerged – had a way of pushing back, questioning power, and correcting its mistakes. Some of the reporting during the Vietnam War and, of course, during Watergate showcased investigative journalism at its finest, leading, indirectly and mediated by institutional forces, to sweeping changes in policy and, in the case of Richard Nixon, the resignation of a president who ruptured democratic processes.

Over the ensuing decades, adversarial reporting, where journalists challenge authorities, became a cause célèbre, in some cases producing an excessive "Gotcha" journalism, where reporters challenged the powers-that-be, as much to get a titillating story as to highlight social injustice. Economic factors, always important to capitalistic media, took on growing significance in the latter decades of the 20th century, as newspapers declined, folded, or were bought by big corporations; cable television monetized first-on-the-scene international crisis coverage; TV newsmagazines, illuminating social inequities, developed an appealing formula to snag viewers; and news focused endlessly on novel crime stories to hook viewers, showcasing how news, often simplistically, constructed the fraught problems of gender, class, and race. At the same time, with the FCC loosening restrictions on cross-media ownership and media mergers becoming a regular part of the news landscape, the nation's citizens were increasingly beset by the discovery that just that a handful of companies controlled the bulk of the media outlets producing news.

But just as scholars became accustomed to this uncomfortable reality, news changed again. A majority of Americans received some news via social media, chiefly Facebook, a distribution channel not created for journalistic ends, a reflection of the increasingly decentralized, fragmented nature of contemporary journalistic gatekeeping.

Alas, the history of news in America is a story of continuities, from bias to news commodification, and changes, from the very nature of news to its reception in different modalities. It is a colorful history, full of triumphs and tragedies, marked by sound and fury (to quote Shakespeare), but, contrary to the Bard, signifying a great deal in the teeming realm of human affairs.

References

Bagdikian, B.H. (2004). *The new media monopoly.* Boston, MA: Beacon Press.

Bai, M. (2014). *All the truth is out: The week politics went tabloid.* New York: Knopf.

Baldasty, G.J. (1993). The rise of news as a commodity: Business imperatives and the press in the nineteenth century. In W.S. Solomon & R.W. McChesney (Eds.), *Ruthless criticism: New perspectives in U.S. communication history* (pp. 98–121). Minneapolis, MN: University of Minnesota Press.

Baldasty, G.J. (2011). American political parties and the press. In B. Brennen & H. Hardt (Eds.), *The American journalism history reader: Critical and primary texts* (pp. 270–296). New York: Routledge.

Barnhurst, K.G., & Mutz, D. (1997). American journalism and the decline in event-centered reporting. *Journal of Communication, 47,* 27–52.

Barnhurst, K.G., & Nerone, J. (2001). *The form of news: A history.* New York: Guilford Press.

Baughman, J.L. (1987). *Henry R. Luce and the rise of the American news media.* Boston, MA: Twayne Publishers.

Bennett, W.L., & Paletz, D.L. (Eds.) (1994). *Taken by storm: The media, public opinion, and U.S. foreign policy in the Gulf War.* Chicago, IL: University of Chicago Press.

Bird, S.E. (2000). Audience demands in a murderous market: Tabloidization in U.S. television news. In C. Sparks & J. Tulloch (Eds.), *Tabloid tales: Global debates over media standards* (pp. 213–228). Lanham, MD: Rowman & Littlefield.

Black, J.E. (2013). In defense of Vespertilio-homo: Finding the truth in the 1835 moon hoax. In D.B. Sachsman & D.W. Bulla (Eds.), *Sensationalism: Murder, mayhem, mudslinging, scandals, and disasters in 19th century reporting* (pp. 223–240). New Brunswick, NJ: Transaction Publishers.

Boczkowski, P., & Mitchelstein, E. (2017). Scholarship on online journalism: Roads traveled and pathways ahead. In P.J. Boczkowski & C.W. Anderson (Eds.), *Remaking the news: Essays on the future of journalism scholarship in the digital age* (pp. 15–26). Cambridge, MA: The MIT Press.

Brennen, B., & Hardt, H. (Eds.) (2011). *The American journalism history reader: Critical and primary texts.* New York: Routledge.

Bromley, M. (2019). "Who are those guys?" The challenge of journalists' identity. *Journalism, 20,* 13–16.

Bulla, D.W., & Sachsman, D.B. (2013). Introduction. In D.B. Sachsman & D. W. Bulla (Eds.), *Sensationalism: Murder, mayhem, mudslinging, scandals, and disasters in 19th century reporting* (pp. xvii–xxxiv). New Brunswick, NJ: Transaction Publishers.

Burns, E. (2006). *Infamous scribblers: The founding fathers and the rowdy beginnings of American journalism.* New York: Public Affairs.

Byfield, N.P. (2014). *Savage portrayals: Race, media, and the Central Park jogger story.* Philadelphia, PA: Temple University Press.

Campbell, R. (1987). Securing the middle ground: Reporter formulas in *60 Minutes. Critical Studies in Mass Communication, 4,* 325–350.

Campbell, R. (1991). *60 Minutes and the news: A mythology for Middle America.* Urbana, IL: University of Illinois Press.

Campbell, W.J. (2013). Yellow journalism: Why so maligned and misunderstood? In D.B. Sachsman & D.W. Bulla (Eds.), *Sensationalism: Murder, mayhem, mudslinging, scandals, and disasters in 19th century reporting* (pp. 3–18). New Brunswick, NJ: Transaction Publishers.

Cappella, J.N., & Jamieson, K.H. (1997). *Spiral of cynicism: The press and the public good.* New York: Oxford University Press.

Carey, J.W. (2007). A short history of journalism for journalists: A proposal and essay. *The International Journal of Press/Politics, 12,* 3–16.

Chambers, D., Steiner, L., & Fleming, C. (2004). *Women and journalism.* New York: Routledge.

Cohen, P.C. (1998). *The murder of Helen Jewett: The life and death of a prostitute in nineteenth-century New York.* New York: Knopf.

Copeland, D.A. (2006). *The idea of a free press: The enlightenment and its unruly legacy.* Evanston, IL: Northwestern University Press.

Copeland, D.A. (2007). A series of fortunate events: Why people believed Richard Adam Locke's "moon hoax". *Journalism History, 33,* 140–150.

Craft, S. (2017). Distinguishing features: Reconsidering the link between journalism's professional status and ethics. *Journalism & Communication Monographs, 19,* 260–301.

Dicken-Garcia, H. (1989). *Journalistic standards in nineteenth-century America.* Madison, WI: University of Wisconsin Press.

Dicken-Garcia, H. (2011). Changes in news during the nineteenth century. In B. Brennen & H. Hardt (Eds.), *The American journalism history reader: Critical and primary texts* (pp. 229–256). New York: Routledge.

Emery, M., Emery, E., & Roberts, N.L. (2000). *The press and America: An interpretive history of the mass media* (9th ed.). Boston, MA: Allyn and Bacon.

Folkerts, J., Teeter, Jr., D.L., & Caudill, E. (2009). *Voices of a nation: A history of mass media in the United States* (5th ed.). Boston, MA: Pearson Education.

Fung, B. (2017, November 16). The FCC just repealed a 42-year-old rule blocking broadcast media mergers. *The Washington Post.* Online: www.washingtonpost.com/news/the-switch/wp/2017/11/16/the… (Accessed: April 6, 2018).

Gilliard, D. (2017, February 7). *James Baldwin's provocative truth.* Online: ctobt.com/james-baldwins-provocative-truth/ (Accessed: April 4, 2018).

Gitlin, T. (1980). *The whole world is watching.* Berkeley, CA: University of California Press.

Hallin, D.C. (1986). *The "uncensored war": The media and Vietnam.* New York: Oxford University Press.

Hallin, D.C. (1994). *We keep America on top of the world: Television journalism and the public sphere.* New York: Routledge.

Hamilton, J.M., & Tworek, H.J.S. (2017). The natural history of the news: An epigenetic study. *Journalism, 18,* 391–407.

Hardt, H. (1995). Without the rank and file: Journalism history, media workers, and problems of representation. In H. Hardt & B. Brennen (Eds.), *Newsworkers: Toward a history of the rank and file* (pp. 1–29). Minneapolis, MN: University of Minnesota Press.

Jirik, J. (2012). Engagement as an emerging norm in international news agency work. In B. St. John, III & K.A. Johnson (Eds.), *News with a view: Essays on the eclipse of objectivity in modern journalism* (pp. 170–186). Jefferson, NC: McFarland & Co.

Kaplan, R.L. (2002). *Politics and the American press: The rise of objectivity, 1865–1920.* Cambridge, UK: Cambridge University Press.

Kaplan, R.L. (2010). The origins of objectivity in American journalism. In S. Allan (Ed.), *The Routledge companion to news and journalism* (pp. 25–37). New York: Routledge.

King, S. (2005). *The Colorado kid.* New York: Dorchester.

Knowlton, S.R. (2005). A history of journalistic objectivity. In S.R. Knowlton & K.L. Freeman (Eds.), *Fair and balanced: A history of journalistic objectivity* (pp. 3–5). Northport, AL: Vision Press.

Lang, K., & Lang, G.E. (1953). The unique perspective of television and its effect: A pilot study. *American Sociological Review, 18,* 3–12.

Leonard, T.C. (1986). *The power of the press: The birth of American political reporting*. New York: Oxford University Press.

Lippmann, W. (1922). *Public opinion*. New York: Free Press.

Maras, S. (2013). *Objectivity in journalism*. Cambridge, UK: Polity Press.

Marzolf, M. (1977). *Up from the footnote: A history of women journalists*. New York: Hastings House.

McChesney, R.W. (1999). *Rich media, poor democracy: Communication politics in dubious times*. Urbana, IL: University of Illinois Press.

Mindich, D.T.Z. (1998). *Just the facts: How "objectivity" came to define American journalism*. New York: New York University Press.

Mindich, D.T.Z. (2000). Understanding Frederick Douglass: Toward a new synthesis approach to the birth of modern American journalism. *Journalism History, 26*, 15–22.

Mott, F.L. (1962). *American journalism* (3rd ed.). New York: Macmillan.

Nadler, A.M. (2016). *Making the news popular: Mobilizing U.S. news audiences*. Urbana, IL: University of Illinois Press.

Nerone, J.C. (1987). The mythology of the penny press. *Critical Studies in Mass Communication, 4*, 376–404.

Nerone, J.C. (1994). *Violence against the press: Policing the public sphere in U.S. history*. New York: Oxford University Press.

Nerone, J.C. (2015). *The media and public life: A history*. Malden, MA: Polity Press.

Nerone, J.C. (2018, May 22). Personal, email communication to Richard M. Perloff.

Patterson, T.E. (1993). *Out of order*. New York: Knopf.

Perloff, R.M. (1998). *Political communication: Politics, press, and public in America*. Mahwah, NJ: Erlbaum Associates.

Perloff, R.M. (1999). Elite, popular, and merchandised politics: Historical origins of presidential campaign marketing. In B.I. Newman (Ed.), *Handbook of political marketing* (pp. 19–40). Thousand Oaks, CA: Sage.

Perloff, R.M. (2000). The press and lynchings of African Americans. *Journal of Black Studies, 30*, 315–330.

Perloff, R.M. (2015, August 23). Emmett Till's killing holds timely lessons. *The Plain Dealer*, E8.

Perloff, R.M. (2017, January 1). Fake and biased news are old stories in politics. *The Plain Dealer*, E2.

Reese, S.D. (2001). Understanding the global journalist: A hierarchy of influences approach. *Journalism Studies, 2*, 173–187.

Roberts, G., & Klibanoff, H. (2006). *The race beat: The press, the civil rights struggle, and the awakening of a nation*. New York: Knopf.

Rosenfeld, S. (2019). *Democracy and truth: A short history*. Philadelphia, PA: University of Pennsylvania Press.

Rovere, R.H. (1959). *Senator Joe McCarthy*. New York: Harcourt, Brace.

Ryfe, D.M. (2017). *Journalism and the public*. Cambridge, UK: Polity Press.

Schiller, D. (1981). *Objectivity and the news: The public and the rise of commercial journalism*. Philadelphia, PA: University of Pennsylvania Press.

Schiller, D. (1987). Critical response: Evolutionary confusion. *Critical Studies in Mass Communication, 4*, 409–412.

Schudson, M. (1978). *Discovering the news: A social history of American newspapers*. New York: Harper.

Schudson, M. (1995). *The power of news.* Cambridge, MA: Harvard University Press.

Schudson, M. (2001). The objectivity norm in American journalism. *Journalism. Theory, Practice & Criticism, 2,* 149–170.

Schudson, M., & Tifft, S.E. (2005). American journalism in historical perspective. In G. Overholser & K.H. Jamieson (Eds.), *The press* (pp. 17–47). New York: Oxford University Press.

Shaw, D.L. (1987). *Critical response*: Why we need "myths". *Critical Studies in Mass Communication, 4,* 412–415.

Sloan, W.D. (1991). *Perspectives on mass communication history.* Hillsdale, NJ: Lawrence Erlbaum Associates.

Sloan, W.D. (2005). *The media in America: A history* (6th ed.). Northport, AL: Vision Press.

Sloan, W.D. (Ed.) (2008). *The media in America: A history.* Northport, AL: Vision Press.

Solomon, W.S. (1995). The site of newsroom labor: The division of editorial practices. In H. Hardt & B. Brennen (Eds.), *Newsworkers: Toward a history of the rank and file* (pp. 110–134). Minneapolis, MN: University of Minnesota Press.

Stabile, C.A. (2005). "The most disgusting objects of both sexes": Gender and race in the episodic crime news of the 1830s. *Journalism, 6,* 403–421.

Standage, T. (2013). *Writing on the wall: Social media – The first 2,000 years.* New York: Bloomsbury.

Steele, R.W. (1985). *Propaganda in an open society: The Roosevelt Administration and the media, 1933–1941.* Westport, CT: Greenwood.

Steiner, L. (1992). The history and structure of women's alternative media. In L. F. Rakow (Ed.), *Women making meaning: New feminist directions in communication* (pp. 121–143). New York: Routledge.

Steiner, L. (1993). Nineteenth-century suffrage periodicals: Conceptions of womanhood and the press. In W.S. Solomon & R.W. McChesney (Eds.), *Ruthless criticism: New perspectives in U.S. communication history* (pp. 66–97). Minneapolis, MN: University of Minnesota Press.

Stephens, M. (2007). *A history of news* (3rd ed.). New York: Oxford University Press.

Streitmatter, R. (2016). *Mightier than the sword: How the news media have shaped American history* (4th ed.). Boulder, CO: Westview Press.

Tillet, S. (2018, April 3). Marching against the glare of the nightly news. *The New York Times,* C1, C6.

Tucher, A. (1994). *Froth & scum: Truth, beauty, goodness, and the ax murder in American's first mass medium.* Chapel Hill, NC: University of North Carolina Press.

Vos, T.P. (2019). Journalists' endangered professional status. *Journalism, 20,* 122–125.

Vos, T.P., & Finneman, T. (2017). The early historical construction of journalism's gatekeeping role. *Journalism: Theory, Criticism and Practice, 18,* 265–280.

Waisbord, S. (2013). *Reinventing professionalism: Journalism and news in global perspective.* Cambridge, UK: Polity Press.

Warren, K.F. (1991). *The juggler: Franklin Roosevelt as war-time statesman.* Princeton, NJ: Princeton University Press.

Weaver, D., & Willnat, L. (2012). Journalists in the 21st century: Conclusions. In D.H. Weaver & L. Willnat (Eds.), *The global journalist in the 21st century* (pp. 529–551). New York: Routledge.

Wilson, C.C., & Gutierrez, F. (1995). *Race, multiculturalism, and the media: From mass to class communication*. London: Sage.

Young, K. (2017). *Bunk: The rise of hoaxes, humbug, plagiarists, phonies, post-facts, and fake news*. Minneapolis, MN: Graywolf Press.

Zelizer, B. (1992). *Covering the body: The Kennedy assassination, the media, and the shaping of collective memory*. Chicago, IL: University of Chicago Press.

Zelizer, B. (1993). Journalists as interpretive communities. *Critical Studies in Mass Communication, 10*, 219–237.

Zelizer, B., & Tenenboim-Weinblatt, K. (Eds.) (2014). *Journalism and memory*. New York: Palgrave Macmillan.

Part II

What Makes News Tick?

Concepts, Controversies, and Conclusions

6 Unpacking the News
Refracting not Reflecting Reality

"You give us 22 minutes, we'll give you the world," a New York City radio station loved to boast. "All the news that's fit to print," *The New York Times* proudly proclaims in the upper left corner of each newspaper's front page, suggesting the editors will publish all the suitable news of the world on a particular day. News holds up a mirror to reality, television executives insisted back in the 1970s. "There is no doubt that television is, to a large degree, a mirror of society. It is also a mirror of public attitudes and preferences," Reuven Frank, a long-time former producer of NBC news, said (Epstein, 1973, p. 13). Nowadays, Facebook offers up a similar claim, professing to be a neutral company, a mere medium by which news can diffuse, get posted, processed, and shared without exerting a whit of influence on the process (Marantz, 2018).

All of these claims presume in some sense that the media are neutral vehicles that transmit a literal rendition of reality, offering up an accurate, mirror-image version of events on the local, national, or international stage. If this is true, some news executives have argued, the media can't be blamed for whatever problems result from their coverage. You can't blame the messenger for the message, they soberly say. But is that true? Does news reflect reality? And if not, what factors determine news? What makes news tick? Or, as Berkowitz (1997) puts it, "why does news turn out like it does?" (p. xii).

The next section of the book, beginning with this chapter, examines these issues, viewing them from multiple perspectives. The focus, beyond the descriptive "who, what, where, and when," is on the deeper layers of "why" – why news covers stories as it does. Why does news ignore certain stories and favor others, frame stories in particular ways, focus on consistent angles, prioritize power, favor celebrities, downplay the mundane and prosaic, and display that fraught, freighted, misunderstood term, bias? Why, in short, is news as it is?

These are exciting questions that cut to the heart of the journalistic enterprise. You may have posed some of these queries yourself or argued about them with friends. The chapters that follow will challenge your opinions by introducing new perspectives and empirical findings. This chapter begins with a comprehensive debunking of the claim that news reflects reality. The second portion examines the complex, multi-layered concept of facts, with a focus on how journalists construct – not simply reflect – events covered in the news. It also revisits the idea of objectivity, acknowledging its flaws, but highlighting its role as a guiding beacon in a world in which facts are under siege.

Does News Reflect Reality? Well, Not Exactly

When a hurricane strikes, news reports it. When a horrific terrorist incident occurs, you receive immediate notification on your phone. News dutifully tells you who won the presidential election. Of course, in a very basic, naïvely realistic sense, news reflects reality. But beyond that, why are some hurricanes, terrorist events, and elections rather than others reported? How do we account for the play they get and the ways stories are covered? In this more fundamental sense, which strikes at the basics of news, news hardly reflects reality. Let's see why.

Valence

The first way news departs from reality is obvious: News is negative, offering an overwhelmingly negative valence – evaluation or affective slant – on public events. News eschews the positive features of life that people frequently experience. Instead, it emphasizes the negative information that grabs attention far more than positive content: a drive-by shooting rather than a festive family reunion, a crime spree rather than neighbors banding together to stop crime, evidence of voter suppression instead of millions voting freely to select the new president, and during Christmas season, of all times, a story of the theft of a statute of the baby Jesus from Bethlehem, Pennsylvania instead of a fabled account of the birth of Jesus in a Bethlehem manger (Shoemaker & Cohen, 2006; Smith, 2018). The focus on negative news is not unique to American media. It emerges abroad as well, including, intriguingly on Al-Jazeera, the prominent Middle East-based global news outlet. More than 80 - percent of the coverage of the U.S. Al Qaeda was negative on both the Arabic-language and English-language websites of Al-Jazeera, research- ers Shahira Fahmy and Mohammed Al Emad (2011) discovered in a thorough content analysis.

At life's personal and social levels, this news does not reflect reality. For most of us, at least most of the time, life is not primarily negative; many of us say we are happy (see 77 percent in developed world are happy, 2014). Communities operate on the basis of normal, predictable routinized procedures. For most people most of the time, life is okay, predictable, certainly not as overcast and stormy as news portrays.

Why is news negative? There are underlying psychological reasons: Negative information is more psychologically memorable and neurologically impactful than its psychological counterpart, attracting both journalists' and readers' attention (Newhagen & Reeves, 1991; Soroka, 2014). Negatively-focused stories agitate and arouse readers (and are commonly believed to recruit more eyeballs to news outlets). There are also important journalistic explanations, chiefly that negative news defies intuitive expectations. Pamela J. Shoemaker and Stephen D. Reese (2014) helpfully note:

> Like the body's autonomic system, most of the systems that run our communities and nations operate unnoticed. Is it good news to know that your heart is still beating, that you are still breathing? Undoubtedly, but who wants a television program devoted to everything that's working okay? We expect things to work properly, but when the levees are about to break, we want to know about it. Journalists' anticipation of problems – worrying about the worst that could happen – may help by gaining the attention of those who can fix problems.
>
> (p. 54)

Negative news is so common and expected a staple of news that when good news happens, it stands out. *The New York Times* actually publishes a weekly list of six positive items under the headline "The Week in Good News" to remind readers beleaguered by negative news that good things did happen over the course of a week, such as a daring rescue of 12 Thai soccer players and their coach from a cave, as well as the 15-year-old girl who came to the rescue of a deaf and blind airline passenger who was having trouble communicating with flight attendants by using sign language, leaving the passenger grateful and "very moved" (Shoe, 2018, A2).

Should there be more positive news? Perhaps. It might help people savor life's pleasures and citizens appreciate elected officials' dedication to public service (Bryant & Veroff, 2007). Indeed, some political communication scholars and devotees of citizen journalism make this argument, noting that bad news about politics dispirits voters and reduces motivation to participate in worthwhile community-enhancement activities. From a broader perspective, though, bad news fulfills normative functions. Negatively framed news that calls attention to calamitous effects of global warming, political injustice, societal breakdowns, urban ills, and colossal failures of government bureaucracy helps institutions to monitor the environment, offers broad feedback on the status quo, and fulfills the essential function of helping society correct systemic problems. If news were all positive, it might make us feel good for a time, but it would exert dysfunctional effects, covering up schemes concocted by the powerful, masking wrongs, and making it high-nigh impossible for activists to discover ways to correct these problems. There is room for disagreement on how much news *should* be negative, especially when bad news is ginned up to elevate ratings. But you will find few journalists or scholars who argue with the normative function negative news performs for citizens and society (though see Hermans & Gyldensted, 2019). To paraphrase Madison, if people were angels, no bad news would be necessary.

Let's return to the news-reflects-reality question. Given that negative news predominates, could the negative news about different walks of public life still accurately depict the reality in these areas? Let's look at the balance sheet of news across contexts (see Table 6.1).

Knowns and Celebrities

News lavishes far more coverage on those who are known than those not well-known, with knowns accounting for approximately 75 percent of the people who appear in national news (Gans, 2004). Famous people, celebrities, the politically influential, and economically connected elites of society receive as much as four times as much news coverage as ordinary people, citizens, and interesting everyday folks doing worthwhile things, but who have not attained social prominence. The marriage of celebrities (like the nonconforming Prince Harry and the delightfully vocal feminist Meghan Markle) get exponentially more coverage than the marriage of ordinary, even other handsome, volubly feminist, couples.

The deaths of celebrities – the rich, famous, artistically celebrated, and outsize personalities of our ubiquitous media era – receive exponentially more coverage than the passing of everyone else. From Aretha Franklin, David Bowie, John F. Kennedy, Jr., and, of course, President George H.W. Bush, media coverage follows the adage of Aristotle that the primary theme of tragedy is "the fall of a great man," or at least a man (or woman) who fits society's canons of celebrity greatness (Mindich, 2002, p. 26; see Figure 6.1). Celebrities, while mortal like everyone, personify broad cultural memes that link disparate, otherwise disconnected individuals (Kitch, 2000). Media

Table 6.1 The News-Reflects-Reality Myth

News Does Not Reflect Reality in:
• Emphasis on the negative
• Focus on known individuals and celebrities
• People profiled in obituaries
• Selection of causes of death
• Crime and race
• Elections
• International coverage: Countries, conflicts, ethnocentric frames

Figure 6.1 When the celebrity British rocker and musical artist David Bowie died in 2016, the news media covered his life and death poignantly and perhaps extravagantly, illustrating the ways news doles out exponentially more coverage to the deaths of known and world-famous people than those of ordinary individuals. In its coverage of who dies and the cause of death, news does not mirror reality, but reflects the values and norms of journalism.

coverage of celebrity deaths fulfills ritualistic functions for society, but is hardly reflective of the vast processional of human deaths that occur each day in the U.S. and other countries.

Indeed, as William McDonald, *The New York Times* obituaries editor (2018), observed, "Some 155,000 people die between each day's print version of *The New York Times* and the next – enough to fill Yankee Stadium three times over. On average, we publish obituaries on about three of them." Although each life is important, *The Times* can't print an obituary for everyone. It can't reflect reality. "We have only so much space in the print newspaper, only so many hands to produce stories and only so many hours in the day to produce them," McDonald said. How do they decide who gets an obituary? "We focus on people who made a difference on a large stage – people who, we think, will command the broader interest. If you made news in life, chances are your death is news, too," McDonald explains (p. 15).

There is a cultural logic. The famous, infamous, and artistically significant have moved people or changed events in ways that ordinary individuals haven't. The singer Aretha Franklin was hailed as a groundbreaking force in music, civil rights, and feminism, who inspired millions of people, particularly African Americans, for whom she symbolized "black-woman magic" (Joseph, 2018, p. C1). Her obituary received significant play.

A sad, but related, dynamic occurs in news of suicides. Some 45,000 Americans committed suicide in 2017, the year before fashion designer Kate Spade and celebrity food journalist Anthony Bourdain killed themselves. Each death was equally tragic, the tragedy compounded when the suicides involved adolescents just beginning their lives, with excitement, verve, but also deadly depression. Yet in 2018, media attention was splashed on Spade and Bourdain, with CNN understandably, but arguably narcissistically, devoting precious time to Bourdain, who hosted a food and travel program on the cable network. The news judgments were consistent with journalistic standards, in both made visible, notable contributions to public life, and it is the public stage that journalism attends to, for good and for ill (Dubied & Hanitzsch, 2014).

Race and gender come into play. For many years, White – and predominately heterosexual – men received the overwhelming majority of obituaries. Why not more people of color, women, as well as gay and transgender individuals, on the obituary pages of *The Times* and other newspapers? Some – like African American entertainment greats like Scott Joplin, the late 19th-century Black ragtime composer, and Oscar Micheaux, gifted filmmaker of the silent movie era – made more significant contributions to public life than garden-variety Whites. The reason news overlooked their deaths is the same reason they neglected them in life: prejudice. For many years White newspaper editors would not publish photos of Black brides, nor print obituaries of Black domestic laborers (Carroll, 2017). With the exception of a handful of women and individuals of color who pushed aside barriers that were closed to them, who received only a fraction of their due in death notices of the era, obituaries reflected the broader values of the culture.

Causes of Death

On Sunday October 1, 2017 a gunman, perched on the 32nd floor of a Las Vegas casino, opened fire on a rollicking crowd of concertgoers at an autumn country musical festival. Stephen Paddock murdered 58 people and wounded scores more. The media covered the story extensively, showing non-stop footage, describing the enormous precautions

Paddock used to elude police, exploring Paddock's predictably troubled background, and profiling the victims felled by his attack.

Equally significant, in the views of their families, were accounts of *the same number of people* – 58 – killed by guns in Chicago in the span of less than a month, in Baltimore in a little over two months, and in Houston over a 3-month period. Yet the Las Vegas story received exponentially more news coverage than the other gun homicides, largely because the attack was unexpected, unusual, and directed at a mass of innocent concertgoers (Buchanan et al., 2017). Some critics found a disturbing racial note in this. The overwhelming majority of victims of the Las Vegas – and other gun massacres – were White, while many of those in Chicago, Baltimore, and Houston, also innocent victims, were people of color.

Consider another example of news coverage that departs from the reality of death statistics in the U.S. One Saturday in 2009, during their high school's homecoming weekend, three 16-year-olds from south Florida were killed in a car crash when their Volkswagen plummeted into a canal, devastating families and friends. There is tragic irony to the story. The students attended Marjory Stoneman Douglas High School in Parkland, Florida, where 17 people were gunned down in a mass school shooting in February, 2018. The mass shooting story received significantly more coverage than the car crash because it comported with journalistic news values (see Chapter 8). Yet it did not reflect the larger reality. Although gun violence is the second cause of adolescent death in America, with 1,675 teenagers murdered in 2016, the leading cause of teenage death is automobile crashes, with a devastating 2,829 American teens killed by motor vehicles in 2016 (Leonhardt, 2018). By contrast, less than 3 percent of homicides of children aged 5 to 18 occurred at schools (Goldstein, 2018).

Crime and Race

Local news feasts on crime, following the sensationalist tradition of the American press. Historically, as news took on an increasingly entertainment-laced edge in the 1990s, newsmagazines like *60 Minutes* and *Dateline NBC* emphasized crime, with more than 80 percent of the programs focusing on crime and about three-fourths of these shows featuring crime as the lead item (Grabe, 1999). While crimes have horrific consequences, once again they are not the only problem facing society. News exaggerates their frequency, particularly violent crimes, where the relatively graphic stories of police use of force depart from empirical data showing that police rarely use physical force to arrest criminal suspects, and when they do, most suspects are not hurt (Ordway, 2018). Clearly, when police do use excessive force, it is the exception to the rule, which is why it makes news.

In the morality play of TV newsmagazines, police officers were traditionally depicted as forces of good, doing their job to protect the neighborhood, while criminals were cast as evil. Lawbreakers were portrayed as guilty and nearly always brought to justice. In the real world the lines are cloudier, with police sometimes on the take and accused criminals less likely to be apprehended; in some cases, people accused of criminal activity turn out to be innocent, framed by prosecutors or victims of a careless, overworked justice system (Feuer, 2018; Glaberson, 2013).

Race exacerbates the problem, adding a troubling layer. Research has shown that local news in multicultural Los Angeles more often depicts Black than White juveniles as perpetrators of crime. Importantly, when the researchers compared TV portrayals to actual crime reports, they discovered that TV significantly overrepresented African Americans as lawbreakers (Dixon & Azocar, 2006; Poindexter, Smith, & Heider, 2003). In a classic finding, with relevance to our era, Entman and Rojecki (2000) reported that Chicago's local TV news showed Blacks more than twice as frequently as Whites under the physical custody of police officers. Police restrained, grabbed, and handcuffed Black suspects, depicting a reality constructed by TV news that suggests Blacks "seem to require physical control or restraint twice as much as Whites," implying they constitute a stereotypically primal threat to society (Entman & Rojecki, 2000, p. 83), a perception that reinforces racial stereotypes.

Politics

If you follow election coverage in the American press, you get the impression the only elections that are held – and certainly the ones that matter most – are the presidential primaries and the penultimate election of the president. The news media lavish vast coverage on the presidential election, beginning as much as two years before Election Day, as candidates begin jockeying for nomination, contenders form advisory committees, and reporters begin the adrenalin-filled coverage of the presidential horse race. News incessantly covers polls, who is ahead, and frames the presidential election as a horse race (Patterson, 1993, 2016). As a consequence, news focuses on poll-driven, high-profile early presidential nominating contests like the Iowa caucuses and New Hampshire primary, even though the demographic features of these states hardly reflect the U.S. population. What's more, there are many third and fourth party candidates who are outside the mainstream Democrat and Republican parties – some goofy, others serious – who attract voters' attention. Yet these candidates get short shrift from a media which dwells on the major party contenders, suggesting that third-party candidates are outside the purview of voter support (Perloff, 2018).

More generally, presidential election coverage eclipses news of state and municipal elections, which are given short shrift. Yet these races can exert a greater impact on people's lives because elected officials make decisions about issues that hit close to home, like schools, neighborhood safety, and property taxes.

Geography: A Limited, Ethnocentric Picture

One of the most telling examples of the failure of the news-reflects-reality thesis can be found in foreign news. If news reflected reality, all countries would get roughly equal coverage, or at least coverage in proportion to incidents that affect their national fabric. It does not work this way. News favors the more powerful countries with strong economies, notably those with White, western citizens; indeed, countries with less international status have long received less prominent news play (Galtung & Ruge, 1965; Segev, 2015). "Core countries (particularly the United States and Western Europe), their international affairs, and their interchanging opponents or enemies have always been at the center of international news," Sandrine Boudana and Elad Segev (2017, p. 316) observed.

Conflicts and wars also predict news coverage, but some conflicts are more relevant than others. Conflicts in the Middle East are more newsworthy than conflicts occurring in Asia or Africa, because the Middle East is more strategically relevant to preeminent western nations. What's more, conflict coverage hinges less on "reality" than on how major media construct the international news flow. News centers on conflicts between western nations and their adversaries; enemies of the U.S. are framed as the "bad guys," with North Korea the most frequently identified provoking country (Boudana & Segev, 2017). While news of North Korean's nuclear weapons testing does indeed reflect an underlying reality for the U.S., news typically neglects to examine North Korea's motives, or dynamics of the U.S.-North Korean conflict, ignoring other aspects of the underlying geopolitical reality.

More generally, certain parts of the world can be hidden, concealed – invisible – in mainstream media coverage. Lives lived and public events experienced in Third World countries off the beaten path of conventional cultural narratives go unreported. To U.S., western, and, truth be told, most global media, these regions constitute geographical "dead grounds," seemingly inert, irrelevant areas that gain life only when interpreted in the context of a colorful, dramatic narrative, which is imposed by news media (Salovaara-Moring, 2009).

What are frequently captured in times of war are photographic images, popularly viewed as "real" and "true" because they seem untainted by human judgments and the mélange of words, but inevitably influenced by photojournalists' judgments about what pictures to shoot, how, and where. Photographs can create false images of reality. News of the 1991 Persian Gulf War – the first U.S.-led war against Iraq – vividly, grandly portrayed Patriot missiles as tremendously successful in intercepting Iraqi scud missiles. However, the patriotic depictions did not mesh with reality; later reports showed the Patriots were far less effective than television news implied (Kaplan, 2003). In other cases, photographers applied deceptive visual techniques to burnish a reality that did not exist, as when a freelance photographer used Adobe Photoshop to enhance the color of smoke spiraling over Beirut from an Israeli strike in 2006. Photographs, with their evocative images of pain and heroism, can influence public opinion, evoke empathy, and trigger historical memories, cueing a particular narrative interpretation of the past (Zelizer, 2017).

Far from a mirror, international news, whether depicted in photographs or online articles, revolves ethnocentrically around the interests and concerns of a particular country – namely, the one in which their journalists reside. The national and even patriotic identity of journalists can influence what gets covered in news (Nossek, 2004). You see this graphically illustrated in news of natural disasters.

The U.S. media blanketed the airwaves and online pages with up-to-the-minute, empathic coverage of Tropical Storm Harvey, which slammed and slashed through Houston in August, 2017. What you would not know from this coverage is that more devastating damage occurred elsewhere in the world during a similar period. During the summer of 2017, floods killed more than 1,000 people in India, Bangladesh, and Nepal; a gigantic mudslide killed or injured some 1,000 residents of Sierra Leone, and, more generally, a shocking 41 million people were directly impacted by floods in South Asia (Beyond Houston, A World Awash, 2017). The effects of natural calamities and climate change wreak havoc across the world, but the U.S. media provides affecting coverage of deaths of Americans.

And then there is terrorism. The evil of September 11 resulted in the unspeakable death of some 3,000 Americans, a horror that received nonstop, immense coverage, much of it laudatory and deeply moving. Unpleasant as it is to consider (and in no way to trivialize September 11), Mindich (2002) reminds us that "ours are not the only deaths. Every day, more than 5,000 people die of AIDS in Africa … Every day, more than five thousand *children* die from tuberculosis, malaria and rotavirus" (p. 25). The American news media did not reflect these realities with the same magnitude of coverage as they devoted to September 11. U.S. news outlets cover global terrorism selectively, basing news judgments on the event's geographical proximity to the U.S. and the target country's affinity with the United States (Sui et al., 2017).

From a normative perspective, important questions emerge. *Should* a particular nation's news media devote the same coverage to calamities in other countries as to tragedies that befall its own citizens, particularly those that result from a horror like 9/11? How does one balance normative emphasis on informational monitoring and truthful reporting with perspectives that emphasize ritualistic reporting (binding citizens together in national tragedies), patriotic responsibilities, and collaborative approaches that argue news should serve government? Should news, in cases like September 11, frame stories sympathetically from the perspective of journalists' home country, or should it offer a more critical, less ethnocentric line? These are tough questions to answer. In any case, a nation's news media are inevitably guided by values and frameworks, not by reality, as if one could objectively assess reality in a world as multitudinous as ours.

Divergent Media Realities and Social Media's Refractive Mirror

A final shortcoming in the news-reflects-reality thesis is the different ways news outlets cover the same story. If news held up a mirror to reality, the coverage across outlets should be the same, resulting from the identical images the mirror held up. Different cable channels can cover events in very different ways, offering more space or time to certain issues and organizing them through different frameworks.

Local, regional, and national newspapers frequently cover the same event – such as the wanton rape of a 16-year-old girl by two adolescent boys in Steubenville, Ohio in 2012 – in dramatically different ways (Gutsche & Salkin, 2016; see also Du, 2016). Blogs, for their part, prioritize different angles and issues than do conventional news outlets (Robinson & DeShano, 2011).

Social media also bends the mirror to fit algorithmic priorities. Facebook has professed, perhaps for public relations purposes or perhaps because it likes to believe this, that it is a neutral company, a mere medium that diffuses news, kindly helping people share information, without making gatekeeping decisions. Of course, this is ridiculous. Facebook's algorithms prioritize messages that stimulate comments, user engagement, and negative emotions like anger and fear rather than mirroring the totality of information or affect out there (Fisher & Taub, 2018; Marantz, 2018).

News as a Process of Construction

If news does not reflect reality, then what determines news? One of the time-honored insights of news scholarship is that news is a construction, not a reflection. Gatekeeping is a process of locating, judging, defining, and ultimately constructing news from disparate bits of information. For more than two centuries, beginning with the penny press and evolving, through fits and starts, over the 20th and 21st centuries, this construction has revolved centrally around the fraught concept of facts. During the late 19th century, as empirical epistemologies began to emerge, reporters were naïve empirical thinkers believing facts were not human constructions, but literally part of the reality itself (Nerone, 2015; Schudson, 1978). This reflected the august status facts held during the 19th and 20th centuries.

Consider, as an example, that Charles Dickens began his classic, *Hard Times*, with Mr. Gradgrind, a school owner, declaring that "Now, what I want is, Facts. Teach these boys and girls nothing but Facts. Facts alone are wanted in life ... Stick to Facts, Sir." (Muñoz-Torres, 2012, p. 566). In the iconic, though by today's standards simplistic, 1950s television show, *Dragnet*, the all-business, verbally laconic Sergeant Joe Friday, would insist that all he wanted was the facts, the reference becoming so famous the super-masculine Friday was famously (though mistakenly) believed to have told female characters that what he wanted was "just the facts, ma'am."

The emphasis on facts roughly coincided with the growth in objectivity, that hallowed journalistic term. Objectivity, as discussed in Chapter 5, became a journalistic norm – a calling, revered philosophical precept – that presumed "facts can be separated from opinion or value judgments, and that journalists can stand apart from the real-world events whose truth or meaning they transfer to the news audience by means of neutral language and competent reporting techniques" (Hackett, 1984, p. 232; Hanitzsch, 2007).

This view – that reporters could easily separate out facts from value judgments – has changed dramatically in light of psychological evidence of the persistence of human biases, the impossibility of anyone standing apart from events without their opinions intervening, and sterility of neutral language in the wake of the dramaturgical license 1960s journalists and nonfiction writers later took with the facts, in books by Tom Wolfe, Norman Mailer, and Gail Sheehy.

There is, alas, no such thing as perfectly objective reporting. Facts just don't exist as literal entities out there in the real world that are detected and scooped up to form a story. Facts are always a matter of some construction by a human observer. Judgments of facts are based on perceptions, and perceptions are formed from prior learning, interposition of acquired concepts, and application of mental shortcuts (Shoemaker & Vos, 2009). As Lippmann (1922) observed a century ago, "for the most part we do not first see, and then define, we define first and then see" (pp. 54–55).

Consider that in the early 1900s, as the objectivity ethos took hold, the ways reporters imposed interpretations on what they saw could be glimpsed in the different ways three New York City newspapers reported a woman's assault on Russian political leader Alexander Kerensky at a New York City theater. "According to the *News*, she struck him on the left cheek with her bouquet. According to the *Times*, she slapped his face three times with her gloves. According to the *Mirror*, she struck him a single blow" (Romano, 1986, p. 64).

Reporters do not just collect facts and base the story on the facts they have collected. Instead, they decide what constitutes a meaningful or accurate fact; their perspective determines how they interpret, assimilate, and build a narrative from the information they weave into a story. In an example of contemporary relevance, for years it was regarded as an objective truth – a *fact* – that a rape victim was at fault if she moved outside the housewife role, knew her attacker, and was pretty. Intimate violence was not generally regarded as a crime (McManus & Dorfman, 2005). Today, in the wake of consciousness of sexual abuse, such statements would be regarded as fictions, reflecting journalistic biases of the time, covering up the painful facts about widespread male perpetration of violence against women. Clearly, facts don't just exist out there, waiting to be discovered, but are defined and adjudicated by journalists.

If journalism is, alas, based on facts, what is a fact? Which facts count most? And how does one evaluate the truth value of an assemblage of facts? These questions cut to the heart of journalism, where, over the course of the 20th and 21st centuries, facts became "God-terms" to reporters and editors (Zelizer, 2004a, p. 100), endowed with mythical status. (The journalistic approach to facts contrasts intriguingly with that of cultural studies scholars, who examine news from the perspective of culture, social construction, and subjectivity [Zelizer, 2004b].)

"Journalism's presumed legitimacy," Zelizer (2004a) notes, "depends on its declared ability to provide an indexical and referential presentation of the world at hand" (p. 103). Journalism derives its legitimacy and authority from its ability to adjudicate and present narratives about what happened, when, how, and even why. This capacity traditionally separated journalism from other societal institutions and, during the course of the 20th century, afforded it epistemological authority.

Yet facts, Bonnie Brennen (2009) notes, "are messy, difficult to determine and they are often dependent on interpretation" (p. 301). The next section offers a case study in this principle, focusing on news of the Middle East, where warring partisans have different interpretations of the facts because the very definition of a fact is a matter of contentious, indeed bloody, disagreement.

Complexity of Facts: Arab-Israeli News as a Classic Example

Decades ago, in classic battles in June, 1982, Israel invaded nearby Lebanon to expel its enemy, the Palestinian Liberation Organization, from the once-beautiful country. Three months of air assaults, pitched battles in Beirut, and a multitude of civilian casualties, including deaths of children, ensued, raising difficult, controversial questions for reporters on what constituted a fact and just how to invoke the fraught term, context, as an explanation for what occurred on a particular day.

Reporting required making judgments about innumerable tragic events. For example, should reporters say that a 7-month-old baby lost both arms when an Israeli plane accidentally crashed into a residential area during an air attack on Palestinian Liberation Organization forces, as the United Press International reported? Or was Israel correct when it produced photographs that showed that the baby had not lost both arms and his injuries were not serious? Was the Israeli report factually suspect?

Were Palestinian militants – and was the word "militant" appropriate, or biased? – correct in arguing that Israel indiscriminately attacked residential buildings and, more cruelly, hospitals? Or did Israel launch such attacks with unusual care and strategic precision because its intelligence indicated that Palestinian forces deliberately hid out in hospitals in an effort to extract maximal public relations damage on Israel? How could reporters, who must depend on sources from both sides (which vary in their credibility), and frequently arrive on the scene long after a pitched battle ended, reach a reasonable judgment about the facts (Muravchik, 1983)? And, more generally, there is the conundrum that in some cases reporters knew that anti-Israel fighters were deliberately disguised as civilians and their deaths were routinely counted as civilian deaths in the death toll. Because reporters could not publish this without jeopardizing their own lives, their reports of the death toll contained artificially-inflated information (Friedman, 2018).

Nearly two decades later, in the autumn of 2000, similar factual conundrums surfaced, as reporters struggled to cover the violent uprisings in Israel, known as the second Intifada. Should participants in the violent rebellions be called "terrorists," "suicide bombers," or "martyrs," the latter the preference of Palestinian activists? Should territories won by Israel after it was attacked in the 1967 Six-Day War, as well as its later settlements in the West Bank, be called "occupied territories," because they are the heart of a future Palestinian state and are viewed by most countries (though vehemently not by Israel) as a clear violation of international law (Kershner & Halbfinger, 2017)? Should they be more neutrally called "disputed territories?" Or is the term "occupation" biased (and factually incorrect) because, as some Orthodox Jews argue, the area historically belongs to the Jews? By choosing certain words, as well as maps that reflect one rather than another geographical perspective, and determining that members of one side were victims rather than aggressors in a given battle, reporters necessarily made judgments about the nature of the facts (Zelizer, Park, & Gudelunas, 2002).

Because violence in the Middle East is seemingly endless, we have ever-more recent examples of the fraught nature of facts, or the difficulty of defining them in ways that are seen as objective by all sides in the contentious Middle East conflict (see Figure 6.2). When Palestinians protested Israel's decade-long economic blockade of the Gaza strip, coinciding in May 2018 with the U.S. moving its embassy to Jerusalem, Israel turned back protesters, unleashing tear gas that seemed to have killed an 8-month-old girl. But was the girl killed, as initially suggested, by tear gas inhalation, a congenital heart defect, or from causes other than the Israeli attack, as Israeli authorities suggested, though without evidence (Walsh, 2018)? "An 8-month-old in Gaza is dead, but that's all they can agree on," *The New York Times* tellingly headlined. Equally tragic was the case of the death of a Palestinian medic, a symbol of the fractious conflict, with both Palestinians and Israelis adhering to compelling, but different, factual narratives. Palestinians said that she was callously shot to death at a Gaza protest when she raised her hands in the air to show she meant the Israeli Army no harm. The Israelis countered that they did their best to avoid civilian casualties in violent

Figure 6.2 Israeli soldiers confront Palestinian activists in a 2017 protest against Israeli policies, in one of innumerable photographs of the decades-long Arab-Israeli conflict. Reporters must constantly struggle with how to describe exactly what happened in particular battles, determine what constitutes a fact, and decide the most appropriate way to adjudicate competing claims from both sides. News of the Middle East is an imbroglio of contested views of history and truth, pointing up the ways journalism must construct facts, inevitably inviting challenges from both sides, no matter how confidently journalists support their claims.

protest situations, but felt she was serving as a human shield for enemy terrorists (Halbfinger et al., 2018).

The facts – how they are defined, which ones are published, how they are framed, and the variability among media outlets in how they contextualize these facts – is a matter of controversy and journalistic debate. From stories of the Middle East to abortion, journalists apply professional judgments – not set in stone, but frequently debated – as they construct a narrative from a mélange of information and source-supplied interpretations (Coddington, 2014).

Constructing the News

Decades of research on the journalistic distillation of facts and objectivity has shed light on inevitable shortcomings in the objectivity norm and the manner in which reporters assemble information (Boudana, 2016; Tuchman, 1978). The scholarly consensus is that news is best regarded as a social construction of reality, subsumed under the label of constructionism. **Constructionism** is a complex concept that emphasizes the active role journalists play in defining news, based on psychological filters and newsgathering routines. It unpacks the ways journalists come to decide what is newsworthy, distilling the factors that determine what they report, how they write what they do, and why (Fishman, 1981; Lau, 2012; Molotch & Lester, 1974; Tuchman, 1972, 1978). There are different views of constructionism, with scholars delving into some pretty philosophical ideas, like the degree to which social reality can ever be known, the extent to which there is some literal reality that forms the foundation of reporter's constructions, and just which journalistic practices exert the strongest impact on reporters' news judgments.

Returning from the Anti-Objectivity Precipice

For years, scholars unpacked the origins of objectivity, explaining its strategic functions, noting the ways reporters construct narratives based on particular perspectives, and subtly emphasizing the objectivity norm's tendency to reinforce the status quo. The viewpoint is helpful, and a constructionist perspective continues to shed light on the bases of conventional reporting. However, the late 20th century, when constructionism dominated, was a time when there were only a handful of major gatekeepers, not the multiplicity of gatekeepers that vary in their integrity and credibility. And for all the omissions and biases in news, there was agreement then on who was a journalist, as well general acknowledgment that reporters were committed to providing what they regarded as a professional product.

This has changed in an era where people can receive posts that primarily agree with their viewpoints via outlets that are not committed to journalistic values, as well as false messages that masquerade as legitimate news. In this new environment, scholars seem poised to revise some of the common "-ist" wisdom. Have we gone too far in implicitly drawing an equivalence between construction, on the one hand, and subjectivity of news, on the other, perhaps throwing out the promising journalistic baby with the worst of the digitally distributed bath water? For all its insights, a total constructionist view leaves us in a quagmire: "If every view is 'socially constructed,' the view that everything is socially constructed is itself socially constructed, and we gain no insights" (Richards, 2005, p. 19). *New York Times* reporters construct news based on reliable – flawed, but time-honored – judgments. Are their constructions no better than abjectly partisan websites or extremist groups filtering politics through their conspiracy-laden constructions?

Scholars usefully harnessed constructionism to puncture the notion that news is objective and free of human judgments. But this puts us in the uncomfortable position of having to justify even the most heinous, untruthful constructions as just another example of how subjective reporters are. One does not want to make a false equivalence between constructions derived from news values and professional routines, on the one hand, and constructions based on ideological extremism or careless, inexperienced reporting, on the other. In today's messy, blurred-line world, one must acknowledge that journalists construct, rather than discover, facts, while not losing respect for solid shoe-leather or data-based reporting.

In the world where journalists decide what's news, there are not absolute, unequivocal facts. But facts exist that pass empirical, or evidence-based, muster. For example, there is scientific consensus that global warming exists, buttressed by a large body of empirical knowledge indicating that climate change has its roots in human, industrial activities. The earth has warmed by approximately 2 degrees Fahrenheit since 1880, the time when global records were first kept; if greenhouse gas continues without restraints, global warming could rise to more than 8 degrees Fahrenheit, an intolerably high level for the planet (Gills, 2017). Yet a highly conservative counter-movement, which rejects environmental science and fears federal regulation, has sought to influence media reports, suggesting that there are two legitimate sides of the story (Boykoff, 2013). While this plays to conventional news values – giving both sides of the story – such so-called balanced reporting ignores the scientific facts that demonstrably show increased global warming (Boykoff & Boykoff, 2004). The false equivalence between the two sides ignores the scientific fact that increased human-caused global warming presents serious environmental threats, even as there can be questions about the degree to which scientific models precisely forecast future environmental conditions that may differ from the assumptions contained in the models.

Responsible journalism cannot throw up its hands and say, "We need to cover both sides of the story, even though one side has the overwhelming preponderance of evidence on its side. After all, who knows what a fact is? It's all constructed." In reaching this judgment, journalism fails us. It blurs the truth, equating a view with no credible evidence with one that has passed scientific muster. In cases where there is incontrovertible scientific evidence that global warming is increasing, to give equal, "even-steven" coverage to both sides, particularly those who deny the science of climate change, actually represents a distortion and a bias (see Schiffer, 2018, for an excellent discussion).

This total rejection of facts and scientific evidence – the idea that facts are 100 percent socially constructed – results in false equivalence in another area, the contentious arena of vaccines and autism. The refusal to acknowledge scientific facts leads one to conclude that news must treat as equivalent fraudulent claims that vaccines cause autism with immense, empirical evidence that vaccines do not have this impact and ward off serious diseases (Mnookin, 2011). In our current environment, where extremist, biased reports can be seen as equivalent to imperfectly objective, but factually-based, responsible reporting, there is a danger that truth can be sacrificed on the altar of nihilistic rejection of con-temporary science. There are many unscrupulous websites that pitch false information to extremist followers all too willing to grab up ideas consistent with their worldviews.

The wanton conspiracy theorist, Alex Jones, peddles faux facts to his army of followers, claiming that the 2012 massacre at Sandy Hook Elementary School was an extravagant hoax contrived by government-supported "gun-grabbers," a lie that caused great pain to families of victims (Williamson, 2018). A postmodern-styled rejection of all facts would treat Jones's lies as equivalent to the truth that a killer shot 20 children at Sandy Hook, an affront to a journalism based on verification and committed to the articulation of truth (Richards, 2005).

Let's be clear: There is no question that objective journalism is high-nigh impossible to achieve in an absolute sense, and can blind journalists to the ways their own cultural and professional habits of heart influence what they write. Yet, as Sandrine Boudana (2011) wisely notes:

> Acknowledging the fact that a situation of 100% objectivity can never be reached does not amount to admitting the failure of objectivity. Instead, it means that, like any other performance, there is always potential for improvement. Objectivity is something that you do and that you can always do better.
>
> (p. 396)

Thus objective journalism can be helpfully viewed as a goal – an open-minded, evidence-based commitment to truth, a beacon to encourage fairness and appreciation of the multiplicity of perspectives that underlie a problem. Objectivity remains an idealized value, a standard toward which professional journalists, broadly defined, can strive. (In fairness, the linkage between idealized objectivity and journalism is particularly prominent in the U.S. In some northern European countries, professional journalism is linked with taking an active interventionist role in political life; see Hallin & Mancini, 2004; Schudson & Anderson, 2009.) One can acknowledge that facts are constructed or assembled, but also recognize that they can provide us with authentic information about the world (De Maeyer, 2019). As historian Sophia Rosenfeld (2019) notes, it is "entirely possible to believe that much of the world we experience is socially constructed without denying the existence of mind-independent facts" (p. 143).

To be sure, it is easier to make confident assertions about facts in areas where there is scientific consensus than in complex policy arenas or politics. Journalists have struggled with how to describe demonstrable presidential misstatements of facts, as when President Trump stated that millions of votes illegally cast by undocumented immigrants cost Trump the popular vote in the 2016 election. Should reporters state that Trump made "incorrect claims" or "statements without evidence?" Or should reporters call them "lies" because of the frequency with which Trump uttered them (journalists documented more than 8,700 false or misleading claims he made over the course of his presidency), and the inference that he intended to deceive others, a linguistic requirement for the invocation of the word "lie" (Barry, 2017; Kristof, 2019; Leonhardt & Thompson, 2017; Qiu, 2018)?

We live in a world of multiple sources of information, including websites that distort facts to promote an ideology and seemingly truthful, but woefully inaccurate tweets, like Rosanne Barr's anti-Semitic falsehood that billionaire and liberal philanthropist George Soros turned in his fellow Jews to be murdered in Nazi concentration camps (Chokshi, 2018). In this non-gatekept world filled with false information masquerading as true, and falsehoods dressed up in the patina of fact, people need to know what is false and what meets conventional standards of truthfulness. Yet the challenge in curating information, based on journalistic and empirical standards, can sometimes be daunting and difficult. There are many views about how journalism should proceed, but even critics of objectivity are careful not to reject empirical methods of establishing truth (Muñoz-Torres, 2012).

Skeptics point out there is no such thing as facts, but journalists have a more nuanced position, recognizing that Absolute Truth may not exist, but their job is to separate out the empirical wheat from the chaff, sort out information that is not likely to be true from what is, and base narratives on information that is credible and in accordance with consensually accepted rules of journalistic evidence. What constitutes credible evidence, and the processes by which these are defined, are part of the tried-and-true methods journalists use to establish knowledge (Ekström, 2002).

Of course, there is variability among journalists in how they go about accomplishing these tasks. Reporters and news organizations vary greatly in their truth-finding epistemologies. Some outlets are sloppy, ideological, prejudicially publish false information, or geared to pleasing the audience. By contrast, the best journalism in the land – which we admire and to which reporters aspire – employs careful truth-testing procedures, presenting its methods transparently. There are different ways to uncover truth, with conventional reporters applying long-established journalistic rules of corroboration, and bloggers viewing truth as coming not from "one autonomous individual," but "from shared, collective knowledge – from an electronically enabled marketplace of ideas" (Goldstein, 2007, p. 164; Singer, 2006). Both aim to discover the elusive truth, recognizing they necessarily rely on information accurately (and inaccurately) supplied by others, and must depend on time-honored, but incomplete, methods to uncover truth.

The best reporters use time-tested procedures – and new ones, guided by social media – to determine the validity of facts and quality of evidence. They collect factual information, evaluate its credibility, and verify the growing assemblage of facts, recognizing that facts vary along a continuum of relative truth and falsehood. Experienced reporters build a narrative structure around the most convincing pattern of evidence, and evaluate alternative explanations and competing narratives before submitting the most compelling storyline they can credibly construct (Ekström, 2002; Ettema & Glasser, 1998). They strive, in all cases, to be fair, self-reflective, and cognizant of the factors that influenced their constructions (Boudana, 2016; Steiner, 2013). They recognize that even though determinations of fact are based on human judgments, in another sense, the facts are out there, the truth lies waiting to be discovered by sensitive journalistic observers. But discovery of these truths – racism that is hidden behind institutional veneers, global warming previously thought to be scattered evidence of record-breaking heat, hypocrisies among Hollywood's liberal elite – require the application of perspectives and evidence-gathering methods acquired through learning and experience, allowing the hitherto-unseen to be penetrated and labeled with new sets of eyes.

In the end, journalism remains an imperfect method to establish truth, but so are all the others. Its shortcomings – and there are many – should not detract from the nobility of the quest.

Conclusions

News executives have long argued that news holds up a mirror to reality, either because they believe this or seek to shield themselves from unpleasant criticisms of their gatekeeping decisions. Of course, news hardly reflects reality, and even if it could, an attempt at media stenography runs afoul of the normative purposes of news.

Decades of journalism scholarship have documented that in its emphasis on negative events, focus on known individuals and media celebrities, demographics of individuals profiled in obituaries, causes of death that receive the most play, and stories of crime, politics, and international issues, news is shaped by cultural and journalistic judgments about what constitutes the most newsworthy stories and frameworks to describe them.

Journalists distill, decide, and construct news, based on micro and macro criteria. For the overwhelming number of issues reporters cover, there is no such thing as an absolute fact, but different versions of truth, which reporters are duty-bound to cover. Reporters do not simply assemble facts, but decide what the facts are, based on a variety of criteria, as well as how to provide the most meaningful interpretations of multifaceted events and perspectives. In the current media milieu, these judgments vary from those that emphasize journalistic verification to less responsible calls, based on the ideology of the writer that pay little heed to rules of evidence or the credibility of information.

The subjectivity of gatekeeping decisions has led many scholars to unpack and criticize the time-honored notion of journalistic objectivity, yielding important insights. Yet in an era of digital falsehoods where it can be difficult to discriminate between professional and unprofessional news outlets, scholars have sought to rescue objectivity from its postmodern precipice. They have noted that objectivity is a worthwhile, if elusive, goal to attain, and emphasized the importance of time-tested journalistic procedures to make judgments about the validity of facts and truthfulness of information, both of which take on particular importance when political leaders falsely and opportunistically castigate legitimate news accounts as fake to shore up their political power.

These are issues surrounding the framing of facts in an age when facts seem to be up for grabs and online news sites can differ in their criteria for truth, even as the best news outlets struggle to publish verifiably factual information. It all is complicated, intricate, and controversial, as discussed in the book (and later Broadway play), *The Lifespan of a Fact*, that chronicled the debate between a fact-checker who insisted on literal truth of a magazine story about a Las Vegas suicide and the writer, who felt that the larger truth about suicide and Las Vegas required taking liberties to depict the more layered human condition. However, in the world of journalism, news, as opposed to magazine nonfiction, involves an attempt to convey facts, valiantly, though imperfectly, constructed by journalists through a variety of time-tested and contemporary digital procedures.

The criteria reporters use – the broader forces that determine news, shape its content, and constrain and expand journalists' choices – are the areas of focus in the book, as I explore demographic, psychological, political, organizational, economic, and ideological forces that lie behind that fuzzy, democratically-enshrined concept of news.

References

77% in developed world are happy but wish life was simpler, says poll. (2014, July 16). *Guardian*. Online: www.theguardian.com/politics/2014/jul/16/most-people-deve. (Accessed: April 19, 2018).

Barry, D. (2017, January 25). In a swirl of "untruths" and "falsehoods," calling a lie a lie. *The New York Times*. Online: www.nytimes.com/2017/01/25/business/media/donald-trump. (Accessed: May 20, 2018).

Berkowitz, D. (1997). Overview: Why a "social meanings of news" perspective? In D. Berkowitz (Ed.), *Social meanings of news: A text-reader* (pp. xi–xiv). Thousand Oaks, CA: Sage.

Beyond Houston, A world awash. (2017, August 31). *The New York Times* (Editorial), A22.

Boudana, S. (2011). A definition of journalistic objectivity as a performance. *Media, Culture & Society, 33*, 385–398.

Boudana, S. (2016). Impartiality is not fair: Toward an alternative approach to the evaluation of content bias in news stories. *Journalism, 17*, 600–618.

Boudana, S., & Segev, E. (2017). The bias of provocation narratives in international news. *International Journal of Press/Politics, 22*, 314–332.

Boykoff, M.T. (2013). Public enemy No. 1? Understanding media representations of outlier views on climate change. *American Behavioral Scientist, 57*, 796–817.

Boykoff, M.T., & Boykoff, J.M. (2004). Balance as bias: Global warming and the U.S. prestige press. *Global Environmental Change, 14*, 125–136.

Brennen, B. (2009). The future of journalism. *Journalism, 10*, 300–302.

Bryant, F.B., & Veroff, J. (2007). *Savoring: A new model of positive experience.* Mahwah, NJ: Lawrence Erlbaum Associates.

Buchanan, L., Griggs, T., Lee, J.C., & Yourish, K. (2017, October 9). Comparing the Las Vegas attack with daily gun deaths in U.S. cities. *The New York Times*, A16.

Carroll, F. (2017). *Race news: Black journalists and the fight for racial justice in the twentieth century.* Urbana, IL: University of Illinois Press.

Chokshi, N. (2018, May 30). It wasn't the only ugly thing she said online on Tuesday. *The New York Times*, A18.

Coddington, M. (2014). Defending judgment and context in "original reporting": Journalists' construction of newswork in a networked age. *Journalism, 15*, 678–695.

De Maeyer, J. (2019). Taking conspiracy culture seriously: Journalism needs to face its epistemological trouble. *Journalism, 20*, 21–23.

Dixon, T.L., & Azocar, C.L. (2006). The representation of juvenile offenders by race on Los Angeles area television news. *Howard Journal of Communications, 17*, 143–161.

Du, Y.R. (2016). Same events, different stories: Internet censorship in the Arab Spring seen from China. *Journalism & Mass Communication Quarterly, 93*, 99–117.

Dubied, A., & Hanitzsch, T. (2014). Studying celebrity news. *Journalism, 15*, 137–143.

Ekström, M. (2002). Epistemologies of TV journalism: A theoretical framework. *Journalism, 3*, 259–282.

Entman, R. M., & Rojecki, A. (2000). *The black image in the white mind: Media and race in America*. Chicago, IL: University of Chicago Press.

Epstein, E.J. (1973). *News from nowhere*. New York: Random House.

Ettema, J.S., & Glasser, T.L. (1998). *Custodians of conscience: Investigative journalism and public virtue*. New York: Columbia University Press.

Fahmy, S.S., & Al Emad, M. (2011). Al-Jazeera vs. Al-Jazeera: A comparison of the network's English and Arabic online coverage of the US/Al Qaeda conflict. *International Communication Gazette, 73*, 216–232.

Feuer, A. (2018, April 27). Tracking graft, from the bootlegger to the mayor. *The New York Times*. Online: www.nytimes.com/2018/04/27/nyregion/tracking-graft -from. (Accessed: May 1, 2018).

Fisher, M., & Taub, A. (2018, April 26). Does Facebook just harbor extremists? Or does it create them? *The New York Times*, A11.

Fishman, M. (1981). Crime waves as ideology. In S. Cohen & J. Young (Eds.), *The manufacture of news: Social problems, deviance and the mass media* (pp. 98–117). London: Constable.

Friedman, M. (2018, May 17). The split-screen fallacy. *The New York Times*, A23.

Galtung, J., & Ruge, M.H. (1965). The structure of foreign news. *Journal of Peace Research, 2*, 64–90.

Gans, H.J. (2004). *Deciding what's news: A study of CBS evening news, NBC nightly news, Newsweek and Time* (25th anniversary edition). Evanston, IL: Northwestern University Press.

Gills, J. (2017, September 19). Climate change is complex. We've got answers to your questions. *The New York Times*. Online: www.nytimes.com/interactive/ 2017/climate/what-is-clim. (Accessed: May 30, 2018).

Glaberson, W. (2013, April 13). Faltering courts, mired in delays. *The New York Times*. Online: archive.nytimes.com/www.nytimes.com/2013/04/14/nyregion. (Accessed: May 1, 2018).

Goldstein, D. (2018, May 23). Grim tally obscures statistical reality: Schools are "safest place" for children. *The New York Times*, A13.

Goldstein, T. (2007). *Journalism and truth: Strange bedfellows*. Evanston, IL: Northwestern University Press.

Grabe, M.E. (1999). Television news magazine crime stories: A functionalist perspective. *Critical Studies in Mass Communication, 16*, 155–171.

Gutsche, Jr., R.E., & Salkin, E. (2016). Who lost what? An analysis of myth, loss, and proximity in news coverage of the Steubenville rape. *Journalism, 17*, 456–473.

Hackett, R.A. (1984). Decline of a paradigm? Bias and objectivity in news media studies. *Critical Studies in Mass Communication, 1*, 229–259.

Halbfinger, D.M., Al-Hlou, Y., Browne, M., Abuheweila, I., & Collier, N. (2018, December 30). A conflict, and a life, laid bare by a bullet. *The New York Times, 1*, 10–12.

Hallin, D.C., & Mancini, P. (2004). *Comparing media systems: Three models of media and politics*. New York: Cambridge University Press.

Hanitzsch, T. (2007). Deconstructing journalism culture: Toward a universal theory. *Communication Theory, 17*, 367–385.

Hermans, L., & Gyldensted, C. (2019). Elements of constructive journalism: Characteristics, practical application and audience valuation. *Journalism, 20,* 535–551.

Joseph, Y. (2018, August 21). Aretha Franklin's imperial magic. *The New York Times,* C1, C4.

Kaplan, F. (2003, March 24). Patriot games. *Slate.* Online: www.slate.com/articles/news_and_politics/war_stories/2003/03/patriot_g. (Accessed: May 29, 2018).

Kershner, I., & Halbfinger, D.M. (2017, October 17). Israel presses forward on West Bank settlement plans, but guardedly. *The New York Times,* A8.

Kitch, C. (2000). "A news of feeling as well as fact": Mourning and memorial in American newsmagazines. *Journalism, 1,* 171–195.

Kristof, N. (2019, February 28). A racist ... a con man ... a cheat. *The New York Times,* A27.

Lau, R.W.K. (2012). Re-theorizing news' construction of reality: A realist-discourse-theoretic approach. *Journalism, 13,* 886–902.

Leonhardt, D. (2018, March 5). Letting teenagers live. *The New York Times,* A27.

Leonhardt, D., & Thompson, S.A. (2017, June 25). Trump's lies. *The New York Times* (Sunday Review), 10.

Lippmann, W. (1922). *Public opinion.* New York: Macmillan.

Marantz, A. (2018, April 16). About Facebook. *The New Yorker,* 19–20.

McDonald, W. (2018, March 11). Why most obits are still of white men. *The New York Times* (Sunday Review), 15.

McManus, J., & Dorfman, L. (2005). Functional truth or sexist distortion? Assessing a feminist critique of intimate violence reporting. *Journalism, 6,* 43–65.

Mindich, T.Z. (2002). September 11 and its challenge to journalism criticism. *Journalism, 3,* 22–30.

Mnookin, S. (2011). *The panic virus: A true story of medicine, science, and fear.* New York: Simon & Schuster.

Molotch, H., & Lester, M. (1974). News as purposive behaviour: On the strategic use of routine events, accidents, and scandals. *American Sociological Review, 39,* 101–112.

Muravchik, J. (1983, January). Misreporting Lebanon. *Policy Review, 23,* 11–66.

Muñoz-Torres, J.R. (2012). Truth and objectivity in journalism: Anatomy of an endless misunderstanding. *Journalism Studies, 13,* 566–582.

Nerone, J.C. (2015). *The media and public life: A history.* Malden, MA: Polity Press.

Newhagen, J.E., & Reeves, B. (1991). Emotion and memory responses for negative political advertising: A study of television commercials used in the 1988 presidential election. In F. Biocca (Ed.), *Television and political advertising, Volume 1: Psychological processes* (pp. 197–220). Hillsdale, NJ: Lawrence Erlbaum Associates.

Nossek, H. (2004). Our news and their news: The role of national identity in the coverage of foreign news. *Journalism, 5,* 343–368.

Ordway, D.-M. (2018). Police use of force: Most suspects are not injured. *Journalist's Resource: Research on Today's News Topics.* Online: https://journalistsresource.org/studies/government/criminal-justice/p. (Accessed: May 8, 2018).

Patterson, T.E. (1993). *Out of order.* New York: Knopf.

Patterson, T.E. (2016, July 11). *News coverage of the 2016 presidential primaries: Horse race reporting has consequences.* Harvard Kennedy School Shorenstein

Center on Media, Politics and Public Policy. Online: http://shorensteincenter.org /news-coverage-2016-presidential-primarie. (Accessed: December 6, 2018).

Perloff, R.M. (2019). *The dynamics of political communication: Media and politics in a digital age.* New York: Routledge.

Poindexter, P.M., Smith, L., & Heider, D. (2003). Race and ethnicity in local television news: Framing, story assignments, and source selections. *Journal of Broadcasting & Electronic Media, 47,* 524–536.

Qiu, L. (2018, December 31). Deciphering the patterns in Trump's lies. *The New York Times,* A14.

Richards, I. (2005). *Quagmires and quandaries: Exploring journalism ethics.* Sydney, Australia: University of New South Wales Press.

Robinson, S., & DeShano, C. (2011). "Anyone can know": Citizen journalism and the interpretive community of the mainstream press. *Journalism, 12,* 963–982.

Romano, C. (1986). The grisly truth about bare facts. In R.K. Manoff & M. Schudson (Eds.), *Reading the news: A Pantheon guide to popular culture* (pp. 38–78). New York: Pantheon Books.

Rosenfeld, S. (2019). *Democracy and truth: A short history.* Philadelphia, PA: University of Pennsylvania Press.

Salovaara-Moring, I. (2009). Dead ground: Time-spaces of conflict, news, and cultural understanding. *The Communication Review, 12,* 349–368.

Schiffer, A.J. (2018). *Evaluating media bias.* Lanham, MD: Rowman & Littlefield.

Schudson, M. (1978). *Discovering the news: A social history of American newspapers.* New York: Harper.

Schudson, M., & Anderson, C. (2009). Objectivity, professionalism, and truth seeking in journalism. In K. Wahl-Jorgensen & T. Hanitzsch (Eds.), *The handbook of journalism studies* (pp. 88–101). Thousand Oaks, CA: Sage.

Segev, E. (2015). Visible and invisible countries: News flow theory revisited. *Journalism, 16,* 412–428.

Shoe, D. (2018, June 30). This week in good news. *The New York Times,* A2.

Shoemaker, P.J., & Cohen, A.A. (2006). *News around the world.* New York: Routledge.

Shoemaker, P.J., & Reese, S.D. (2014). *Mediating the message in the 21st century: A media sociology perspective* (3rd ed.). New York: Routledge.

Shoemaker, P.J., & Vos, T.P. (2009). *Gatekeeping theory.* New York: Routledge.

Singer, J.B. (2006). *Truth and transparency: Bloggers' challenge to professional autonomy in defining and enacting two journalistic norms.* Paper presented to the annual convention of the Association for Education in Journalism.

Smith, M. (2018, December 23). Cameras, bolts and an elusive goal: To sleep in heavenly peace. *The New York Times, 1,* 22.

Soroka, S.N. (2014). *Negativity in democratic politics: Causes and consequences.* New York: Cambridge University Press.

Steiner, L. (2013). Less falseness as antidote to the anxieties of postmodernism. In B. Brennen (Ed.), *Assessing evidence in a postmodern world* (pp. 113–136). Milwaukee, WI: Marquette University Press.

Sui, M., Dunaway, J., Sobek, D., Abad, A., Goodman, L., & Saha, P. (2017). U.S. News coverage of global terrorist incidents. *Mass Communication & Society, 20,* 895–908.

Tuchman, G. (1972). Objectivity as strategic ritual: An examination of newsmen's notions of objectivity. *American Journal of Sociology, 77,* 660–679.

Tuchman, G. (1978). *Making news: A study in the construction of reality.* New York: Free Press.

Walsh, D. (2018, May 17). An 8-month-old in Gaza is dead, but that's all they can agree on. *The New York Times*, A8.

Williamson, E. (2018, May 24). Sandy Hook suits target fabulist and online "post truth" culture. *The New York Times*, A1, A16.

Zelizer, B. (2004a). When facts, truth, and reality are God-terms: On journalism's uneasy place in cultural studies. *Communication and Critical/Cultural Studies, 1,* 100–119.

Zelizer, B. (2004b). *Taking journalism seriously: News and the academy.* Thousand Oaks, CA: Sage.

Zelizer, B. (2017). *What journalism could be.* Cambridge, UK: Polity Press.

Zelizer, B., Park, D., & Gudelunas, D. (2002). How bias shapes the news: Challenging *The New York Times*' status as a newspaper of record on the Middle East. *Journalism, 3,* 283–307.

7 Do Journalists' Personal Attributes Shape News?

Myths and Realities

What makes news tick? Do hippie-dippy liberal reporters inject their biases into news? Why do some stories get big play, while others never see the light of day? What role does the almighty dollar play in today's news?

These are some of the questions you may have asked about news. There are also others: Does news harbor a distinct political bias? What are news sources, and why are they the lifeblood of journalism? How has social media changed the way journalists report news? And then the most subtle, insidious, broad-based of them all: Do media serve the status quo and ruling elites? Or do they serve as powerful instruments of change, prodding society's leaders into action?

The next four chapters address these and a host of related questions, as I examine the multifaceted determinants of news, beginning with a comprehensive model of news that will guide discussions in the chapters that follow. This chapter examines the first layer of the model, taking us through the impact on news of broad individual-level factors, like race and social class, as well as the role played by reporters' partisan attitudes, the focus of one of the most famous memes – a myth with complex aspects: the notion that news in America has a liberal bias.

Gatekeeping and a Model of News

A central question in news scholarship revolves around gatekeeping, the process by which journalists cull through countless messages to decide which information will pass through society's gates. As discussed in Chapter 2, in the 19th and 20th centuries, news editors at media outlets were the primary keepers of those informational gates, deciding which information people viewed and sculpting it into stories in line with broad values of the epoch. Early research reflected the simplicity and male domination of the process, as it explored how the wire editor of a small-town newspaper, aptly called "Mr. Gates," explained why he chose not to print 90 percent of the wire service copy that cascaded across the clickety-click teletype machines (White, 1950).

Over the past digitally dominated decades, a seismic sea change has occurred. A multitude of gatekeepers, varying in their commitment to journalistic professionalism, have emerged, breaking down the gatekeeping process, yanking power from the old media, expanding choices, while raising questions about the credibility of information that passes through mediated gates. Yet, as Chapter 2 noted, conventional media still exert considerable power, with mainstream news outlets producing much of the news content that appears on social networking sites. What determines the choices news outlets make? Which factors most strongly determine the types of information that passes through their mediated gates? What is prioritized, minimized, or even ignored? How do journalists decide which information – visual and verbal – will form the basis of the public narrative called news?

We begin with a model. Researchers develop models to describe and explain phenomena. People and institutions, particularly media, are so complicated we need to go beyond our everyday armchair philosophizing and speculations about news, many of which (let's be honest) are filtered through a host of preconceived stereotypes and biases. The most robust model – or conceptual framework – in news scholarship is a hierarchical influence perspective developed by Pamela J. Shoemaker and Stephen D. Reese (1991, 2014), recently adapted to the contemporary online networked public sphere (Reese, 2016). The model is nifty because it proceeds from micro to macro, from mentally focused psychology to societal-centered sociology and the broader social system.

You know from Chapter 6 that news does not simply reflect reality. So, which factors shape its content? As Figure 7.1 shows, albeit simplifying a little based on Shoemaker and Reese's scholarship, news is shaped by four forces, distinct but overlapping levels of conceptual analysis. Shaping news on the first level are individual-level attributes, such as race, gender, and demographic and psychological characteristics of journalists. The individual factor, the focus of this chapter and linked in many people's minds with reporters' biases, is commonly believed to be the major – or sole – determiner of news. It can be important, but is frequently overshadowed by other forces. The second factor focuses on the routines, or professional practices, journalists employ to do their jobs. These exert a profound impact on news, as they call on time-honored news-gathering values and norms. Moving up the sociological hierarchy to more macro forces, one glimpses other broad factors, organizational and economic forces. Finally, the most systemic and sometimes insidious: the role played by ideology, elite leadership, and the overall social system on news.

These four broad factors can also be viewed as levels of analysis that scholars apply to study determinants of news. Factors can overlap, as when male editors (individual level of analysis), who have internalized a gender-stereotyped, patriarchal ideology (systemic view) disparage the

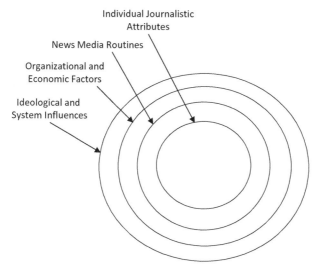

Determinants of Political News

Figure 7.1 A model of news and gatekeeping (adapted from Shoemaker & Reese, 1996).

work of female journalists. Overlap can also occur when a secular, indifferent-to-religion reporter (individual level) overlooks the views of deeply religious citizens, so as to curry favor with the agnostic values of the news outlet's owners (organizational level). Or a reporter, relying on a journalistic routine (second-level factor in the model), turns to official, high-level Pentagon authorities to report on a pending military raid, but fails to give as much play to dissenters who oppose the foray, thereby giving the national leadership favorable publicity, in line with the social system level.

For the most part, however, the discussion that follows will separate out these factors so you can appreciate their singular power, while suggesting interesting overlaps when appropriate. This chapter examines individual-level factors; Chapter 8 describes the critical ways routines – news values, sources, and the everyday business of doing journalism – inform and influence news. Chapter 9 examines core organizational and economic organizational factors. Chapter 10 looks at the ever-controversial, systemic, ideological factors that influence news, exploring the extent to which news props up the status quo. Viewing news through the lenses of the model, we can appreciate the hierarchy of different, overlapping influences on news, as they operate through conventional, partisan, and social media, highlighting ways that power diffuses, is contested, and changes hands through society's digitally mediated spaces (Reese, 2016). The focus, given their continued influence and the preponderance of research, is on mainstream, conventional news organizations; however, the roles played by citizens news outlets and social networking sites are also discussed in appropriate places in the next chapters.

Individual-Level Influences on News

Race and Gender

Let's begin with the obvious: The ethnicity, gender, gender identity, social class, and psychological characteristics of the individual journalist matter. Each, singly and in combination, has exerted profound effects on news gathering. During the Jim Crow and racist eras of the 19th and 20th centuries, when newsrooms were demarcated White-only, lynching of Blacks was covered in despicably prejudiced ways, with stories sensationalized so they would appeal to White readers, the guilt of the Black victim frequently assumed (Perloff, 2000). A number of mainstream Northern newspapers did not even cover the lynching epidemic of the late 19th century, and photographs of the horrific acts were rarely published (Cotter, 2018). For much of the 20th century, news was plagued as much by indifference to the racism that oppressed African Americans as by insidious stereotypes, some of which continued into the late 1990s and early 21st century (Entman & Rojecki, 2000). The predominance of White journalists and lack of appreciation of minority cultures ensured that racial biases would intrude into news.

Of course, there have been enormous changes, beginning with the press's coverage of the civil rights struggles of the 1960s, with its illumination of racism's stains in words, televised pictures, and forceful editorials (Roberts & Klibanoff, 2006). There have been ups and downs in racial coverage over the years; it is a complex, multifaceted story. Suffice it to say that stories now profile achievements of individual Blacks and other minorities, while prominently describing continued structural problems Blacks face, such as landlord eviction from rental housing.

The sea change in coverage was evident in routine news stories describing ABC's decision in 2018 to cancel Roseanne Barr's wildly popular television sitcom after she posted a racist tweet that called a former aide to President Barack Obama the offspring of "muslim brotherhood & planet of the apes." In decades past, news would have shied away from labeling the tweet as prejudiced, let alone racist. Yet, by all standards and psychological definitions of the term, it fit the racist bill.

Over the past decades, news outlets have worked hard to hire more ethnic minorities, hoping to provide news consumers with a more diverse chorus of voices telling America's stories. Ethnic minorities comprise approximately

17 percent of all newsroom employees, with 23 percent employed at metropolitan daily newspapers (The ASNE Newsroom Diversity Survey, 2017). Over the past decade, there has been some improvement in minority representation in U.S. news outlets, notably of Asian Americans and African Americans; however, Blacks continue to be underrepresented in the journalism craft (Weaver, Willnat, & Wilhoit, 2019; Willnat, Weaver, & Wilhoit, 2017). Critics lament that there are not more minorities working in journalism. Many members of ethnic and racial minorities do not choose to pursue journalism and don't advance to leadership positions, for a constellation of reasons ranging from their preference for other career paths to racial to social-structural impediments.

Gender has served up another scourge. Newsrooms were long bastions of male power. Male journalists schooled in the chauvinism of yore demeaned women reporters and failed to write stories exposing patriarchal oppression of women (Steiner, 2009). Presumably, their gender – that is, the prejudices with which male reporters were raised – impeded efforts to expose institutional sexism. Sexism continues apace, as graphically apparent in the 2017 revelations that luminary journalists – Matt Lauer, Bill O'Reilly, Mark Halperin, and Charlie Rose – engaged in sexual harassment, including nudity and wanton sexual advances, revelations that cost them their jobs (Steiner, 2019).

Once again, news has made significant progress, as these exposés of male sexual abuse were reported in the media, in many cases the dirt dug up by female reporters. We are long past the journalistic sexism of years past, where female writers of newspaper advice columns upheld gendered attitudes. In one case an advice columnist counseled women who complained that their husbands were brutes against pursuing divorce. "My heart bleeds for you. But will you be any better off if you are divorced? A beast of a husband is no worse than the wolf at the door," she wrote (Weisberg, 2018, p. 5).

The #MeToo movement, galvanized by news exposés and stimulating a multitude of online news stories showcasing female empowerment, is a testament to the distance women have travelled from the long-ago era of newswomen subservience. Women now account for close to 40 percent of U.S. journalists, the exact proportion depending on the survey; this is nearly double the percentage in 1971, and a higher proportion than in other professional occupations (The ASNE Newsroom Diversity Survey, 2017; Willnat & Weaver, 2014; Willnat, Weaver, & Wilhoit, 2017). In nearly two-thirds of American newspapers, a woman journalist was a top editor, although, for individual and structural reasons, the majority of bosses at U.S. newspapers are men (Jurkowitz, 2014).

From a philosophical perspective, these findings raise the difficult question of the degree to which newsrooms *should* reflect demographics in the larger society, and whether news organizations should place greater priority on hiring women reporters and journalists of color, as opposed to, for example, reporters from working-class and more reli-gious backgrounds. This raises the freighted issue of affirmative action, and arguments can be given on both sides, with legitimate, but different values underlying the pro and con positions (Schuck, 2017). Suffice it to say that the consensus among many journalists is that the ability to sensitively describe problems facing people who have faced discrimina-tion over the years is enhanced by the presence in the newsroom of those who have experienced these problems themselves.

Besides race and gender, the sexual orientation of reporters has influenced news. In June, 1969, conventional – presumably heterosexual – male reporters missed the significance of the Stonewall uprising, the violence that erupted after police raided New York City's famous Stone-wall Inn, a gay bar in Greenwich Village, presaging the emergence of the gay rights movement. Openly engaging in homosexual behavior was generally illegal at the time, so gay men flocked to bars like Stonewall. When the police decided to crack down on Stonewall on June 29, 1969, violence ensued. "Hundreds of young men went on a rampage," *The New York Times* reported, with a pro-police slant, adding that men were arrested for not wearing gender-appropriate clothing. The headline – "4 Policemen hurt in 'Village' Raid" – focused on injuries to the police (On This Day in History, 2018).

In a similar vein, more than a decade later, the press ignored or marginalized the onset of the AIDS epidemic, with its devastating impact on gay men (Kinsella, 1988). Even the editorially liberal *New York Times* did not permit the use of the descriptor "gay," at that time, preferring "homosexual," with its negative connotations (Altman, 2018). Of course, this has changed exponentially over time, as gay deaths from AIDS were covered with great compassion. LGBT Pride Month, held in June to coincide with Stonewall, is covered extensively, particularly in *The Times*, which devoted a special celebratory section to the event.

On the individual level of analysis, one might wonder about the impact of being a minority or a woman reporter, or both, on a particular reporter. To the extent that membership in a broad social category lends empathy to the problems of the group, minority and female reporters may gather and write news that is more closely in tune with the challenges these groups face in American society. However, minority and women reporters are also *reporters* with journalistic pas-sions and values, and they balance their race or gender with professional values. The intersection between demographic categories and the indivi-dual reporter's journalistic perspective are not always predictable, nor do they necessarily result in simple, politically correct outcomes.

Case in point: *New York Times* reporter John Eligon is a sensitive writer who happens to be Black and has personally experienced racial profiling. In covering the tragic aftermath of the police shooting of Michael Brown, a Black teenager, in Ferguson Missouri in 2014, Eligon did not sugarcoat or explain away Brown's troubled upbringing, based on liberal sympathies. On the contrary, in an affecting profile piece of Brown after the controversial shooting, he described Brown's stealing cigars from a convenience store, pushing the clerk into a store display case, and his use of alcohol and drugs. He described the 18-year-old Brown as "no angel," two pejorative words that provoked outrage on the Internet, suggesting to some that Brown was partly responsible for his unjust shooting. Eligon later regretted his choice of words (Sullivan, 2014). Others might argue that the word choice was journalistically appropriate, because it was ironically intended to play off an opening paragraph in the article, in which Brown told his father he saw the form of an angel in dark clouds that hovered overhead after a storm.

Gender also exerts unexpected effects when it intersects with the highly professional values of a top-notch female reporter, in this case Amy Chozick, who covered Hillary Clinton's 2016 presidential campaign for *The New York Times*. You might think it would all be sweetness and light for the Clinton campaign, with a stalwart female reporter covering the campaign of a long-time feminist candidate. Not exactly. Clinton aides criticized Chozick for referring to Clinton's ambition, or for claiming Clinton acted in a "secretive" way. Clinton supporters told her "you're jealous, you want to take another woman" or "you're a mean girl." Chozick, her professionalism shining through, said that she didn't think being secretive had anything to do with a candidate's gender. "I mean, she's running for president," Chozick said. "If she's being secretive by keeping a private [email]server in her basement ... I don't think that has to do with gender," she added.

At the same time, people who did not necessarily support Clinton also criticized Chozick, claiming she was all in for Hillary, charging that she was "in the tank" for Hillary simply because she and Clinton were both women (Covering Hillary Clinton, 2016). Gender came to the foreground, but not by blindly causing Chozick to cover issues in a gender-correct way. If anything, gender was less important than the reporter's carefully honed professionalism. So, when it comes to broad demographic categories like gender and race, their effects are always complicated by the personality and values of a reporter, and the context in which the reporting occurs.

Social Class

Reporting used to be a working-class gig. Far more than today and certainly in celebrated movies, journalists were depicted as hard-bitten, working-class stiffs, with a rough exterior and a big heart – "rude, many times divorced, hard-drinking, cigarette-smoking, social misfits who will do anything for a front-page byline" (Gersh, 1991). The rude, social misfits part may still be true, and the desire to do anything for a byline –

a big ego craving attention – sometimes seems like an entrance requirement to the field!

During the first half of the 20th century, journalists were more
likely to grow up in a working-class background (Shoemaker & Reese,
2014). Over the past decades, the socioeconomic status of journalists
has unquestionably increased. In the early 1970s, nearly six in ten
U.S. journalists were college graduates. However, by 2013, 92 percent
of American journalists earned college diplomas, compared to 30 percent in the U.S. as a whole (Kreiss, 2019; Willnat & Weaver, 2014;
Willnat, Weaver, & Wilhoit, 2017). Given that reporters are more
likely to have a college education than the average American, you
can appreciate why some of those who didn't go to college might
resent reporters, even if their charges, as will be discussed, are open
to serious question.

Does the social class background of individual journalists serve as
a filter through which they report the news? Certainly, many journalists
felt this way themselves, feeling in 2016 that they missed – or failed to
cover until it was obvious – the story of Trump's support among Rust
Belt and working-class voters. Arguably, journalists' middle- or upper-
middle-class upbringing could have blinded them for a time to exploring
reasons for the strong support Trump received in working-class quarters.
On the other hand, many experts, some undoubtedly from working-class
backgrounds, missed this story until it was obvious, too.

In any case, the impact of class on newswork is complex, with little
empirical support for grand generalizations. What is more interesting is
the public *perception* that reporters are part of a high-SES, liberal elite and
this influences how they cover the news. This brings us to one of the
biggest media-crazed roller-coaster rides of this book, a trek through the
never-ending, "can't-get-away-from-it" charge that news reflects a liberal
bias, a result of reporters' reputed liberal attitudes and the way they
intrude into their reporting. The main question here is simple: Is it true?

Unpacking the Liberal News Bias Myth

It is an article of faith among conservatives, a veritable fact – an obvious
aspect of the media landscape, akin to observing that more than 70 percent of the Earth's surface is covered by water, the idea that we are
surrounded by a liberal media with a patently liberal bias. Sean Hannity,
the Fox anchor who is a strong supporter of President Donald Trump,
constantly warns viewers about The Media, by which he means not the
wildly popular conservative Fox News, but the liberal news outlets that,
in his view, blanket the airwaves. Sarah Palin, the television commenta-
tor and 2008 Republican vice-presidential candidate, invented a term to
mock the mainstream media: the "lamestream" liberal news media,
which propagates liberal Democratic views.

To conservative author and television personality Ann Coulter, "the media are so partisan that many people are under the impression that they must take their marching orders directly from the Democratic National Committee" (Coulter, 2008, p. 19).

A Republican bumper sticker (circa 1992) laid out the charge plainly and bluntly: "Annoy the Media – Reelect Bush."

Charges of liberal news bias are hardly new. They date back to Republican Vice President Spiro Agnew's accusations in 1969 about the power of "a small band of network commentators and self-appointed analysts" who were hostile to President Richard Nixon (Gitlin, 2018). Popularized by conservative intellectuals in the 1990s, the liberal bias thesis encouraged the formation of conservative news outlets, like the magazine, *The Weekly Standard*, and Fox News, which touted the notion that the media harbor a love for liberalism or passion for progressivism, to make the point alliteratively, in the tradition of the late conservative columnist William Safire, who popularly penned some of these notions.

The terms "liberal bias" and now "fake news" are part of the political lexicon, popular memes. Egged on by these popular narratives, of the many Americans who perceive the news is partisan, 64 percent believe it favors Democrats; just 22 percent say it favors Republicans (Edsall, 2018). You have undoubtedly heard the charges raised and perhaps conjured up evidence yourself that supports the claim of liberal press bias. But are the charges correct? Do they have empirical support?

Two issues are frequently conflated. The first is the political loyalties of journalists; are reporters predominately liberal? The second is whether news flows from, or is determined by, journalists' liberal biases. At first blush it may seem that if the first is true, the second must be as well. As you will see, the entire matter of liberal news bias is intriguingly more intricate than what it appears. For to convincingly demonstrate that at the individual level of analysis, the psychological beliefs of reporters are of consequence, we must demonstrate that reporters march to a liberal political drummer, *and* this drummer crucially determines the sounds that news emits. One must show not only that reporters harbor a liberal viewpoint, but that their liberal viewpoint is an important influence on the content of news.

Myth 1: All Reporters Are Liberal Democrats

At first blush, this statement appears to be true – until you look at the breadth of the research. Research indicates that the Washington press corps – the journalists who cover the corridors of power, the elite journalists who cover the White House and national issues – do have liberal political attitudes, in some cases even voting for Democratic rather than Republican presidential candidates (Groseclose, 2011;

Groseclose & Milyo, 2005; Kuypers, 2014; Lichter, Rothman, & Lichter, 1986). These findings offer support for conservative critics' charges.

But here's the thing. When you look carefully at journalists outside the Beltway, from across the United States, as David H. Weaver and his colleagues (2007) have, in prodigious research over the past decades, you find abundant evidence that journalists are a fairly diverse political group (see Figure 7.2). Averaging across the years, more than twice as many journalists were Democrats (36.4 percent) than Republicans (17.2 percent), a finding that congeals with conservatives' criticism of liberal bias in the news. Yet the highest, by a nose (for news – no doubt!), percentage of journalists are Independents (37.7 percent), with the rest falling into miscellaneous categories.

Clearly, many more journalists are Democrats than Republicans (four times as many when the survey was taken in the second decade of this century). However, in the same study, more than half of the journalists

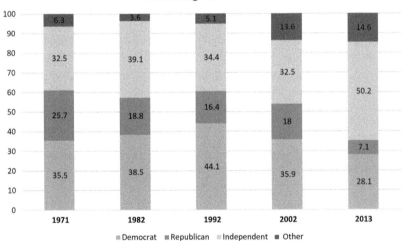

Party Affiliation
Percentage of Journalists

Figure 7.2 A higher percentage of journalists are Democrats than Republicans. However, the percentage of journalists who indicate they are Democrats declined in 2013. Significantly, there is political variation among journalists, with more than 50 percent of journalists calling themselves Independents in 2013, the latest national survey by David H. Weaver and his colleagues. This contrasts with the cartoon meme that all journalists are liberal Democrats, pointing up differences and complexities in the political attitudes of American reporters. (From Willnat & Weaver, 2014.)

(50.2 percent) indicated that they were neither liberal Democrats nor conservative or moderate Republicans, but Independents, a complex, but meaningful, political identification signifying dissatisfaction with the ideologies of both parties, as well as likely acceptance of some positions of both Republicans and Democrats – in essence, perhaps the most neutral affiliation you can locate.

"Overall," Lars Willnat and David Weaver (2014) helpfully conclude, "U.S. journalists today are much more likely to identify themselves as Independents rather than Democrats or Republicans – a pattern not observed before 2002." Indeed, the researchers note there has been a substantial increase in the percentage of reporters who regard themselves as "middle of the road" politically, reflecting a dissatisfaction with the political extremes, particularly the far-right, but the left-of-center perspective as well (Weaver, Willnat, & Wilhoit, 2019; Willnat, Weaver, & Wilhoit, 2017).

Viewed another way, the data show that over the years, an average of 64 percent of journalists did not regard themselves as Democrats. If more than six in ten journalists in America do not consider themselves as liberal Democrats, then it is hard to make the argument that the press is overwhelmingly liberal. And while you can find leading journalists like Paul Krugman who are liberal (actually he isn't a reporter, but a columnist, so the thesis breaks down there), you can find many prominent news media opinion leaders who are conservative, ranging from Sean Hannity to Laura Ingraham, as well as Rush Limbaugh, who reaches more people than print columnists like Krugman.

When you take a national perspective on the press, you can readily understand the range of journalists' opinions about politics. Many reporters work in Red States, conservative bastions, and small towns, not just the liberal Northeast. They hail from different backgrounds and may take conservative positions on certain issues, like tariffs or the war on terrorism. In addition, reporters aren't the only ones who work for the news media. There are graphic designers, research assistants, and assistant editors. They may not be liberal at all. What's more, their bosses – executives and out-of-town owners who ultimately control content – are business types who aren't necessarily liberal. They are the antithesis of social justice warriors. Indeed, as we will see in Chapter 9, these news media execs are concerned with corporate profits and hewing the financial bottom line.

One other point: When you broaden the definition of a news outlet to include the host of citizen journalistic sites, you probably have an even more politically diverse group of journalists. These citizen editors may be liberal on some issues, less so on others. They are undoubtedly devoted to the communities in which they reside, but are not necessarily more favorably disposed to Democratic rather than Republican elected officials, or take liberal positions on issues, like abortion or gun control.

In sum, it is hard to argue that reporters are left-wing ideologues, as the popular caricature notes. There has been a noteworthy swing to the middle of the political distribution in recent years. Complicating matters, the latest definitive research by Willnat, Weaver, and Wilhoit (2017) also shows that when compared to the rest of the American public, reporters do lean more to the liberal and less to the conservative direction than the rest of the population. So, reporters have more sympathy with a social reformist agenda than most Americans – but, again, the fact that less than one in three journalists, in the most recent survey, identify with the Democratic Party makes it hard to argue they are card-carrying liberal Dems.

Myth 2: Overall, News in America Reflects a Left-Liberal Bias

Once again, it is not simple. Scholars have acknowledged that news coverage of social issues, for example, homelessness, gay rights, religion, and gun control, may drift to the liberal side of the political spectrum (Entman, 2010). And liberal writers have acknowledged instances in which the national press seemed to present a liberal slant. These include offering up more positive references to pro-choice than pro-life activists, focusing on the large number of innocent people condemned to death rather than the suffering of families of murder victims (Alterman, 2003), and, in some instances (this is complicated), emphasizing the negative rather than positive aspects of President Donald Trump's presidency. For example, a *New York Times* headline about his signature meeting with North Korea's supreme leader in 2018 noted that the two sides were far apart rather than that this was the first time an American president met with the supreme leader of North Korea (Landler, 2018).

The examples above are taken from the national press, and in coverage of social issues, national newspapers like *The New York Times* and broadcast networks like CBS, have sympathetically covered liberal perspectives. They have cast the media searchlight on issues close to liberals' heart – like civil rights and problems faced by those left behind in America – rather than problems conservatives traditionally emphasize, such as abortion and welfare fraud. Here's the rub: Even granting that national newspapers sometimes cover problems liberals emphasize more than conservatives – and making the liberal/conservative distinction is messy in an era when Donald Trump has opposed positions conservatives usually favor – it is not clear that this is true for news outlets in the country's heartland, and, of course, Fox News (Brock & Rabin-Havt, 2012).

The larger point is that we can't determine whether news has liberal bias based on anecdotal, cherry-picked examples, like the ones above. When conservative critics offer up examples of liberal bias, such as on abortion or homelessness, they may be ignoring instances in which news amply covered the pro-life position or offered negative reports on home-less individuals. While *The New York Times* headline above may have focused unduly on the negative side of Trump's meeting with North Korean leader Kim Jong-un (and that's a matter of debate), other portions of the article and stories the next day noted the historic, positive aspects of the meeting.

On the other hand, *The Times* has described Trump as "mercurial" and "impulsive," negative qualities that may reflect bias, even going so far (arguably too far) to describe him as "the always-about-me presi-dent," and referring to "his demagogy on race" (Baker, 2018, p. A1; Martin, 2019, p. A1). These comments cross a line, providing informal evidence of liberal bias. Yet other individuals have used some of the same terms to describe Trump, with a former CIA director calling his claims of "no collusion" with Russia during the 2016 campaign as "in a word, hogwash" (Brennan, 2018). However, the CIA director referred to Trump's behavior, rather than making attributions about his personality, as *The Times* did. Taking note of *Times* coverage in recent years, some writers argue that the newspaper has unabashedly moved in a more liberal direction in the era of Donald Trump (Pressman, 2018).

At the same time – and this is an important point – *The New York Times* also broke many stories digging up dirt on Democratic politicians, including exposing Hillary Clinton's misuse of emails, which morphed into a scandal that may have doomed Clinton's presidential prospects. What's more, *The Times*, although influential, is only one of many news outlets in the U.S., many of which trend in varied political directions. And in 1998, *The Times* and other news outlets also gave lavish coverage to her husband's scandalous behavior with White House intern, Monica Lewinsky, which cast him in a negative light. Was the press then biased against Hillary and Bill Clinton, or perhaps in all these cases, doing its job by holding political leaders' feet to the fire?

It depends, of course, on the meaning of that popular term, "bias." Based on the scholarly literature, **news bias** can be defined as the *consistent* pattern in media presentation of an issue, person, or problem, in a way that reliably favors one perspective of an issue, while minimizing or distorting the other sides, for reasons that arguably have at least some of their roots in partisanship or ideology (see also Schiffer, 2018).

Stories about the financial melt-down that occurred under Republican President George W. Bush's watch placed Bush in a negative light but didn't necessarily show bias because they had their roots not in ideol-ogy – reporters weren't trying to "get" Bush – so much as in journalistic obligation to cover a big story that tapped into the economic founda-tions of the country. By the same token, positive news about Republican president Ronald Reagan's presidency, which called attention to an improving economy, many Americans' affection for Reagan, and Rea-gan's ability to massage the media, did not necessarily display news bias in favor of Reagan. These were legitimate stories that bore on tangible issues, like Americans' economic fortunes and their attitudes toward the president, as well as new political communication strategies, such as adroit White House news management techniques. In this case, *liberal* critics thought the news was biased against their side, but that wasn't necessarily so.

To demonstrate bias, we need to have consistent evidence and reliable inferences of partisan intent. Intent is difficult to assess, but if there is strong evidence that a news outlet consistently favors one side over another in the volume and tone of news – doing so significantly more than other comparable outlets, in this way putting aside norms of fairness – we can probably conclude that the newspaper, television network or website displays political bias in its coverage.

Research Evidence

Researchers have examined these issues by conducting **content analyses,** or systematic studies of news content that categorize news based on scientific procedures. Content analyses offer little or no support for the liberal bias thesis. In a meta-analysis, or statistical examination of many studies of an issue, D'Alessio and Allen (2000) explored whether presidential campaign news in elections from 1948 through 1996 favored Democrats over Republicans. By and large, it didn't. Biases in newsmagazines were minimal, although there was a slight pro-Republican bias in coverage. Television news showed a modest, though not entirely consistent, trend that favored Democratic candidates.

A more recent, innovative content analytical study of political news in major news outlets obtained complementary findings. Researchers found that news organizations describe political issues in primarily nonpartisan terms, showing no bias toward Republicans or Democrats, except to depict both sides negatively, reflecting, if anything, a "pox on all sides" bias (Budak, Goel, & Rao, 2016). During the white-hot presidential primary campaign of 2015–2016, when Trump's supporters perceived that the liberal media were biased against Donald Trump, the news, infatuated by Trump's celebrity status, gave Trump more coverage than his Republican challengers. As Table 7.1 shows, for the most part, he gained a plurality or strong majority of coverage from July, 2015 through April, 2016. Even the supposedly liberal CNN and the definitely liberal MSBC gave Trump more than 65 percent of the coverage during the spring months. "Incredibly, Trump received more coverage than any opponent on the combined cable networks *every single day* between July 2 and October 29," Adam J. Schiffer concludes (Schiffer, 2018, p. 104). Cable news covered Trump because his unexpected victories and Twitter-based support were newsworthy, guaranteeing audience interest.

Table 7.1 Donald Trump's Proportion of Total Republican Party Candidate Mentions during Presidential Primary Campaign of 2016

	All channels	CNN	Fox	MSNBC
June (partial)	31.3	33.5	32.3	26.4
July	57.8	69.8	54.1	54.5
August	57.1	65.3	50.5	57.2
September	47.9	52.3	43.7	46.4
October	42.2	48.7	38.0	39.3
November	35.5	41.2	32.7	38.0
December	57.8	60.9	56.3	56.6
January	55.7	60.3	50.0	55.9
February	45.2	46.4	44.0	42.9
March	66.7	68.3	65.5	65.9
April	69.3	69.9	68.5	68.7

From Schiffer (2018, p. 105).

Seemingly complicating matters, other content analytic studies appear to provide evidence of liberal news bias (Groseclose & Milyo, 2005). In an effort to provide a yardstick, against which to compare possible press bias, Groseclose and Milyo (2005) compared the frequency with which news outlets – and liberal and conservative members of Congress – cited think tanks of different ideological persuasions. Think tanks or policy groups included the Brookings Institution and the NAACP on the liberal side, and the Heritage Foundation and National Right to Life Committee on the conservative side. While legislators cited both liberal *and* conservative think tanks, news organizations primarily cited liberal think tanks. This seemed to suggest that the news preferred the liberal to the conservative side of the issue.

Wait a minute, though. On closer analysis, problems emerge. First, Congressional legislators are an odd yardstick to employ as a media comparison. Congressional representatives are bound to be political, perhaps making an effort to cite think tanks from both political persuasions to enhance their credibility; they also have a different mission than the press, which ideally strives to present truth. Second, the findings were more nuanced, sensitive to the particular think tanks that were examined and on closer analysis, trending more conservative over the course of the study (Schiffer, 2018). In fact, the press actually cited the conservative National Right to Life Committee and National Rifle Association *more frequently* than did members of Congress. And the liberal American Civil Liberties Union was cited frequently by both legislators and the media, perhaps because a campaign finance law the ACLU opposed was a topic of national interest. This suggests the results reflected the particular think tanks that were examined, and factors other than ideological bias determined media citations. And just because the news cites a group more frequently does not tell us how favorably or unfavorably news media citations are, or how the favorability level comports with those of comparable elite institutions.

In addition, when you look systematically at news media coverage, by topic and across the multitude of U.S. media outlets, you find a picture that is actually more conservative than critics suggest. Examine news coverage of foreign affairs, particularly wars and military attacks, and you see plenty of favorable, chest-pounding, status quo-affirming news, not simply liberal anti-war critiques. This emerges in stories about Vietnam, the 1991 Persian Gulf War, the Iraq war, and Trump's 2017 missile attack on a Syrian airbase (Bennett, 1994; Hallin, 1986; Rich, 2006; see Chapter 10).

Of course, you can find striking examples of apparent liberal bias, just as you can locate stunning instances of conservative bias. For example, some commentators appropriately pounced on apparent hypocrisy in the Roseanne Barr episode of years back. ABC canceled Barr's program after she posted a racist tweet, describing a former African American adviser to President Obama as the offspring of an ape. Yet the TBS cable network refused to fire comedian Samantha Bee after she used the "c" word to describe First Daughter Ivanka Trump. To be sure, one can argue Barr's insult is immeasurably worse than Bee's, given the content of the remark and its long-standing association with institutional racism. Or you can see both comments as equally derogatory and rightly object to TBS's decision not to fire Bee.

There are several complicating issues here. First, these were entertainment programs, so whatever bias did or did not exist does not bear on news. Second, the news media *widely* covered the stories, so readers could judge for themselves whether ABC was correct or incorrect, and if TBS was hypocritical. These too were individual cases; as noted earlier, the determination of news bias rests on examining patterns of coverage over time on many issues across different news outlets.

Critics – they're usually conservative when it comes to this issue – like to refer to the liberal media, as if there were no other. And newspapers like *The New York Times* and *The Washington Post*, along with CBS News, have had a liberal slant on some issues, choosing to frame domestic (though, not always, foreign policy) issues from a liberal perspective (Groseclose, 2011). But there are legions of right-leaning or right-wing websites, political radio (Rush Limbaugh), conservative newspapers like the venerable *Wall Street Journal,* and of course, Fox News.

Conservative talk radio programs and Fox News recruit an audience of about 50 million (Draper, 2016). Overall, Fox has been the most heavily viewed cable news network in prime time and over the 24-hour-day period since 2002, recruited larger audiences than CNN and the liberal MSNBC, as well as generating more than $1 billion in advertising each year. Fox host Sean Hannity, who regularly promotes President Trump's message, recruits an audience of more than 3 million viewers, the largest in cable news (Grynbaum, 2018). Doesn't this count? How can you call the news media liberal, but exclude the biggest – conservative – platform of them all? With wildly popular conservative news outlets like Fox recruiting millions of viewers each night, as influential with their partisans as liberal hosts are with theirs, and, in the case of Fox News, inspiring one president (Donald Trump) to regularly post tweets based on their stories, it's silly to suggest that the media as a whole are predominately liberal.

The coup de grace is the psychological bias that critics bring to their allegations. Social psychologists have documented that news bias is, to a considerable degree, in the eye of the impassioned beholder. When people have strong political attitudes, they attribute a hostile media bias to the news, presuming that news coverage is biased against their side and in favor of their antagonists (Vallone, Ross, & Lepper, 1985). Conservatives perceive that the news harbors a liberal bias; liberals presume news favors Republican politicians and a pro-military, pro-capitalism status quo. Pro-Israeli partisans believe that television news is biased against Israel and in favor of their Palestinian foes, while pro-Palestinian supporters perceive the mirror-image opposite (Perloff, 2015). When people have strong passions about an issue, they are sensitive to any perceived slight or critical commentary, psychologically primed to worry that The Media (as they think of it) will blow the negative information out of proportion and depict their side in a negative light. There are many reasons for this, including partisans' psychological tendency to perceive the news through the lenses of their own biases, ways they sharply contrast news coverage from their own perceptions of what they see, and their oversensitivity to news that casts their side in a negative light. Of course, sometimes liberals and conservative partisans get it right: News does display a bias against their side. But, in the overwhelming number of instances, their perceptions tell us more about their own perspectives – bias in the eye of the beholder – than about news.

In sum, empirical studies and scholarly analyses leave little doubt that the liberal news bias idea is more meme than reality, more myth than truth. There have been instances of liberal bias, just as there are cases of conservative news bias, and they are important to pinpoint and understand. But it is high-nigh impossible, particularly given the diverse, networked public panoply of news today, to pin a particular political label on all news.

Summing up, let's return to the original question that stimulated this discussion: Do individual journalists' liberal political attitudes or biases shape the overall, aggregate content of American news? By and large, the answer is no, because journalists are not primarily liberal, and news does not reflect a consistent, prevailing liberal slant. What's more, on many conventional news outlets, journalists can get fired for expressing a liberal view, as it detracts from the newspaper's or television network's mission, undercuts the news company's brand or alienates viewers who harbor a different point of view. For their part, reporters emphasize that they work hard to separate their political attitudes from their reporting, noting that this is part of a professional identity they deeply value.

In addition, reporters' attitudes are only one of many determinants of news. In fact, they are greatly overshadowed by more sociological factors, like news routines and organizational forces, that strike at the heart of how news is gathered (Shoemaker et al., 2001). Partisanship does play a role in news content, but not in the way critics frequently assume. Generally speaking, it is not that liberal or conservative *reporters* inject their individual views into news so much as *news organizations* with strident political and business slants place their stamp on news. Academically, this highlights the importance of the level of analysis, addressing the particular domain of news – individual or organization – that is most relevant. It also speaks to the fragmentation of the audience and ways that some cable channels in particular, along with websites, deliver up news, showcasing a particular political perspective to reach like-minded viewers, helping them recruit a reliable market share. This is an organizational issue at the heart of so many of the problems that roil news today, and it *is* a cause of news bias, as I will discuss in Chapter 9. But it is a *different* type of bias than the individual-level slant popularly associated with news.

The final section of this chapter looks at the role individual-level reporter attitudes exert on news in the ubiquitous platform that both journalists and the politicians they cover love: Twitter.

Individual Factors Redux in an Age of Twitter

In the old days readers would have no clue about how reporters felt about what they covered, let alone their opinions about people in the news. Occasionally, a television journalist would make an untoward comment on a talk show, or display a broad smile or unseemly frown when a candidate's name was mentioned, suggesting the reporter harbored a positive or negative attitude. But that was about it. This has changed in the Twitter era, where reporters post tweets conveying feelings and opinions, in some cases those with a decidedly partisan bent.

Reporters love Twitter because It allows them to communicate with a large audience, as well as keep up with breaking news and scoop competitors. Editors like it too, prizing its capacity to help a journalist display their personality, as well as building a brand that can encourage readers to follow the news outlet online (Lakshmanan, 2017). Reporters tweet all sorts of messages, some serious, some flippant, some showcasing their work, others offering political observations, and, yes, some showcasing personal or professional opinions (Lasorsa, Lewis, & Holton, 2012).

Occasionally, egged on by the informal spontaneity of the platform, reporters go too far. *New York Times* reporter Hiroko Tabuchi expressed her frustration with Toyota's press relations by posting on Twitter that Toyota's president "took very few questions, ignored reporters (including) me who tried to ask a follow-up. I'm sorry, but Toyota sucks." The tweet was widely disseminated, causing the newspaper's business editor to consider yanking her off the Toyota story (Hohmann, 2011). However, he relented when he concluded (rightly or wrongly) that the reporter was frustrated with Toyota's press operations, not its business, and did not detect any bias in her stories.

In other cases, journalists have been fired for displaying strong opinions, strident attitudes, or prejudice in tweets. A Canadian sports reporter lost his job for posting a tweet against gay marriage, and a CNN senior editor was fired for tweeting in favor of a vehemently anti-Israel cleric who favored suicide bombings against innocent Israeli citizens (Zak, 2011). In a celebrated example, ESPN co-anchor Jemele Hill left her job in the wake of her controversial tweet calling President Trump "a white supremacist," and "the most ignorant, offensive president of my lifetime." In these cases, media executives felt the reporters had offended their audience, tarnished the company's image, or simply could not be trusted to display impartial views.

Notice that the tweets cut across the political spectrum, reflecting conservative and liberal views. Once again, this suggests that journalists do not tweet in one (liberal) voice, and even when they do, more business-minded journalistic editors reign them in toward a more mainstream perspective. Do reporters' tweets telegraph a bias they display in their stories? In some cases, quite probably, yes. In the main, though, most journalistic tweets are nonpartisan, observational, and even cute. They rarely showcase partisan attitudes. And even when they do, they usually don't lead reporters to undercut the journalistic obligation to be fair, or at least the desire not to be fired for steering into partisan territory (unless you are a Fox or MSNBC anchor, where partisanship is rewarded, a different realm; see Chapter 9).

Consider that *New York Times* political reporter Amy Chozick posted a tweet in which called Donald Trump "an alleged sexual abuser," – but proffered the same comment about Bill Clinton (Dowd, 2017, p. 9). But a bias against Trump was not reflected in her political reporting during the 2016 election, where she covered Clinton so critically that Clinton's aides denounced her, calling her "a mean girl" (Covering Hillary Clinton, 2016). Nor did it deter her from aggressively – and, by her own admission, ambitiously – covering the treasure trove of WikiLeaks-released emails that revealed politically toxic aspects of Clinton's campaign (Chozick, 2018).

Let's face it: Reporters have opinions, like everyone else. They can be snarky and catty, annoyed and adulatory, full of petty, partisan, as well as thoughtful, views about public life. The best reporters have more than personal opinions, but (undergirded by enduring commitment to journalistic values) deep empathy with people oppressed by social forces, as well as contempt for leaders on both sides of the aisle who exploit the powerless. We want reporters to bring these personal viewpoints to their reporting; we don't want boring, stenographic bot-like observers. Outstanding reporters, like *The Times*'s Dan Barry and N.R. Kleinfield call on these values. "To keep a reporter's prejudices out of a story is commendable," writer Irving Kristol observed. "To keep his judgment out of a story is to guarantee that the truth will be emasculated," he added (Lepore, 2019, p. 20).

The narrow question before us here is whether partisan viewpoints displayed in tweets (and other personal commentaries) influence reporting. Of course, they can, telegraphing the risks of the more personalized Twitter-sphere. However, they usually don't; most journalists subscribe to professional standards and recognize that they will earn the wrath of management if they cross a political line. More thoughtful, nonpartisan observations do inform reporters' news stories, and they should.

News organizations balance their desire to encourage reporters to develop a popular online presence with recognition that perceived reporter bias can detract from the credibility of the larger news outlet. Some news outlets have developed specific guidelines – do's and don'ts of how reporters should use social media platforms in their journalistic work. The standards, another example of gray areas or fuzzy borders between journalistic categories, are an attempt to navigate the elusive fine line between spontaneous, personal online messaging and time-honored journalistic respect for verifiable reporting (Hermida, 2012). Thus, news organizations emphasize that reporters should "assume everything you write online will become public," including something written "behind someone's wall," particularly information written on a Facebook page intended for friends and family. Even as reporters build personal brands they are advised to "beware of perceptions," recognizing that revealing too much personal information about themselves can tarnish their brand and the news organization (Hohmann, 2011).

Conclusions

When you ask people what makes news tick, they think of news bias emphasizing the first factor in Shoemaker and Reese's model: individual-level variables, such as race, gender, social class, and partisan attitudes. From a historical perspective, these factors have been important. Domination of journalism by White men produced horrific examples of racist reporting. Nowadays, the effects of race are interwoven with other factors, such as the journalistic values of the reporter and news outlet. The issues are similar with gender, where male reporters for decades overlooked (or affirmed, with a wink and a nod) sexual abuse of women. Heterosexual male reporters displayed insensitivity to gay men in their early coverage of the gay rights movement, tending also to marginalize the AIDS epidemic, with its devastating impact on gay men. From a conservative perspective, secular reporters have undoubtedly showed insensitivity to the role religion plays in people's lives.

In recent years, there has been a reassessment, with considerable, sympathetic focus on issues germane to religious people, as well as female, gay, and transgender individuals. But a woman or gay reporter working for a responsible news outlet is not likely to slant the news to simplistically take positions favorable to women or gay individuals (and, given the diversity of these demographic groups, it is not always clear what such positions would be).

Once again, the impact of gender and sexual orientation on a particular journalist's reporting is a mixture of the individual reporter's personal attitudes and the political and journalistic values of the news organization. In general, these latter factors – particularly news values, and the host of macro sociological, economic, and systemic variables to be discussed in subsequent chapters – exert more significant influences on news than individual-level demographics or reporters' partisan views.

Still, the most popular meme of journalism may be "liberal bias" – the notion that reporters are all liberal and twist news so it takes liberal positions. This is a grand simplification and myth.

Content analyses, and a thorough review at the voluminous research in this area, provide little evidence of partisan bias. To be sure, there are prominent liberal news outlets and celebrated liberal commentators. However, the bulk of journalists, and especially their bosses, on the whole are not left-liberal. To be sure, reporters, particularly on the national level, do lean more to the liberal direction, a consequence of their social-reformist values, and this much does confirm conservatives' suspicions. But the increase in political middle-of-the-roaders, and the fact that more than six in ten journalists do not regard themselves as liberal Democrats, makes it hard to argue that reporters are card-carrying liberal Democratic Party zealots.

In any case, news takes on a variety of shades besides pro-Democratic blue, notably patriotic red-white-and-blue when it comes to national security threats to the U.S. On many issues the news favors the pro-business, pro-nationalist political perspective, hardly a reflection of liberal bias (see Chapter 10). One can certainly find anecdotal evidence that national newspapers like *The New York Times* or *The Washington Post* push issues consistent with a liberal perspective, and this understandably animates critics. However, when you look at the entire American media and examine a wide range of issues, the liberal bias thesis falls apart. The political tone of news coverage is complicated, reflecting the type of media outlets, issues under consideration, and public opinion on the topic. Those who accuse news of partisan bias are not unbiased themselves, displaying a tendency to perceive hostile intent in reports they don't like, an example of the classic tendency whereby bias is in the eye of the beholder. Indeed, to many observers, this is the most interesting issue – that members of the public so confidently attribute or project their own political biases onto the complex collage of news.

Let's be clear: There are unquestionably political biases in the news, intensified by the growth of partisan news outlets, but they aren't reduced simply to a predilection to bleed liberal blue. And, once again, the partisan biases of reporters are probably less important than their broader journalistic values, such as whether they believe news should serve as an adversary of government, proffer interpretations, accurately and quickly disseminate information, or motivate people to get involved in public issues, as in the deliberative democratic dialogue role discussed in Chapter 4 (Willnat, Weaver, & Wilhoit, 2017).

And even when individual reporters inject partisan bias into the news, it remains only one type of news bias (Schiffer, 2018). There is bias stemming from intrusion of sensational content, bias resulting from an emphasis on the strategic political game, bias that results from emphasizing click-bait stories that prioritize funny lists, bias emerging from playing up lucrative urban developments, bias toward the home town sports team, and, of course, toward the home country when it is under attack. Not all these biases are bad from a normative perspective, and journalists have to straddle the always-blurred lines between normative values that favor one versus another bias. Ultimately, the use of the term "bias," so centrally part of the public's wheelhouse, to describe news, falls short because the term is so general that it becomes useless as a descriptor. The term "bias" is an exclamation that lambasts news ("it's biased, it's bad; you see!") rather than a concept that helps us understand and improve journalism.

What makes news tick is an important question to ask, both intellectually and for citizens in a democracy. The answers are different than one might think, as you will appreciate when you turn to the next chapter, with its focus on core factors that shape news, forces that are much different than the media memes we frequently encounter.

References

Alterman, E. (2003). *What liberal media? The truth about bias and the news.* New York: Basic Books.

Altman, L. (2018, April 22). What no one could have predicted *T· The New York Times Style Magazine*, 88.

Baker, P. (2018, September 14). Trump rejects a storm's tally as winds roar. *The New York Times*, A1, A20.

Bennett, W.L. (1994). The news about foreign policy. In W.L. Bennett & D. L. Paletz (Eds.), *Taken by storm: The media, public opinion, and U.S. foreign policy in the Gulf War* (pp. 12–40). Chicago, IL: University of Chicago Press.

Brennan, J.O. (2018, August 16). John Brennan: President Trump's claims of no collusion are hogwash. *The New York Times*. Online: www.nytimes.com/2018/08/16/opinion/john-brennan. (Accessed: December 11, 2018).

Brock, D., Rabin-Havt, A., & Media Matters for America. (2012). *The fox effect: How Roger Ailes turned a network into a propaganda machine.* New York: Anchor Books.

Budak, C., Goel, S., & Rao, J.M. (2016). Fair and balanced? Quantifying media bias through crowdsourced content analysis. *Public Opinion Quarterly, 80*, 250–271.

Chozick, A. (2018, April 22). They were never going to let me be president. *The New York Times (Sunday Review)*, 1, 6.

Cotter, H. (2018, June 3). Remembering lynching's toll. *The New York Times (Arts & Leisure)*, 1, 14.

Coulter, A. (2008). *Guilty: Liberal "victims" and their assault on America.* New York: Crown Forum.

Covering Hillary Clinton. (2016). A candidate "forged in the crucible" of conflict. *NPR Politics*. Online: www.npr.org/2016/07/27/487620196/covering-hillary-clinton-a-candidate-forged-in-the-crucibleofconflict. (Accessed: March 4, 2019).

D'Alessio, D., & Allen, M. (2000). Media bias in presidential elections: A meta-analysis. *Journal of Communication, 50*, 133–156.

Dowd, M. (2017, December 10). Roadkill on Capitol Hill. *The New York Times (Sunday Review)*, 9.

Draper, R. (2016, October 2). How Donald Trump's candidacy set off a civil war within the right wing media. *The New York Times Magazine*, 36–41, 54–55.

Edsall, T.B. (2018, March 15). One thing Donald Trump would like is freedom from the press. *The New York Times*. Online: www.nytimes.com/2018/03/15/opinion/trump-press-freedom-fake-news.html. (Accessed: June 7, 2018).

Entman, R.M. (2010). Framing media power. In P. D'Angelo & J.A. Kuypers (Eds.), *Doing news framing analysis: Empirical and theoretical perspectives* (pp. 331–355). New York: Routledge.

Entman, R.M., & Rojecki, A. (2000). *The black image in the white mind: Media and race in America.* Chicago, IL: University of Chicago Press.

Gersh, D. (1991, October 5). Stereotyping journalists: Whether in movies from the 1930s or the 1980s, newspeople are usually portrayed as rude, divorced, hard-drinking, cigarette-smoking misfits. Online: www.questia.com/read/1G1-11383674/stereotyping-journalis. (Accessed: March 4, 2019).

Gitlin, T. (2018, February 12). From "liberal media" to "fake news". *The American Prospect*. Online: prospect.org/article/liberal-media-fake-news. (Accessed: June 7, 2018).

Groseclose, T. (2011). *Left turn: How liberal media bias distorts the American mind.* New York: St. Martin's Press.

Groseclose, T., & Milyo, J. (2005). A measure of media bias. *The Quarterly Journal of Economics, 120,* 1191–1237.

Grynbaum, M.M. (2018, July 1). Fox and Trump: It's a friendship without equal. *The New York Times, 1,* 20.

Hallin, D.C. (1986). *The "uncensored war": The media and Vietnam.* New York: Oxford University Press.

Hermida, A. (2012). Social journalism: Exploring how social media is shaping journalism. In E. Siapera & A. Veglis (Eds.), *The handbook of global journalism* (pp. 309–328). Malden, MA: Wiley-Blackwell.

Hohmann, J., & The 2010–2011 ASNE Ethics and Values Committee. (2011, May). *10 best practices for social media: Helpful guidelines for news organizations.* Online: www.asne.org/Files/pdf/10_Best_Practices_for_Social_Media.pdf. (Accessed: July 9, 2018).

Jurkowitz, M. (2014, July 30). ASNE: Two-thirds of U.S. newspapers employ women in top editing jobs. *Facttank: News in the Numbers (Pew Research Center).* Online: www.pewresearch.org/fact-tank/2014/07/30/asne-two-thirds. (Accessed: August 23, 2018).

Kinsella, J. (1988). *Covering the plague: AIDS and the American media.* New Brunswick, NJ: Rutgers University Press.

Kreiss, D. (2019). The social identity of journalists. *Journalism, 20,* 27–31.

Kuypers, J.A. (2014). *Partisan journalism: A history of media bias in the United States.* Lanham, MD: Rowman & Littlefield.

Lakshmanan, I. (2017, September 20). Twitter dustups are a reminder: Journalists, you are what you tweet. *Poynter.* Online: www.poynter.org/news/twitter-dustups -are-reminder-journalist.. (Accessed: June 19, 2018).

Landler, M. (2018, June 12). 2 sides far apart as Trump and Kim meet to end crisis. *The New York Times,* A1, A11.

Lasorsa, D.L., Lewis, S.C., & Holton, A.E. (2012). Normalizing Twitter: Journalism practice in an emerging communication space. *Journalism Studies, 13,* 19–36.

Lepore, J. (2019, January 28). Hard news. *The New Yorker,* 18–24.

Lichter, S.R., Rothman, S., & Lichter, L.S. (1986). *The media elite.* Bethesda, MD: Adler & Adler.

Martin, J. (2019, February 4). Pushed by Trump, opponents try to set example. *The New York Times,* A1, A13.

On This Day in History (2018, June 29). *The New York Times,* A2.

Perloff, R.M. (2000). The press and lynchings of African Americans. *Journal of Black Studies, 30,* 315–330.

Perloff, R.M. (2015). A three-decade retrospective on the hostile media effect. *Mass Communication and Society, 18,* 701–729.

Pressman, M. (2018). *On press: The liberal values that shaped the news.* Cambridge, MA: Harvard University Press.

Reese, S.D. (2016). A media sociology for the networked public sphere: The hierarchy of influences model. *Mass Communication and Society, 19,* 389–410.

Rich, F. (2006). *The greatest story ever sold: The decline and fall of truth from 9/11 to Katrina.* New York: Penguin Press.

Roberts, G., & Klibanoff, H. (2006). *The race beat: The press, the civil rights struggle, and the awakening of a nation.* New York: Knopf.

Schiffer, A.J. (2018). *Evaluating media bias.* Lanham, MD: Rowman & Littlefield.

Schuck, P.H. (2017). *One nation undecided: Clear thinking about five hard issues that divide us.* Princeton, NJ. Princeton University Press.

Shoemaker, P.J., Eichholz, M., Kim, E., & Wrigley, B. (2001). Individual and routine forces in gatekeeping. *Journalism & Mass Communication Quarterly, 78,* 233–246.

Shoemaker, P.J., & Reese, S.D. (1991). *Mediating the message: Theories influences on mass media content.* White Plains, NY: Longman.

Shoemaker, P.J., & Reese, S.D. (1996). *Mediating the message: Theories of influences on mass media content* (2nd ed.). White Plains, NY: Longman.

Shoemaker, P.J., & Reese, S.D. (2014). *Mediating the message in the 21st century: A media sociology perspective* (3rd ed.). New York: Routledge.

Steiner, L. (2009). Gender in the newsroom. In K. Wahl-Jorgensen & T. Hanitzsch (Eds.), *The handbook of journalism studies* (pp. 116–129). Thousand Oaks, CA: Sage.

Steiner, L. (2019). Addressing sexual harassment in journalism education. *Journalism, 20,* 118–121.

Sullivan, M. (2014, August 25). An ill-chosen phrase, "no angel," brings a storm of protest. *The New York Times.* Online: https://publiceditor.blogs.nytimes.com /2014/08/25/an-ill-chosen-phr.. (Accessed: June 21, 2018).

The ASNE newsroom diversity survey (2017, October 10). Online: asne.org/diver sity-survey-2017. (Accessed: June 1, 2018).

Vallone, R.P., Ross, L., & Lepper, M.R. (1985). The hostile media phenomenon: Biased perception and perceptions of media bias in coverage of the Beirut massacre. *Journal of Personality and Social Psychology, 49,* 577–585.

Weaver, D.H., Beam, R.A., Brownlee, B.J., Voakes, P.S., & Wilhoit, G.C. (2007). *The American journalist in the 21st century: U.S. news people at the dawn of a new millennium.* Mahwah, NJ: Erlbaum Associates.

Weaver, D.H., Willnat, L., & Wilhoit, G.C. (2019). The American journalist in the digital age: Another look at U.S. news people. *Journalism & Mass Communication Quarterly, 96,* 101–130.

Weisberg, J. (2018, April 29). Dear Abby, #MeToo. *The New York Times (Sunday Review),* 5.

White, D.M. (1950). The "Gate Keeper": A case study in the selection of news. *Journalism Quarterly, 27,* 383–390.

Willnat, L., & Weaver, D.H. (2014). *The American journalist in the digital age: Key findings.* Bloomington, IN: School of Journalism, Indiana University. Online: archive.news.indiana.edu/releases/iu/2014/05/2013-american-journalist-key-fin. (Accessed: June 12, 2018).

Willnat, L., Weaver, D.H., & Wilhoit, G.C. (2017). *The American journalist in the digital age: A half-century perspective.* New York: Peter Lang.

Zak, E. (2011, May 23). 8 journalists who were fired for tweeting, Part 1. *AdWeek.* Online: www.adweek.com/digital/8-journalists-who-were-fired-for-tweeting. (Accessed: June 20, 2018).

8 Journalistic Routines and Why They Matter

For years, it was an open secret, known by the starlets and studio cognoscenti in shimmering Hollywood circles that Harvey Weinstein, the Miramax mogul, was a letch – a depraved, middle-aged rich man who would prey on aspiring actresses and coerce them into performing sexual acts. But few outside the elite corners of the movie industry knew. Reporters for the fabled Tinseltown magazine, *The Hollywood Reporter*, tried to break the story, but couldn't get the journalistic goods (Rutenberg, 2017). Weinstein used his power to tempt, woo, or threaten people who wanted to talk or write about his serial sexual misconduct. A cravingly unethical succession of actions had occurred, but it was not public knowledge. Formally speaking, it was not news.

This changed in October, 2017 when two courageous, enterprising *New York Times* reporters, Jodi Kantor and Megan Twohey, assembled the journalistic evidence to break the story, leading to a series of stories across the media outing other famous men alleged to have engaged in sexual harassment – spanning "Today" co-host Matt Lauer, TV journalist Charlie Rose, hip hop music mogul Russell Simmons and comedian Louis C.K. – prompting the formation of the online #MeToo movement. The actions that Weinstein and other men performed had all happened, but until sources talked and the journalistic exposés landed on newsstands or pinged on people's phones, it was not, for the hundreds of millions of Americans who had viewed Weinstein's films or seen the other men on TV or YouTube, news.

Overview

The concept that is at the root of the production of the sexual abuse exposés and news more generally is a prosaic, familiar one, with immense journalistic significance. The key word – the gatekeeping factor underpinning so much of news – is **routines.** Routines are the everyday practices of journalistic work, "rules – mostly unwritten – that give the media worker guidance," or more exactly, the "patterned, repeated practices, forms, and rules that media workers use to do their jobs"

(Bantz, McCorkle, & Baade, 1980; Shoemaker & Reese, 1996, pp. 164, 165).

Think of it this way. You have routines in your job, whether a part-time job at the university library or a full-time job in a factory, business, doctor's office, or fitness facility. These routines influence how you do your job, the decisions you make, the work you turn out, and the way you communicate with co-workers at the office. It is the same with reporters. Routines, as a levels of analysis in the study of journalism, operate somewhere between the individual level discussed in Chapter 7 and the organizational level to be discussed in Chapter 9. As workaday aspects of reporting, they are job-related dimensions of newswork, with cultural and sociological overtones, overlapping with the organizational ethos of the news organization (Shoemaker & Vos, 2009).

Routines are the guts of news – the basics of news decisions that reflect journalists' ethical and occupational precepts. They draw on the fundamental norms of journalism. They are the foundations of how newswork is conducted – the foundational processes by which reporters construct facts and weave data, sources' comments, and conclusions into a verifiable narrative. They help journalists do their jobs, offering a simplifying roadmap of how to gather and write up information on deadline. "News organizations and news workers are faced with an overwhelming stream of events and information that must be culled and crafted into news. Routines economize effort," Shoemaker and Vos (2009, p. 60) explain (see also Berkowitz, 1997). Routines operate in conventional news outlets, online newsrooms, citizen journalism sites, and blogs, though they can differ with the modality (e.g., Paterson & Domingo, 2008). At one level, routines are functional because they help reporters do their jobs efficiently and generate hard-hitting investigative stories. They become dysfunctional or problematic when they lead to publication of stories that circulate misleading information or prop up the status quo.

This chapter discusses core journalistic routines, with the first section describing classic news values, as well as news values in the digital age. The second section discusses the routine channels on which journalists depend to get information, focusing on formal channels and information subsidies. The third section provides in-depth exploration, with classic and recent case studies, of the critical role sources play in journalism, beginning with reliance on status quo-confirming official sources, as well as more entrepreneurial reporting via leaks and anonymous sources. The final section takes a digital direction, examining how online and social media have changed journalists' information-gathering routines, altered their reliance on the usual group of powerful government actors, and exerted a host of effects on routine reporting, both positive and negative. As you read about routines, you will appreciate how ordinary aspects of reporters' daily activities take on extraordinary significance in shaping news.

News Values

Let's begin by reaffirming that news is not something objective that just exists, but is "a social artifact: the product, the output of journalistic routines" (Shoemaker & Cohen, 2006, p. 337). News is constructed, shaped, and sculpted by people working in newsrooms that are both conventional and contemporary. Journalists, broadly defined, decide which of the billions of incidents that occur each day are actually covered in the news media or defined as news. "Events are not inherently newsworthy; only people can decide whether an event is newsworthy," Pamela J. Shoemaker and Tim P. Vos (2009, p.25) remind us.

So, how do reporters make these gatekeeping judgments of what constitutes news? They draw on **news values**, a series of time-honored, professionally honed, culturally adapted notions of what constitutes news. News values are important because they signify the professional, cultural, and even ideological maps that reporters call on to make sense of political and public life. In this way, they provide a window on the deeper structure of news (Harcup & O'Neill, 2001, 2017). Two values are central: **deviance** and **social significance** (Shoemaker & Cohen, 2006).

Although deviance frequently has a negative connotation – calling to mind a deviant or social misfit – it does not have this meaning in news research. Deviance refers to events that differ from the norm, deviating from expectation – normatively, through breaking laws or social conventions (which can be a good or bad thing), and statistically, by differing from the average or typical instance. Social significance is, as it suggests, the degree of societal importance of the event, or news item. Events can be politically, economically, and culturally significant or have significant implications for public health. Importantly, deviance and social significance can intersect so events can be high or low in deviance and high or low in social significance.

As Figure 8.1 shows, a story is most newsworthy when it is high in both deviance (deviating from what is expected) and social significance, as in 9/11, the shocking CIA-led operation that killed Osama bin Laden in 2011, the surprising, consequential election of Donald Trump in 2016, and devastating effects of natural disasters like Hurricane Harvey in Houston in 2017. Interestingly, newsworthiness drops, but remains high when an event deviates significantly from normality, but is low in social significance, such as the 2018 marriage of Prince Harry to Meghan Markle, a biracial, divorced American actress who brought English royalty into the multicultural 21st century; the cataclysmic death of Princess Diana in 1997; and deaths of celebrity artists, like Prince in 2016. These events have no tangible effects on individuals, but are highly symbolic, public events that bring together celebrity, media-age values, and the intense emotions of many members of the public.

		Deviance	
		Low	High
Social Significance	Low	**Low Newsworthiness** *(Member of Congress gives speech in House of Representatives; Routine City Council meeting in a suburban community)*	**High Newsworthiness** *(Prince Harry marries Meghan Markle; Surprise soccer victory of a nation's football team in Word Cup)*
	High	**Medium Newsworthiness** *(Expected approval of school levy to fund new elementary school; Temperature rises, though not breaking records, increasing global warming)*	**Highest Newsworthiness** *(CIA-led mission kills Osama bin Laden; Hurricane Harvey devastates Houston)*

Figure 8.1 Deviance and social significance as determinants of newsworthiness (adapted from Shoemaker & Cohen, 2006, p. 9).

In addition, events can be of moderate to high newsworthiness when social significance is high and deviance is relatively low. Reports that the national budget deficit will swell to record-breaking levels is not surprising, but of considerable economic and social significance. In a local community, voter approval of a routine school levy increasing property taxes to fund a school is hardly deviant, but of high community significance. The national budget funds health and social welfare programs, and school levies keep schools running effectively for children and educationally focused parents. In the environmental arena, scientific evidence that a particular year is one of the hottest in recent years is not shocking, given calamitous climate change, but of considerable global significance. Finally, when both significance and deviance are low, as in an ordinary day of Congressional speech-making or a city council meeting, newsworthiness recedes to its lowest level.

It says a lot about news that events that are of no little material or tangible significance, but great symbolic deviance, are newsworthy. News does not necessarily play up the most substantial or socially significant events, but sometimes those that titillate and intrigue because they are different, deviating from what everyone expects should or will happen. Sport offers another example. A nation's surprise victory in the World

Cup soccer tournament is high in deviance, but generally low in social significance, if we define social significance based on the tangible, political and economic consequences of events for citizens and a nation.

Such is the nature of news, a public, symbolic artifact, with fraught relationships with truth. And yet from a journalistic perspective, there is consensus on what constitutes news. Research shows there is strong agreement across different countries on the types of events, people, and ideas that epitomize news, highlighting anew the importance of news values (Shoemaker & Cohen, 2006). To be sure, there are complications. American and British journalists, as a group, overtly champion political values less than their German and Italian counterparts (Hanitzsch, 2009). And reporters' news values aren't the only determinant of news; source routines, organizational imperatives, and ideological pressures also shape news. But news values, broadly defined, exert an important influence on journalistic gatekeeping.

Core News Values

Building on deviance and social significance, as well as other scholarship (e.g., Caple & Bednarek, 2016; Galtung & Ruge, 1965; Harcup & O'Neill, 2001; Shoemaker & Reese, 1996), one can identify a variety of specific news values. These in turn offer a window into the construction processes of journalism and the deeper structures of news. Scholars have identified a host of key news values that continue to influence the production of news (see Table 8.1). I begin with the time-honored classic: novelty.

Novelty

Novel events, which deviate from expectation, are the crux of news. In the classic aphorism, a dog who bites a man is rarely news, because it is

Table 8.1 Classic and Contemporary News Values

Classic Values	*Contemporary Values*
Novelty	Online Immediacy
Threats to the Social and Moral Order	Interactivity
Elitism and Prominence	Participation
Conflict and Controversy	
Dramatization and Personalization	
Visuals	
The Big Story of the Moment	

not unexpected. However, if a man or woman bit a dog, that is news because it is unexpected, deviating from the norm. (Men have actually bitten dogs! Some years back, a man in southern India wrestled down a rabid dog and bit the dog in the throat. Needless to say, it was news!) Sudden, cataclysmic earthquakes, crime waves, and mysterious epidemics, on the negative side, and human achievements, from scientific discoveries to the *first* (media love *firsts*) double-amputee, Oscar Pistorius, to run in the Olympic Games, are by definition news. In the latter case, the news value was doubled when another dramatically unlikely event involving Pistorius transpired: Pistorius fatally shot his girlfriend, claiming he mistook her for an intruder in his home, and the heavily covered trial resulted in a guilty verdict.

Events that are novel and infused with positive emotions, from empathy to euphoria – such as the daring rescue of 12 boys, all soccer players, trapped in a cave in Thailand in July, 2018 (and the rescue of Baby Jessica from a well in Texas 31 years earlier) – also generate news, in the former case news across the world from posts on Facebook to print newspaper articles. These events call on the quintessential features of news – novelty, drama, and emotions common to parents and children in countries spanning the globe – even as equally tragic deaths of children stricken with cancer and everyday efforts to save their lives are deemed less newsworthy, lacking the cardinal values that underpin news, notably novelty and drama.

Social changes that fall under the novelty rubric are also news. These span 1960s student protests, feminist demonstrations, the backlash from conservative pro-life supporters, gay men's uprisings, and joys of transgender individuals, including the story of a trans man, Tanner, who was born female, transitioned to male in his teenage years, and gave birth to a playful baby girl, Paetyn (Molloy & Grady, 2018).

Threats to the Social and Moral Order

As suggested above, news focuses on events that threaten the social, political, and moral order (Gans, 2004). These are newsworthy both because they deviate from expectation – people are expected to obey, not disobey, the law – and they have significant consequences for society as a whole. Revolutionary or popular uprisings (like the Arab Spring of 2011), populist waves of opposition to a country's president, as in the French yellow vest protests in 2018, and widespread demonstrations against police killings of innocent African Americans are the stuff of news.

More important than the mere coverage is how these stories are highlighted or framed (Entman, 2004; see Chapter 10). Is a police shooting described as justified self-defense, a terrible accident, or another racist killing? Coverage is not monolithic, but depends on the nature of the event, the people journalists can reach out to, how leaders frame the incident, the degree of partisanship of the news outlet, and the larger media system (social responsibility-democratic, or pro-government collaborative).

Elitism and Prominence

Just as news focuses on threats to the established order, it also revolves around the way order is maintained by those who wield power in a society. Because news is a narrative account of issues of public importance, it necessarily focuses on people and groups who control the public space and resources. Elites – those influential individuals who wield power and, in a democratic capitalist society, political leaders and owners of mega-corporations – are newsworthy, a fixture in news.

The U.S. president, as the leader of the most powerful country on the planet, is newsworthy. Empirical studies documented that news gave abundant coverage to the president in the 1970s through the 1990s (e.g., Smoller, 1990), and the president dominates the news today, especially when he makes controversial statements or posts emotive tweets that generate conflict and controversy. There is debate about whether presidential news is slavishly favorable, giving the president a propagandistic platform to promulgate policies to the public, or critical, full of digs by a confrontational press. The answer, complicated and contextual, depends on a host of factors, including the president's popularity, the chief executive's communication skills, and the degree to which the issue resonates with elites and the public.

Members of the high-powered financial elite – the 1 percenters, as they are sometimes (pejoratively) called – are particularly likely to be in the news when their actions have highly significant economic consequences, or deviate from expectation. When two CBS media moguls, Leslie Moonves and Shari Redstone – who had known each other for years and watched the Super Bowl in the CBS Box together – suddenly became involved in a highly visible battle over a possible merger between CBS and Viacom, their corporate split was big news (de la Merced & Koblin, 2018). Although the squabble between two multimillionaires is of little tangible consequence to readers, who can only dream of making a fraction of what they are worth, it influences financial markets, corporate politics, and Big Media. Yet it can also produce public perceptions that the news is an elite, out-of-touch force.

News later lavishly covered multiple allegations of Moonves' sexual abuse, leading to his resignation from CBS. Prominent, not always influential, individuals – the rich, famous, celebrities of different occupations, races, and creeds – are also featured because they recruit a public audience. In some cases, when a prominent individual commits a pratfall, has an affair, or makes an unusual (novel and stupid) statement, he or she is covered. Some years back, Fox News online covered 60s actor Peter Fonda's offensive tweet that we should rip President Trump's son "Barron Trump from his mother's arms and put him in a cage with pedophiles and see if his mother will stand up against the giant asshole she is married to." Fonda's apology and criticisms from others brought more news. This example – and there are countless others, such as Kanye West's controversial comment that 400 years of slavery sound "like a choice" – become news not because they are socially significant, partly because they are unusual, but, critically, because the statements were uttered by a celebrity, who is in the public eye. As discussed earlier in the book, news creates, builds, and feeds off celebrities, documents their abilities to attract adulating fans, and fervidly covers their downfall, if and when it occurs. The comments of the prominent – silly or serious – are news, for better (given they are a major part of the cultural scene), and frequently worse (when you consider what else news could be covering).

Conflict and Controversy

This is a classic component of news. News naturally gravitates, like the earth revolves toward the sun, toward conflict. These include conflicts between political parties, government and dissidents, and individuals whose battles over deep, symbolic values (for example, abortion, guns, and accusations of sexual abuse) spill over into the public arena. Conflicts bespeak stories – different stories and narratives about the nature of social reality, and these have implications for understanding the public world, of which news is a central component. Conflicts frequently involve power, and journalism has an obligation to cover issues involving the powerful, along with threats to the social order in a town, city, nation, or online. Conflicts, because they bear on attitudes audience members hold and are filled with dramatic stories, interest and intrigue, drawing in readers and viewers.

In addition to the conflicts described earlier – between police and community members, protesters and elected leaders – an emblematic conflict for news involves politics, particularly the competition between candidates for public office, especially battles over political tactics, and the incessantly competitive presidential game (Patterson, 1993; Perloff, 2018).

Political news coverage relentlessly focuses on controversies – Trump's tweets, Democrats' outrage, drama between the two political parties, the high-stakes hearings involving accusations of sexual abuse in 2018 – because they fit time-honored news values: conflict, novelty, and drama. News is especially likely to thrive on controversy when the rumpus concerns the media itself, as when news prior to President Trump's announcement of a Supreme Court justice in 2018 centered on how effectively the White House was keeping its choice secret from the news media, an instance of "treating the shell game like a proxy test of governance" (Poniewozik, 2018, p. A14). National news was similarly agog about the tell-all revelations of the former reality TV program star and Trump White House aide, Omarosa Manigault Newman, who claimed that Trump employed a racial slur to denigrate Blacks and that he was in a state of mental decline. The dust-up that followed when Trump disparaged his former aide, calling her a dog, was grist for many stories over the news cycle, showcasing the ways frequently trivial inside-the-Beltway conflicts dominate news.

Stories about Trump and politics fit the conflict news value like a glove, classically focusing on political frictions, broadly informing the public about the body politic, particularly when they involve issues that cut to the heart of government, such as Special Counsel Robert Mueller's investigation of Russian cyber-involvement in the 2016 election. Yet these stories frequently favor superficial, ratings-driven, one-side-versus-another disputes, as well as stories of trivial tweets and equally silly retorts that elide deeper cultural and intellectual undercurrents that are more difficult for conventional news to comfortably cover. And they encourage politicians adept at generating conflict to dominate the news cycle, ensuring more news about political trivia than deeper, if more fraught, political substance.

No better recent example of the press's obsession with controversy – and scandals – is the vast amount of television time and online news space devoted to the Mueller investigation of whether Trump colluded with the Russians to defeat Clinton in the 2016 election. The probe of Russian election meddling was the second most frequently covered news story of 2018 (Tyndall Report, 2019). Consumed by the conflict and absorbed by the machinations of a presidential scandal, reporters could not get enough of the titillating intrigue and the possibility of indictments. While this was a legitimate story, and much reporting served the public interest, too much time was spent on idle speculation and exploiting the controversy for ratings, "a seduction delusion" (Manjoo, 2019) that sucked up air time from more substantial stories.

Dramatization and Personalization

Complementing its focus on controversy, national news in America tells a dramatic story of big personalities: a president; his colorful staff (Kellyanne Conway, who popularized the problematic term "alternative facts," and Anthony Scaramucci, aka "The Mooch," who was fired after talking up a stream of obscenities); conflicts with other Big Personalities, like James Comey, the FBI director who was fired by Trump, Oprah Winfrey, whose speech at a 2018 Hollywood awards dinner stoked journalistic speculation that she might run for president (she didn't), and the indefatigable Hillary Clinton; Trump's enemies (North Korean supreme leader, Kim-Jong un for a time, the "fake news media," and Special Counsel Mueller; frenemies (Russian president Vladimir Putin); and, of course, the made-for-television high-stakes "he said she said" 2018 Senate hearings drama between Judge Brett Kavanaugh and the woman who accused him of sexual abuse, Dr. Christine Blasey Ford.

News focuses endlessly on "high stakes" personality duels. In the case of Trump, drama played out every night on cable news with endless prattle about what Trump tweeted, why he tweeted it, how his tweets played with supporters and opponents; and what effect it would have on public opinion and the presidential election. When Trump deliberated on who to nominate to replace retiring Anthony Kennedy on the Supreme Court, the news "turned the selection process into a kind of Supreme Court sweepstakes," tracking the candidates like they were contestants in a beauty queen extravaganza, following the candidates as Trump promised "a blockbuster choice," transforming The Decision into a television reality drama, focusing more on drama than the candidates' legal positions or judicial philosophy (Landler & Haberman, 2018, p. A15).

A similar dynamic has occurred in the United Kingdom, with much of the coverage of the tempestuous 2016 British vote to withdraw from the European Union focused on personalities, like the circus-like performers in British elite circles, than the complex economic and political issues that faced UK voters (Rusbridger, 2019).

You can praise this coverage, arguing that politics really is a show biz reality show about big, outsize personalities who prattle around a big stage, or criticize it, noting that news puts style over substance and focuses on trivial drama rather than exploring deeper social issues. The news cycle, or agenda of national issues that the president emphasizes and the press covers, accelerated during Trump's administration, creating a magic trick by which Trump could (sometimes) escape scrutiny for the latest problem by making his latest tweet the subject of conversation, news could move onto the next ratings-driven story, and thoughtful analysis of larger implications was lost (Flegenheimer, 2017).

In addition to all these major news norms are other values conventional journalists emphasize. These include *firsts*, in which a news outlet strives to be first to break a story, call an election, or announce which of several candidates a president has nominated to the Supreme Court. From a normative perspective, citizens gain little when a news organization breaks its backside to be the first in any of these categories. It is chiefly about entertainment and attracting audiences, a nod to the 19th-century penny press and yellow journalism in which news announced some superficially big event to all who cared to read about it. With the diffusion of social media and its capacity to stream out the latest crisis information long before journalists get to the scene, the news value of firsts has diminished, although in the realm of election projections, the value is alive and well.

Another prominent value emphasizes *visuals*, such as heart-rending pictures of Syrian refugees in 2015, and crying young children separated from their parents and sent to special shelters in the wake of a presidential directive toughening policy toward unauthorized immigration in 2018. Visual images also dominate coverage of domestic protests, particularly heavily charged racial protests. Photos, including those tweeted by news organizations in the wake of violence that erupted in Ferguson, Missouri after a White policeman shot an unarmed African American teenager in 2014, depicted crowds of Blacks wrecking property, but also riot gear-clad police throwing tear gas into crowds of protesters (Blackstone, Cowart, & Saunders, 2017). Visuals can drive news, focusing on the personal, dramatic, and conflicted aspects of public life.

Pictures offer a narrative that is heart-rending and compelling, but sometimes misleading because they elide historical or political background. Indeed, scholars frequently counsel that journalists should avoid coverage of "catastrophic images in favor of describing political, structural, and natural root causes and contexts" (O'Neill & Harcup, 2009, p. 170). This advice is routinely rejected for fear more in-depth news will turn off audiences, although there is little evidence to support such fears.

Lastly, news dwells on the Big Story of the Moment, *the news in the glare of the current agenda.* After the financial crisis of 2008, news focused on the consequences and fall-out of the financial markets, subprime mortgages, a global banking crisis, huge bailouts of banks, and implications for a quaking international financial system. After Trump's election, news examined the plight of the working class, how Trump capitalized on working-class voters, and the reasons why White working-class voters gravitated to Trump. In the wake of investigations of sexual abuse by Harvey Weinstein, an outpouring of news followed, documenting other high-powered male harassment of women, spanning newscasters, politicians, elite restaurant chefs, and blue-collar factory workers.

Once an issue catapults to the top of the media agenda, similar stories follow, driving a feeding frenzy of journalistic output on the issue, begging the question of why it took so long to bring these issues out into the open. It is only when the story has become national news that reporters rush to the scene of the fire, covering en masse what they missed and should have been covering to begin with. Once leading journalists deem these outside-the-box problems worthy of coverage – the onset of HIV/AIDS in the 1980s, the 2007–2009 global banking crisis, and the shattering opioid problem of recent years – feeding frenzies of reporters arrive on the scene, focused on covering news in the glare of the current agenda, writing helpful stories, uncovering facts, exposing malfeasance. There are, of course, a number of reasons why journalists missed these stories to begin with, explanations rooted in journalistic routines, and the economics and ideology of news (see Chapters 9 and 10).

News Values in the Digital Age

Complementing these classic news values, three contemporary notions of news, rooted in long-standing values of the past, play an important role in gatekeeping. Articulated by Nikki Usher (2014) in a captivating account of how news is constructed at today's *New York Times* and, by extension, other media, the new news values are **immediacy, interactivity**, and **participation**.

Immediacy has long guided gatekeeping decisions, as glimpsed in the discussion about reporters' determination to be the first to get a story. But it takes on new trappings in an age of online editing, constant updates, and reader participation (Karlsson, 2011). Immediacy emphasizes the value of freshness, speed, getting news as quickly as possible, instantly – when it happens. Breaking news has morphed from the next edition of a newspaper later in the day to television bulletins, breaking news, which became famous in the 1980s with CNN's global network news service and the Fox-inspired news crawler on the bottom of the screen, to phone apps that deliver crisis news as it happens.

News organizations strive to update stories, constantly changing the look of a newspaper's home page, so the form and content of the page breathe a freshness that propels readers to come back. For example, a *New York Times* lead paragraph on a story about national unemployment changed several times over the course of the morning, beginning with a first post at 8:47 a.m. that stressed job losses were less than expected and shifting to a late morning post providing more context, comparing monthly job losses to those of a year earlier. Reporters at big news outlets are constantly tweeting updates to stories. In the online world of news, the push for immediacy – and publishers' economically based desire that reporters' tweets propel website traffic – deliver up-to-the-minute relevance, while also leading to unforced errors, incorrect information, and unsubstantiated rumors.

In addition to delivering updated content to consumers, online journalism seeks to engage users interactively, involving readers in the experience of multimedia storytelling. Multimedia newspaper journalists, who may view themselves more as documentary filmmakers or video game makers than old-fashioned scribes (notebooks in hand), produce short news videos for the website, available for viewing as a mobile app. In one case, journalists produced a striking series on cell phone-distracted driving that included a gaming simulation in which users guided an online car through highway toll booths while texting about their favorite desserts, showcasing the perils of texting while driving in a way that a print narrative could not. Journalists have won awards for multimedia storytelling, although the quality can vary as a function of the size and resources of the news outlet.

The digital age has also breathed new life into a third contemporary news value, participation, a news orientation that dates back to letters to the newspaper editor and news organizations' soliciting of reader involvement through public journalism ventures. Nowadays, users can play a more active role in the construction of news, reflected in the blurring of the distinction between news consumers and producers in creation of online content, what Bruns (2008) felicitously calls "produsage." Projects highlighting the value of citizen participation include a Connecticut newspaper's newsroom café, where community members can sip coffee and offer up contributions to local news, and a Canadian news outlet that updated public journalism of the 1990s with collaborative efforts that gave community members input into the coverage of unfolding news stories (Usher, 2016). These participatory projects, probably easier to cultivate in smaller communities, must be evaluated to determine the degree to which they involve a majority of citizens, rather than just tried-and-true activists, and the extent to which they actually produce more enriching, deeper knowledge of community events than conventional journalistic accounts. They are great ideas, but we don't know how well they work and how many people they reach.

In larger news outlets, the value of participation takes on different forms. It involves readers commenting in ever-popular Twitter accounts of columnists and reporters; news organizations' Facebook pages where individuals interested in politics or artsy topics can form like-minded communities, with links to the larger news organizations; and organizations' profit-driven encouragement of users' sharing content with (say) non-*New York Times*-oriented friends, who can be lured to the *Times* site and once there, invited to suggest stories to *their* friends via Facebook, in this way increasing the number of people accessing the news site (Usher, 2014). As will be discussed in the next chapter, money, while not the whole story, is never far from the genesis of innovation in journalistic values.

Importantly, as online immediacy, interactivity, and participation have become incorporated into journalists' roles, they have become routinized, emerging as expected parts of the patterned ways reporters gather and diffuse information. Like all news values, they are filled with pros and cons. Some have pointed out that the ability to update via immediacy allows news to correct mistakes and increase up-to-the-minute accuracy. However, critics note, the result is speed for speed's sake; reporters are akin to hamsters running ceaselessly on the hamster wheel, moving quickly, but offering little by way of insight or narrative depth (Boczkowski, 2010; Starkman, 2010). And while participation allows for greater citizen involvement, in theory broadening perspectives, readers who actively participate in news outlets are frequently those with strong partisan attitudes, glomming to both sites and journalists who merely confirm what they already believe.

Digital media do expand the contours of these three news values, infusing news with an adrenalin, richness, and involvement inconceivable in the analog days of yore, in these ways demonstrating how time-honored verities persist but bend with new technologies. The online milieu showcases the increased role citizens play in news, balancing the loss of journalistic authority over gatekeeping with new potential for a broader, more enriched news experience.

The next section moves away from citizens to the time-honored role that power plays in news routines, as I discuss the ways authorities continue to influence news through journalistic routines, as well as how this is changing in the social media milieu. Table 8.2 summarizes main concepts discussed in the next portions of the chapter.

Formal Channels and Information Subsidies

Formal channels are the channels of officialdom: the conveyance of information through official sources, planned events, and press releases. In the past, businesses, governments, entertainment companies, non-profit agencies, and PR agencies disseminated promotional information via press releases. Brands and PR firms have adapted to the digital era by emailing or tweeting the information to reporters, placing links in news releases, or posting it on their websites, using social media to drive traffic to the sites (Scott, 2015). Although they don't rely on news media exclusively, as in the past, PR firms still actively seek out reporters through social media or interpersonally, recognizing that news is a vehicle to promote clients' products.

In these ways, as Oscar Gandy (1982) perceptively noted, public relations practitioners (and other information providers) offer up an **information subsidy** to news organizations, transmitting visual, verbal,

Table 8.2 Important Components of Journalistic Routines

Classic Factors	*Internet and Social Media Routines*
Formal Channels	Tapping into Blogs
Information Subsidies	Social Media Snooping
Sourcin	Crowdsourcing
Official Sources	Monitoring and Posting on Twitter
Leaks	
Anonymous Sources	

video, or socially mediated information that promotes a product or service their client has produced. This constitutes a kind of subsidy on the part of PR practitioners to news organizations, providing not money, but information that offers journalists a reward for relatively little work on their part: the promise of a bylined story.

The news organization receives for no charge the accoutrements of news, freeing it from expending scarce journalistic resources to dig up a story that attracts audiences and advertisers. For its part, the PR agency has transmitted information that advances the client's cause through the publicity furnished by a news story. Intriguingly, Franklin, Lewis and Williams (2010) found that 60 percent of published newspaper stories relied entirely or primarily on content derived from public relations materials.

Although public relations subsidies are frequently criticized in journalism circles, more of which below, it is instructive to note that they do perform functions for news and consumers. PR specialists can generate news features about products and services that consumers find informative and useful. People like to know the best restaurants in town, the most interesting cuisines, the newest apps, the coolest start-ups, to say nothing of new albums by rock stars, new smartphones, and ecologically friendly gadgets. You can get this information from social media, but also by reading PR-generated news stories. There is even a new name for some of these stories: service journalism, which focuses on providing information on products, businesses, and trends that serve consumers' needs, giving informational nuggets, while also offering a platform to sell goods and services.

News based on social media PR posts is not inherently problematic; they do provide a service to consumers and can usefully publicize entrepreneurial startups that want to challenge more established brands. Where they become journalistically dysfunctional is when news outlets don't do their homework or, because of budgetary crunches or a desire to please advertisers, simply list in an online listicle popular retail establishments – let's say new restaurants – assembled from online public relations posts, giving them high marks, failing to consider shortcomings or consumer complaints about health hazards. Similarly, an article that accepts without question promoters' claims about a new fitness or dietary regimen without checking to see if the new techniques actually improve health, raises journalistic questions. Lewis, Williams, and Franklin's (2008) study suggests this is all too common, with seven in ten newspaper and broadcast stories failing to corroborate or verify claims offered up in PR releases. Public relations performs important functions for society, but journalism's job is not to parrot that back, but to let the public know if the services PR promotes do what they say they are doing, and if not, how they fall short. As scholar Jane B. Singer (2010) acerbically observes:

It is frustrating, to journalists and to readers, to see newspapers filled with unimportant items taken straight from press releases or official pronouncements – and that are old news by the time they appear in print. It is frustrating, too, to know that people who might provide a much more valuable service cannot do so because all their time and energy goes into processing this junk food and feeding it to a beast with multiplying, incessantly demanding mouths: a print mouth, an online one, maybe a mobile one.

(p. 284)

If digital technologies "lead to the spread of the 'cut and paste' culture in which journalists not only use PR to inform their stories, but increasingly 'gobble up' stories written and published online by fellow journalists," then online technologies have hardly improved the status quo, as Franklin (2011) notes (p. 104). What's more, by providing information subsidies in the form of free publicity to companies with the greatest online resources, "those with economic power are able to maintain their control over a capitalist society" (Gandy, 1982, p. 8).

This points up a larger issue. From a broader perspective, the problem with gaining information through formal channels is journalistic dependence on established sources upholding the status quo, the focus of the discussion that follows.

Sources: The Lifeblood of News

News is not what happens, but what someone says has happened or will happen. Reporters are seldom in a position to witness events firsthand. They have to rely on the accounts of others.

(Sigal, 1986, p. 14)

Leon Sigal's pointed observation – "news is not what happens, but what someone says has happened or will happen" – is one of the most famous quotes in journalism scholarship. It underscores a major mechanism by which journalism seeks truth. By soliciting information from sources – that is, people in government, business, entertainment, and other occupations who talk to reporters – journalists provide verifiable information that is the foundation of news.

In the 19th century, long before the development of the objectivity norm, routine reliance on sources to obtain factual information was virtually nonexistent. Stories were partisan, emerging implicitly from politicians who shared the newspaper's political view or funded the paper. Over time, as reporters built a more evidentiary basis for their stories, turning to sources became a way to get information, as well as to suggest that stories were credible and high-nigh objective, even if the facts, as always, could be open to interpretation. Dependence on sources for information and the broader negotiated relationships between reporters and sources are core journalistic routines in all media systems, although there are variations as a function of the degree to which the system favors authoritarian, libertarian, or collaborative values (Berkowitz, 2009).

You have probably noticed references to sources in news articles you have read, as when a reporter attributes a statement to "highly-placed sources," to "sources in the State Department" or to a "source who requested anonymity given the sensitivity of the information" (this is controversial). Not surprisingly, a subtle gender bias lurks behind the use of sources. Showcasing gender stereotypes and male domination of the political hierarchy, sources in both conventional news and reporters' tweets are usually men (Armstrong, 2004; Artwick, 2014).

Source Reliance: Strengths and Shortcomings

Sourcing, as it is known in everyday journalism, is a strength of contemporary newswork. It insists that before a news story is published, broadcast or streamed, it have a demonstrable factual, evidentiary basis. Sourcing holds news's feet to the fire by demanding it be backed up by the perspectives of credible others. But there is a catch.

Reporters can rarely report without turning to sources who are knowledgeable about what goes on in government, a corporation, or other institutions. This means reporters frequently rely on – cultivate relationships with – sources who have formal or official roles in these organizations, in short those who have institutional power. This in turn raises journalistic questions. One must ask "Who speaks through the news? Which voices get heard?" (Carlson & Franklin, 2011, p. 1). Who has political power and who does not? Do the sources the news media rely on affirm or challenge the powers-that-be? These questions, glimpsed in this chapter and explored in Chapter 10, require an appreciation of the dynamics of sourcing.

On the other extreme, when reporters solicit information from whistle-blowers (sources determined to blow the cover off government deceptions), their investigative reports serve as a watchdog on government abuse. Aggrieved individuals have disclosed confidential information to reporters, acting as sources whose identities journalists promise to protect, producing the litany of journalistic exposés from Watergate to #MeToo. And while journalistic investigations have complex roots (Ettema & Glasser, 1998) and sources rarely act from altruistic motives, the truth that emerges from whistle-blowing sources provides a necessary corrective on institutional overreach, ensuring that government, business, and social institutions are held morally and legally accountable for their crimes.

This, of course, is the best of journalism: exposés produced by sources willing to talk for the public good and reporters who goad them into talking for the public record. It's the great romance of journalism, the stuff of movies like *Post*, which retold the Pentagon Papers saga, showcasing journalism's inspirational role as a knightly agent of change. The reality is soggier and messier. News frequently does not turn to the whistleblowers, but relies on sources who are frequently available, easy to contact, and savvy at exploiting reporters for their own needs. These sources are all-too-often those official sources in positions of authority. The offer journalistic efficiency, but at a cost: Reliance on official sources can lead to propping up the powers-that-be, reifying the status quo, an informational subsidy of official source control.

To richly illustrate this aspect of source power – the role established sources play in disseminating information through formal channels – I offer two classic examples, one domestic, the other involving a controversial foreign war (e.g., Bullock, 2008; Sigal, 1986).

The Allure of Official Police Sources

New York City Police Officer Nector Martinez took his oath to tell the truth, the whole truth, and nothing but the truth, and then proceeded to lie.

Officer Martinez testified in a Bronx courtroom that after a shooting, he began to search an apartment to obtain evidence, then noticed a woman in the doorway, holding a laundry bag. When he picked up the laundry bag and plunked it down, he heard a thud and clunk, and found a 9-millimeter handgun. He informed the woman, Kimberly Thomas, she was under arrest (Goldstein, 2018).

But there was a problem. The woman was not a criminal. A surveillance camera in the hallway of the apartment building showed there was no laundry bag, let alone a gun, in the doorway. A gun was found in the apartment, but could not be linked to Ms. Thomas. New York police officers have a word for what Officer Martinez did next. They call it "testilying." It's a term that dates back at least 25 years, pointing up a relatively common practice in the NYPD by police officers trying to build a case against someone they presume is guilty, but who, in the view of police, would be hard to arrest because of legal roadblocks (Goldstein, 2018). Stretching – or fabricating – the truth is a simpler way to snare one of the many bad guys, in the view of police, who encounter many criminals every day. Needless to say, this assumes the police are right and the person is actually guilty.

The story about police testilying in the Kimberly Thomas case appeared six months after the actual incident, giving reporters time to locate the all-important facts that exonerated Ms. Thomas. Had the story about the shooting, the laundry bag and handgun been published the day after Thomas was arrested, it probably would have led with the arrest of a woman presumed to be a criminal. Based on reports by official police sources, it would likely have favored the police's – false – account, correcting it when new information from the surveillance camera emerged, but after readers had lost interest in the story and presumably concluded that it was yet another instance of police nabbing a guilty victim. Police, as dutiful symbols of the social order, are frequently the first sources for these stories; they are also easier to contact than victims, who may be fearful their words will get them in trouble.

In his classic paper, Sigal (1986) cites a news story, based on police and housing department sources, that described how a 67-year-old woman, Eleanor Bumpurs, who was "being evicted from a city housing project for nonpayment of rent, was fatally shot by a police officer yesterday after she slashed at another officer with a butcher knife" (p. 9). However, two days later another story questioned this version of the facts. Mrs. Bumpurs' daughter, Mary, questioned the police's view, saying her mother suffered from arthritis and high blood pressure, could not move quickly, and was fearful of people who might break into her apartment. "Shotguns are for elephant hunting, not for an old woman who was terrified by people breaking into her apartment," she said (p. 11).

The Bumpurs' case proved to be an enduring, emblematic example of the intersection of crime, poverty and race. Critics later questioned the police officer's statement that Mrs. Bumpurs, an older Black woman with a history of mental illness who struggled to pay her monthly rent, could have threatened a police officer with the knife. They suspected racial prejudice influenced the White officer's decision to shoot Bumpurs twice with a 12-gauge single-barrel shotgun. The officer, who had little training in how to nonviolently subdue individuals with emotional problems, was charged with, and later cleared of, manslaughter (Feuer, 2016).

From a source perspective, the point is this: The original Bumpurs story contained none of this ambiguity; instead the reporter based the account on the police source's version, giving the established authorities a critical first attempt to frame the complex issue. Over time, stories based on other sources were published, and you could say it evened out in the end, as different sources questioned and criticized the police version. However, for those readers who only read the first story, or processed later stories in terms of the framework of the first one, the damage was done, and they never learned the more multifaceted truth.

The primacy of official source deceptions is probably less pervasive nowadays, when cell phone videos that challenge the police version are streamed on line and reporters can update the story immediately when new facts come to the fore. However, official sources can still dominate the frameworks reporters use to describe events, as the example in the next section and later chapters suggest.

Official Source Deceptions in the Run-Up to the 2003 Iraq War

It looked to be an easy call, a slam-dunk. In fact the basketball metaphor was exactly what CIA director George Tenet used in 2002 to describe the evidence that Iraqi president Saddam Hussein had weapons of mass destruction (WMDs). In the view of the upper reaches of the administration of President George W. Bush, there was little doubt that Iraq had acquired unconventional biological and chemical weapons, and was on the fast track to obtain nuclear weapons. The administration concluded that a war to oust Saddam Hussein was necessary, particularly given the grave dangers the country faced in the wake of 9/11. Thus, the White House pulled out all stops, harnessing every informational and persuasive weapon it could exploit to make the case.

A key instrument was the press. If reporters could be persuaded there was strong evidence Hussein was poised to acquire WMDs, and the news media could furnish stories that attested to the global threat Iraq posed, the table would be set – the handiwork provided, a casus belli obtained – for the Bush administration to gain Congressional approval to take military action against Iraq, ousting Saddam and eliminating the WMDs.

It turns out that a number of journalists were all too happy to comply, dutifully turning to official Bush Administration sources, then writing up news stories that made the case Iraq had pushed up its effort set to obtain WMDs. A particularly compliant – and later controversial – reporter was Judith Miller of *The New York Times*, who ironically was not a passive, "go along with others" person by nature, but quite the contrary – ambitious, aggressive to the point of being rude to colleagues and also the impressive recipient of major journalistic honors for her top-notch reporting. But when it came to Iraq war coverage, her desire to be the first to get the big story had the opposite impact. She became famous – or infamous in journalistic circles – for writing a series of stories that took official sources at their word that Saddam Hussein was set to acquire WMDs, when, as definitive evidence showed later, he hadn't, and the sources were unequivocally wrong.

Sources who claimed to have personal knowledge of Hussein's attempts to obtain nuclear weapons told Miller that Iraq sought to import large numbers of high-powered aluminum tubes, whose sole purpose was for use in centrifuges designed to enhance uranium, a critical step in developing an atomic bomb. "This was dramatic news," journalism critic Michael Massing (2004) noted. "If true, it would represent a rare piece of concrete evidence for Saddam's nuclear aspirations."

Emboldened by knowledge obtained from highly placed, seemingly impeccably informed sources, Miller and her *Times* colleague Michael Gordon confidently stated, in a September 8, 2002, article, that "Iraq has stepped up its quest for nuclear weapons and has embarked on a worldwide hunt for materials, to make an atomic bomb." The claims were bolstered and dramatized with "colorful quotes from administration officials who feared a 'mushroom cloud' if Saddam's mad arms march was not stopped" (Boehlert, 2006, p. 223). It gained its journalistic imprimatur from the key information that followed, the attribution of the so-called facts and claim to Bush Administration officials, prominently showcasing the role played by official sources in providing the information.

The information, however, was faulty and incorrect, communicated either because officials sincerely believed the evidence or, more cynically, because they were willing to go to deceptive lengths to oust Hussein from power. As later reports made abundantly clear, Iraq did not have WMDs that posed a threat to the security of the U.S. or its allies (Erlanger & Sanger, 2016). Experts argued that its high-strength aluminum tubes were not intended for use in atomic weapons, but for less threatening conventional weapons (Massing, 2004). The evidence corroborating the much-publicized claim Iraq had stepped up its quest for nuclear weapons that could produce deadly mushroom clouds was sparse, if non-existent. Facing an outpouring of criticism for its reporting, *The Times* issued an apology of sorts, taking responsibility for reporting that placed too much credence on sources – Iraqi defectors and informants – who should have been more carefully vetted, while giving insufficient play to skeptics who questioned the validity of evidence that Iraq had intensified its push to acquire WMDs (The Editors, 2004).

When the Iraq war, which succeeded in toppling Hussein from power, had a series of unforeseen consequences, leading to the devastation of the country's infrastructure, hundreds of thousands of Iraqi deaths, and more than 4,000 American soldiers killed, critics lambasted Miller and *The Times*. They suggested that if journalists had refused to accept information propagated by official sources, news stories would have presented a more skeptical version of the Bush Administration's push toward war, possibly pushing Congressional legislators to have opposed what critics viewed as an ill-fated military venture.

Conundrums of Source Routines: Leaks and Anonymous Sources

These two examples illustrate the dangers of relying on official sources. Although reporters frequently resort to this routine, they don't always. Reporters seek out credible sources, often surrounding themselves with a group of regular officials who dominate their news field (Reich, 2011), but don't rely slavishly on status quo authorities in all instances.

In fact, official sources, pervasive as they are, do not always dominate news. Power does not always speak with one voice. Sources from one government domain frequently challenge, counter, or contradict one another. Reporters, for their part, seeking political dirt, often try to circumvent official versions relayed through information subsidies. They seek out information by nudging sources to leak information, with the understanding the source's identity will remain anonymous, or the information will be vaguely attributed to a highly placed government authority talking on background. Both leaks and anonymous sourcing are laudable news routines, but they raise journalistic, ethical, and legal issues.

The Dynamics of News Leaks

Why Sources Leak

Leaks are information sources deliberately reveal to reporters, with the understanding their identities will be protected. Leaks are indispensable to journalism because they illuminate underlying realities that are not revealed by official sources. A dramatic example of a leak was the tantalizing revelation in 2018 of an "incident" that allegedly involved then-Judge, now Supreme Court Justice, Brett Kavanaugh and a girl while both were in high school, published in The Intercept, an online news publication (Grim, 2018). Washington, D.C. was agog about who leaked the story. Pointing up the critical role leaks can play in politics, Christine Blasey Ford, who would later accuse Kavanaugh of sexual assault before the Senate Judiciary Committee, went public days after the leak appeared. To some the leak was dirty politics, to others a necessary method to surface the serious issue of sexual assault.

Sources – the people who talk to reporters in public life – leak information for a multitude of reasons. First, government officials leak information to cultivate policy options. For example, they may want to publicize the dangers that foreign adversaries pose to the U.S. in order to protect U.S. national security. This is one reason why government officials revealed bundles of information to reporters about Russia's attempts to digitally subvert the 2016 election (though see Boyd-Barrett, 2019).

Sources also leak to cultivate a specific policy option among Washington, D.C. power elites. For example, American national security officials revealed abundant examples of how North Korean hackers had developed a program of cyberwarfare (spanning "digital sleeper cells" in the South Korean defense ministry and computerized heists from banks) that netted the North Korean regime hundreds of millions of dollars, while helping Pyongyang achieve its strategic objectives (Sanger, Kirkpatrick, & Perlroth, 2017). The sources hoped to reveal threats posed by North Koreans, probably to push a particular policy option among their peers in the politicized government bureaucracy.

Second, in a related fashion, officials, particularly in Washington, D. C., frequently leak stories to "get back" at others in government, whom leakers believe are thwarting their preferred policy position, or are part of a rival faction. Early in his term, especially as Special Counsel Robert

Mueller's investigation of possible collusion between Trump's election campaign and the Russian government heated up, there were leaks galore, so much so one writer observed that "ever since Donald Trump became President, the White House has leaked like a sieve" (Cassidy, 2018). Leaks have long been part of informal White House communications, plaguing presidents long before Trump. However, their frequency in Trump's White House illustrates the ways that an administration led by a president who thrives on conflict encourages leaks.

Rival factions within Trump's, and other administrations, use leaks "to discredit their internal opponents," leaking strategically and aggressively to promote their in-group and undermine opposing groups inside or outside the White House (Cassidy, 2018). For example, in the wake of Trump's refusal to endorse the U.S. government's assessment that Russia had digitally interfered in the 2016 presidential election, after a Helsinki summit meeting with the Russian leader in 2018, government intelligence experts were aghast. The United States president was siding with a foreign enemy, erroneously too. Three days after the meeting, a front-page story in *The New York Times*, based on leaks from about a dozen intelligence officials, revealed that Trump had in fact been shown classified materials demonstrating that Putin had directed a disinformation, hacking campaign to disrupt the election in January, 2017. This revelation restored the reputation of intelligence experts, indicating they had long known of Putin's involvement, while raising questions about Trump's criticism of their work and his own credibility (Sanger & Rosenberg, 2018).

A third reason that officials inside government leak stories is to test-market possible policy plans, examining how they play with leading elites and the public. Even if most Americans follow political news only casually, the political class closely attends to reports in conventional and online media. Presidential aides have leaked stories about controversial policy options as well as candidates for Supreme Court and Cabinet posts to gauge elite and public opinion in advance of official pronouncements.

And then there is the final reason, the most noble and altruistic. Sources leak information to disclose abuses of power in the corporate, technology, and, most prominently, national political world. Animated by a sense of justice, sources are whistleblowers, who leak information to the press to spur investigative stories that will elicit outrage and propel reform on issues ranging from sexual harassment to Facebook's privacy violations. This view of source leaks is famously exemplified in Watergate, where the source known as "Deep Throat," in a pun that played off the double entendre between his vocal revelations and the pornographic movie of the early 1970s, spoke to *Washington Post* reporters to reveal spectacular abuses of power in the Oval Office. Yet even in this storied example, one finds ambiguity, evidence that sources, like all human beings, act from a confluence of motives.

"Deep Throat," whose identity was kept secret for more than 30 years, until his family revealed his role in Watergate in a magazine article, turned out to be none other than W. Mark Felt, the second most high-ranking official at the FBI in the early 1970s. Historical research has cast some doubt on the beatific purity of Felt's motives suggesting that, incensed by President Richard Nixon's decision not to appoint him FBI director, he retaliated by leaking critical details of the Nixon White House's role in Watergate to *The Post* (Holland, 2012). However, the evidence for this view is circumstantial and incomplete, even as it suggests that sources' motives are more complexly determined than commonly believed. Indeed, one should not be too cynical about altruistic motives that propel some source revelations. Many people have come forward to report corporate, police, political, and sexual abuses by authorities, revealing this information to reporters so that others do not have to endure what they faced.

Evaluating News Leaks

When sources leak information, they can subtly break confidences with bosses and colleagues, ratting on them for reasons both selfish and altruistic. Reporters assure anonymous sources they will not reveal their names, a promise with legal ramifications. Journalists argue that the revelations provide valuable information the public needs to know, although this is self-serving, as journalists benefit by scooping competitors. Nonetheless, as advocates emphasize, without leaks about government abuses, society's information pores would be closed, blocking public understanding of what actually occurs in the dark recesses of the modern state.

Leaks are a distinctively American journalistic gambit, protected by the First Amendment, in sharp contrast with the United Kingdom, where the Official Secrets Act (the name sends shudders down the spines of First Amendment advocates) permits government to suppress publication of official secrets, even advocating punishment for both leakers and reporters (Shane, 2017). Of course, in the U.S., and all countries where officials leak, there remain perennial questions of how to balance the need for a free flow of information with the impetus to protect national secrets central to the nation's security. The press is four-square on the side of the first normative value, but there are gray areas, as you know.

One of those gray arenas involves digitized leaks conducted by foreign governments, released through a proxy, as occurred during the 2016 presidential campaign when Russian cyber-spies hacked into the Democratic National Committee's computer system. Journalists published these leaks, raising a host of questions (Shane, 2018). Should news outlets without question publish such leaks, basing publication solely on whether the information is true and relevant? How can they be sure that foreign agents do not digitally alter some documents and falsify others? When journalists publish these leaks, have they allowed themselves to become vehicles for manipulation by America's enemies? And if that's a problem, what is the difference between publishing leaks from foreign agents and publishing domestic leaks, in which reporters also become instruments of exploitation, by rival political groups? Even legal experts confess they don't have easy answers to these questions.

Ethics of Anonymous Sourcing

You can't have journalism without anonymous sources, but they come with headaches and costs. Whistleblowers, as well as those who have access to classified information but reveal it for more self-serving motives, must be confident their anonymity will be protected. If anonymous sources fear their names will be revealed, they will stop talking, causing the well of revelations about corruption to go dry, blocking pathways for truth to cleanse the system. Without the protection of anonymity, there would have been no Watergate, because Mark "Deep Throat" Felt would have never squealed, for fear of losing his job or facing official retaliation. Or, if the information had been revealed, without Felt's leads and confirmation, it might have been less accurate and therefore less likely to have exerted the impact it did on legislators investigating the Nixon White House. The multitude of investigative stories since Watergate – exposés of massive federal government wiretapping and revelations of sexual abuses in the Catholic Church – have necessarily relied on anonymous sources, helping to bring about social and political change.

However, anonymous sourcing is not without problems. It implicitly violates the journalistic value of transparency, providing only vague information about the source, in some cases offering questionable reasons why anonymity was given to begin with (Carlson, 2011). Sources granted anonymity may feel disinhibited from moral constraints, feeling more comfortable lying or distorting truth for self-serving reasons. Or, in rare instances anonymous sourcing can encourage unsavory journalists to fabricate information, attributing it to faux anonymous sources. Balancing pros and cons, news outlets regard anonymous sourcing as "a last resort," according to *The New York Times* style manual, though a journalistic necessity (Sullivan, 2013). When reporters should give sources anonymity, as opposed to demanding they provide some identification of who they are, is always a judgment call.

In early 2017, news organizations wrestled with whether they should publish information from anonymous sources who claimed the Russian government colluded with the 2016 Trump presidential campaign. A number of news organizations opted not to publish it because the claims were not substantiated and had not been independently verified, leaving them open to problems if the information turned out to be false (Ember & Grynbaum, 2017). However, BuzzFeed published it, arguing that transparency could only shed light on the dark recesses of possible collusion, noting that its publication helped the public learn more about how seriously the U.S. government treated the report (Smith, 2018). At the same time, some journalists, while admiring BuzzFeed's decision, worried that they had no way to determine whether the sources could be trusted because they did not know who they were. They also noted that the report on which the story was based had been authorized by Trump's opponents, raising questions about its authenticity (Fargo, 2017).

The Society of Professional Journalist's Code of Ethics provides guidance instructing journalists, in the main, to clearly identify sources, consider their motives before offering anonymity, and provide anonymity only to sources who could face harm if their names were identified. Editors usually insist that reporters vouch for the credibility of the anonymous source, describe the source's probable motivation for revealing the information, and offer some general information that establishes the source's domain of expertise.

Legal Dimensions and Broader Issues

There are also critical legal issues at stake. The government has an interest in protecting national security and has sought to pry classified national security information from reporters, who have confidentially obtained it from sources. Reporters valorously emphasize the broad benefits that anonymous source protection affords society, ensuring that future sources, knowing their identities will be kept secret, will deliver important informational goods when reporters come tweeting.

The White House has gone to great lengths to compel reporters to reveal their sources on national security matters, arguing that the information is critical to national security. Journalists doubt this, arguing that much information is unnecessarily classified and the administration wants to shut down dissent. The Obama Administration, despite its vaunted image of transparency, mounted some of the most aggressive efforts in recent history to intimidate reporters, gain access to their sources, discourage officials from talking to reporters, and prevent leaks (Downie, 2013).

Should reporters be legally protected from having to reveal the identities of confidential sources to government agencies? Journalists, rightly fearing that government may demand their sources for trumped-up political reasons not rooted in national security, have strenuously argued that source identity should be protected, period. They have couched their arguments in the Constitution, asserting that the First

Amendment shields journalists from being forced to disclose the identities of confidential sources. The courts have been sympathetic, up to a point.

In a precedent-setting 5–4 decision in 1972, later affirmed in related cases by appellate courts, the Supreme Court ruled that the First Amendment does not afford reporters blanket protection against being forced to reveal their sources' names to a grand jury. In its key opinion, the Court ruled that the average citizen – including a reporter – is not constitutionally protected "from the disclosing to a grand jury information that he has received in confidence" (Pember & Calvert, 2015, p. 402). However, the key justice brokering the close vote, appreciating the need for reporters to publish confidential information, noted that the 1972 decision was a very narrow one and suggested there were instances in which reporters had a First Amendment right to protect a source's identity. The four dissenting Supreme Court justices also staked out conditions under which reporters should be shielded from revealing their sources, including when the government lacks a compelling reason to gain the information, and there is no probable cause to believe that the reporter has information that bears on violation of a specific law.

As is always the case with the law, the case in question matters a great deal in determining whether a court will affirm the right of a journalist to refuse to reveal his or her sources. For example, courts, arguing that reporters do not have the privilege to refuse to testify before grand jury proceedings, have generally required that reporters reveal their confidential sources to grand juries. Journalists have sometimes refused to comply with court rulings, even going to jail to protect their sources. The reporter Judith Miller, who aroused such controversy for reliance on sources in the Iraq WMD stories, made the principled decision to go to jail – and was imprisoned for 85 days – rather than revealing a confidential source involving the leak of the name of a CIA officer.

In other cases, government investigators have employed other coercive methods to pursue national security leaks. They invaded the privacy of reporter James Risen to try to locate his source for a story about CIA efforts to disrupt Iran's development of a nuclear program, gaining access to his phone calls and personal bank records (Gerstein, 2011). The Trump Administration seized a reporter's phone records in the wake of the reporter's romantic involvement with a source who had access to classified information. The romantic entanglement showed poor judgment, but the seizure of personal information arguably interfered with the reporter's First Amendment right to investigate her own government's activities.

Presidents, particularly Barack Obama (again, in stark contradiction to his liberal image), have prosecuted government officials for sharing classified information with reporters (Liptak, 2012). Journalists, determined to protect their access to classified information they believe the public needs to know, have pressed for state shield laws that give reporters some legal protection against having to disclose confidential sources' identities. At present, 49 states (Wyoming is the sole exception) have shield laws, though reporters' protection varies greatly by state, as well as in the degree to which protection is extended to conventional reporters or citizen journalists, such as those using websites to disseminate information.

Source protection is essential to the craft of journalism, but, as the foregoing discussion indicates, there are other viewpoints, notably those emphasizing that reporters are citizens, who have responsibilities to the larger society (Carlson, 2011). Investigative reporting is filled with ethical and legal conundrums and is most certainly not meant for the faint of heart. Yet when stories are reported expertly, thoroughly, and relentlessly, they can influence public opinion and policy. These stories call on well-honed source routines in investigative reporting, whereby reporters recruit not one source but several sources to make the same allegation, as *Washington Post* reporters did, in locating different women who said that 2017 Alabama Senate candidate Roy Moore had initiated sexual or romantic contact when they were teenagers and he was in his 30s. News that reported on the repulsive sexual abuses of Larry Nasser, the former team doctor for USA Gymnastics, gained credibility because it was based on graphic accusations made by more than 160 women – women who were willing to offer their stories and reveal their names in public, despite the emotional turmoil it caused.

As the foregoing discussion indicates, the legal, ethical, and professional issues involving sources are longstanding, broadly understood as emerging from the dynamic social relationship between sources and reporters. It is a strategic interpersonal relationship, with sources and reporters both feeling they gain professionally from the interaction. In a reporter's case, it is a story, byline, shot at a journalistic prize, an opportunity to right an ethical wrong. In the source's case, it is an opportunity to push a policy option, influence the bureaucracy, extract revenge, set the record straight, or expose social injustice.

The ethically nuanced and frequently compromised relationship between sources and reporter is at the heart of journalism, as "a struggle over the boundaries of the public sphere; a struggle over what information becomes public and what remains in the private realm, and which topics are discussed openly and which remain concealed" (Broersma, den Herder, & Schohaus, 2013, p. 388). Reporters and sources are constantly renegotiating their roles, and we want their negotiations to serve the public interest by revealing information that is of significant import to citizens and policymakers. It is all complex, controversial, and in flux, particularly in the wake of the advent of digital technologies, the focus of the final section of our exploration of contemporary journalistic routines.

Internet, Social Media, and Routines

Active shooter ... down at the baptist church in Sutherland Springs down my road, be careful everybody!!!!

The horrifying tweet on Dataminr, an online news platform that searches Twitter for breaking news, instantly captured the attention of *New York Times* Express Team reporters on Sunday November 5, 2017. It came with a "Flash," the highest importance level. Was it true? How could they confirm this? There weren't likely to be any reporters in the small Texas town, and the police weren't giving details. Combing social media, reporters went to work, viewing the town on Google Maps, examining public records to see if there were residents they might call. Each time they tried, they hit a brick wall. Reporter Christopher Mele located a church Facebook page and left a message for Sandy Ward, one of the parishioners; no reply. As Mele (2017) relates, "I could feel a pit in my gut as the minutes ticked by ... Our goal at The Times is always to first be right, and *then* be first" (p. A2).

Then a break. The reporter, through Twitter, reached someone near the church, and he indicated he would snap pictures and email them. Then another reporter was able to reach a town constable, who confirmed that, yes, a shooting had taken place at the First Baptist Church of Sutherland Springs, Texas, with reports of children shot. A call came through from Sandy Ward, the parishioner the reporter had contacted hours earlier. The two spoke for five minutes when she told him that three of her grandchildren and a daughter-in-law had been hit at the church; she asked him for prayers, he felt his voice beginning to crack, but knew there was more work to do before they could complete the story, truly a horrible one, 26 people dead, the worst mass shooting in Texas.

The reporters posted the story later in the day. They may not have been first, but, using social media, they did their best to authenticate the facts to make sure they were right.

The story-behind-the-story exemplifies the central role social media and the Internet play in contemporary journalism. It is at once a truism and misleading to state that online media have changed journalistic routines. It is a truism because without question reporters rely on social media to gather information for news stories, supplanting much (though by no means all) of the face-to-face interviews of yore with online messaging and digital sleuthing. Reporters gravitate to social media to check for breaking news stories, find out what other news organizations are doing, and identify new story ideas (Willnat & Weaver, 2014). Social media have become real-time, information sensors, an early warning system that detects events and offers streams of data as breaking news occurs (Hermida, 2012). Twitter is the most commonly used social networking site, monitored by reporters for breaking news stories spanning accidents, shootings, and terrorist attacks, often with the aid of TweetDeck, a social media dashboard that enables efficient tweeting and replying in a single interfaced system (Brandtzaeg et al., 2016).

However, the statement that online media have changed journalistic information-gathering suggests a "Gee whiz, it's all different now" when classical routines – news values, formal channels, and official sources – are still employed. They are the categories that subsume online strategies, the old bottles in which the new online wine (or perhaps beer, given its storied association with journalism) is contained.

Thus, journalists receive formally conveyed information from official sources, but the information can come via tweets (Bane, 2019). Interestingly, while citizen news media also use official sources or official tweets, they rely on them less than conventional news outlets, sometimes preferring linked reports to quoting officials, in this way providing a more diverse array of sources than some traditional outlets (Cui & Liu, 2017; Robinson & DeShano, 2011). At the same time, aggressive, entrepreneurial reporting is very much alive and well in the contemporary investigative realm, through journalistic examination of dissenters' whistle-blowing blogs or their snooping relevant Facebook, Twitter, or Instagram posts.

An enterprising 45-year-old blogger, Alexandria Goddard, put these stalking skills to use, getting to the bottom of a shocking rape of a 16-year-old West Virginia girl in Steubenville, Ohio in August, 2012 by two star high school football players. With local media seemingly downplaying the story because of its nefarious implications for Steubenville football, a crazily popular sport in the small city, Goddard combed social media sites, locating a horrific Instagram photograph showing the victim being carried by the two perpetrators. Her head drooped backward toward the floor; one of the boys was smiling. Outraged, Goddard posted the picture online, attracting attention from mainstream reporters, but also Anonymous, the international hacking group, which went even further than Goddard, hacking into the high school football team's website and promising vigilante justice, showing how online sleuthing raises ethical red flags (Levy, 2013). Nonetheless, were it not for aggressive reporting via social media, thanks to Goddard, the facts of the story might never have been widely diffused.

Another way social media has been used to bolster investigative reporting involves **crowdsourcing**, where reporters solicit information from online communities, turning to a broader swath of investigators than they would have obtained in the old days – fellow journalists, volunteers, activists, and experts, who supply information that online reporters subsequently verify for accuracy (Aitamurto, 2016). These two techniques have netted information, as well as major reporting awards.

Talking Points Memo became the first blog to win a major journalism honor back in 2008 for disclosures obtained through tips from thousands of readers across the U.S., as well as document searches. The blog established that George W. Bush's administration fired eight U.-S. attorneys for purely political reasons (Marshall, 2011). The *Washington Post*'s David Fahrenthold received a Pulitzer Prize, in part for his 2016 crowdsourced reporting that showed Trump's claims about his generous philanthropy were mostly a façade. Unlike most reporters, who tend to be guarded about their news-gathering techniques, Fahrenthold went public, turning to his Twitter followers, asking for their help in obtaining evidence of Trump's philanthropy, as he sought to discover if Trump had actually made donations to veterans' groups, as he claimed. None of the groups Fahrenthold contacted said they received gifts from Trump, and the gap between Trump's claim and reality helped spawn other crowdsourced stories identifying ethical problems in Trump's charitable-giving (Gillmor, 2016).

Technologies like crowdsourcing have expanded routines available to reporters, allowing them to tap into the views of more people, taking news beyond the usual suspects frequently quoted through formal channels. News outlets can use social media to reach individuals who aren't often quoted, enhancing the diversity of stories that get told. For example, by sending out messages through social media, a news outlet asked teachers to relate experiences in classrooms. The newspaper received more than 4,000 responses from teachers across the U.S., authenticated the identities of contributors, and published their stories, offering a panoramic view of crises in American education, one that richly enhanced what could have done been done in the analog, foot-on-the-pavement era (Van Syckle, 2018). In a similar fashion, reporters writing a story on sexual harassment of National Football League cheerleaders sent a digital message to former and current cheerleaders, gaining a much wider range of responses than would have been possible in earlier times.

Journalistic Costs and Benefits of Social Media Routines

Social media channels offer reporters much quicker and broader access to sources and breaking news than was imaginable in earlier eras, when journalists were constrained by their feet or the service of telephones. Sites like Twitter have also changed the pace of news, speeding up the news cycle, allowing news outlets to cover events instantly without reporters on the scene. They have altered the grammar too. The who-what-where-when linear news story of the old days has been replaced by a multi-media, multi-authored package – "a constantly updated stream of text, audio, and video from both journalists and amateurs" (Hermida, 2012, p. 315).

Twitter has become a beat, a routine journalists rely on to communicate with sources and fellow reporters, as well as to access information in fast-breaking crises. Twitter offers many broad social benefits, notably democratizing the playing field in which news-gathering occurs. There has been an expansion of sources quoted on Twitter. Official sources still count; they have a strong, tweeted presence. However, a variety of sources who might not have been quoted before, from professionals to activists to ordinary people, are quoted in news stories, as well as in journalists' tweets, showcasing the ways reporters today are more apt "to open the gates to non-professional participants in the news production process," as Lasorsa and his colleagues note (Broersma & Graham, 2013; Lasorsa, Lewis, & Holton, 2012, p. 31; Paulussen & Harder, 2014, though see Blackstone, Cowart, & Saunders, 2017). In a celebrated example, National Public Radio's Andy Carvin posted hundreds of news-tweets each day about the Arab Spring uprisings of 2011, giving more priority to alternative, non-elite sources than the usual journalistic or official communicators (Hermida, Lewis, & Zamith, 2014).

On the other hand, routine reliance on social media has drawbacks, chiefly in verification, a key function of journalism. Real-time informational posts, despite their air of authenticity and seeming veridicality, are inevitably incomplete and can never be totally vetted or verified. Social media-routinized reporting, with news based on Twitter reports, has produced major inaccuracies, partly because the stories come from unofficial, sometimes incredible sources. While social media sites can make errors more transparent (Berkowitz & Liu, 2016), they can also magnify the impact of erroneous information, as when early media reports of the school massacre in Newtown, Connecticut in 2012 misidentified the name of the gunman and incorrectly claimed there was a second shooter (Mele, 2017). It can also be difficult to assess the background of sources from Twitter posts, including whether they have conflicts of interest that imperil their credibility.

Citizen journalists, with their visible online presence, offer new opportunities, as well as challenges to traditional journalistic routines and values. By offering a fresh epistemology that is less dependent on official sources and more open to different perspectives obtained through online engagement with community members, citizen journalists can expand the range of perspectives on a problem, particularly in smaller communities with a history of citizen involvement in government (Carpenter, 2008). While, to their credit, citizen journalism sites frequently rely on links and academic reports, with solid documentation, some citizen reporters acknowledge they publish rumors, opinions, and avoid fact-checking, part of a different "sense of etiquette for information production" (Carpenter, 2008; Robinson & DeShano, 2011, p. 974). To the extent that this information is inaccurate and spreads across online communities, the etiquette is problematic, raising questions about citizen news site accuracy.

Conventional news outlets increasingly incorporate citizen-shot videos into blogs or news reports, broadening the range of reporting by involving citizen journalists in news gathering. However, the videos can vary in quality and clarity of their narrative (Wall & El Zahed, 2015), as well as in the degree to which they offer opinionated claims not backed up by reasonably authenticated facts.

Conclusions

Journalistic routines are the everyday, patterned practices of newswork, the rules and conventions that journalists use to gather and produce news. People don't think of routines when they reflect on news or news bias. They usually turn to simple, dramatic factors like partisan bias or the ways that a star anchor, simplistically viewed as the exemplar of news, seems to skew news in an ideological direction. As suggested in the previous chapter, this perspective on news has serious shortcomings, understating the ways that prosaic, but commonly accepted, news practices influence news content.

A key routine involves journalists' news values, culturally honed determinations of what constitutes a newsworthy story (though the relationship between news and newsworthiness is complex; see Shoemaker & Cohen, 2006). News judgments can be divided into the degree to which they are socially significant and deviant, with a story that fits squarely into both camps accorded the highest news value and receiving the best play.

Core news values include novelty, threats to the social and moral order, events involving elite and prominent individuals (showcasing the ways that power arrangements influence news decisions), as well as conflict, controversy, drama, and personalization of political issues. The emphasis on these news values, which occur in different national contexts, does not necessarily mean that the most important or socially meaningful issues are covered in the news. Trivial issues that strikingly deviate from what is expected, events involving famous personages who strut across the public stage, heart-rending visuals that nonetheless understate the complexity of events, and issues that congeal with the agenda du jour – which in the case of opioids or sexual abuse by powerful men were neglected by media until they became The Big Story – receive outsize attention. News values, agreed on by journalists across different geographical regions and media, constitute a routine that helps reporters make sense of the warp and woof of public life. In many cases, news values do call attention to issues of public significance, but they frequently neglect deeper cultural and social underpinnings, which are layered with normative perspectives and complex, rendering them difficult to cover without charges of bias or boredom, the latter a ratings killer.

In recent years, the online milieu has added three news values – immediacy, interactivity, and participation. Although emphasis on these news values can replicate the old problems, such as speed over depth and participation of elites rather than ordinary people, they have potential to improve the quality and range of journalism by extending the breadth of storytelling to the digital age.

A second key routine involves the channels by which reporters receive information, a routine that overlaps with reporter reliance on sources for information. Journalism is unthinkable without the information sources provide and their capacity to lend credibility to reporters' hunches. Sources also allow reporters to cross-check facts by determining if the same interpretations are proffered by sources with different expertise and motivations to divulge information. News, alas, is never what "objectively" happened, but, instead, what someone – a whistleblower, information leaker or, more frequently, a government or business official – says has happened and is willing to share with reporters.

In the case of formal channels, where information is released through officially planned events or public relations specialists working for an organization, news outlets are provided with an information subsidy, a low-cost informational product that PR specialists offer to reporters in exchange for publicity. Although formal PR releases, conveyed today by links, website posts and tweets to drive social media traffic, have wide informational benefits, they can, when not treated critically by journalists, offer unduly positive information about an organization's product or practice. When journalists fail to corroborate claims contained in formally conveyed releases, they fail to fulfill the key informational function of news, neglecting to inform citizens about the costs, drawbacks, or hazards of a product that a public relations specialist pedals.

A related problem is reporters' reliance on official sources, who have a vested interest in protecting their organization, often to the detriment of the public. As the examples of reliance on sources in the NYPD and the run-up to the 2003 war in Iraq illustrate, journalistic dependence on this simple informational routine can prop up officials, service the status quo, and in the process offer a distorting narrative that misleads citizens and policymakers.

It is complex. Reliance on sources can reinforce, but also challenge the powers-that-be. While the sourcing routine can be misused, as when journalists depend too heavily on official sources, it can also yield investigative fruit, as seen in the wealth of exposés of business and government that had their origins in revelations of dirt via leaks and anonymous sources.

Sources leak for a variety of reasons – typically self-serving, but on occasions to blow the whistle on immoral behavior. Reliance on anonymous sources raises a hornet's nest of issues. While a journalistic necessity in cases where sources would face severe financial or personal hardship if their names were revealed, reliance on anonymous sources can encourage reporters to take the easy route, publishing questionable information just because a source of impressive provenance says it. Thus, the SPJ Code of Ethics offers specific guidelines on when to offer anonymity to sources.

There are also key legal issues at stake. Journalists appropriately argue they should be able to protect their promise to guarantee source anonymity. However, government, seeking source names for national security (and, truth be told, trumped-up political reasons), has taken journalists to court. Courts have ruled that the First Amendment does not offer blanket protection to reporters against being forced to reveal their sources. During a time when governments are increasingly seeking to squelch journalists' initiatives, First Amendment advocates have increasingly pressed for state shield laws, which give reporters varying degrees of protection against demands from overzealous government officials.

The final issue discussed in the chapter involves ways that source routines have changed in the wake of social media. The old verity – reliance on sources – has not disappeared, but has been adapted to Twitter, where official sources can tweet official pronouncements. At the same time, social media offers new avenues for aggressive, watchdog reporting, harnessed by citizen and conventional journalists through blogs, crowdsourcing, and online sleuthing. And journalists are frenetically active on Twitter, sharing information more quickly and with more colleagues than they could in earlier times.

Like all innovations, online and social media-focused routines come with benefits and drawbacks. The former include the capacity to instantly update stories, enabling news to be current and more accurate, as well as offering greater input from users outside the groups to which reporters usually turn. The degree to which Twitter facilitates greater reliance on non-elite sources remains a work in progress, with the story type (government pronouncement versus grass roots protest) influencing sourcing decisions. Like all strategies, routine reliance on social networking sites has shortcomings that raise red flags about the degree to which journalism can fulfill its verification function. Dependence on sources of questionable credibility and routinized reliance on social media-posted information has led to errors in accuracy, misinforming citizens already awash in too much information of questionable provenance.

Routines, constantly evolving, are the heart of journalism, as seen in the newspapers of the 20th century and websites of today. Routines can lead to superficial stories reaffirming the powers that be, as well as deep investigations that shake up the status quo. Although frequently disparaged as "history on the run," journalism – and the news that is its main focus – continues to be of the utmost importance to citizens. "If journalism is sometimes inaccurate and often inadequate, ignorance would not be preferable," writer Thomas Griffith (1959) observed (p. 66), an apt warning in an age when political leaders label news that they don't like "fake" and political leaders across the world are happy to demonize the press.

References

Aitamurto, T. (2016). Crowd-sourcing as a knowledge-search method in digital journalism: Ruptured ideals and blended responsibility. *Digital Journalism, 4,* 280–297.

Armstrong, C.L. (2004). The influence of reporter gender on source selection in newspaper stories. *Journalism & Mass Communication Quarterly, 81,* 139–154.

Artwick, C.G. (2014). News sourcing and gender on Twitter. *Journalism, 15,* 1111–1127.

Bane, K.C. (2019). Tweeting the agenda. *Journalism Practice, 13,* 191–205.

Bantz, C.R., McCorkle, S., & Baade, R.C. (1980). The news factory. *Communication Research, 7,* 45–68.

Berkowitz, D. (1997). Non-routine news and newswork: Exploring a what-a-story. In D. Berkowitz (Ed.), *Social meanings of news: A text-reader* (pp. 362–375). Thousand Oaks, CA: Sage.

Berkowitz, D. (2009). Reporters and their sources. In K. Wahl-Jorgensen & T. Hanitzsch (Eds.), *The handbook of journalism studies* (pp. 102–115). New York: Routledge.

Berkowitz, D., & Liu, Z.M. (2016). Media errors and the "nutty professor": Riding the journalistic boundaries of the Sandy Hook shootings. *Journalism, 17,* 155–172.

Blackstone, G.E., Cowart, H.S., & Saunders, L.M. (2017). TweetStorm in #ferguson: How news organizations framed dominant authority, anti-authority, and political figures in a restive community. *Journal of Broadcasting & Electronic Media, 61,* 597–614.

Boczkowski, P.J. (2010). *News at work: Imitation in an age of information abundance.* Chicago, IL: University of Chicago Press.

Boehlert, E. (2006). *Lapdogs: How the press rolled over for Bush.* New York: Free Press.

Boyd-Barrett, O. (2019). Fake news and "RussiaGate" discourses: Propaganda in the post-truth era. *Journalism, 20,* 87–91.

Brandtzaeg, P.B., Lüders, M., Spangenberg, J., Rath-Wiggins, L., & Følstad, A. (2016). Emerging journalistic verification practices concerning social media. *Journalism Practice, 10,* 323–342.

Broersma, M., den Herder, B., & Schohaus, B. (2013). A question of power: The changing dynamics between journalists and sources. *Journalism Practice, 7,* 388–395.

Broersma, M., & Graham, T. (2013). Twitter as a news source: How Dutch and British newspapers used tweets in their news coverage, 2007–2011. *Journalism Practice, 7,* 446–464.

Bruns, A. (2008). *Blogs, Wikipedia, Second Life, and beyond: From production to produsage.* New York: Peter Lang.

Bullock, C.F. (2008). Official sources dominate domestic violence reporting. *Newspaper Research Journal, 29,* 6–22.

Caple, H., & Bednarek, M. (2016). Rethinking news values: What a discursive approach can tell us about the construction of news discourse and news photography. *Journalism, 17,* 435–455.

Carlson, M. (2011). Whither anonymity? Journalism and unnamed sources in a changing media environment. In B. Franklin & M. Carlson (Eds.), *Journalists, sources, and credibility: New perspectives* (pp. 37–48). New York: Routledge.

Carlson, M., & Franklin, B. (2011). Introduction. In B. Franklin & M. Carlson (Eds.), *Journalists, sources, and credibility: New perspectives* (pp. 1–15). New York: Routledge.

Carpenter, S. (2008). How online citizen journalism publications and online newspapers utilize the objectivity standard and rely on external sources. *Journalism & Mass Communication Quarterly, 85*, 531–548.

Cassidy, J. (2018, May 15). How game theory explains the leaks in the Trump White House. *The New Yorker*. Online: www.newyorker.com/news/our-columnists/how-game-theory-explains-the-leaks-in-the-trump-white-house. (Accessed: August 5, 2019).

Cui, X., & Liu, Y. (2017). How does online news curate linked sources? A content analysis of three online news media. *Journalism, 18*, 852–870.

de la Merced, M.J., & Koblin, J. (2018, May 18). Two moguls vie for power in CBS fight. *The New York Times*, A1, A8.

Downie, Jr., L. (2013, October). The Obama administration and the press: Leak investigations and surveillance in post-9/11 America. *CPJ: Committee to Protect Journalists*. Online: https://cpj.org/reports/2013/10/obama-and-the-press-us-leaks-surve... (Accessed: October 19, 2018).

Ember, S., & Grynbaum, M.M. (2017, January 10). BuzzFeed posts unverified claims on Trump, igniting a debate. *The New York Times*. Online: www.nytimes.com/2017/01/10/business/buzzfeed-donald-trum. (Accessed: July 11, 2018).

Entman, R.M. (2004). *Projections of power: Framing news, public opinion, and U.S. foreign policy.* Chicago, IL: University of Chicago Press.

Erlanger, S., & Sanger, D.E. (2016, July 6). Chilcot report on Iraq war offers devastating critique of Tony Blair. *The New York Times*. Online: www. nytimes.com/2016/07/07/world/europe/chilcot-report. (Accessed: July 3, 2018).

Ettema, J.S., & Glasser, T.L. (1998). *Custodians of conscience: Investigative journalism and public virtue.* New York: Columbia University Press.

Fargo, A. (2017, January 23). How should you read unnamed sources and leaks? *The Conversation*. Online: http://theconversation.com/how-should-you-read-unnamed-sources-an... (Accessed: July 15, 2018).

Feuer, A. (2016, October 19). Fatal police shooting in Bronx echoes one from 32 years ago. *The New York Times*. Online: www.nytimes.com/2016/10/20/nyregion/fatal-police-shooting... (Accessed: July 1, 2018).

Flegenheimer, M. (2017, December 30). The year the traditional news cycle accelerated to Trump speed. *The New York Times*, A16.

Franklin, B. (2011). Sources, credibility, and the continuing crisis of UK journalism. In B. Franklin & M. Carlson (Eds.), *Journalists, sources, and credibility: New perspectives* (pp. 90–106). New York: Routledge.

Franklin, B., Lewis, J., & Williams, A. (2010). Journalism, news sources and public relations. In S. Allan (Ed.), *The Routledge companion to news and journalism* (pp. 202–212). New York: Routledge.

Galtung, J., & Ruge, M.H. (1965). The structure of foreign news. *Journal of Peace Research, 2*, 64–90.

Gandy, O. (1982). *Beyond agenda setting: Information subsidies and public policy.* New York: Ablex.

Gans, H.J. (2004). *Deciding what's news: A study of CBS Evening News, NBC Nightly News, Newsweek and Time* (25th anniversary edition). Evanston, IL: Northwestern University Press

Gerstein, J. (2011, February 24). Feds spy on reporter in leak probe. *Politico*. Online: www.politico.com/story/2012/02/fed-spy-on-reporter-in-leak... (Accessed: July 14, 2018).

Gillmor, D. (2016, December 21). How one reporter turned to his readers to investigate Donald Trump. *The Atlantic*. Online: www.theatlantic.com/politics/archive/2016/12/what-journalists... (Accessed: July 15, 2018).

Goldstein, J. (2018, March 19) "Testilying" by police persists as cameras capture truth. *The New York Times*, A1, A16, A17.

Griffith, T. (1959). *The waist-high culture*. New York: Harper and Brothers.

Grim, R. (2018, September 12). Dianne Feinstein withholding Brett Kavanaugh document from fellow Judiciary Committee Democrats. *The Intercept*. Online: https://theintercept.com/2018/09/12/brett-kavanaugh-confirmation-... (Accessed: October 8, 2018).

Hanitzsch, T. (2009). Comparative journalism studies. In K. Wahl-Jorgensen & T. Hanitzsch (Eds.), *The handbook of journalism studies* (pp. 413–427). New York: Routledge.

Harcup, T., & O'Neill, D. (2001). What is news? Galtung and Ruge revisited. *Journalism Studies, 2*, 261–280.

Harcup, T., & O'Neill, D. (2017). What is news? News values revisited again. *Journalism Studies, 18*, 1470–1488.

Hermida, A. (2012). Social journalism: Exploring how social media is shaping journalism. In E. Siapera & A. Veglis (Eds.), *The handbook of online journalism* (pp. 309–328). Malden, MA: Wiley-Blackwell.

Hermida, A., Lewis, S.C., & Zamith, R. (2014). Sourcing the Arab spring: A case study of Andy Carvin's sources on Twitter during the Tunisian and Egyptian revolutions. *Journal of Computer-Mediated Communication, 19*, 479–499.

Holland, M. (2012) *Leak: Why Mark Felt became deep throat*. Lawrence, KS: University Press of Kansas.

Kantor, J., & Twohey, M. (2017, October 5). Harvey Weinstein paid off sexual harassment accusers for decades. *The New York Times*. Online: www.nytimes.com/2017/10/05/us/harvey-weinstein-harassment-allegations.html. (Accessed: August 5, 2019).

Karlsson, M. (2011). The immediacy of online news, the visibility of journalistic processes and a restructuring of journalistic authority. *Journalism, 12*, 279–295.

Landler, M., & Haberman, M. (2018, July 10). Former Bush aide is Trump pick for Court: Kavanaugh could cement a majority on the Right. *The New York Times*, A1, A15.

Lasorsa, D.L., Lewis, S.C., & Holton, A.E. (2012). Normalizing Twitter: Journalism practice in an emerging communication space. *Journalism Studies, 13*, 19–36.

Levy, A. (2013, August 5). Trial by Twitter. *The New Yorker*. Online: www.newyorker.com/magazine/2013/08/05/trial-by-twitter. (Accessed: December 15, 2018).

Lewis, J., Williams, A., & Franklin, B. (2008). A compromised fourth estate? UK news journalism, public relations and news sources. *Journalism Studies, 9*, 1–20.

Liptak, A. (2012, February 11). A high-tech war on leaks. *The New York Times.* Online: https://www.nytimes.com/2012/02/12/sunday-review/a-high-tech-war-on-leaks.html (Accessed: August 5, 2019).

Manjoo, F. (2019, March 26). Collusion was a seductive delusion. *The New York Times.* Online: www.nytimes.com/2019/03/25/opinion/colluion-mueller-t ... (Accessed: March 28, 2019).

Marshall, J. (2011). *Watergate's legacy and the press: The investigative impulse.* Evanston, IL: Northwestern University Press.

Massing, M. (2004, February 26). Now they tell us. *The New York Review of Books.* www.nybooks.com/articles/2004/02/26/now-they-tell-us/. (Accessed: July 1, 2018).

Mele, C. (2017, November 10). A firsthand account in a crisis. *The New York Times*, A2.

Molloy, J., & Grady, D. (2018, June 18). Yeah, I'm a pregnant man. What? *The New York Times*, A14.

O'Neill, D., & Harcup, T. (2009). News values and selectivity. In K. Wahl-Jorgensen & T. Hanitzsch (Eds.), *The handbook of journalism studies* (pp. 161–174). New York: Routledge.

Paterson, C., & Domingo, D. (Eds.) (2008). *Making online news: The ethnography of new media production.* New York: Peter Lang.

Patterson, T.E. (1993). *Out of order.* New York: Knopf.

Paulussen, S., & Harder, R.A. (2014). Social media references in newspapers: Facebook, Twitter and YouTube as sources in newspaper journalism. *Journalism Practice*, *8*, 542–551.

Pember, D.R., & Calvert, C. (2015). *Mass media law* (19th ed.). New York: McGraw-Hill.

Perloff, R.M. (2018). *The dynamics of political communication: Media and politics in a digital age* (2nd ed.). New York: Routledge.

Poniewozik, J. (2018, July 11). Made-for-television rollout, slick and substance-free. *The New York Times*, A14.

Reich, Z. (2011). Source credibility as a journalistic work tool. In B. Franklin & M. Carlson (Eds.), *Journalists, sources, and credibility: New perspectives* (pp. 19–36). New York: Routledge.

Robinson, S., & DeShano, C. (2011). "Anyone can know": Citizen journalism and the interpretive community of the mainstream press. *Journalism*, *12*, 963–982.

Rusbridger, A. (2019). *Breaking news: The remaking of journalism and why it matters now.* New York: Farrar, Strauss & Giroux.

Rutenberg, J. (2017, October 6). Harvey Weinstein's media enablers. *The New York Times.* Online: www.nytimes.com/2017/10/06/business/media/harvey-weinstein (Accessed: July 12, 2018).

Sanger, D.E., Kirkpatrick, D.D., & Perlroth, N. (2017, October 16). North Korea deploys corps of hackers bent on chaos. *The New York Times*, A1, A8, A9.

Sanger, D.E., & Rosenberg, M. (2018, July 19). From start, Trump has muddied clear message: Putin interfered. *The New York Times*, A1, A13.

Scott, D.M. (2015). *The new rules of marketing and PR: How to use social media, online video, mobile applications, blogs, news releases, and viral marketing to reach buyers directly.* Hoboken, NJ: John Wiley & Sons..

Shane, S. (2017, May 25). Leaks: A uniquely American way of annoying the authorities. *The New York Times*. Online: www.nytimes.com/2017/05/25/world/europe/manchester-bom... (Accessed: July 9, 2018).

Shane, S. (2018, May 13). When spies hack journalism. *The New York Times* (Sunday Review), 4.

Shoemaker, P.J., & Cohen, A.A. (2006). *News around the world: Content, practitioners and the public*. New York: Routledge.

Shoemaker, P.J., & Reese, S.D. (1996). *Mediating the message: Theories of influences on mass media content* (2nd ed.). White Plains, NY: Longman.

Shoemaker, P.J., & Vos, T.P. (2009). *Gatekeeping theory*. New York: Routledge.

Sigal, L. (1986). Who: Sources make the news. In R.K. Manoff & M. Schudson (Eds.), *Reading the news* (pp. 9–37). New York: Pantheon.

Singer, J.B. (2010). Journalism in the network. In S. Allan (Ed.), *The Routledge companion to news and journalism* (pp. 277–286). New York: Routledge.

Smith, B. (2018, January 9). I'm proud we published the Trump-Russia dossier. *The New York Times*. Online: www.nytimes.com/2018/01/09/opinion/im-proud-we-published. (Accessed: July 11, 2018).

Smoller, F.T. (1990). *The six o'clock presidency: A theory of presidential press relations in the age of television*. New York: Praeger.

Starkman, D. (2010, September/October). The hamster wheel: Why running as fast as we can is getting us nowhere. *Columbia Journalism Review*. Online: https://archives.cjr/org/cover_story/the_hamster_wheel.php. (Accessed: August 19, 2018).

Sullivan, M. (2013, August 27). Anonymous sources on Syrian weapons and mayoral politics brings criticism. *The New York Times*. Online: https://publiceditor.blogs.nytimes.com/2013/08/27/on-syrian-weapons. (Accessed: July 12, 2018).

The Editors. (2004, May 26). From The Editors; *The Times* and Iraq. *The New York Times*. Online: www.nytimes.com/2004/05/26/world/from-the-editors-the-times. (Accessed: July 3, 2018).

Tyndall Report. (2019). Top twenty stories of 2018. *Tyndall Report: 2018 Year in review*. Online: tyndallreport.com. (Accessed: March 28, 2019).

Usher, N. (2014). *Making news at The New York Times*. Ann Arbor, MI: University of Michigan Press.

Usher, N. (2016). *Interactive journalism: Hackers, data, and code*. Urbana, IL: University of Illinois Press.

Van Syckle, K. (2018, July 20). The power of the crowd. *The New York Times*, A2.

Wall, M., & El Zahed, S. (2015). Embedding content from Syrian citizen journalists: The rise of the collaborative news clip. *Journalism*, *16*, 163–180.

Willnat, L., & Weaver, D.H. (2014). *The American journalist in the digital age: Key findings*. Bloomington, IN: School of Journalism, Indiana University. Online: archive.news.indiana.edu/releases/iu/2014/05/2013-american-journalist-key-fin. (Accessed: November 23, 2018).

9 Organizational and Economic Influences

Let's see. There was the Harvard graduate who had the bright idea to warm his socks in the newsroom microwave, destroying the microwave and leaving a putrid smell in the process. There was the drama critic who broke into a colleague's car with a military-style slingshot in broad daylight, under the watch of the newspaper's security cameras. And let's not forget the award-winning female journalist who mastered the newspaper's nonverbal code, tugging at her sleeve when she wanted to furtively communicate she was walking across the street to imbibe at the paper's official watering hole, aptly called the Headliner. When she wanted to slip out of the newsroom to get a cold one, she knew the drill: Leave your coat behind, walk nonchalantly out of the building tugging on your shirtsleeve to communicate that you were heading to the Liner, as it was affectionately known (Mazzolini, 2018; Theiss, 2018, Davis & Mazzolini, 2018).

These were among the delightfully eclectic reporters who worked during the 1990s and 2000 at the fabled newsroom of the Cleveland *Plain Dealer*, chronicling their stories in a book edited by two former investigative reporters, Dave Davis and Joan Mazzolini (2018). One journalist called the newsroom "the Island of Misfit Toys," where

> there was tolerance for weirdness, crankiness and dissent, even the occasional tantrum. Editors yelled across the newsroom. Reporters argued with editors over assignments and rewrites. Clashes spilled into the managing editor's office all the time. To management's credit, you could disagree, and they didn't hold a grudge.
>
> (Spector, 2018a, p. 167)

Or at least some of the time, for editors could be arbitrary, vindictive, and, of course sexist.

But there was, within the confines of a hierarchical news outlet, a rough democracy in the newsroom. Reporters had freedom to argue and could persuade editors to acquiesce, using persuasive strategies ranging from sweet-talking and negotiation to cogent arguments defending the journalistic integrity of the story.

The newsroom at a major metropolitan daily illustrates the role that organizational factors play in news. The decline of *The Plain Dealer*'s newsroom in recent decades, like those of other newspapers, highlights another theme of the chapter: the role economic factors play in news, particularly the ways that market factors, plummeting advertising, and the financial bottom line have taken a toll on journalism, especially at the local level.

This chapter tales a macro turn, examining news determinants that extend beyond the usual individual and professional journalistic suspects. The first portion of the chapter explores the impact on news of organizational structures and processes, encompassing newsroom architecture, social stress, gender intersections, and news outlets' political biases. The second section describes the market forces that have exerted punishing effects on newspapers, as well as the economic intersections between news and social media. The third portion brings organizational and economic issues together by focusing on local news, a classic, frequently overlooked component of news that has robust implications for democracy.

Organizational Forces

Traditionally, when you worked for a newspaper or television station, you worked in a crowded newsroom, full of clacking typewriters or humming computers, punctuated by stimulating conversations, shouting matches, a captivating flow of adrenalin, and the unadulterated thrill of finishing a story on deadline. The kick of a byline and news story completed on deadline remain, but the breadth of organizational factors has expanded, influencing the news product in many ways (see Table 9.1). Let's examine each of these factors.

First, *the organizational structure and nature of the newsroom matter* (Altmeppen, 2008). Working for an old-fashioned conventional newspaper, with an authoritative, hierarchical chain of command, exerts different organizational strains than writing for a smaller citizen journalism website,

Table 9.1 Key Organization Influences on News

1. Nature of the news organization and newsroom
2. Stresses and work changes produced by multimedia news emphasis
3. Organizational culture of news outlet
4. Owners' political ideologies that explicitly or subtly influence news

with a more communal atmosphere and relaxed deadline structure (albeit with less frenetic excitement). Laboring in a crowded, high-octane, newsroom exerts different organizational pressures than reporting for a more contemporary online-focused newspaper, with less buzz, fewer silos and walls, and more open space to encourage connectivity, at least in theory (Coester, 2017).

Newsrooms at conventional media outlets have changed over the years. Many have been restructured, with online editors moved to the center of the newsroom and older-style metro editors shifted to the back of the newsroom, signifying a change in power relations (Robinson, 2011). The news organization is now staffed by social media and digital editors, showcasing the central role that online content, with its constant need for updates, plays in daily journalism.

Yet, as more news outlets have moved from physical to virtual newsrooms, and more reporters work offsite, cost-saving benefits that accrue to news organizations may be accompanied by social costs, such as reduced camaraderie and diminished commitment to the organization. Journalists are not passive participants in workplace technology changes; they define and construct the technological change process, integrating changes with their preferred ways to report and write up news on deadline (Boczkowski, 2004). Old habits die hard. For a number of reporters, the storied, routine focus on raw immediacy may be more important than a broader organizational focus on interactivity with online users (Domingo, 2008), showcasing how routines and organizational factors can clash.

A second organizational factor is *the increased emphasis on multimedia news*. Journalists are now expected to multitask in diverse realms, encompassing traditional reporting, continuous online updates, interactive graphics, and self-promotion on Twitter. The increasingly diversified, rapidly paced news cycle can place considerable pressure on reporters, who must constantly switch from one mental orientation and task to another, cognizant that they must abide by the time-honored accuracy norm to get their facts right. *New York Times* reporters interviewed by Usher (2014) reported that they were stressed and exhausted by trying to simultaneously work on traditional print and contemporary online routines. "The immediate needs of all the news all the time on the Web has taken over," one reporter said.

> We are now asked to do a lot of things, get news out very fast, feed the Web site, the *International Herald Tribune*, and do eight or nine versions ... This is not what you would have done ten years ago. There are more demands on time.
>
> (Usher, 2014, p. 138)

These new multimedia job demands, amplified by deadline pressure, and exacerbated when management is insensitive to the pressures reporters face, causes stress, even burnout. When editors, not traditionally known for their deep levels of social empathy, fail to provide reporters support at the organizational level, their lack of sensitivity can compound stress. This in turn can magnify family conflicts over work issues, even causing burnout, a problem that young women reporters (given gender-stereotyped pressures that women still face) are particularly likely to experience (MacDonald et al., 2016). News organizations can be exciting, but stressful places to work, given intense financial pressures, low salaries, and intra-organizational conflicts, exemplified by ever-increasing union-ization of journalists, pitting reporters concerned with stagnating wages against news outlets with a gimlet-eyed focus on bottom-line profits.

A third broad organizational factor that influences news is *organizational climate or culture, the shared values and meanings that animate a particular newspaper, television network, or citizen journalism outlet's workaday ethos* (Bantz, 1997; Hanitzsch, 2007; Schultz, 1994; Wilkins, 2014). News organizations differ in their cultural values, institutional traditions, and occupational values. For example, some news outlets convey a long tradition of Pulitzer Prize-winning investigative journal-ism, where competition for awards may dominate the culture, fueled by big-name, self-promoting, reporters. At other news outlets, a cooperative norm can flourish, and at still others the atmosphere is cold, indifferent, and dominated by fear of layoffs by corporate owners. At smaller news organizations, the ethos can favor identification with the community and boosting local traditions, spanning local sports teams, downtown devel-opments, and, more negatively, historical relics, like statues of Confeder-ate soldiers. The news organization's cultural lineage filters down to reporters, who become socialized into the occupational values and roles of the news organization, internalizing occupational norms of the parti-cular news outlet to get along, get ahead, and do their jobs seamlessly and efficiently (Breed, 1955; Tuchman, 1972).

Gender, as always, comes into the fray. An organizational glass ceiling persists, hampering the ability of qualified women journalists to advance toward executive positions, subtly maintained through formal and infor-mal mechanisms, including lack of support networks for women repor-ters (Robinson, 2008). To be sure, as more women assume executive positions in news organizations, less hierarchical, more collaborative approaches to newswork, traditionally congenial with women's approaches to problem-solving, can characterize the newsroom culture (Everbach, 2006). At the same time, there are undoubtedly complex intersections between the type of female boss and the organization she is leading. Even so, a masculine, male-focused newsroom culture persists, exerting gendered influences via organizational structures, assignment to particular beats, and everyday interpersonal communication (Chambers,

Steiner, & Fleming, 2004). What's more, the legacy of sexual abuse in new outlets, documented graphically in #MeToo posts and exposés of famous male journalists' lecherous behavior, serves as a cautionary note, reminding us that long-time patriarchal patterns can exert ugly effects on the working lives of aspiring female journalists.

And then there is *politics, the controversial, and in many ways most intriguing, influence of news organizations on content.* As discussed in Chapter 7, on the individual level, reporters at conventional news outlets rarely display partisan bias. On the organizational level, it can be a different story, where competition for an ever-dwindling conventional news audience and the emergence of niche programming that appeals to staunch partisans have led some news organizations to color news with a right-wing or left-wing hue. The role of news organization owners and organizational political culture, writ large, is deserving of extended discussion, presented below.

You will note that there is much more discussion of the conservative biases of the Fox News than those of liberal news outlets like MSNBC and *The New York Times.* This does not reflect any bias I harbor, against (or for) Fox News, I hasten to add, appreciating that some readers might understandably view it in this light! There is simply more empirical evidence that documents Fox News's political biases than those of the other news outlets. What's more, Fox, as the most highly watched cable news network, exerts a larger impact on the national conversation (and the president, in the case of Donald Trump) than its liberal competitors. In fact, scholars refer to the "Fox News Effect" to describe its empirical impact; viewing Fox News propelled Republicans and even some Democrats to support Republican candidates, an effect that MSNBC did not exert on a comparable group of voters (Benkler, Faris, & Roberts, 2018).

The point here is not Fox per se, so much as the ways that news organization owners' political perspectives influence the ways reporters do their jobs, and in this way shape news content.

Organization-Level Political Biases

On the liberal side of the spectrum, there are examples and evidence of bias on the part of MSNBC News, whose prime time host Rachel Maddow proudly communicates left-of-center political sentiments. In 2019, MSNBC televised a town hall-style meeting marking Democrat Nancy Pelosi's return to Congressional power as Speaker of the House, offering the Democrats a handout in free publicity (Stolberg, 2019). In 2016, Democratic officials had a direct pipeline to MSNBC, as the head of the Democratic National Committee arranged meetings with MSNBC executives to develop relationships that would encourage the cable network to provide Hillary Clinton with more favorable press (Grynbaum, 2016). In 2012, less than 5 percent of MSNBC's news stories about

Republican nominee Mitt Romney were positive, while 71 percent were negative (Peters, 2012).

Long-time observers of *The New York Times* have detected a shift to the left in *Times* coverage since Trump was elected through the use of unfavorable adjectives to describe Trump, like "mercurial," as well as negative attributions of his political success, as in a story describing his successful 2016 election campaign as "laden with Trump falsehoods and scurrilous innuendo," and his "blindsiding the public" with his executive orders on immigration and foreign policy (McFadden, 2018, pp. 16–17; Pressman, 2018). A more conservative news organization would have written this differently, calling Trump bombastic, not mercurial, referring to Hillary Clinton's misleading statements on her email server, in contrast to Trump's punchy, pointed policy statements, and describing his muscular executive orders as president that reversed unpopular policies on immigration.

Yet, as consistent as these examples from *The Times* seem to observers, they are not drawn systematically from a population of the newspaper's news stories, some of which have offered favorable coverage of the economy during Trump's years in office and offered critical news about Bill Clinton's impeachment saga. On the other hand, there are news outlets that unquestionably trend toward liberal values (*The New York Times* is clearly in this group), and one would be naïve, as well as oblivious to research, to deny the impact their organizational norms exert on some gatekeeping decisions.

The Fox Factor

Although Fox is a bona fide news network, whose reporters cover the White House, it projects distinctive biases. Empirical research shows that across different elections, Fox favors – even slants – news to favor Republican candidates (see Brock, Rabin-Havt, & Media Matters for America, 2012). Even during the 2006 election campaign, when real-world events legitimately generated more bad news for Republican than Democratic candidates, Fox was the only news outlet where there were about as many even-handed or positive stories about Republicans as negative ones (Groeling, 2008; Iyengar & Hahn, 2009).

To understand Fox you have to dig into the biography of Roger Ailes, the bombastic, offensive former chairman and CEO of Fox News, who started out as a producer on a daytime talk show, then harnessed his timely recognition that politics is entertainment, as well as conservative political philosophy, to engage in landmark political consulting for Presidents Richard Nixon, Ronald Reagan, and George H.W. Bush, all of whom profited handsomely from the blunt Ailes' cynical, but canny, wisdom about how to exploit news for political ends (see Figure 9.1). During the 1990s, Ailes once called CNN the "Clinton News Network" –

Figure 9.1 Roger Ailes (left), the late chairman and CEO of Fox News, who insistently, successfully, but controversially, pushed a conservative agenda at Fox that served as an organization-wide, biasing influence on news.

which was not exactly true, but served his political agenda. Sure enough, Fox milked the 1998 Clinton-Lewinsky sexual scandal for ratings gold, harnessing "Fox's prime-time stars, Bill O'Reilly and Sean Hannity … as cultural bulwarks against a growing number of contemptible influences: Bill Clinton's libido, the media, environmentalism, gay activists you name it" (Sherman, 2014, p. 225).

Over the past three decades, Fox branded itself as a network opposed to the dogmatic liberal line supposedly pursued by the mainstream media (or the "lamestream" media, as 2008 Republican vice presidential candidate Sarah Palin amusingly called it), drawing on unabashedly (and to supporters, refreshingly) conservative stars like Palin, Glenn Beck, Sean Hannity, and Bill O'Reilly, the latter a magnet to millions of viewers, until he was fired under a cloud of sexual harassment in 2017. Anchors like Beck, who once said that Obama was a racist, "a guy who has a deep-seated hatred for white people," drew more than two million viewers a day, recruiting huge advertising revenues (Berry & Sobieraj, 2014, p. 53; Sherman, 2014). Fox broke the mold with its obtrusive approach, although, from a historical perspective, you could find parallels in the partisan press of the 19th century and Henry Luce's *Time Magazine*, with its patently pro-American perspective, despite alternative views of complex 20th-century events.

Fox's news, frequently intermingled with commentary (as is the case with other cable news programs), has focused endlessly on issues that appealed to conservative viewers, framing controversies in ways that made conservatives look good and liberals appear bad or stupid. Fox gave enormous coverage to the conservative Tea Party groups that raucously challenged President Obama in 2009; went full hog on the birther conspiracy theory issue that falsely claimed Obama had not produced his original birth certificate, not-so-subtly suggesting that the African American Obama was not a bona fide American citizen; and in 2018 gave substantial news play to the horrific murder of an Iowa college student by an undocumented immigrant, playing up the factually incorrect storyline that immigrants are more likely to commit violent crime than native-born Americans (e.g., Savillo & Groch-Begley, 2014; Schroeck & Johnson, 2011).

Indeed, over the course of Trump's presidency, Fox crossed even its own highly partisan line, lavishing so much favorable coverage on the Trump White House that "it can be hard to determine, during a particular news cycle, which one is following the other's lead" (Mayer, 2019, p. 40). Fox anchor Hannity freely fraternized with Trump Administration officials (even hugged a Cabinet official), and former co-host Kimberly Guilfoyle worked on Trump's 2020 reelection campaign, even dating his son, Donald Trump, Jr.!

The Sinclair Phenomenon

Conservative media, aggressively courting viewers in their hiring and content decisions, have been more successful than partisan liberal conglomerates in capturing major shares of the market. Like Fox, the Sinclair Broadcast Group is a telecommunications giant, owning more than 190 television stations in 89 markets, the most in the U.S. Their news reaches nearly four in ten American television viewers, and it has a decidedly, consistent slant: pro-Trump, reliably conservative, no-bones-about-it anti-liberal (Kolhatkar, 2018).

During the 2016 campaign, Sinclair's chairman took a chapter from Ailes's book, telling Trump "we are here to deliver your message. Period" (Kolhatkar, 2018, p. 31). They did so during the election and afterwards, actually requiring anchors to read from a prepared script that echoed Trump's (inaccurate) claims about biased, "fake news," an act so outrageous that it led the website Deadspin to satirically remix the broadcasts of anchors into a segment where all of the anchors in different cities spoke the same words simultaneously. The video went viral, eliciting a firestorm of protest against Sinclair, tempering the telecommunication giant, but only for a time. Attesting to the company's impact, research finds that once Sinclair has purchased local stations, stations adopt a national focus, skewing predictably to the right (Kolhatkar, 2018).

Such news not only showcases organizational biases; it also pinpoints a cynical marketing strategy rooted in the owner's political views. By delivering a news commodity that plays to conservative audience members' political biases, stations offer a nostrum that stokes viewers' values, recruiting people who share Sinclair's political perspective. Fox has pursued this strategy, but so too has MSNBC, and perhaps *The New York Times.*

Thus, the ideological biases of owners can skew certain cable and broadcast stations in political directions, producing a bias befitting the definition offered in Chapter 7. The bias is more pronounced at conservative Fox and Sinclair-owned stations, as well as at the more liberal MSNBC, than at other cable and online news outlets, that strive, however imperfectly, to steer clear of consistent political biases, partly to avoid alienating a broad, politically heterogeneous audience. This may be changing, as more news outlets use news as a niche marketing tool to recruit like-minded consumers, pitting the economics of news against the quintessential values of objectivity and journalistic responsibility. The battle between economic sustainability and responsibility continues apace, showcased by the role contemporary economics plays in gatekeeping decisions.

Economic Influences

You cannot understand news without appreciating money. That's probably a statement that holds for just about everything, except maybe love and marriage, although you would get an argument from some economists, who take an economic perspective toward selecting a spouse and deciding how many children to bear (Hershey, 2014). Economic issues, spanning supply and demand, pricing, and market factors, impact news in any economic system, but the effects are frequently more striking in a capitalistic economy, where news is a commodity in which advertising, audience demand, and monopolistic influences exert outsize effects. This section discusses the role of economics, focusing on their dramatic effects on newspapers and news in the social media milieu.

I begin by reviewing the steep decline in newspapers, once a bastion of muscular financial strength. To be sure, most people, particularly students perusing this book, probably don't read a print paper at all. But for journalism devotees, who admire legendary investigative print reporters, and scholars, who appreciate the pivotal political impact of newspapers, newspapers offer a fitting first window to glimpse the economic influences on news.

Gloom and Doom in the Newspaper World

The name of the website says it all: *newspaperdeathwatch.com.* The telltale bluntness of the site elicits a smile, but the news is grim. The site regularly lists newspapers that have gone out of business, as well as

WIPs, Works in Progress, daily papers that cut back or adopted new cost-cutting interventions. Research bears out these pronouncements.

Print newspapers grew by enormous leaps and bounds in the 19th century and dominated news for the first half of the 20th century. They were profitable enterprises, "cash cows" that gave lucrative returns to investors and owners, with advertising revenues increasing from 1985 to 2005 at an annual rate of $1.1 billion (Soloski, 2013). Then things changed.

Newspaper profits plummeted, beginning in the first decade of the new century, as ad revenues plunged by more than 55 percent, dropping dramatically in 2007; total advertising profits fell $26.7 billion from 2005 to 2011 (Kovach & Rosenstiel, 2014; see Figure 9.2). What's more, during the first decade of the 21st century, as seismic technological and financial changes impacted print, daily print newspaper circulation in the U.S. tumbled, falling by 11 percent between 2002 and 2012. Circulation and advertising revenue have markedly declined by an annual rate of about 10 percent, according to one recent estimate, portending more cutbacks and deficits in the quality of news (Newspapers Fact Sheet, 2018).

These revenue losses took a huge toll on journalism. The number of journalists employed in U.S. newsrooms dropped by about a third from 2000 to 2012 (with particularly heavy losses in the newspaper industry),

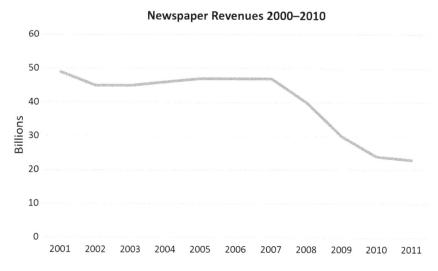

Figure 9.2 Declining newspaper revenues, 2000 to 2010. During the first decade of the 21st century, print newspaper advertising revenues plunged, dropping dramatically in 2007 and continuing to plummet over the ensuing years (from Soloski, 2013)

diminishing the quality of national and local reporting (Anderson, 2013; Pickard, 2019; see Figure 9.3). Indeed, journalists, particularly those working for daily newspapers, have experienced decrements in their ability to get important issues covered in news articles (Weaver, 2009).

The ever-increasing cemetery of print newspapers includes tombstones for the storied *Rocky Mountain News* in Denver and Seattle's *Post-Intelligencer* (now available only online; Hargreaves, 2014; see also Alexander, 2016). *The Philadelphia Inquirer* went through bankruptcy and hand-offs by four different owners over a five-year period. The once-mighty Tribune newspaper chain was sold to a real estate magnate, who slashed news budgets, only to experience bankruptcy in the wake of poor management and financial difficulties (Usher, 2014). In a dramatic symbol of the devastation, *The New York Daily News*, that rough-and-tumble tabloid with shirtsleeves-rolled-up appeal to the city's working class, the daily that was a model for *The Daily Planet* (particularly reporters Lois Lane and Clark Kent), slashed its newsroom staff by half in July, 2018 (Peiser, 2018a).

All told, from 1970 to 2016, the year the American Society of News Editors stopped counting, some 500 daily newspapers went belly-up, and the rest reduced news coverage, trimmed the size of the paper, or terminated the print edition (Lepore, 2019).

Not to be outdone, the British landscape is also littered with the debris of declining newspapers. As Figure 9.4 shows, national newspaper circulation in the UK fell by more than 35 percent from 2003 to 2014. Similar hemorrhaging occurred across Western Europe, although certain

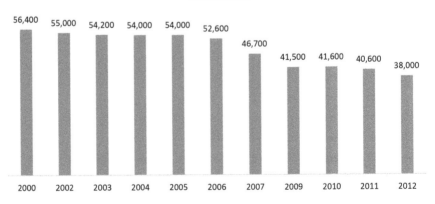

Journalists Employed in American Newsrooms

Figure 9.3 Reduction in number of journalists employed in American newsrooms during critical period of newspaper decline (from Hargreaves, 2014)

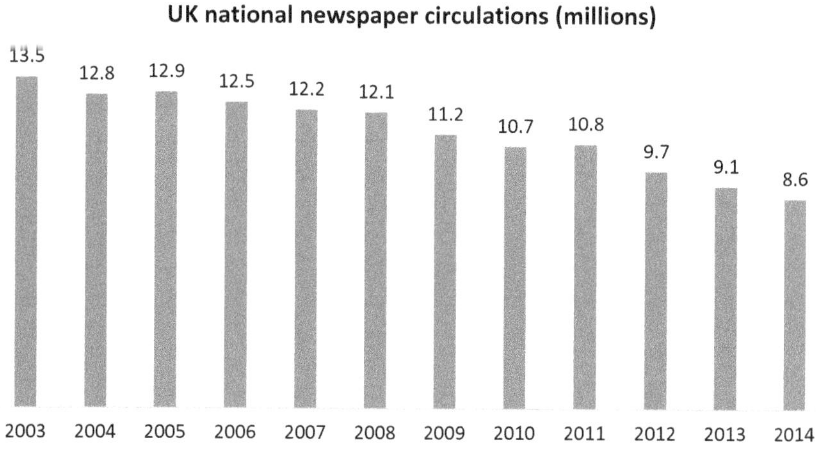

UK national newspaper circulations (millions)

Figure 9.4 Reduction in UK national newspaper circulation during critical period of newspaper decline (from Hargreaves, 2014)

countries, like France, were insulated because the press is more subsidized by government (Ryfe, 2017).

All this raises the central academic question: Why? What factors led to the decline of newspapers and the collapse of financial fortunes in the print newspaper industry? Scholars have identified a number of explanations (see Table 9.2). The key factors are:

- *Emergence of the Web and social media.* News (broadly defined) reported on websites and then on Twitter has encouraged people to bypass newspapers and other conventional media. In the old days, when traditional news outlets were the only portals for information about the larger world, they were the only game in town, the sole gatekeepers that provided access to news. That is no longer the case, and it has changed the economic and social foundations of news. Scarcity of news content could drive up advertising rates, but this hardly characterizes the online world (Freedman, 2010). Indeed, there is so much public affairs content on the Internet (albeit, of questionable value) that it is hard for newspapers to charge advertisers high prices for news.
- *Popularity of Craigslist, the classified advertising website.* Craigslist gradually made newspaper classified ads, a major source of revenue, irrelevant and, for most papers, killed them off, significantly reducing revenues.

- *Reduction in display advertising revenue.* In the old days, newspapers gained a majority of their funding from business display ads. However, their online equivalents are placed at cheaper prices than in print, generating only 5 to 10 percent of the profits of print ads. Newspapers have lost money from the emergence of online advertising and marketing, and online ads have not brought in the revenue stream publishers expected (Picard, 2011; Sneed, 2013; Soloski, 2013). Indeed, the decline in revenue from print ads has greatly outstripped gains in online digital revenue, aggravated by Google gobbling up display ads from print (Bell & Owen, 2017; Pickard, 2017).
- *Lack of profit for outlets that actually gather the news.* As Jones (2009) notes, search engines like Google and social media sites are

'free riders,' who get the benefit of offering their audience a range of reported news that has been generated by newspapers and other media. But the originating news organizations get little if any enduring traffic to their own sites … Google, in other words, makes money from the news article while the newspaper does the work

(Jones, 2009, p. 187)

- *Collapse of a distribution model to replace the delivery of newspapers on the doorstep and in newsstands.* In the main, newspapers have failed to develop a successful online funding model. Struggling with the web in the early years, newspapers faced a dilemma: They could put news stories online for free, but this encouraged subscribers to drop subscriptions, reducing circulation-based revenue. If they charged for news, readers would opt instead to read news on sites that did not charge for content (Jones, 2009). After many newspapers allowed users to read stories online for free, it became difficult to charge people for what they thought was their right in a "free for all" online era (van der Wurff, 2012).
- *Difficulties with paywalls.* Paywalls emerged as a way to solve this problem. As the name suggests, a paywall is a device that limits access to news stories to paid subscribers. A tough or hard paywall requires users to subscribe to the newspaper in order to gain any access to the site. Although in theory it replenishes money lost from dropped print subscriptions, it is easy for people to circle around it, turning to news sites that, while perhaps less comprehensive, deliver information for free. A softer or metered paywall lets online users read a certain, specified number of articles before demanding they subscribe to the online news outlet. Although there is evidence that some news outlets have experienced increased circulation profits from paywalls, questions remain about their viability in the current milieu (Franklin, 2014), whether paywalls can sustain smaller newspapers with less established brands, and if audiences accustomed to getting news for free will shell out money for news over the long haul (van der Wurff, 2012).

How have news outlets reacted to these changes? In the main, they have turned online for readers, recognizing this is where the action is. Aggressively recruiting readers to build circulation, like the 19th-century press (Wu, 2016), newspapers have made changes in content and delivery, hyping trivial, but engaging content, famously exemplified by the buzz created by BuzzFeed's "What Colors Are This Dress" post about a dress a Scottish mother purchased to wear at her daughter's wedding (white and gold, or black and blue?). BuzzFeed also raised journalistic hackles over its widespread use of sponsored posts that can be hard to differentiate from news, deliberately, deceptively blurring the lines between advertising and news.

One area in which profit frequently collides with journalistic quality is clickbait. **Clickbait** refers to a seemingly titillating headline or story that encourages people to click on a link that promises more content than it delivers. The headline, the bait that encourages users to click, is the same come-on that yellow journalism used in the 19th century and local eyewitness news exploited in the 20th century to induce consumers to tune into crime or bizarre, novel events. Examples of clickbait headlines include: "Cabin crew take secret pictures, you won't believe the results"; "The must-see technology that is changing the way you listen"; "32 Pictures That Will Make You Say Awwwwwwww," and "He put garlic in his shoes before going to bed and what happens next is hard to believe." More prosaic stories can also generate clicks, like lists of top restaurants or weekend resorts.

Like a tickle, the headline invites the reader to click on the link to the news story. Of course, the headline is sensationalized and misleading, as the story may have little do with the headline, or if it does pick up on the headline, frequently concerns a trivial, though captivating issue. The publisher's goal is simple: invite users to click, count the clicks, and relay this to advertisers so news outlets can charge more money for advertisements. This is particularly

Table 9.2 Primary Economic Factors Explaining Newspaper Declines and Broader Changes in News

1. Collapse of standard news distribution model
2. Craigslist effects on classifieds
3. Decreases in display advertising revenue
4. Difficulties in developing successful online funding model, including paywall problems
5. Challenges in monetizing Facebook
6. Outsized emphasis on profit by out-of-town group owners

important for newspaper sites without paywalls, as these newspapers depend primarily on advertising revenue (Everett, 2018).

Given the demise of so many newspapers and declining circulation, one can certainly appreciate why news outlets would develop clicks as online bait. In fact, there is evidence that audience clicks do influence editors' selection of news, pushing editors to choose the most viewed articles (Welbers et al., 2016). But clickbait cheapens news. Like the odor of a delicious meal that turns out to foretell a fatty high-caloric dinner, clickbait disappoints and deceives. As a long-time journalist, Harlan Spector, former Cleveland *Plain Dealer* reporter and leader of its union, observed:

> My take on clickbait in news is more about playing up and promoting fluff stories, celebrity stories, sexy stories, trending nonsense, partially reported stories, etc. – content likely to generate clicks – at the expense of arguably more important stories that don't generate desired traffic. It's concerning, in my opinion, if news decisions are based more on a desire to maximize clicks than on journalistic merit. In Cleveland, we've seen a proliferation of non-stories masquerading as news, and a de-emphasis of serious reporting about public institutions of Northeast Ohio.
>
> (Spector, 2018b)

But there's the thing: News outlets don't need clickbait to bolster revenues. Journalism scholar Philip Meyer (2004) has shown that the more readers perceive newspapers as credible, the stronger their circulation. Publishing informative news stories, empathy-inducing features, and investigative reports can help the bottom line. Unfortunately, these goals are seen as more difficult to pursue than the simpler clickbait. Publishers who agree with Meyer argue that they don't have the economic luxury to assign reporters, or hire new ones, to write these stories. In many cases their reluctance stems from underestimating readers' interest in substantial news, fear that the costs will be too high, or refusal to consider options that would reduce their profits. Even storied newspapers like *The New York Times* have moved to blur lines that would never have been crossed, engaging in subtle, sedate clickbaiting, publishing funny videos that have nothing to do with news, like people doing yoga with goats, and goading the business and news departments to work together more, as when an idea for a new focus in the Styles section came from the advertising department (Abramson, 2019).

Social Media, News Economics, and Normative Issues

Two-thirds of Americans receive some of their news from social media, such as Twitter, YouTube, the ever-innovative Snapchat, and particularly Facebook (Shearer & Gottfried, 2017). More than two-fifths of traffic to news sites comes via Facebook (Isaac & Ember, 2016). Consequently, news organizations have had to confront the role Facebook plays in distributing news they once distributed themselves via print and online news sites.

As Facebook has become an ever-important gatekeeper, publishers grappled with a dilemma. They could build up their websites, gaining potentially smaller audiences, but preserving control over profits and brand identity, an increasingly important factor in contemporary news (Holton & Molyneux, 2017). Alternatively, they could cede control over publishing to technology companies by posting more content on social media platforms, as many have done (Rashidian, Brown, & Hansen, 2018).Traditional, elite news organizations like *The New York Times*, which emphasize loyalty, have focused on the former, gaining traffic from direct visitors to their site. Increasingly, though, news outlets have gravitated to the second approach, viewing Facebook and its billions of users as a path toward recruiting new readers and increasing revenues. By sharing links to stories that appear on news outlets' websites, news organizations hope to drive users to their website, gaining page views and advertising. However, with a few exceptions, the capacity of social media to drive traffic to news organizations' websites and increase advertising revenue has not proved impressive, in part because Facebook and Google are underpaying news organizations, which, of course, create the content that is shared (Ju, Jeong, & Chyi, 2014; Rusbridger, 2018).

News organizations also have pursued more targeted approaches, trying to partner with Facebook and tailor content to the social networking site (Isaac & Ember, 2016). For example, a news outlet could designate a story for Facebook's Instant Articles, allowing users perusing Facebook in a mobile app to read the article, complete with interactive features, within Facebook. News media outlets could monetize the app by selling ads in the article and pocketing the money, or gaining access to Facebook advertisers with Facebook's Audience Network.

But the formula has met with mixed success. A number of media outlets showed lackluster interest in Instant Articles, partly because Facebook began to deemphasize content from news publishers (Brown, 2018). While Facebook for years encouraged news organizations to rely more on the social media site to increase audience size, the company changed its algorithm, favoring posts from friends and family over public content from publishers. Facing criticism about whether its content has negative effects and that its algorithms may have assigned higher priority to fake news in News Feeds, Facebook deemphasized "passive content," like news stories people simply click to read, in favor of posts and videos family and friends share that makes them feel good, not bad, after visiting the site (Isaac, 2018). To Facebook, high quality content was all about engagement – stories that stimulated users to post a comment or share it with friends. Engaging in these activities was presumed to increase the chances users noticed the all-important advertising that adjoined the story. Pages that earned high engagement would advance in Facebook rankings, meaning that they would be shown to many followers, presumably increasing their advertising panache (Abramson, 2019). Engagement, via its assumed impact on number of eyeballs viewing advertisements, could deliver more money to news publishers.

This raises normative concerns. Facebook, never intended to be a publisher or gatekeeper of news, makes decisions based on commercial criteria, not journalistic social responsibilities. Perusing positive information on Facebook is not the same as receiving critical, frequently negative and nuanced, information that citizens need to evaluate leaders, and leaders need to serve constituents. If news becomes dumbed down so it includes a smartphone announcement that there is a really cool burrito restaurant downtown, news may not exactly be fulfilling its broader responsibilities (Taplin, 2017, p. 169)! This underscores the conundrum that occurs when social media become gatekeepers, and the largest social networking sites are placed in the uncomfortable position of curating the role that news plays in a democratic society.

Summary

From a journalistic perspective, the issues are survival and growth of online news outlets. Although it once seemed that digital news would simply replace the mainstream news media dinosaurs, accumulating healthy profits from the masses of millennials perusing their phones, it hasn't worked that way. Digital news outlets have faced challenges in making a sustainable profit from news and devising a workable model to monetize news content. Online news organizations have experimented with sponsored posts and branded content, which blur lines between advertising and news, as well as with different collaborations with Facebook and paid subscriptions (Abramson, 2019). It is a mixed, uncertain picture. Some sites like Vox Media and Axios have reported financial gains, while others (AOL and Yahoo) have laid off employees (Lee, 2019). Just like their print counterparts – some of which, like *The Washington Post* and *The New York Times* have grown as they accommodate to online readers – digital outlets face gnawing economic challenges in the disruptive news market.

The Case of Local News

These issues – organizational, economics, and normative – volatilely come to the fore in the case of local news. If "all politics is local," as former U.S. House Representative Tip O'Neill famously said, so too has journalism developed from local foundations. Newspapers grew as cities expanded. In the 19th century newspapers helped socialize immigrants to

American urban life. During the 20th century newspapers, read on subways and discussed in diners, were part of the social tapestry of residential life. They commanded considerable loyalty from urban residents, who avidly read their sports pages and developed love/hate relationships with columnists (Kaniss, 1991). In small towns, print papers had a loyal following and had a symbiotic relationship with town leaders, the newspapers depending on leaders to provide official access to reporters, the leaders relying on newspapers to support their civic and political projects.

Sociological Issues

Communication researcher Phillip Tichenor and his colleagues viewed these issues through the lens of functional theory, which emphasizes that society consists of complex webs of relationships, with media and communities performing interrelated roles that have societal functions. The particular function a newspaper performs depends in part on the size of the community (Tichenor, Donohue, & Olien, 1980). In small towns, newspapers historically steered clear of conflict, providing relatively little coverage of disputes among leaders or between leaders and influential members of the public

According to the functional view, the culture of small-town newspapers favored cooperation between political leaders and reporters, who knew each other and endorsed similar pro-town values. What's more, small-town norms did not favor open dissent or opposition, which could imperil the solidarity and cohesiveness of the community (Perloff, 1998). For example, the newspaper covered up conflicts that erupted at a city council meetings, presenting instead a mythical view of the legislative process through a respectful narrative that depicted the council as a sober, authoritative body that reached decisions dispassionately and efficiently (Paletz, Reichert, & McIntyre, 1971). And, of course, in the case of virulent racism, small-town papers were loath to describe the prejudice that African Americans faced, for fear of uprooting the status quo (see Box 9.1 for a contemporary example of status quo affirmation on the part of the local press in the online age).

Box 9.1 Coverage of the Steubenville Rape Case through the Lens of Functional Theory

We gain insight into the complex, current dynamics of local news, viewed through Tichenor and his colleagues' functional approach, by examining how different media covered the horrific case of a 16-year-old girl who was raped by two high school football players during a rowdy night of partying in Steubenville, Ohio on August 11, 2012. In a fascinating, thorough study of how the national, regional, and local press covered the story, Robert E. Gutsche Jr. and Erica Salkin (2016) found that different newspapers invoked different moral and cultural narratives, in keeping with their divergent missions, audiences, and economic underpinnings.

Intriguingly, national newspapers focused on the adolescent girl as a victim, the cruelty she experienced that resulted from the community's "hero worshipping" of the football culture. The regional press acknowledged the girl's victimhood, but suggested she was partly responsible for attending a party without her parents' permission; yet the newspapers suggested the community bore responsibility for what happened. In sharp contrast, local newspapers in the Steubenville, Ohio area tended to blame the victim for her sexual abuse, presenting her as "faceless and person-less," while offering more humanizing, personifying portrayals of the boys as "student-athletes, " for whom the sexual attack was "completely out of character" (Gutsche & Salkin, 2016, p. 463).

As Tichenor and his colleagues' work on community news suggests, the local Steubenville newspapers found it functional to offer defensively protective coverage of Steubenville, an economically depressed steel town that basks in the reflected glory of the Steubenville High School Big Red football team, its legendary athletic performance, and desire to symbolically keep "Steubenville on the map" (Macur & Schweber, 2012). However, the local newspapers' coverage was insensitive, even cruel to the female victim. The researchers emphasized how proximity of readers to news events shaped the "mythical archetypes" and narratives used to explain what happened; the local press, focusing on the Youngstown audience, cast the victim as a "disturbance to local community values" (Gutsche & Salkin, 2016, p. 467). The national press, farthest removed from the city's community myths, could point to problems in the football culture, while the regional press, proximally in between the national and local newspapers, offered coverage that was both critical of, and sympathetic with, the community.

Intriguingly, it took a blogger unconnected with the politics and economics of local news outlets to shine a light of truth on the problem.

The blogger, Alexandria Goddard, was a former resident of Steubenville, whose early, honest reporting helped bring the issue to national attention. Goddard posted screenshots of caustic comments football players made about the teenage girl at parties, posts by high school girls who disparaged the victim's reputation, tweets from students who vowed to support the boys who were arrested, and an Instagram photo of the two boys carrying the victim, while nude, appropriately blurring the image that blocked the victim (Preston, 2013). Goddard's blog, clearly journalism in the bravest, most investigative sense of the word, helped propel the more cautious conventional newspapers to cover the story and frame the story in ways that were more empathic toward the victim. Tichenor and his colleagues' approach suggests that a blog, freed from the need to appeal to the cultural values of a local audience, found it functional to shine a truthful light on the cruelty of the players, as well as the ways that a young girl was physically victimized and morally shamed. In this way, online media can compensate for the shortcomings of conflict-averse local news, fulfilling informational and watchdog functions that call attention to an urban travesty.

In contrast to small town newspapers, big city papers, serving different sociological functions, provide abundant coverage of conflicts and social problems in both their news and editorial pages (Chang, 2015; Demers, 1998). Conflict is endemic to metropolitan areas, characterized as they are by large diverse populations, a broad range of groups contesting power, and more open expression of frustrations caused by socioeconomic inequalities. City leaders, finding it more difficult to work out conflicts through interpersonal channels than their homogenized small town counterparts, leak stories, hoping to use the news to settle a conflict in a preferred direction. Urban interest groups and protest leaders harness media to promote their causes, seeking to use publicity to set the agenda and frame issues in ways that will force leaders' hands. Conflict, a classic news value, is routinely played up in metropolitan news outlets. Big city news media profit handsomely from showing conflict, as protests and crime news recruit readers and draw interest from social activists.

Boosterism

Complicating matters in intriguing ways, metropolitan newspapers, in some instances, also play down conflict, offering unabashedly, patriotic coverage of city causes and institutions. News media in cities (as well as small towns) dole out lavishly supportive – and biased! – coverage of local sports teams, playing the role of cheerleader rather than critic, particularly when a high school, college or professional city team is in the championships. Similarly, when it comes to civic projects, like a downtown convention center in Chicago, a redevelopment project in Los Angeles, a proposed convention center in Philadelphia, and the rock and roll hall of fame in Cleveland, the local press has rolled over – and rocked in the latter case – for the projects, singing their praises, accepting official sources' problematic estimates of total project costs in the

Philadelphia case, and offering up a chorus of good, rather than critical, news (Kaniss, 1991; Perloff, 1998).

As organizations, news outlets showcase their cultural identification with the growth of the community. Economically, newspaper owners, maintaining that "what is good for the city is good for the paper," recognize that new projects bring jobs, outside visitors, new branded images, and prestige, all of which can recruit more residents (potential subscribers) and businesses, which can be tapped for advertisements. This self-serving news logic offers up pro-business coverage that boosts community elites, while simultaneously discouraging less powerful groups from challenging the community agenda (see Gutsche, 2015 for an interesting discussion).

It should be noted that much of this research was conducted in the 1980s and 1990s, and journalism has changed considerably since that time. Conflict is probably more common in smaller town and suburban newspapers, given the increased acceptance of conflict and protest in the U.S. over the past decades. Still, you are much less likely to see conflict displayed in news outlets in small towns than in bigger, more sociologically pluralistic cities. And, congenial with Tichenor and his colleagues' model, ethnic, and religious newspapers, hewing to a harmony-based approach, tend to be allergic to rocking the boat, offering few stories of conflict between groups or exposés of questionable, corrupt practices on the part of religious federations. But the big story of local news today concerns economics, returning us to the core role money plays in local news, particularly in an era rocked by technological transformations.

Economic Hemorrhaging

Even as local TV news continues to attract a large viewing audience (Matsa, 2018), local newspapers are in an acute state of crisis, facing financial hardship for the reasons discussed earlier in the chapter. National newspapers like *The Washington Post* and *The Wall Street Journal* have established brands, recruited affluent readers and obtained advertising from big businesses. They can count on their reputations, and excellent reporting (underwritten by proportionately larger budgets than local outlets) to recruit readers to subscribe to their websites, share stories via Facebook, and harness online apps.

Local – metropolitan and smaller city – newspapers cannot count on these resources and have struggled, trimming pages, cutting staff, and reducing the quality of content in favor of the journalistically despised clickbait. Many metropolitan dailies that once employed hundreds of reporters now employ only several dozen journalists. More than 1,300 U.S. communities that had vital newspapers in 2004 have no local news coverage whatsoever (A future without the front page, 2019). In two of many examples, *The Ithaca Journal* in upstate New York reduced an editorial staff that once boasted more than 20 journalists to just two reporters (Lee, 2016). In May, 2018, the 125-year-old *Denver Post*, which earned nine Pulitzer Prizes, announced plans to cut 30 staffers, part of a reduction of a staff of more than 250 to fewer than 100. The paper's esteemed reporters were so outraged they took an unusual step, denouncing by name the New York-based hedge fund owner, describing the harm to Colorado journalism the reductions would cause, noting that management enjoys heathy profits and didn't have to take this rash step (Ember, 2018). This example highlights an entirely different economic influence than those discussed earlier – the ways newspaper management has opted to cut staffers and made financial decisions that shamelessly placed profits ahead of the pursuit of local journalism.

Prioritizing Profit

Throughout the 20th century, print newspapers were owned by families and private companies, frequently housed in the same city as the newspaper. Newspapers could be hugely profitable enterprises, and corporations gradually took notice. Over the years, newspapers were gobbled up by chains or group owners, located in different cities from the paper, which functioned as either beneficent managers, or ruthless absentee landlords. Just a handful of big news corporations – Gannett, Digital First Media, and GateHouse Media – own about a fourth of all daily papers in the U.S. (Doctor, 2017). Indeed, chains, coupled with the increasing number of publicly held newspapers, have captured or control the preponderance of newspaper circulation in the U.S.

News media are free enterprise, capitalistic institutions that offer owners opportunities to make big profits, if they can manage the companies efficiently in an era of digital churn. While there is money to be made (and it has been), owners face daunting challenges in the digital era. Stock values have plunged, market values of newspapers have plummeted, and shareholders of news companies have placed pressure on owners to sell papers that don't make as much profit as they deem desirable (Dominick, 2013). Given the economic tremors the news industry faces, it is eminently reasonable for newspapers to harness contemporary corporate capital-maximizing strategies and appoint board members affiliated with successful financial institutions.

In some instances, the new financial arrangements are win-wins for the billionaire magnates and journalists. In several cases, the modern tycoons who bought newspapers have revitalized the news organizations, infusing them with journalistic energy, steering clear of making editorial decisions (Gelles, 2018). Once again on a national level, Amazon's Jeff Bezos purchased *The Washington Post*, increased the size of the newsroom, refrained from dabbling in news decisions, and seems to have made journalism a priority in his overall economic mission. Unfortunately, this is not the norm.

Companies like Tribune, McClatchy, and Avista Capital Partners, which own many smaller American newspapers, behave more like Wall Street companies consumed by the bottom line than groups committed to advancing a free press. For these publicly owned newspaper companies, which control a sizable proportion of U.S. daily newspaper circulation, "the business of news is business, not news. Their papers are managed and controlled for financial performance, not news quality" (Cranberg et al., 2001, p. 9). Their focus, pure and simple, is on revenue growth and pleasing their institutional investors (Soloski, 2013). Investors typically value a high rate of financial return, and management favors short-term goals at the expense of thoughtful long-term planning. One can study the financial reports of the newspapers and have no inkling that the businesses are newspapers, as opposed to hotels or expensive real estate.

The owners of big newspaper companies are primarily institutional investors, such as bank trust departments, insurance companies, and investment firms, which may make decisions based more on capital investment than classic news values (Picard, 1994). Investment firms, which manage financial securities for investment and profit, are currently the largest owners of American newspapers (Soloski, 2019). Unlike newspaper owners of the past, who sought to make a profit off journalism, investment companies are in business to satisfy customers with little concern about journalistic values – i.e., customers like commercial banks, mutual funds, and pension funds. Strong stock performance, maintaining a solid credit rating, conformity to market demands, and – above all – increased profit have become the driving force of many media companies, causing them to steer clear of controversy, avoid risky journalistic exposés, rely instead on safe, status quo-enhancing stories, and shove quality journalism aside (An & Jin, 2004; Cranberg, Bezanson, & Soloski, 2001).

Critics argue that many newspapers have double-digit profits, but, choosing to run their companies like lucrative financial firms, have opted to cut jobs and reduce news quality. Scholars lament that if owners were less concerned with their personal or corporate profit margin and emphasized long-term journalistic goals, they could plow back profits into hiring more reporters and embark on innovations that could enhance journalism, while also building circulation. For reporters who work at these absentee corporate owner-controlled city newspapers, the issues are not just dollars and cents. They're personal (see Box 9.2).

Box 9.2 The End of the Line

Harlan Spector worked for nine years at *The* (Cleveland) *Plain Dealer*'s metro desk before moving into reporting. He was proud he earned a job at Ohio's largest daily newspaper and loved the daily churn of the newsroom: the excitement, unpredictability, and even big egos. "Very few boring people work in newsrooms," a colleague observed (Theiss, 2018, p. 153). But as the newspaper business faced mounting technological and economic problems, some of its own making, his enthusiasm dampened. "It stops being fun when you see workers pay dearly for owners' bad decisions," he related, recalling both a senior editor who proclaimed that the Internet would never supplant newspapers and the series of decisions by management that eroded newspaper quality (Spector, 2018a, p. 169).

The Plain Dealer struggled to cope with the changing news scene during the 1990s, strategically emphasizing zoning, or tailoring news content to specific suburban communities, not to enhance journalistic quality, but to lure readers and advertising, even though experts doubted it could achieve these lofty goals. As it became clear *The Plain Dealer* was facing daunting economic challenges, for reasons discussed earlier in the chapter, the newspaper's owner, Advance Publications (a major national media company), acted. It reduced the editorial staff with a generous buyout in 2006, and in 2008 fired 50 members of the newspaper's reporters' union, the Guild, while terminating not one of the paper's managers. A year later management returned, with what seemed like a compromise that would avert a pyrrhic victory for reporters and the union. If the newspaper unions agreed to a 12 percent wage reduction, they could avoid laying off more than 60 reporters, printers, and other employees.

Reflecting back on the quandary, Spector, chairman of the newspaper's union or guild at the time, noted that he and other members of the newspaper guild were appalled by the ultimatum, but felt they had little choice. Management held a gun to their heads. They opted to go along, simply to save jobs. "I was never so proud of our union," Spector confessed (p. 169). Then reality came crashing down. Advance Publications, the out-of-town corporate owner, feeling it had to make more cuts to preserve the paper, cut quality in draconian ways, reducing the number of days the paper was home-delivered, and shifting staffers and resources to its non-unionized online outlet, Cleveland.com, to further trim costs.

Although management did keep its bargain – it didn't lay off reporters, photographers, page designers, and other staffers when the union accepted the 12 percent wage reduction – as time went on, Spector recalled, Advance failed to deal with the union in the good faith manner it promised. The company, he noted, violated portions of the contract, for example, cutting jobs and giving union work to company managers. The focus increasingly was on cost-cutting, clickbait, and publishing a newspaper that reporters felt compromised journalistic integrity. A community-based "Save *The Plain Dealer*" campaign and *60 Minutes* report could not stanch the bleeding. Layoffs continued, and, for many employees, sticking around in the face of the journalistic losses, insecure future employment prospects, and a stressful work environment wasn't worth it.

In the end, on July 30, 2013, after decades of reporting experience, Spector and other Guild members, with similar service, opted to leave. The Guild received decent terms: funding for pensions and health care. But reporters felt they had been forced out of journalism. Yet there were other ways the newspaper could have handled its financial travails. Management at *The Plain Dealer* could have could have called staffers to democratically determine how best to adapt to the online milieu by emphasizing content that could recruit readers while not sacrificing quality. They could have increased revenues by erecting a paywall, which requires users to subscribe to the newspaper in order to gain access to the site. Or Advance's top brass could have trimmed their high salaries so that reporters didn't take as much of a hit. None of the solutions was easy or pain-free, but might have provided a middle ground between profit-maximization and journalism.

While *The Plain Dealer* continues, to its credit, to publish daily, the size of the paper is a shadow of what it used to be. The behemoth of a news staff, some 400 reporters, editors, and other staffers in the newsroom at the paper's zenith in the 1990s, is a fraction of that today.

On that somber July afternoon, their last day in the storied newsroom, many reporters felt speechless and distraught, their journalistic spirit vacuumed out by an omnivorous force they could not realistically confront. "I walked around the newsroom in a daze for a while," Spector confessed, feeling numb, hugging old colleagues, reflecting on the good old days that were no longer.

Online Local Journalism: Grounds for Hope?

The macro picture, experienced up-close at Cleveland's daily newspaper, raises concerns. The economic downturn, aggravated by profits-over-news developments, have spawned concerns about the viability of local news, even with its tendency to cheerlead for flawed downtown developments. Local news can ideally serve social responsibility functions, including informational monitoring, watchdog journalism, and facilitating civic dialogue. Given the economic distresses local news outlets face, can digital innovations preserve some semblance of informative local news?

To some degree, online sites have helped sustain regional journalism. Undaunted by the hedge fund owners' staff cuts at *The Denver Post*, some of the *Post*'s former reporters and editors created a new online website, *The Colorado Sun*, that developed a financial base by partnering with a New York start-up and selling stakes in ownership to the public to prevent a group of rich investors from gaining control (Peiser, 2018b). Citizen journalism sites have also proliferated, providing coverage of local issues that can compensate for the shortage of such stories in conventional media.

Hyperlocal journalism, encompassing websites and apps that focus on issues of concern to a local area or smaller neighborhood, has grown in recent years (Shaw, 2007). In the arena of local sports, which is close to residents' hearts, *The Athletic*, a sports website and app, includes the latest coverage of local sports in at least 15 cities (Draper, 2017). Hyperlocal sites vary in quality and utility, with some content uncritically promoting neighborhood activities and other content emphasizing investigative stories, such as those in Fort Meyer, Florida's *The News-Press*, which blew the whistle on unreasonable cost increases in water and sewer hookups. The stories led to a 30 percent fee reduction and the resignation of a city official (Shaw, 2007). Similarly, as noted in Chapter 2, a homegrown Brooklyn, New York digital news site exposed neighborhood problems, notably a 27,000 gallon oil spill that authorities had not disclosed, propelling a city council member to introduce a bill that required agencies to immediately inform city officials of pollution risks. A fresh New York City nonprofit website, *The City*, was formed to offer in-depth investigative journalism on local issues in New York neighborhoods (Peiser, 2018c). In these cases, hometown reporters, citizen groups (and nonprofit foundations) stepped in to fill the gap left by the city press.

But these sites are not without problems. Some news sites can allow opinion to intrude into news coverage in ways that conventional news outlets would not allow. The economics of hyperlocal sites run hot and cold. Seizing the opportunity to reach new markets, big companies like Gannett, *The New York Times*, and MSNBC have purchased or partnered with sites (Rogers, 2017; Shaw, 2007). However, in a number of cases, hyperlocal sites are short of funding, operating on small budgets, lacking business models, as in the case of Patch, AOL's hyperlocal websites, or so reliant on local businesses that they can be tempted to cheerlead rather than criticize (Kennedy, 2013).

Predicting the future of local news, in light of economic tribulations, is difficult to make with confidence. Increasing numbers of community and city newspapers will go under, others moving totally online. New websites, like the sports outlet, *The Athletic*, which opportunistically pledges to let papers "continuously bleed until we are the last ones standing" (Draper, 2017, p. B7), are likely to grow by gaining funding from venture capital start-ups and subscriptions. But in the Darwinian app-eat-app world, only those online outlets that have a niche audience and can monetize the new milieu will survive. There remain questions about how beholden news organizations will be to venture groups that pay the piper.

Advertising is likely to play a diminished role in comparison to years past as reader-payment economic models become more prevalent. As one scholar presciently observed in 2003, "media content will become less a reflection of advertisers' audience preferences and more a reflection of the preferences of those audience segments with the greatest willingness to pay" (Napoli, 2003, pp. 180–181). Yet journalistic questions loom regarding the quality of news and the degree to which local news organizations will offer the deep, probing, investigative stories communities need to grow and reinvent themselves, as well as human interest features that profile role models championing urban change. News will continue, but, absent resources to delve into the underpinnings of local governance and the guts of social problems, it may be more glitz than substance, more puff than interpretive, in these ways neglecting the critical issues communities must confront to grow and prosper.

Conclusions

Broad, macro forces, such as organizational dynamics and market-based factors, exert important influences on news. The hierarchical versus egalitarian organizational structure, constellation of job demands, newsroom culture, and top-down political priorities (which play a more prominent role in some news outlets than in others) shape news content. Working in a contemporary newsroom, with more open space to encourage connections among workers, can improve the quality of work, perhaps encouraging collaboration among staffers. On the other hand, other contemporary organizational factors – for example, off-site work with little connectivity with colleagues, and a rapidly-paced news cycle requiring constant updates – can stress journalists, producing burnout.

One troubling, though long-standing, organizational factor concerns the insidious influences of the owner's political philosophy. All owners have political viewpoints, and these can filter down to staffers, just like other aspects of the organizational environment. The question is how much, and to what degree owner-enforced, organization-wide political ideologies intrude into news, overcoming journalists' commitment to dispassionate, fair-minded reporting, as well as their reliance on routine professional news values. The impact of organizational-level political values comes into play most clearly in cable television: MSNBC, with a more liberal ideological bent, and particularly Fox, which has unabashedly pushed a conservative political agenda in its news programs.

Of course, television news was never apolitical. During the 1960s–1990s, the big three broadcast news networks adopted a seemingly moderate, middle-of-the-road approach that affirmed homogenized, mainstream White culture-dominated values, in some cases pushing agendas embracing liberal causes, but also conveying a status quo bias, particularly in the area of U.S. military ventures (Gans, 2004; see Chapter 10). However, Fox and other news outlets, notably Sinclair-owned TV stations, seamlessly merge fact and opinion more explicitly and obtrusively than the broadcast networks of the late 20th century. Such biases occur more on the organizational level than at the level of individual reporters, as discussed in Chapter 7. These biases are not just driven solely by owners' politics, but instead represent a clear economic strategy to build a large, niche audience composed of like-minded political viewers.

Economic factors exert significant influences on news, particularly in a capitalist society where news is a commodity that must make profits to survive and prosper. Focusing on the stark decline of newspapers, as good an exemplar of economic effects as you will find, the chapter enumerated key factors that have shaken the newspaper industry to its core. Factors include: (1) Internet-based evisceration of classified advertising and reduction in display advertising revenue; (2) difficulties in developing a successful online funding model; (3) challenges in finding ways to monetize online news use; and (4) indifference to journalistic values on the part of institutional investors.

Confronted by new gatekeepers, particularly social media, with its popularity-based algorithms that do not center on journalistic values, news outlets have scrambled to make money. They have resorted to listicles and clickbait, where a headline provides a dramatic, misleading summary of a story to invite readers to click on the site, bringing in readers and advertising dollars. (BuzzFeed might counter-argue that the profits are plowed into news-gathering, but that remains speculative.) Increasingly, legacy news outlets have partnered with Facebook, tailoring content to the social networking site, with mixed economic success, particularly as Facebook has deemphasized content from news publishers, favoring social posts from family and friends over news articles shared by news outlets. And while these problems are not new – news outlets have always had to devise hooks to recruit readers and advertisers who underwrote more substantive journalistic content – the challenges are particularly acute today.

Conventional news organizations, particularly print and online news outlets, face a precarious future as print newspapers struggle to survive, and news remains a difficult commodity for conventional news outlets to monetize on digital platforms (Picard, 2015). Some scholars believe the advertising-dependent economic model for journalism is no longer viable, raising questions about the degree to which news can continue to thrive as a public good (Pickard, 2017). Others warn that journalists should be wary of becoming economically dependent on social media platforms, whose algorithms favor affect rather than classic news values journalism prioritizes (Crilley & Gillespie, 2019). These critics worry that digital technology gurus who speak the language of "content delivery" are seizing control of time-honored journalistic routines, emphasizing breadth of online audience reach at the expense of information or investigation.

Still others, noting that journalism has always rebounded from market failures, and seeing untapped economic potential in hunger for digital news, are more optimistic, particularly as they point to ways that legacy brands like *The Washington Post* and *The Atlantic* have adapted their economic models to the news habits of digital readers (Lee, 2019). Optimists also point to the energizing addition of more than 200 non-profit news organizations in the U.S. that can provide in-depth analysis and investigative muscle. Some of these outlets will survive, others won't, but they showcase the vitality of news in troubling times.

A common thread in discussions of current news is the importance of local news coverage, despite its tendency, particularly on the small-town level, to favor stories that sing the community's praises rather than offering up a medley of more critical voices. At its best, local news touches the lives of community residents directly, and it can serve informational, interpretive, investigative, and civic enhancement functions. As local newspapers have faced dire economic woes, online outlets, featuring blogs, citizen news sites, and hyperlocal journalism, have stepped into the breach, providing welcome coverage of local issues. Questions remain about whether these sites can fulfill the deep interpretive and investigative functions that the best local news provides, as well as the long-term viability of their funding mechanisms.

In the end, the frequently asked question, "Will journalism survive?" underscores a multifaceted reality. The endurance of news over centuries past gives cause for optimism. News will endure. The question is in what form, number, and diversity of news outlets, and whether the content will serve informative, interpretive, watchdog, and deliberative democratic functions. Will it offer deep coverage of critical issues or devolve to BuzzFeed's watermelon detonation described in Chapter 1, stories about the Walmart shopper who licked an ice cream container and returned it to the freezer, and a collection of shared, liked, but not belief-challenging, news articles? Will new, refined economic models develop to enable news to reach, inform, and puncture the biases of citizens? The questions are not new, but are raised in every historical epoch, as technology and economics clash with broader democratic goals. Nonetheless, the answer is important because the news is not a game of trivia; it is the essence of democracy (Harris, 2000).

References

Abramson, J. (2019). *Merchants of truth: The business of news and the fight for facts.* New York: Simon & Schuster.
Alexander, J.C. (2016). Introduction: Journalism, democratic culture, and creative reconstruction. In J.C. Alexander, E.B. Breese, & M. Luengo (Eds.), *The crisis of*

journalism reconsidered: Democratic culture, professional codes, digital future (pp. 1–28). New York: Cambridge University Press.

Altmeppen, K. D. (2008). The structure of news production. The organizational approach to journalism research. In M. Löffelholz & D. Weaver (Eds.), *Global journalism research: Theories, methods, findings, future* (pp. 52–64). Hoboken, NJ: John Wiley & Sons.

An, S., & Jin, H.S. (2004). Interlocking of newspaper companies with financial institutions and leading advertisers. *Journalism & Mass Communication Quarterly, 81*, 578–600.

Anderson, C.W. (2013). *Rebuilding the news: Metropolitan journalism in the digital age*. Philadelphia, PA: Temple University Press.

Bantz, C.R. (1997). News organizations: Conflict as a crafted cultural norm. In D. Berkowitz (Ed.), *Social meanings of news* (pp. 123–137). Thousand Oaks, CA: Sage.

Bell, E., & Owen, T. (2017, March 29). The platform press: How Silicon Valley reengineered journalism. *Columbia Journalism Review*. Online: www.cjr.org/tow_center_reports/platform-press-how-silicon... (Accessed: September 13, 2018).

Benkler, Y., Faris, R., & Roberts, H. (2018). *Network propaganda: Manipulation, disinformation, and radicalization in American politics*. New York: Oxford University Press.

Berry, J.M., & Sobieraj, S. (2014). *The outrage industry: Political opinion media and the new incivility*. New York: Oxford University Press.

Boczkowski, P.J. (2004). The processes of adopting multimedia and interactivity in three online newsrooms. *Journal of Communication, 54*, 197–213.

Breed, W. (1955). Social control in the newsroom: A functional analysis. *Social Forces, 33*, 326–335.

Brock, D., Rabin-Havt, A & Media Matters for America. (2012). *The Fox effect: How Roger Ailes turned a network into a propaganda machine*. New York: Anchor Books.

Brown, P. (2018, February 2). More than half of Facebook Instant Articles partners may have abandoned it. *Columbia Journalism Review*. Online: www .cjr.org/tow_center/are-facebook-instant-articles-worth... (Accessed: September 13, 2018).

Chambers, D., Steiner, L., & Fleming, C. (2004). *Women and journalism*. New York: Routledge.

Chang, Y.-L. (2015). Framing of the immigration reform in 2006: A community structure approach. *Journalism & Mass Communication Quarterly, 92*, 839–856.

Coester, D. (2017, October 18). A matter of space: Designing newsrooms for new digital practice. *American Press Institute*. Online: www.americapressinstitute.org /publications/reports/strategy-s... (Accessed: August 22, 2018).

Cranberg, G., Bezanson, R., & Soloski, J. (2001). *Taking stock: Journalism and the publicly traded newspaper company*. Ames, IA: Iowa State University Press.

Crilley, R., & Gillespie, M. (2019). What to do about social media? Politics, populism and journalism. *Journalism, 20*, 173–176.

Davis, D., & Mazzolini, J. (Eds.) (2018). *Plain Dealing: Cleveland journalists tell their stories*. Cleveland, OH: MSL Academic Endeavors (Cleveland State University).

Demers, D.K. (1998). Structural pluralism, corporate newspaper structure, and news source perceptions: Another test of the editorial vigor hypothesis. *Journalism & Mass Communication Quarterly, 75*, 572–592.

Doctor, K. (2017, July 6). Newsonomics: There's a newspaper chain that's grown profits for the past 5 years, and it's looking to buy more papers. *NiemanLab*. Online: www.niemanlab.org/2017/07/newsonomics-there's-a-newspaper-chain. (Accessed: September 20, 2018).

Domingo, D. (2008). Interactivity in the daily routines of online newsrooms: Dealing with an uncomfortable myth. *Journal of Computer-Mediated Communication, 13*, 680–704.

Dominick, J.R. (2013). *The dynamics of mass communication: Media in transition* (12th ed.). New York: McGraw-Hill.

Draper, K., (2017, October 24). They're out to kill every paper's sports section. *The New York Times*, B7, B11.

Ember, S. (2018, April 8). *Denver Post*, gutted by layoffs, prints rebuke of its ownership. *The New York Times, 1*, 19.

Everbach, T. (2006). The culture of a women-led newspaper: An ethnographic study of the *Sarasota Herald-Tribune*. *Journalism & Mass Communication Quarterly, 83*, 477–493.

Everett, R. (2018, October 5). Email to author.

Franklin, B. (2014). The future of journalism: In an age of digital media and economic uncertainty. *Journalism Studies, 15*, 481–499.

Freedman, D. (2010). The political economy of the "new" news environment. In N. Fenton (Ed.), *New media, old news: Journalism & democracy in the digital age* (pp. 35–50). Thousand Oaks, CA: Sage.

A future without the front page. (2019, August 4). *The New York Times* (Special section), 1–11.

Gans, H.J. (2004). *Deciding what's news: A study of CBS evening news, NBC Nightly News, Newsweek and Time* (25th anniversary edition). Evanston, IL: Northwestern University Press.

Gelles, D. (2018, September 20). As tycoons rescue media, risks remain. *The New York Times*, B1, B5.

Groeling, T. (2008). Who's the fairest of them all? An empirical test for partisan bias on ABC, CBS, NBC, and Fox News. *Presidential Studies Quarterly, 38*, 631–657.

Grynbaum, M.M. (2016, July 25). Ego clashes exposed in Democratic National Committee emails. *The New York Times*, A25.

Gutsche, Jr., R.E. (2015). Boosterism as banishment: Identifying the power function of local, business news and coverage of city spaces. *Journalism Studies, 16*, 497–512.

Gutsche, Jr., R.E., & Salkin, E. (2016). Who lost what? An analysis of myth, loss, and proximity in news coverage of the Steubenville rape. *Journalism, 17*, 456–473.

Hanitzsch, T. (2007). Deconstructing journalism culture: Toward a universal theory. *Communication Theory, 17*, 367–385.

Hargreaves, I. (2014). *Journalism: A very short introduction* (2nd ed.). Oxford, UK: Oxford University Press.

Harris, J. (2000). In What is missing from your news? W. Serrin (Ed.), *The business of journalism: Ten leading reporters and editors on the perils and pitfalls of the press*. New York: The New Press.

Hershey, Jr., R.D. (2014, May 4). Gary Becker, 83, Nobel Laureate dies; applied economics to everyday life. *The New York Times*. Online: www.nytimes.com /2014/05/05/business. (Accessed: August 28, 2018).

Holton, A.E., & Molyneux, L. (2017). Identity lost? The personal impact of brand journalism. *Journalism, 18*, 195–210.

Isaac, M. (2018, January 11). Facebook overhauls news feed to focus on what friends and family share. *The New York Times*. Online: www.nytimes.com/2018/01/11/technology/facebook-news-feed... (Accessed: September 6, 2018).

Isaac, M., & Ember, S. (2016, June 29). Facebook to change news feed to focus on friends and family. *The New York Times*. Online: www.nytimes.com/2016/06/30/technology/facebook-to-cha... (Accessed: September 6, 2018).

Iyengar, S., & Hahn, K.S. (2009). Red media, blue media: Evidence of ideological sensitivity in media use. *Journal of Communication, 59*, 19–39.

Jones, A.S. (2009). *Losing the news: The future of the news that feeds democracy.* New York: Oxford University Press.

Ju, A., Jeong, S.H., & Chyi, H.I. (2014). Will social media save newspapers? Examining the effectiveness of Facebook and Twitter as news platforms. *Journalism Practice, 8*, 1–17.

Kaniss, P. (1991). *Making local news.* Chicago, IL: University of Chicago Press.

Kennedy, D. (2013, August 12). Salvaging something from the rubble of Patch. *Media Nation*. Online: https://dankennedy.net/2013/08/12/salvaging-something-from-the-... (Accessed: September 8, 2018).

Kolhatkar, S. (2018, October 22). Breaking the news. *The New Yorker*, 30–31, 34, 36–40, 42.

Kovach, B., & Rosenstiel, T. (2014). *The elements of journalism* (3rd ed.). New York: Three Rivers Press.

Lee, E. (2019, February 5). Digital media hit a rut. What's next? *The New York Times*, B1, B4.

Lee, T.B. (2016, November 2). Print newspapers are dying faster than you think. *Vox*. Online: www.vox.com/new-money/2016/11/2/13499004/print-news... (Accessed: September 7, 2018).

Lepore, J. (2019, January 28). Hard news. *The New Yorker*, 18–24.

MacDonald, J.B., Saliba, A.J., Hodgins, G., & Ovington, L.A. (2016). Burnout in journalists: A systematic literature review. *Burnout Research, 3*, 34–44.

Macur, J., & Schweber, N. (2012, December 16). Rape case unfolds on web and splits city. *The New York Times*. Online: www.nytimes.com/2012/12/17/sports/high-school-football-... (Accessed: September 8, 2018).

Matsa, K.E. (2018, January 5). Fewer Americans rely on TV news; What type they watch varies by who they are. *Facttank: News in the numbers*. Pew Research Center. Online: www.pewresearch.org/fact-tank/2018/01/05/fewer-americans-rely-on-tv...(Accessed: September 7, 2018).

Mayer, J. (2019, March 11). Trump TV. *The New Yorker*, 40 53.

Mazzolini, J. (2018). Health care, the "sleeve," and life in the PD newsroom. In D. Davis & J. Mazzolini (Eds.), *Plain Dealing: Cleveland journalists tell their stories* (pp. 155–160). Cleveland, OH: MSL Academic Endeavors (Cleveland State University).

McFadden, R.D. (2018, August 26). A symbol of course in half a century of battles. *The New York Times, 1*, 16–18.

Meyer, P. (2004). *The vanishing newspaper: Saving journalism in the information age*. Columbia, MO: University of Missouri Press.

Napoli, P.M. (2003). *Audience economics: Media institutions and the audience marketplace*. New York: Columbia University Press.

Newspapers Fact Sheet (2018, June 13). Pew Research Center (Journalism & Media). Online: www.journalism.org/fact-sheet/newspapers/. (Accessed: September 5, 2018).

Paletz, D., Reichert, P., & McIntyre, B. (1971). How the media support local government authority. *Public Opinion Quarterly, 35*, 80–92.

Peiser, J. (2018a, July 24). *Daily News*, lean but brassy New York staple, cuts staff in half. *The New York Times*, A1, A19.

Peiser, J. (2018b, June 18). *Denver Post* defectors and blockchain start-up team up in news outlet. *The New York Times*, B4.

Peiser, J. (2018c, September 28). Website revs up, with magazine's help, to cover more New York news. *The New York Times*, B3.

Perloff, R.M. (1998). *Political communication: Politics, press, and public in America*. Mahwah, NJ: Lawrence Erlbaum Associates.

Peters, J. (2012, November 6). Dueling bitterness on cable news. *The New York Times*, A10, A11.

Picard, R.G. (1994). Institutional ownership of publicly traded U.S. newspaper companies. *Journal of Media Economics, 7*(4), 49–64.

Picard, R.G. (2011). *The economics and financing of media companies* (2nd ed.). New York: Fordham University Press.

Picard, R.G. (2015). Economics of print media. In R.G. Picard & S.S. Wildman (Eds.), *Handbook on the economics of the media* (pp. 151–164). Cheltenham, UK: Edward Elgar Publishing.

Pickard, V. (2017). Rediscovering the news: Journalism studies' three blind spots. In P.J. Boczkowski & C.W. Anderson (Eds.), *Remaking the news: Essays on the future of journalism scholarship in the digital age* (pp. 47–60). Cambridge, MA: The MIT Press.

Pickard, V. (2019). The violence of the market. *Journalism, 20*, 154–158.

Pressman, M. (2018). *On press: The liberal values that shaped the news*. Cambridge, MA: Harvard University Press.

Preston, J. (2013, March 18). How blogger helped the Steubenville rape case unfold online. *The New York Times*. Online: https://thelede.blogs.nytimes.com/2013/03/18/how-blogger-helped-... (Accessed: September 9, 2018).

Rashidian, N., Brown, P., & Hansen, E. (2018, June 14). Friend and foe: The platform press at the heart of journalism. *Columbia Journalism Review*. Online: www.cjr.org/tow_center_reports/the-platform-press-at-the h... (Accessed: September 13, 2018).

Robinson, G. (2008). Journalism as a symbolic practice: The gender approach in journalism research. In M. Löffelholz & D. Weaver (Eds.), *Global journalism research: Theories, methods, findings, future* (pp. 79–89). Hoboken, NJ: John Wiley & Sons.

Robinson, S. (2011). Convergence crises: News work and news space in the digitally transforming newsroom. *Journal of Communication, 61*, 1122–1141.

Rogers, T. (2017, May 20). What is hyperlocal journalism? *ThoughtCo*. Online: www.thoughtco.com/what-is-hyperlocal-journalism-2073658. (Accessed: September 9, 2018).

Rusbridger, A. (2018). *Breaking news: The remaking of journalism and why it matters now*. New York: Farrar, Straus and Giroux.

Ryfe, D.M. (2017). *Journalism and the public*. Malden, MA: Polity Press.

Savillo, R., & Groch-Begley, H. (2014, September 16). REPORT: Fox's Benghazi obsession by the numbers. *Media Matters*. Online: www.mediamattters.org/research. (Accessed: August 30, 2018).

Schroeck, E., & Johnson, M. (2011, April 20). Fox News goes full birther. *Media Matters*. Online: www.mediamattters.org/research. (Accessed: August 30, 2018).

Schultz, M. (1994). *On studying organizational cultures: Diagnosis and understanding*. Berlin: Walter de Gruyter.

Shaw, D. (2007, April/May). Really local. *American Journalism Review*. Online: http://ajrarchive.org/Article.asp?id=4308. (Accessed: September 8, 2018).

Shearer, E., & Gottfried, J. (2017, September 7). *News use across social media platforms 2017*. Pew Research Center (Journalism & Media). Online: www.journalism.org/2017/09/07/news-use-across-social-med... (Accessed: September 6, 2018).

Sherman, G. (2014). *The loudest voice in the room: How the brilliant, bombastic Roger Ailes built Fox News –And divided a country*. New York: Random House.

Sneed, T. (2013, April 9). Pay Walls could be print's salvation online. *U.S. News & World Report*. Online: www.usnews.com/news/articles. (Accessed: September 5, 2018).

Soloski, J. (2013). Collapse of the US newspaper industry: Goodwill, leverage and bankruptcy. *Journalism, 14*, 309–329.

Soloski, J. (2019). The murky ownership of the journalistic enterprise. *Journalism, 20*, 159–162.

Spector, H. (2018a). Welcome to *The Plain Dealer*. In D. Davis & J. Mazzolini (Eds.), *Plain Dealing: Cleveland journalists tell their stories* (pp. 167–171). Cleveland, OH: MSL Academic Endeavors (Cleveland State University).

Spector, H. (2018b, October 1). Email to author.

Stolberg, S.G. (2019, January 3). Same gavel, but whole new challenge for Pelosi. *The New York Times*, A1, A11.

Taplin, J. (2017). *Move fast and break things: How Facebook, Google, and Amazon cornered culture and undermined democracy*. New York: Little, Brown.

Theiss, E. (2018). The road to a big-city daily and life at Ohio's largest newspaper. In D. Davis & J. Mazzolini (Eds.), *Plain Dealing: Cleveland journalists tell their stories* (pp. 146–154). Cleveland, OH: MSL Academic Endeavors (Cleveland State University).

Tichenor, P.J., Donohue, G.A., & Olien, C.N. (1980). *Community conflict and the press*. Thousand Oaks, CA: Sage.

Tuchman, G. (1972). Objectivity as strategic ritual: An examination of newsmen's notions of objectivity. *American Journal of Sociology, 77*, 660–679.

Usher, N. (2014). *Making news at The New York Times*. Ann Arbor, MI: University of Michigan Press.

van der Wurff, R. (2012). The economics of online journalism. In E. Siapera & A. Veglis (Eds.), *The handbook of global online journalism* (pp. 231–250). Malden, MA: Wiley-Blackwell.

Weaver, D.H. (2009). US journalism in the 21st century – What future? *Journalism, 10*, 396–397.

Welbers, K., van Atteveldt, W., Kleinnijenhuis, J., Ruigrok, N., & Schaper, J. (2016). News selection criteria in the digital age: Professional norms versus online audience metrics. *Journalism, 17*, 1037–1053.

Wilkins, L. (2014). My newsroom made me do it: The impact of organizational climate on ethical decision-making. In W.N. Wyatt (Ed.), *The ethics of journalism: Individual, institutional and cultural influences* (pp. 33–53). London: I.B. Tauris & Co.

Wu, T. (2016). *The attention merchants: The epic scramble to get inside our heads.* New York: Knopf.

10 News and the Social System
Conformity or Change?

Now comes the big question, the elephant in the newsroom, the center-piece for so many scholars, the one that lurks beneath the ordinary queries for so many others. It's the most insidious, provocative, funda-mental, and in some ways most interesting question of them all. Does news prop up the powers-that-be, upholding a nation's social system, insulating it from systemic reforms, or is it a mechanism of change, a force that subverts the status quo, and ushers in basic political reform? To radical theorists (famously Herman & Chomsky, 2002), the answer is obvious: News preserves the economic and political status quo, stifling fundamental change, doing the bidding of the power elite. To conserva-tive critics, news, au contraire, is an endless source of change, under-mining authorities by hyping the bad (e.g., Robinson, 1976), legitimizing domestic protests, and focusing inappropriately, and sometimes inaccu-rately (Braestrup, 1978), on U.S. military paralysis or shortcomings in foreign wars (Kuypers, 2006). Journalists, of course, perhaps because they are egocentric or have particular insights into the nature of what they cover, emphasize the ways the news can profoundly change social norms, as in the case of news of racial prejudice in the 1960s (Roberts & Klibanoff, 2006). Scholars are all over the map, emphasizing modest, sizable, and subtle media influences, while consistently highlighting the powerful influences of the social system on news (Hallin, 1986; McCombs, 2004; Shoemaker & Reese, 2014).

This chapter focuses on the **social system**, the fundamental structure of society that is composed of subsystems, notably the ideological, economic, political, cultural, and media subsystems of a nation's foundational whole. The social system view emphasizes that you cannot understand the role of a particular subsystem – for us, news – without appreciating the broader economic, political, cultural, and ideological contours of society-as -a-whole, in both the U.S. and the multitude of nations abroad (Hallin & Mancini, 2004; Shoemaker & Reese, 2014). Thus, to understand what makes American news tick, you have to appreciate the key subsystems in which it operates: the nature of its economic subsystem (e.g. capitalism, with concentration of wealth among the richest sectors); the political subsystem (democratic rule and protection of civil liberties, with questions about how effectively this works in practice); and, to some degree, the cultural subsystem (flourishing artistic and entertainment industries that transmit cultural values, controversially in cases of violence, sex, and ethnic identities). Coursing through these is ideology, not the individual's worldview or constellation of beliefs, but ideology that operates as a macro, societal-level force of influence.

Working on the systems level, Shoemaker and Reese describe ideology as "a symbolic mechanism that serves as a cohesive and integrating force in society" (2014, p. 70). Williams (1977), in a thoughtful definition, views ideology as "a relatively formal and articulated system of meanings, values, and beliefs, of a kind that can be abstracted as a 'world view'" (p. 109). Ideology encompasses the broader frames of reference that govern how individuals perceive events, what they "see as 'natural' or 'obvious'" (Becker, 1984, p. 69) and the broader values that course through institutions, organizations, and societal subsystems.

Ideology is a subtle, important influence, even if it can be difficult to measure. Theoretically, it is believed to operate across contexts, working in concert with economic, organizational, routine, and individual-level factors like a sweeping wind that leaves its potent particles at each of these domains. For example, in the U.S., the ideology of capitalism pervades media economics; news organizations' conformity to status quo community values exerts a conservative socializing influence on reporters; government national security policies in the wake of terrorist threats can mandate reliance on official sources; and individual reporters, while frequently questioning national policies, may fall back on well-learned patriotic values during national crises. That at least is the theory, though, as we will see, it is more complex in practice.

There are different theoretical perspectives on ideology, power, and the larger social system (Shoemaker & Reese, 2014). Some approaches emphasize how the system is sustained by its underlying structure, along with functions that media perform to maintain the status quo. Others take a Marxist approach emphasizing class factors, as well as the ideological power of the ruling class to influence workers' material and mental states. Still other perspectives stress the ways political and economic factors determine media content or how cultural processes grant media somewhat more autonomy. A centerpiece of these social system approaches, and one that has stimulated a great deal of scholarly interest, is the concept of hegemony.

Hegemony, the intriguing – and controversial – focus of this chapter, stipulates that news is a systemic handmaiden of the status quo, propping up the forces-that-be in subtle, not always coercive, ways. Broadly speaking, the chapter describes hegemony, offers compelling examples, explains how it works in concert with other news determinants described in the book, and discusses strengths and key shortcoming in the hegemonic perspective. The first portion of the chapter examines the thesis that news is shaped by system-wide economic forces, while the second explores the ways that news props up the political status quo by harnessing core news determinants discussed in earlier chapters. After discussing shortcomings in a simple hegemonic, system-based view, the chapter turns to the concept of framing, refinements in framing, current dilemmas involving online investigative organizations like WikiLeaks, and a critical assessment of the hegemonic perspective in the current milieu.

The Hegemonic Social System Perspective

Hegemony. This frustratingly abstruse, but fascinating, concept dates back to the early 20th-century philosopher Antonio Gramsci. Influenced by radical political philosophies of the time, notably Marxism, Gramsci (1971) argued that society's ruling group typically maintains power not though coercion, brute force or overt dominance, but by harnessing shared values and cultural institutions to ensure public acquiescence to its policies. Hegemony is the way that ruling groups systematically manufacture "mass consent to the established order" or the predominant structure of society (Condit, 1994; Gitlin, 1980, p. 253; Reese, 1990). Hegemonic theorists emphasize that democratic societies are governed by powerful economic and political groups and elites. These groups wield their influence not coercively but indirectly, through institutions and the symbolic power of media. The news, Shoemaker and Reese (2014) suggest, serves:

> a hegemonic function by continually producing a cohesive ideology as a unifying force, a set of commonsense values and norms that reproduce and legitimate the social system structure through which the subordinate classes ultimately participate in their own domination.
>
> (p. 82)

The rap is this: By accepting the common frameworks purveyed by official sources and delegitimizing voices that fall outside established circles, news props up the status quo, ensuring that the dominant groups maintain power, the oppressed continue to be oppressed, and, except for window dressing and small changes, the status quo chugs on. The approach emphasizes that **elite leaders** – the president, key members of Congress, and rich influential capitalist leaders – exploit their influence to dominate, even control, the ways news presents political issues, in sharp contrast to journalistic ideals (Goss, 2009). As you can see, it's a radical theory, one highly critical of news, and it excites some theorists, irritates others, yet is intriguing in its conceptual sweep.

Integrating different strands of scholarship, especially Herman and Chomsky (2002), we can identify two main components of the hegemonic, social system-based thesis.

First, concentration of media ownership, advertising, and corporate domination ensure that news upholds the preeminent economic hierarchy, marginalizing criticism of monopoly capitalism.

Second, journalistic routines, such as those prioritizing official government sources and PR doled out by powerful leaders, pushes news toward favoring ruling groups, protecting the interests of those in power, and limiting exposure to dissenting views.

As a result of these propulsive forces, the theory asserts, news manufactures consent (Table 10.1).

It is important to keep in mind that the hegemonic, systemic thesis argues that powerful economic and political constraints operate in all economic and political systems, not just capitalism or the U.S. The bulk of the criticism has focused on the U.S., given its global power (and perhaps scholars' political predilections). Our focus, in line with the purposes of this book, is hegemony's implications for American journalism, a large undertaking in and of itself. In discussing this, you will find that the various processes underlying news – the determinants of news

Table 10.1 Concept Of Hegemony

Hegemony: Social system-based model stipulating that news media maintain the status quo, propping up the powers-that-be or dominant ruling elites, by ensuring public consent with – or acquiescence to – their policy mandates.

HEGEMONY WORKS, IN THEORY, VIA NEWS DETERMINANTS:

Ideology	Economic	Organizational Forces	Routines	Individual Level Factors
Formal, broad symbolic system of meanings and values that operates across contexts, as a cohesive force underpinning news	Advertising; need to attract an audience; owners' focus on status quo news strengthening investment portfolios	Organizational culture; conformity with editors' values; socialization to roles and conventional orientations	Reliance on official sources; dependence on formal channels; focus on news values emphasizing drama and conflict rather than deeper structural issues	Journalists' professional orientation favoring objective journalism norm that subtly affirms status quo

incisively articulated by Shoemaker and Reese – offer helpful insights into the ways a social system influences news gathering. Let's now examine the two components of the broad hegemonic approach, with illustrative examples.

System-Level Economic Factors

As noted in Chapter 9, news media are, bottom-line, financial institutions for whom "the business of news is business, not news" (Cranberg, Bezanson, & Soloski, 2001, p. 9). A handful of groups own large numbers of newspapers, concentrating ownership in a relatively small number of (typically, white male) hands. A small number of conglomerates boast monopolistic control over most of the dominant firms in the different sectors of the media industries, notably news, extending their reach across national borders (McChesney, 1999, 2013; Reese, 2008). It's a now-familiar story, whereby the institutional investors who own news outlets place a premium on capital investment, profit margins, stock values, and financial performance. Advertising, long the financial underbelly of news, also plays an important role in journalistic decisions (Coddington, 2015). Indeed, advertising's influence on news dates back to the 19th century when newspapers arranged contracts with advertisers to offer favorable news or included reading notices, a precursor to today's native advertising that deceptively appears alongside online news and is deliberately disguised so it looks just like news stories (Shoemaker & Vos, 2009).

In more recent times, advertisers have sometimes canceled campaigns when television or newspapers ran displeasing stories about their businesses. For example, when WCCO, a CBS news affiliate in Minneapolis, aired an investigative series on automobile safety flaws, local automobile dealers pulled their advertising with the station. And what did the automobile dealers do next? They placed their ads on the CBS station's Twin Cities competitor, WKARE, an NBC affiliate. WKARE's good fortunes lasted until one of its reporters did a story on automobile thefts and car dealers. Fearing advertising reprisal, the station's management yanked the story.

Illustrating the power advertising exerts, particularly in smaller markets more dependent on local business largesse, about 90 percent of newspaper editors in one study acknowledged that advertisers had tried to influence news content, and more than a third said they had caved to advertisers' pressure (Soley & Craig, 1992). In one infamous case, the storied *Los Angeles Times* gave a Sunday magazine spread to the Staples Center when it opened years back, going so far as to split advertising profits the Sunday issue garnered with the Staples arena. The content gave a bonanza of free press to the Staples Center, suggesting that those who pay the piper can control the content (Atal, 2018).

Advertising pressure may be particularly likely to compromise journalistic editorial integrity at smaller papers that face financial strain (An & Bergen, 2007). Advertising also cultivates social class biases, as John H. McManus (2009) notes:

> Rational advertisers seek the upscale and those in prime buying years. Market-driven editors will commit scarce reporting resources to please those groups at the expense of the others because advertisers contribute about 80% of paid newspaper revenues and 100% of free paper and broadcast revenues.
>
> (p. 227)

Advertising, although still impactful, exerts a more complex effect on news content nowadays, given that online marketing has supplanted advertising as a product-promotion strategy, and in light of changes in news funding models. Lines between editorial and advertising functions blur, as, for example, British reporters have worked as advertising copywriters, serving on a branded content campaign to promote a consumer product on healthy living (Atal, 2018).

On a broader level, the economic component of hegemony emphasizes interconnections between the news and financial power centers in society. The news media and informational gatekeepers are controlled by a small number of global telecommunication powerhouses, which frequently join forces in massive mergers, such as between AT&T and Time Warner several years back.

As a media technology specialist observed:

> A handful of technology companies, the Frightful Five – Apple, Google, Microsoft, Facebook and Amazon – ... control the most important digital infrastructure, while a handful of broadband companies – AT&T, Charter, Comcast and Verizon – control most of the Internet connections in the United States.
>
> (Manjoo, 2017, 2018)

In the UK, just four companies, run by media magnates, control 90 percent of daily newspaper circulation (Fenton, 2019). In the U.S., six major investment firms, focused on managing high-profile financial securities rather than journalistic social responsibilities, own more newspapers than the 16 biggest private newspaper companies and three largest public newspaper groups (Soloski, 2019).

Critics of news have long highlighted the journalistic and democratic shortcomings of this hyper-capitalistic control of media (Bagdikian, 2004; McChesney, 1999). In many books over the years, Robert W. McChesney, beginning with his exquisitely-titled *Rich media, poor democracy* (1999), has argued that the news media oligopoly, where a handful of massive media companies dominate the market, has plutocratically placed profits over the broad interests of citizens. According to this view, the rich diversity of informational outlets on the Internet is a chimera, a façade:

> But of all those seemingly independent outlets, most of those attracting the largest audiences are owned by a few transactional companies and serve a commercial purpose, selling audience eyeballs to advertisers. Not surprisingly, content that empowers citizens and reports critically on government – and particularly corporate – power is rare. What media cover least … is their own concentrated ownership and hypercommercialism.
>
> (McManus, 2009, p. 223)

It is a broad-based, damning thesis. Is it true?

Critical Assessment

At first blush, there is considerable evidence in support of the thesis. Think of it this way: Every day, with reports constantly available online, news trumpets the Dow Jones Industrial Average that shows the average of the nation's most significant stocks, traded in a regular session on the stock market. It consistently mentions the New York Stock Exchange and Nasdaq, the latter a stock market index you probably have heard of, an acronym for the National Association of Securities Dealers Automated Quotations. The stock markets are viewed as natural parts of the American regime; to not hear the Dow Jones average on a given day is like missing the weather report. It is part of the natural, accepted order of things.

Newspapers have business sections that each day report how corporate, tech, and mom and pop businesses fare in the marketplace. American Public Media even produces a special show called *Marketplace*. The magazines, *Bloomberg Businessweek, Fortune,* and *Inc.*, with the latter's focus on startups, tout the vitality and vicissitudes of American finance. Not only does the content prominently associate business with success and classic American virtues, but the names themselves, for example, *Fortune*, convey pro-business, pro-capitalist values. There are no American business-related magazines called *Misfortune, The Week in Business Oppression,* or *Karl Marx's Marxetplace*!

Beyond this, the larger question is whether news consistently affirms capitalism, offering predominately positive coverage of business, while minimizing or even ignoring news of the economic system's fundamental flaws.

We gain insight into the pathways by which the economic system influences news, as well as how news missed a big economic story, by examining the failure of the news media to sound the alarms that the world financial system was in trouble before the global economic crisis occurred in 2007–2008. Commercial incentives played a role; Reuters, the international news organization, has diversified its operations so that about 90 percent of its revenues come from expert or specialist financial data services rather than reporting, let alone investigative journalism (Manning, 2013). Thus, there was no incentive at Reuters to dig deep into the financial crisis.

Journalistic routines played an important role in reporters' failure to anticipate the likelihood of a global financial collapse. Business reporters, dutifully consumed by standard news values like dramatization and personalization, wrote about Wall Street executives' personalities, gaining information *from* powerful investors rather than *about* them via inside sources (Starkman, 2014). They emphasized the tried-and-true, firms' stock prices and financial returns, doing this very well, but neglecting deeper moral issues involving predatory lending because these stood outside the established routines that fill news holes and television news time on business programs.

At international news agencies like Bloomberg News and Reuters, workaday demands and short-term deadlines for everyday stories on mergers and acquisitions are of paramount importance, making it difficult for reporters to find time to do investigative work. In addition, business reporters, dependent on high-powered banking sources to explain complex aspects of subprime loans and collateralized debt obligations, failed to get beyond formal business reporting routines to expose the underbelly of the problem. Official financial sources may have been reluctant to break down the problem or disclose key details (Usher, 2013).

An organizational factor – news editors' lack of knowledge of the global financial system – made it harder for reporters to persuade editors to let them pursue the story (Manning, 2013). On the organizational level, reporters become socialized into the prevailing business perspective they cover on the financial beat, internalizing the pro-business beliefs of the financial community (Schiffrin, 2011). At the individual level, business reporters at the public radio show, *Marketplace*, view their role as providing entertaining, comprehensible stories about the global economy, not serving as investigative watchdogs (Usher, 2013). To be sure, journalists were hardly the only ones who missed or failed to forecast the crisis. And there was – and is – insightful business reporting. However, to the extent that reporters serve as the veritable antennae of a culture, calling attention to problems on the horizon, their failure to do so in 2008 provides a signature example of the economic corollary of the hegemonic thesis. Journalist Dean Starkman (2014) described it as "the watchdog that didn't bark."

There is another side that complicates matters. As the financial crisis unfolded, was tamed, and when normal times returned, reporters provided penetrating coverage of the 2008 systemic failure, full of thoughtful, critical accounts. Journalists' books on the crisis, described in the press, emphasized the roles played by systemic greed, irresponsible risk-taking, and regulatory corruption (e.g., Morgenson & Rosner, 2011). An investigative magazine story focused on the inexplicable, unethical failure of the system to imprison only one investment banker rather than holding Wall Street financial institutions legally responsible for the largest epic economic disaster since the Great Depression (Eisinger, 2014). A 10-year retrospective described a crisis that "broke a social contract between the plutocrats and everyone else," a charade economy, and its long-term political impact (Sorkin, 2018), while other stories documented that the crisis magnified class inequalities and increased concentration of wealth.

Thus, you can't paint a simple picture of news affirmation of the financial powers-that-be. Ritualistic journalistic biases, and the nature of American journalism, discouraged early investigations, in concert with the hegemonic account. But later coverage provided a more negative portrait, suggesting that the varied explicit and implicit pressures placed on news by the larger economic system are not so severe to block exposure of critical fissures. American journalism is not so slavishly controlled by the economic hegemons that it can't provide critical accounts that point to systemic shortcomings and failure to hold powerful people accountable. As it has with past economic crises, news articles after the fact illuminated the multifaceted problems in the financial structure that caused the crisis, fulfilling informational, interpretive, and watchdog functions with stories that highlighted Wall Street's failures. Yet even its valiant reporting, in the wake of the crisis, was not sufficient to result in retribution for elite financial institutions.

American news amply covers capitalist excesses, in defiance of a simple hegemonic model. Even so, news conglomerates exert considerable control over the market by leveraging economic and political resources. A case in point is the Sinclair Broadcast Group, whose political biases were described in Chapter 9. Despite widespread exposés and viral ridicule of Sinclair news, the company continues its domination of the market, owning more than 190 stations in the U.S., circumventing regulations in the number of stations a company can own by creating shell companies that appear to be separate broadcast units but are actually controlled by Sinclair, and currying favor with the chair of the Federal Communications Commission, possibly causing him to have bent the rules to help Sinclair (Kolhatkar, 2018). The economic conglomerates did not act as one: competing conservative media barons like Rupert Murdoch were motivated to reduce Sinclair's influence, helping derail a planned Sinclair merger with the Tribune Media Company, which would have put Sinclair stations into 70 percent of American homes. Still, Sinclair has exploited its power so that it reaches nearly four in ten American viewers and is poised to expand its influence, attesting to the ways powerful economic elites can restrict the range of viewpoints Americans receive.

Let's turn to the contemporary economic nexus of news and social media. Viewing the economic hegemony perspective critically, you may rightly note that news has provided considerable critical coverage of the big digital behemoths that control so much of the news people see on digital platforms. There has been no end of news stories on shortcomings at Facebook, with its invasion of Americans' privacy, stories of Google protecting its elite technology leaders accused of sexual misconduct by paying them lucrative exit packages, and articles about Amazon's poor wages and working conditions, in contrast to the gargantuan fortunes of its chief executive, Jeff Bezos (e.g., Wakabayashi & Benner, 2018). The American news media is not a monolith that simply parrots back the priorities of the technology companies that provide the audiences for online news. It is a separate power center, with its own priorities.

And although some scholars don't like to admit it, news can also spotlight positive things American business does for society, such as technological innovations, spanning shared workspaces for entrepreneurial cultures (e.g., WeWork), exercise apps on watches, and virtual assistants (hello Alexa). Of course, there are always questions about how equitably these innovations are diffused across classes, and news can exert a powerful – and inequitable – impact on dissemination of business innovations.

But how much power does news wield? To what degree can news be coopted or "captured" by the digital powerhouses that convey its content and provide audiences for online news (Nechushtai, 2018; Schiffrin, 2018; Siapera, 2013)? The Google Digital News Initiative has donated nearly $200 million for digital journalism projects; Facebook introduced its Facebook Journalism Project that promises to increase collaboration with news outlets. It has reached the point that Facebook and Google exert important influences on the very production of news, as a reporter can talk to a source on Google's Android phone, call on data gathered through Facebook- or Google-based tools, publish the article via a Facebook format, and then find that readers connect with the story on Facebook (Nechushtai, 2018).

This raises questions about the degree to which these high-tech platforms control the economics of news production. They distribute news stories, providing news organizations critical access to audiences, which are the source of online advertising revenue. At present, major news organizations are holding their own, maintaining journalistic autonomy, holding social networks' feet to the fire with widely diffused exposés about their exploitation of consumers' privacy for profit (e.g., Dance, LaForgia, & Confessore, 2018). However, the hegemonic perspective raises questions about cooptation in the future, and whether journalism will bend to the economic power of digital platforms.

Propping up the Political Power Structure

Let's turn to the second part of the hegemonic thesis. This proposition stipulates that the country's ruling elite uses the news media – and the news media lets itself be used – to boost dominant political interests and marginalize dissenting views via source routines, public relations subsidies and classic news values. This thesis can strike some students as one-sided and radical, out of sync with their experience of feisty, no-holds-barred online news. Some people object to its strident, seemingly anti-American, or anti-news focus. Of course, other observers who focus on systemic problems that plague the U.S. view the thesis as so obvious and true that it seems bizarre to question it. Our job is to put gut feelings aside and analytically examine a conceptual thesis to see if it holds water. This is the task of the scholar, probing journalist (and open-minded person). Let's start with several classic, affecting examples.

Racial Issues

Beginning with race, there is no question that, during the 19th and much of the 20th century, news covered race in a deeply prejudiced manner, showcasing how the social system influenced news through reporters' racial biases, dependence on racist official sources, news organizations' indifference, and even economics, as gruesome news of 19th-century lynchings sold papers (Perloff, 2000). It all flowed out of the social system's ideology – time-honored resistance on the part of the social and the political system to racial equality, the system-wide manifestation of Myrdal's (1944) famous American dilemma: the glaring inconsistency between liberal values, like equality and civil liberties, and rampant racism. Working through the processes emphasized in Shoemaker and Reese's hierarchical influence model, news coverage neglected racism in institutions spanning housing, education, business, and social justice.

World War II Holocaust

During World War II, the news media downplayed or neglected news of the massacre of millions of Jews at the hands of the Nazis in Europe, placing stories about the systematic extermination of Jews on the inside pages, rather than Page 1, even shrouding the truth in doubt (Leff, 2005; Lipstadt, 1986). Why? It seems mind-boggling now. The White House, under the famously (but not in this case) liberal policies of President Franklin D. Roosevelt, turned a blind eye toward rescuing Jews imprisoned in Nazi concentration camps, as a result of anti-Semitism and dubious beliefs that rescue efforts would have been impossible or lacking in military value (Wyman, 1984). Given the prejudice and government callousness, there were few official government sources who would or could reveal this information to the reporters; dissidents horrified by the policy were marginalized, with little access to mainstream journalists. How could the story get out? Who could tell it reliably? News organizations themselves were reluctant to question the White House in the midst of a world war. Thus, they bought the party line, failed to ask tough questions, and did not seek to independently verify reports, in this way failing to adequately cover one of the monumental tragedies of the 20th century. It was, former *New York Times* executive editor Max Frankel observed, "the century's bitterest journalistic failure" (Denby, 2019, p. 66).

9/11

More than 50 years later, during the first year of the 21st century, another tragic event occurred, illustrating once again how news can march to the beat of the power elite's drummers, serving up news that conforms with dominant political interests. In this case, news did not deny or minimize; rather, it played up and lionized, as the news media offered red, white and blue coverage in the wake of 9/11, patriotically playing up the Bush Administration's policies. To many, such coverage may be understandable, even justifiable in light of the horrific events of that day. That's a reasonable, indeed empathic, position, one some scholars would share. But the hegemonic approach takes a different tack, lamenting that news slavishly parroted back the official U.S. line. At the time, it was painful to look critically at these events; to do so seemed almost sacrilegious – but with the healing effects of time, and the academic necessity to view events from unpopular perspectives, we gain insight into the nature of news about September 11.

News coverage in the immediate aftermath of 9/11 fulfilled ritualistic, nation-healing functions, as discussed in Chapter 4. It affirmed national identity, emphasizing "patriotic declarations of unity and national purpose" and time-honored virtues in the American character, as reporters called on patriotic language to create "journalism that would become a memorial keepsake as well as an official record" (Hutcheson et al., 2004; Kitch, 2011, p. 127; Zelizer & Allan, 2011, p. 19). Yet, from the perspective of any of the key social responsibility functions of journalism, news was problematic, repeating without question the Bush Administration's policies, depending on official sources rather than seeking out dissident viewpoints, providing little if any questioning coverage of the U.S. war in Afghanistan, parroting, then reifying the White House meme, "war on terrorism," and offering simplistic, good-versus-evil descriptions of Muslims and "Islamic violence" (Karim, 2011; McChesney, 2011; Reese & Lewis, 2009, though see Nacos & Torres-Reyna, 2003). As CBS news anchor Dan Rather said at the time, "George Bush is the president, he makes decisions, and, you know, as just one

American, whenever he wants me to line up, just tell me where" (Kumar, 2006, p. 58).

Wrapping itself in the flag, the news elided a focus on drawbacks of the Bush policy, emphasizing a jingoistic type of patriotism rather than a patriotism based on dissent or empathy (Waisbord, 2011). To be sure, in the wake of 9/11, the White House, Congress, major U.S. institutions, and the American public all supported the Bush Administration's policies, propelling the news media to follow suit. Such news congealed with most news organizations' patriotic perspectives, adhered to an economic logic (dissenting perspectives would not fly well with an understandably aggrieved public), tapped into reporters' ethnocentric biases, called on news values, like conflict, immediacy, and classic reliance on official sources, recruited audience interest, boosting revenues, and clearly flowed from the pressures and ideology of a political system – and society – in crisis. Notice that the leaders did not pressure or coerce the news to embrace these perspectives on news. They flowed naturally from systemic constraints on news, the functions journalism performs for the larger culture, and ways that a nation's news media system gatekeeps information when the social system faces external threats that pull different forces together in a cohesive, ideological manner.

Of course, from a normative perspective, this is nuanced. Journalism has responsibilities to the country that supports and sustains them. You can persuasively argue that, in the face of 9/11, patriotic news helped citizens cope, fulfilling communal and national values. But, to critics news went overboard, ignoring its watchdog role. Both of these functions – ritualistic and watchdog – are important to democracy. We wouldn't want a journalism that provided relentless criticism after a searing national tragedy; we need journalism to help us memorialize and mourn. At the same time, news shouldn't close its eyes to leaders' mistakes. Maintaining a balance between these very different functions is a challenge, a moral, professional imperative.

Complexities

The jingoistic coverage that occurred in the wake of 9/11 did not last. Gradually and increasingly, over the next several years, news offered critical coverage, including news of a high-ranking official's accusation that Bush had ignored warnings about the threat of Al Qaeda attacks, Congressional opposition to the 2003 Iraq War, reports of policy mistakes in the Iraq and Afghanistan wars, and blockbuster investigations of the Bush Administration's violation of U.S. citizens' privacy as a questionable cost of war. This was by no means the first time that monolithic coverage of a foreign war turned into a mélange of critical stories. It happened in the case of previous military conflicts, notably Vietnam.

Thus, a simple hegemonic view requires refinements. Media scholar Daniel Hallin (1986) has argued that the degree to which news marches in line with dominant interests depends on the nature of the issue and the political domain into which it falls. He proposed that news can fall into one of three ideological domains: **the sphere of consensus, sphere of deviance**, and **sphere of legitimate controversy** (see Figure 10.1). The first two regions – consensus and deviance – preserve ideological harmony, maintaining the system's values by celebrating societal norms in the case of consensus and marginalizing dissident views, in the case of deviance.

News that falls into the sphere of consensus is the region of "motherhood and apple pie," where "journalists do not feel compelled either to present opposing views or to remain disinterested observers. On the contrary," Hallin (1986) explains, "the journalist's role is to serve as an advocate or celebrant of consensual values" (p. 117). News that falls into the sphere of consensus includes U.S. victories in the Olympics, popular wars, and, on the local level, as discussed in Chapter 9, downtown, community-enhancing projects or victories of city sports teams in championship games. You won't find stories nitpicking or blasting the team or the nation. It is all rah-rah. News of terrorist attacks and natural disasters in the home country, where citizens have suffered grievous losses and the nation bands together to work as one, fall into this sphere as well.

In the sphere of deviance, journalism "plays the role of exposing, condemning, or excluding from the public agenda those who violate or challenge the political consensus" (Hallin, 1986, p. 117). The term "deviance" is not used to criticize, but, as noted in Chapter 8, it describes events that differ from the norm, as well as individuals outside the culturally dominant mainstream. News of AIDS in the 1980s fell into the sphere of deviance. The plight of gay men was off the radar screen in

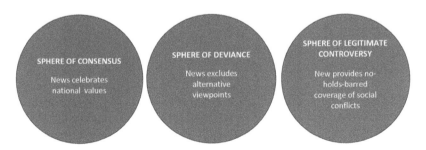

Figure 10.1 Spheres of Consensus, Deviance, and Legitimate Controversy

those days, and systemic forces colluded to keep the spread of the AIDS epidemic outside the news agenda for several years (Dearing & Rogers, 1992). Working through now familiar mechanisms – individual-level reporter prejudice, as when editors tossed around words like "queer" in editorial meetings (Kinsella, 1988); lack of official sources to quote, in light of the Reagan Administration's low priority of AIDS; and cultural ideology, given the national resistance to make AIDS a political priority – AIDS got short shrift, a clear instance in which a problem and its victims fell into the social system-sanctioned sphere of deviance. One might make a similar case for stories about the opioid epidemic. The stories were given lower priority since the victims were poor, and the greed of the big pharmaceutical firm, Purdue Pharma, was covered only later (Macy, 2018).

The sphere of legitimate controversy is the wide-open, no-holds-barred familiar region of conflict, controversy, and animus between political adversaries. Elections, Supreme Court battles, racial and gender-focused disputes, and controversies about celebrities from Bill Cosby to political figures encompassing the Clintons, President Obama, and President Trump are the rich reservoir of news in this domain. News that falls into the sphere of legitimate controversy is considered fair game for the rough-and-tumble, partisan fights of contemporary democratic society. Most political stories are legitimate grist for this domain, provided they don't threaten the dominant ideology or promote dissident perspectives.

The three spheres notion invokes system-based logic to explain why news covers and ignores certain issues. It rejects a simple social system-based hegemonic model that says the news never covers viewpoints that clash with the powers-that-be. It also articulates broad conditions under which such coverage is more or less likely. However, from a conceptual perspective, it is descriptive, not predictive. The spheres' concepts do not stipulate a priori the factors that should cause an issue to fall into one of these categories, nor why a problem might fall into the sphere of consensus or deviance in one era and then emerge as a legitimate source of controversy at another time.

In order to gain more specificity and articulate factors that help us determine more clearly which domains news coverage falls into, we need to call on a contemporary perspective, framing. Framing identifies key factors at work in contemporary systemic influences on news.

Framing

Framing cuts to the core of how power is wielded in democratic societies. Groups that control the frame – i.e., the interpretation or slant on a complex problem – can potently influence public opinion and policy. **Frames**, short for frameworks, highlight certain aspects of a multifaceted, freighted issue, connecting the political dots so as to favor a particular way of defining the problem, and pointing toward a specific evaluation and remedy (Entman, 2004; Hertog & McLeod, 2001; Nisbet, 2010). Does poverty result from lack of individual initiative or broader injustices in capitalist economics? Do school shootings stem from lax policies on gun control or failure to arm teachers? Are downtown developments good for cities, or do they promote social inequities?

News can promote specific frames by calling on certain news values, quoting particular sources rather than others, and offering up a narrative that showcases one interpretation rather than others. The system-based hegemonic thesis argues that news frames issues in ways that favor the dominant ruling elite, reinforcing the status quo. However, as suggested above, there are shortcomings in this simple view, and refinements, based on framing, have been put forth. The next sections, based on framing, examine two refinements of hegemony that emphasize more fluid effects of news on policy (see Table 10.2).

Indexing

The indexing thesis offers a congenial, but important, modification in the hegemonic approach. It emphasizes that news indexes coverage so that it closely matches the range of voices expressed by leading political elites (Bennett, 1994; Bennett, Lawrence, & Livingston, 2007). News media calibrate coverage so it reflects the assertions and frameworks expressed by leading policymakers, while excluding or marginalizing viewpoints that fall outside the boundaries of officialdom (Gitlin, 1980; Speer, 2017). Importantly, if government officials are in general agreement, the media

Table 10.2 Alternatives to Simple Hegemonic Model

Framing: Overarching frameworks and interpretations that influence news-gathering and news production, with different news outlets adopting different frames.

Indexing: News reflects the dominant elite when the leadership is in agreement, but when there are differences among policy elites, news is indexed to reflect these different frames.

Cascading Activation: News is not passive, but an active force. It is less beholden to elites than indexing suggests. News can influence political elites and the public, particularly when events are ambiguous or dramatic. Public opinion can cascade upward, influencing elites, as well as being influenced by them. Elite leaders are important determinants of news, but news does not always index coverage to them.

Revised Cascading Activation: Elite leaders can bypass mainstream news by reaching followers on partisan news outlets, promoting elites' frames or viewpoints. But followers can also influence leaders via Twitter and social media.

---

emphasize the predominant government frame on the issue, in line with hegemony. However, indexing departs from hegemony when government is divided on a policy issue, and different leaders and interest groups frame the issue differently. When policy elites (for example, members of Congress) are divided or object to policies articulated by the ruling group (e.g., the White House), news reflects this, presenting the diversity of elite debate. Let's see how this works in the case of three foreign conflicts that initially fell inside the sphere of consensus and in this way provide an interesting elaboration of the hegemony model.

Vietnam

During the Vietnam War, with Congress and the White House four-square behind the war effort, news supported President Johnson, in the manner of old-style coverage of the "good wars" – World War II and the Korean War. Reporters referred to the North Vietnamese as the enemy and described the war as a "national endeavor," an "American tradition" (Hallin, 1986, p. 175). However, as national leaders, like Senator Robert F. Kennedy, increasingly opposed the war on moral and pragmatic grounds, pointing to its savage loss of life, news began to cover the war differently, highlighting the views of those who favored withdrawal from Vietnam, giving dissenting views television air time.

Persian Gulf War

Arguing that Iraq's 1990 invasion of Kuwait represented an unlawful threat to the world order (as well as to the world's oil supplies), President George H.W. Bush moved decisively on the diplomatic, military, and rhetorical fronts. Working in strategic image management, and in concert with a global public relations firm, the Bush Administration repeatedly compared Iraqi President Saddam Hussein to Hitler and exploited testimony from a teenage Kuwaiti girl who claimed that Iraqi soldiers pulled hundreds of babies from incubators and killed them (Manheim, 1994). (It turned out that the girl, a daughter of the Kuwaiti ambassador to the U.S., had been coached by PR executives in front of video cameras at the company's Washington office, and her claims were untrue, though grist for effective management of public opinion.)

News picked up on these frames, with a magazine calling Hussein "Baghdad's bully," a television station placing an American flag behind the news anchors' set, and TV dramatizing the war, with patriotism-inspiring music that affectively transformed TV news of battles into a mythic movie (Hallin & Gitlin, 1994). Once again, as legislative opposition to the war increased, news prominently covered the Congressional debate, including highly placed criticisms, indexing elite disagreements and divisions among elites and the American public. In the final analysis, there was no "hegemonic media operating entirely at the disposal of the state," Entman and Page (1994, p. 96) observed, even though supportive war frames received more coverage then than opposing frames, and Bush Administration officials received a great deal of airtime.

Iraq War

This brings us to the 2003 war against Iraq that followed in the wake of the September 11 attacks. The White House ostensibly initiated the war to prevent Iraq from using its feared (but largely nonexistent) weapons of mass destruction against the U.S.

In the aftermath of the 9/11 horrors, the nation's leaders and public took a uniformly pro-U.S. stance, supporting President Bush's war on terror and backing the war to destroy the Taliban in Afghanistan. News media followed suit. In the absence of significant criticism from Congressional or other political elites, news indexed the coverage of intervention in Afghanistan to reflect the hawkish national consensus. In 2002, the Bush Administration's plan to attack Iraq had strong backing in Congress, as well as overwhelming public support (see Public Attitudes Toward the War in Iraq, 2008). News – famously Judith Miller's *New York Times* stories, quoting official sources – passively indexed the dominant approach, giving free (information-subsidized) publicity to the Bush Administration's erroneous WMD claims, building up support for the war, as discussed in Chapter 8.

Indexing news to the dominant elite consensus in favor of the Iraq war, network television news reports quoted Bush administration officials twice as frequently as competing sources. Opposing Democratic legislators "were barely audible, and the overall thrust of coverage favored a pro-war perspective" (Hayes & Guardino, 2010, p. 59). But oppositional frames were covered, with officials from foreign governments who advocated a diplomatic settlement quoted on network news reports (Hayes & Guardino, 2010). Over time, dissenting voices received bigger play, as policy experts expressed increasing criticism in 2003 and 2004, and the late Senator John McCain, himself a victim of torture during the Vietnam War, led a Congressional debate on torture and terrorism in 2005. This gave reporters an opening, one that drew on routine reporting through formal news channels, to describe a hearing that offered criticism of Bush administration policies. As Congressional opposition to the war grew, news covered different aspects of the debate. With national leaders increasingly divided on the war, news indexed coverage to reflect these differences, covering both the White House and opposition perspectives on the war.

Summary

The indexing approach emphasizes that hegemony oversimplifies and does not accurately describe news that emerges in the wake of pluralistic opposition from elite leaders in Washington. The ruling elite does not act as a monolith, but is plural, with different elite influences – Congressional opponents, military leaders, and interest group lobbies – gaining coverage when consensus breaks down. Indexing offers a thoughtful counterpoint to a simple hegemonic view. However, indexing has limits as well, underestimating the role played by public opinion and ordinary citizens, who also influence news and public policy. Moreover, indexing assumes news simply *reflects* what political leaders say, though we know news does not mirror political reality. In addition to reflecting differences among the nation's leadership forces, news interjects new factors into the political milieu. This is the focus of another, more media-centric approach to news and the policy process.

Cascading Activation Model

Robert M. Entman's (2004) cascading activation approach assigns media and public opinion a more active role than does the indexing perspective. In line with the social system-based hegemonic model, his cascading activation view stipulates that frames, like a surging waterfall, flow downward, with powerful elites influencing the ways that the media and public frame issues. However, contrary to a simple hegemonic model, which suggest news parrots back official pronouncements, cascading activation emphasizes that news frames and public opinion flow upward to influence top political leaders (Handley, 2010). The media is not shackled to the views of official sources. Instead, it increasingly acts as an independent power center, shaping the range and content of public debate, adopting alternative frames when mid-level news sources suggest alternative interpretations, and unexpected dramatic events occur that require new ways of interpreting issues. Let's look at how cascading activation views news during the three wars – Vietnam, Persian Gulf and the Iraq War – that initially fell in the sphere of consensus, but spiraled out in complex ways.

Vietnam

In addition to indexing news of Vietnam to reflect differences among national leaders, news exerted independent effects on public opinion and policy, although the extent is a matter of scholarly debate. After the pivotal North Vietnamese Tet Offensive in 1968, a surprise attack on more than 100 cities, news took a decidedly negative tone toward the war, a function of reporters' access to the battlefield and the impact of unfavorable assessments of esteemed journalists, like Walter Cronkite. Far from taking a hegemonic tone, news focused graphically on the battlefield brutality, going so far as to suggest, in some dispatches, that the war could not be won, a conclusion that understandably frustrated conservative partisans, who controversially argued this impeded the war effort. Over the ensuing years, coverage became more negative, noting decreasing morale of U.S. troops, drug abuse in the military, the shocking massacre of hundreds of Vietnamese civilians by U.S. soldiers at My Lai, and massive protests by anti-war opponents. Even so, some critics argued that news simplified anti-war demonstrations, predictably focusing on action, violence, and creating celebrities out of savvy protest leaders, while overlooking the broader framework that propelled dissenters, or failing to pose basic questions about what, if any, long-term national interest the U.S. had in the war (Gitlin, 1980; Hallin, 1986).

Persian Gulf War

Indexing also does not fully account for news coverage of the 1991 Persian Gulf conflict. In addition to duly reporting policy elites' differences, news exploited new visual technologies to show riveting real-time coverage of Patriot missile attacks on Iraqi forces, graphic displays of light-up-the-sky missile attacks, and dramatic play-by-play reports from CNN star correspondents in Baghdad as U.S. bombs dropped from the sky (Iyengar & Simon, 1994). Emboldened by the technology and elated by audience interest in high-tech news, TV journalism provided immensely positive reports of the war, exaggerating the success of the Patriot missiles, focusing on the real-time missile attacks partly because the military (having learned from Vietnam) restricted reporters' access to the battlefield, lavishly covering home front support of the war through yellow ribbon-filled pro-war demonstrations, and, for a time, repeating the Bush Administration framing of Iraqi leader Hussein as comparable to Hitler (Kellner, 1993).

Iraq War

The third war in the triad – Iraq, beginning in 2003 – presents a more complex picture of news coverage. After the procession of patriotic coverage in the wake of 9/11, followed by critical stories indexed to opposition from members of Congress, news cascaded to influence public opinion and policy, with a decidedly negative spin. Journalists provided blockbuster coverage of U.S. soldiers' sexual and physical abuse of Iraqi prisoners at an Abu Ghraib prison that included a widely distributed photo of an Army private pulling a dog leash attached to a naked prisoner. Investigative journalists dug up the story and the images were newsworthy, highlighting the way news acts a power center unto itself, complementing, but independent of, indexed elite political leaders. (News of Abu Ghraib was controversial, reporting the gruesome images, to be sure, but favoring the less pejorative term, "abuse," rather than the more accurate "torture," reflecting journalists' caution about employing the stronger term, as well as acquiescence to the Bush administration's use of the less pejorative "abuse" frame; see Bennett, Lawrence, & Livingston, 2007; Jones & Sheets, 2009.)

In the wake of Abu Ghraib, continued battlefield deaths, and questions about high-level military decisions, the press harnessed frames other than the 9/11-initiated Bush Administration "war on terror" perspective. Pulitzer Prize-winning stories revealed serious human and civil rights abuses, notably the CIA interrogating terrorism suspects in covert "black site" prisons in eight countries across the world, and the Bush Administration's secret authorization of the National Security Agency to eavesdrop on Americans for possible terrorist activity without acquiring court-ordered search warrants. The press now reframed the war, no longer stressing the U.S.-under-attack theme, or that Hussein's weapons of mass destruction justified the invasion of Iraq. Instead, the new frames frequently suggested that the peril to America lay inward, in the ways the U.S. government endangered the civil liberties of its own citizens to fight terrorism, a frame increasingly – but by no means universally – shared by Americans (McLeod & Shah, 2015). Rather than being tightly indexed to – or influenced by – White House elites, news broke free, emphasizing frames other than Bush's war on terrorism (Speer, 2017).

Thus, cascading activation says that politics is more fluid than the simple hegemonic or even the indexing approach suggest. With so many digital outlets and frames cascading upward in unpredictable ways, elite leaders can no longer be guaranteed the control over media frames they had when conventional media ruled the roost.

In a revised cascading model that takes into account digital technologies, algorithms, and online media platforms, Entman and Usher (2018) highlight how elite leaders can bypass mainstream media, influencing followers' political beliefs by disseminating messages on ideological news outlets. Conservative leaders, diffusing messages through Fox and Breitbart News, and liberal leaders, via MSNBC and Salon, can communicate frames that reinforce partisans' preexisting attitudes (in some cases in defiance of factual evidence), stimulating partisans to energetically talk up the frames online.

Once again, the arrows can also stretch from followers to leaders, as was the case in the 2016 election, when grassroots Republican voters rejected elites' directives to support established candidates, going instead for insurgent candidate Donald Trump, their tweets and retweets exerting a bottom-up impact on his campaign (Leland, 2016; Perloff, 2018).

While followers were hardly pushing for a non-elite candidate in billionaire Donald Trump, the cascading model emphasizes that public opinion influences news, in a more democratic fashion. The model also suggests that there are multiple, increasingly dynamic influences on news and policymaking in the current era. One such influence is global, the internationalist trend in investigative reporting

Cascading International Journalistic Exposés

Investigative journalism now extends beyond national borders. Chapter 4 discussed the controversial revelations of WikiLeaks, the international online organization dedicated to transparently sharing classified documents. I also described news exposés in British and American news outlets of Edward Snowden's blockbuster revelations about massive surveillance by the U.S. government. In addition, the International Consortium of Investigative Journalists, a worldwide network of reporters and news organizations, has broken big stories, providing news outlets with leaked documents from a Panamanian law firm in 2016. The documents identified politicians, business executives, and celebrities across the world engaged in shadowy financial activities. The news articles documented how the law firm helped well-heeled American clients legally evade U.S. financial disclosure and tax laws, hiding millions in shell companies abroad, showcasing jaw-dropping exploitation of the system by the rich and powerful (Lipton & Creswell, 2016).

International journalism organizations can elide conventional news gatekeepers, giving them a capacity inconceivable before the digital age to release documents worldwide. WikiLeaks did this, revealing clandestine aspects of U.S. wars in Iraq and Afghanistan, such as evidence that hundreds of civilians were killed by U.S. troops in Afghanistan, as well as documents showing that Big Pharma forced developing countries to keep drug prices high, penalizing dying, poor patients (Christensen, 2016). More controversially, in 2016 it dumped thousands of emails, many about Hillary Clinton, from the Democratic National Committee, that had been gathered by Russian cyber-hackers, arguably disrupting a presidential election by revealing documents stolen by a U.S. adversary. WikiLeaks' disruption of a democratic election, and possibly inappropriate contacts with the 2016 Trump presidential campaign, have raised questions about the moral and journalistic character of the organization (Buchanan & Yourish, 2019).

Another example of exposés that transcend national borders involve the classified documents leaked by Edward Snowden, a former analyst at the National Security Agency, in 2013. The documents revealed secret U.-S. government orders that required the telecommunications conglomerate Verizon to hand over phone records of all its users to the federal government. Contrary to President Obama's claim that the NSA surveillance focused only on foreigners, the phone records consistently included American citizens living in the U.S. The news was first reported in the British newspaper, the *Guardian*, based on Snowden's communication with a sympathetic reporter, Glenn Greenwald, and then in *The Washington Post*.

Whatever you think about these revelations, they are broadly inconsistent with hegemony. These internationalist exposés clearly threaten the elite hegemonic fabric on foreign policy, as the classified documents reveal secret government war-time decisions, jaw-dropping business evasion of laws, and massive government surveillance of citizens suggestive of a surveillance state. Snowden's revelations concerned the Obama Administration so much that it charged Snowden with violating the Espionage Act and stealing U.S. government property, although defenders applauded his revelations of Big Brother's snooping, arguing it served democracy (Christensen, 2016). The exposés also show that conventional news gatekeepers continue to be important, as the whistleblowers partnered with news organizations to gain widespread dissemination of their documents.

Journalists' frames of the revelations also came into play. Mainstream British newspapers tended to frame the leaks around surveillance, legitimizing surveillance, even defending it on national security grounds. By contrast, blogs focused on transgression of citizens' rights, challenging mass surveillance (Wahl-Jorgensen, Bennett, & Taylor, 2017). Some mainstream news framed Snowden's revelations of massive government surveillance in terms that favored governmental control, while articles about Snowden in a leading British and American paper were most likely to be categorized with the accurate, but defiant "whistleblower" label, as opposed to "hero" or "villain" (Di Salvo & Negro, 2016). *The New York Times* and *The Washington Post*, attuned to the corridors of elite power, consulted with U.S. intelligence agency officials while covering the WikiLeaks and Snowden stories, exerting gatekeeper control over decisions that concerned withholding sensitive information (Woodall, 2018). Critics argued this could have allowed authorities to "capture," co-opt, or control information that was published.

On a broader level, the emergence of WikiLeaks and the cross-national investigative journalist consortium point to ways non-conventional news organizations have exposed important classified documents that, in the view of defenders, serve democratic functions for society (Christensen, 2016), and, in the view of detractors, thwarted legitimate government needs in an age of terrorism. Yet "journalism after Snowden," as scholars put it, raises new questions, including the pervasiveness of government surveillance, how news goes about reporting such massive revelations, and the ethics of such disclosures (Bell & Owen, 2017). In the face of government invasions of citizen privacy and private sector businesses that secretly prop up authoritarian governments (Bogdanich & Forsythe,

2018), documents provided by WikiLeaks, as well as other groups, serve important watchdog functions, showcasing how news continues to challenge the powers-that-be.

Critiques and Overall Assessment of Hegemony

Over the past decades, and coinciding with the development of new online platforms that provide alternatives to news, scholars have robustly debated the hegemony approach, notably Herman and Chomsky's framework (Mullen & Klaehn, 2010). The virtue of the hegemonic model is its sweep, breadth, and emphasis on how news coverage fits into the larger social system and can protect the interests of dominant institutions and political elites (Herring & Robinson, 2003; Klaehn, 2002). However, the model has generated considerable criticisms that emphasize its limits and shortcomings (Corner, 2003; Evans, 2002; Lang & Lang, 2004; see Table 10.3).

Is the hegemonic view correct? This is a complex question. Certainly, it does capture strong kernels of truth, and highlights the powerful role economic and political elites play in news, particularly when there is overwhelming policy consensus. The model also calls attention to egregious news omissions and biases of the past. It aptly describes news conformity to the powers-that-be in less democratic regimes than the U.S. However, its claim to fame – and most interesting feature – is its

Table 10.3 Hegemony Pros and Cons

Strengths	Shortcomings
Calls attention to the impact of social system on news	Assumes news induces conformity, when news also produces change
Illuminates news coverage in outside-the -box ways, providing criticisms frequently overlooked	Assumes social system speaks with one voice
Provides a theoretical perspective that explains how news reproduces the status quo	Presumes all the institutional forces work in harmony, minimizing the extent to which institutions disagree and news covers dissenting viewpoints
	Has less validity in an age of internationalist investigative groups and non-conventional digital news outlets that bring many voices to the online public square, and where elites have less control over media than in the past

contention that hegemony operates in countries like the U.S. that pride themselves on their democratic characteristics; according to strong pro-ponents, hegemony operates in these nations, just more subtly. But it is here that hegemony runs afoul.

Philosophically, hegemony advocates are prone to make claims that are not falsifiable, or not capable of being proven false, a canon of social science. They do this by dogmatically arguing that evidence inconsistent with hegemony is an unusual exception or is flawed, irrelevant, or even has been put forth by those who don't understand its precepts. This makes hegemony non-falsifiable – a rubbery statue that its proponents hold up in the face of torrents of criticism, refusing to acknowledge that, like all theories, it has shortcomings. As Lang and Lang (2004) note, Herman and Chomsky's framework "obliterates all distinctions," offer-ing up the incredulous claim that that American media offer up propa-ganda for the ruling class that does not differ from that of a totalitarian state (p. 97).

Hegemony oversimplifies. As Bourdieu's (2005) field theory empha-sizes, the field of journalism is attuned to power, part of a broad field where power politics is wielded, but a field composed of different forces and political struggles. Noting that field theory rejects Herman and Chomsky's mechanistic, capitalism-focused approach, Benson and Neveu (2005) point out that journalism does not always prop up the status quo, but can transform relations among powerful groups, as when news indexes coverage to Congressional, rather than White House, elites, or provides sympathetic coverage to powerful activists, such as the Black Lives Matter movement, rather than high-level police officials. Powerful political and economic interests influence media, but, contrary to the simple hegemonic approach, there is more than one power elite in America.

What's more, as Entman (2004) acknowledges, elites no longer possess the power they had during the Cold War. Policy differences among powerful political groups "are no longer the exception but the rule" (p. 5). National leaders still have power, but lack the hegemonic influence of yore, when they could push news coverage into the spheres of consensus or deviance.

Indeed, in the current era of multiple digital outlets, just about every-thing seems to be fair game for the sphere of legitimate controversy. It is difficult to find areas where news strictly protects elites in a sphere of consensus or – in an era where gay rights are universally accepted, violence against transgender Americans is widely reported, and stories about transgender experiences are richly described – where dissidents' perspectives are marginalized as they were in the sphere of deviance in years past. Yet debate persists, with scholars emphasizing that elites can still dominate news and influence frames adopted by the mass public (Entman, 2017).

Herman and Chomsky, for their part, acknowledge that the Internet, blogs and podcasts, which challenge traditional media by diffusing dissident views, can weaken the plausibility of a hegemonic analysis (Mullen, 2009). However, they doubt this will occur because the traditional news media are the dominant providers of news, have the most resources, and other platforms are focused on social, rather than political, connections. Their arguments have some merit. Yet they were published in 2009, well before the penetration of Facebook, Twitter, and new online platforms that have eroded the power of conventional news. Hegemony remains a problem, in certain autocratic countries and under certain conditions in democratic nations, but it is no longer the dominant issue in the study of journalism, supplanted by concerns about extremist groups' manufacturing niche consensus through fake news (Frenkel, 2018). The focus has changed from concerns about top-down influence by power elites to bottom-up influence from extremist fringe groups that spread falsehoods through fake accounts that may be viewed by millions of Facebook users.

Does news prop up the powerful or tear it down? Does news sustain the economic and political status quo or change it? Is it a force of system maintenance or system change? These are big questions that speak to the central importance of a social system approach. The hegemonic perspective traditionally emphasized that there is one dominant political elite, but supportive scholarship (Evans, 2002), along with pluralistic approaches, emphasize there are many centers of power that vie for influence. Clearly, hegemonic economic and political elites have powerful ways to influence news coverage, more ways at their disposal than the less politically connected, and mechanisms built into the system that privilege elites. But this does not mean they always succeed.

The news has instigated change on issues such as civil rights, feminist struggles, and liberties of LGBTQ individuals (MacKinnon, 2018; Roberts & Klibanoff, 2006), as well shaping the agenda, framing issues, and challenging the powers-that-be on foreign wars, the presidential nomination process, and abuse of presidential power during Watergate, the Clinton impeachment, Obama-era civil liberties transgressions revealed by Snowden, and the Mueller investigation of President Trump (Bell & Owen, 2017; Lang & Lang, 1983; McCombs, 2004; Patterson, 1993). What's more, hegemony assumes that the system is bad and corrupt, and news sustains this system. While so many problems plague contemporary politics that it is hard not to agree with some of the critiques, it is important to remember that political systems have virtues, ranging from free, if imperfect, elections to robust participation of different political parties. Conservatives emphasize the positives in the American political system, and they traditionally find the hegemonic approach over-the-top and neglectful of comparative strengths in the U.S. political-economic framework.

The debate – and it is probably not resolvable, given different conceptual definitions and ideological sentiments that shape the discussion – focuses on the degree to which news has propelled societal change. Hegemonic critics rightly note that some of the changes news instigated were only modest reforms that have not struck at the heart of the system. News neglected the global economic crisis of 2008, covering it in depth only after it happened. And yet, journalists provided a wealth of stories that took capitalist actors and institutions to task for their role in the crisis, as they did in cases of other systemic economic problems, writing stories that were "contrary to the interests of the corporate world" and challenged capitalism's assumptions (Shoemaker & Vos, 2009, p. 132).

There are also prominent, powerful cases in which news has led to social change. A telling example is the social and political muscle extended by the #MeToo movement, a spontaneous, unstructured social media-diffused crusade that was inspired by news revelations about sexual assaults by powerful men in the entertainment and media industries (e.g., Farrow, 2017; Kantor & Twohey, 2017). News exposés helped form and catalyze the national movement – a systemic rejection of a key component of the social system, the male-dominated patriarchy. Emboldened by the palpable strength of the #MeToo cause, activists and followers challenged the nomination of Brett Kavanaugh to the Supreme Court after he was accused of sexual assault as a teenager, showcasing how the movement's dynamics had begun to push their way into the upper reaches of American society (Zernike & Steel, 2018).

What's more, as a leading lawyer in sexual harassment observed, by publicly challenging gender inequalities that have long undermined legal recourse for victims of sexual abuse, "the #MeToo movement is accomplishing what sexual harassment law to date has not" (MacKinnon, 2018, A19). The intersection of news, #MeToo conversations, and changes in public opinion helped realign the male management hierarchy. Just a year after the news exposés, 200 prominent men in different industries lost their jobs in the wake of accusations of sexual harassment, nearly seven times as many as a year before, with more than 40 percent of the men replaced by women (Carlsen, Salam, & Miller, 2018).

Mainstream news coverage, and the resultant social media-based activism, conveyed via liberal online platforms, produced social change opposed by powerful patriarchs. Broadly put, a feminist journalism (Steiner, 2009) or, more aptly, a journalism-facilitated feminist social network helped change the status quo. To be sure, it didn't smash the patriarchy, as writer Susan Faludi (2017) notes. However, news does not have the power to undo a social system in and of itself. Its impact on toppling powerful high-profile sexual abusers is a significant media effect, one that over time may help promote a more egalitarian gender role structure.

For their part, traditional hegemonic theorists (typically men) would acknowledge these patriarchal effects, but would probably argue that capitalist economics, not gender dominance, is the basis of how power is wielded on the public and media in contemporary society. But this begs the question of just which influence – economics, politics, gender, or race – is most influential in American society. Clearly, news exposed a problem and provided new frames, catalyzing social media expressions of #MeToo. Social media outrage at sexual abuse in turn influenced news coverage through standard media routines, leading to more outing of sexual abusers, illustrating how news complexly produces social change, at least in this area of American life.

Conclusions

This chapter took on the big issue central to the study of news – the role of the social system in shaping news content. The social system, composed of political, economic, and ideological subsystems, influences news profoundly, working through the individual, routine, organizational, and economic determinants discussed throughout this book. These influences occur in different countries – not just the U.S. – and are moderated by a nation's political, electoral, and economic subsystems.

Influenced by the insightful philosopher-critic Gramsci, critics have long argued that news props up the dominant interests in society, helping to manufacture consent by covering issues in ways that reaffirm the preeminent ideology of ruling groups, while marginalizing dissent. It is a controversial, important thesis that has riled scholars, contains nuggets of truth, makes claims that are not supported by evidence, and is no longer as salient today, in era of global, online news sites. However, hegemony directs us to an appreciation of the ways ideology intrudes in the gatekeeping process.

There is no question that American news outlets are bottom-line capitalistic institutions that prioritize profit and increasingly place a premium on stock portfolio importance, frequently sacrificing high-quality news on the altar of financial investments. Advertisers, a major, if somewhat declining influence on news, can influence news content directly, by threatening to cancel advertising in the face of critical articles and indirectly, by encouraging news organizations to focus on upscale audiences to whom advertising is directed. On the other hand, advertisers have taken on controversial causes that provoke the political establishment, illustrated by Nike's marketing campaign centered on Colin Kaepernick, whose kneeling during the national anthem as a protest against racism was condemned by conservatives, including President Trump. Contrary to hegemony, advertising does not speak in one pro-system, monolithic voice.

On an everyday level, and in exceptional instances like the global economic crisis of 2007–2008, news has played down, even failed to aggressively pursue stories that threaten the economic fabric. Organizational, role socialization, and routine-level factors built into journalism militate against journalists doing the aggressive reporting that could have exposed systemic economic malaise.

It gets more complicated when one considers the mountain of journalistic work that has gotten to the bottom of such crises, including after-the-fact stories that explained the role of greed and regulatory corruption. What's more, journalists have won many major awards for investigations of capitalistic failures, such as bribery at Walmart to control the Mexican market, a shadowy Florida property insurance system, and fraudulent claims about blood tests perpetrated by Theranos, a health technology firm, that was forced out of business as a result of the news exposés. Hegemony proponents would respond that these stories do not cut to the core of the capitalist system, which may be true, but also represents an instance of theorists refusing to abide by disconfirming evidence. In any case, one could argue that, bit by bit, story by story, journalistic investigations illuminate systemic economic shortcomings.

On the macro political front, hegemony has received tragic support in the deeply prejudiced way news covered race over the course of two centuries and failed to cover the Holocaust in any meaningful way. These are among the examples of how the social system, working in a subtle, cohesive way, produced news that propped up the powers-that-be, helping to manufacture consent on the part of the public and policy elites. A similar pattern emerged in the wake of 9/11, with news understandably offering a patriotic view of the terrorist attacks that nonetheless provided one-sided views of the broader international picture. However, there are cases that don't fit the bill so simply – instances of vociferous news criticism of political leadership – that require the invocation of different domains of reporting: the spheres of consensus, deviance, and legitimate controversy.

Consistent with the sphere of consensus notion, early coverage of major foreign wars – Vietnam, the 1991 Persian Gulf conflict in particular, and Iraq – fits a hegemonic pattern. However, news of these wars increasingly became conflicted and critical, failing to provide rah-rah coverage of the ruling elites, and falling into the sphere of legitimate controversy, in a way that does not support a simple hegemonic model.

Clarifying these three broad domains, scholars have emphasized the concept of framing, where news provides a particular interpretation, slant, or evaluation of a complex issue. According to one view, news indexes events to fit elite policymaking, with coverage emphasizing the dominant frame when the leadership is in agreement, but covering a range of frames, including dissenting perspectives, when the national or community leadership disagrees about how to pursue a problem.

Indexing helps explain the range of critical stories that emerged in coverage of foreign wars, as well as domestic issues. However, its neglect of the autonomous role played by news and grassroots public opinion helped generated a cascading activation model.

Cascading activation highlights the ways news offered critical coverage of White House war-time policies, not parroting back policy elites, as hegemony suggests, or simply indexing stories to reflect high-level disagreements. A number of examples – coverage of the North Vietnamese Tet Offensive in 1968, Abu Ghraib torture during the Iraq War, and changing frames focusing on civil liberties violations in the wake of the 2003 Iraq war – showcase the role news plays in promoting dissenting frames, a far cry from manufacturing consent. Cascading activation also has been refined to explain how political elites bypass mainstream media, directing messages to biased ideological media. News coverage and public opinion can also cascade upward, influencing national leaders, illustrating the dynamic nature of news effects in the current ecosystem.

In the present era, with internationalist investigative journalism, such as the controversial WikiLeaks and a worldwide consortium of investigative reporters that produced the 2016 Panama Papers exposé, news is less beholden to a nation's powerful political hegemons. The Snowden leaks, published in the British and American press, attest to the ways that news can expose massive government surveillance that threatens the fabric of democratic civil liberties. These investigative pathways, coupled with the many digital news outlets, suggest that a nation's power elite has fewer ways to control news and manufacture consent, to repeat Herman and Chomsky's felicitous phrase, than in decades past.

Increasingly, the assumption of a conformist news media that yields to dominant elites is out of step with the disruptive, fragmented digital times, in which people distrust established, officially-sourced news or can receive information from alternative, ideologically-based sources of dubious character (Bennett & Pfetsch, 2018).

And yet power elites exist and matter, and for these reasons hegemony offers an insightful starting point – and sometimes metaphor – for a systemic analysis of contemporary news. However, hegemony has been justifiably criticized for making grandiose claims that cannot be proven false, pejoratively painting American media with the disparaging label of propaganda, and suggesting that the social system operates as a monolith, when, in all but the most unusual circumstances, it operates as a siege of competing power centers, of which the media (and many fractious online outlets) are disruptive fields of power.

There are also many instances in which, far from manufacturing consent, news has the opposite effects, sowing discontent or change, as when news exposed Facebook's privacy violations, leading to widespread distrust of the tech behemoth, and covered the conservative Tea Party movement and radical inequality-focused Occupy Wall Street, diffusing anti-government and inequality frames respectively. And, of course, hegemony assumes that the system's effects are predominately negative, a claim that some scholars would accept, but not others, particularly those who emphasize the virtues of American business, commercial innovations, and the political inventiveness of American democracy.

However, the central question remains whether news maintains the political status quo or produces change. Importantly, the basics of the system – capitalist economy, two-party political system, wide-reaching entertainment-focused culture, ideology of individualism and commitment to egalitarianism, tainted by time-honored failures to implement equality in practice – are impervious to influence by even the most impactful of news ventures. And the degree to which news that fundamentally challenged the basics of a social system could, in and of itself, change social institutions and public opinion is a matter of theoretical debate in the field of political communication. But there is little doubt that news has had powerful effects in *changing* racial attitudes (Goldman & Mutz, 2014), electoral politics (Patterson, 1993), the conduct of foreign wars, and, most recently, patriarchal norms of sexual abuse.

To be sure, the degree to which news produces change depends on what we mean by "change," and the hegemonic approach is wise to remind us that systemic factors have a tendency to yoke institutions back into the comforts of the status quo. But, in the main, in most western democracies, in a fragmented, pluralistic online age, the hegemony thesis has key shortcomings. Yes, the social system profoundly influences news, requiring an appreciation of the politics, economics, and culture of a particular system and the structure of its news media (Hallin & Mancini, 2004). Yet ideology, while a pervasive influence, does not always speak in one voice, and even when it does speak in monolingual fashion, it is not always heard by individuals attuned to their own social networks or apps, let alone believed. In America, policymaking elites press upon the complex media field (Benson & Neveu, 2005), moderating and influencing news decisions. But the broader journalistic field and the critical construct of gatekeeping (Shoemaker & Vos, 2009) are too variegated to be influenced only by elites. The news is a relatively autonomous power center – or series of power centers – in which the variety of news determinants described in this book intersect and overlap, producing a commodity called news that is as central to democracy as it is multifaceted, the product of a particular historical age, with its own sensibilities and contradictions.

References

An, S., & Bergen, L. (2007). Advertising pressure on daily newspapers: A survey of advertising sales executives. *Journal of Advertising*, *36*(2), 111–121.

Atal, M.R. (2018). The cultural and economic power of advertisers in the business press. *Journalism*, *19*, 1078–1095.

Bagdikian, B.H. (2004). *The new media monopoly.* Boston, MA: Beacon Press.

Becker, S. (1984). Marxist approaches to media studies: The British experience. *Critical Studies in Mass Communication, 1,* 66–80.

Bell, E., & Owen, T. (with S. Khorana & J.R. Henrichsen) (Eds.) (2017). *Journalism after Snowden: The future of the press in the surveillance state.* New York: Columbia University Press.

Bennett, W.L. (1994). The news about foreign policy. In W.L. Bennett & D. L. Paletz (Eds.), *Taken by storm: The media, public opinion, and U.S. foreign policy in the Gulf War* (pp. 12–40). Chicago, IL: University of Chicago Press.

Bennett, W.L., Lawrence, R.G., & Livingston, S. (2007). *When the press fails: Political power and the news media from Iraq to Katrina.* Chicago, IL: University of Chicago Press.

Bennett, W.L., & Pfetsch, B. (2018). Rethinking political communication in a time of disrupted public spheres. *Journal of Communication, 68,* 243–253.

Benson, R., & Neveu, E. (2005). Introduction: Field theory as a work in progress. In R. Benson & E. Neveu (Eds.), *Bourdieu and the journalistic field* (pp. 1–25). Cambridge, UK: Polity Press.

Bogdanich, W., & Forsythe, M. (2018, December 16). Turning tyranny into a client: How McKinsey helps autocrats rise, countering U.S. interests. *The New York Times, 1,* 8–10.

Bourdieu, P. (2005). The political field, the social science field, and the journalistic field. In R. Benson & E. Neveu (Eds.), *Bourdieu and the journalistic field* (pp. 29–47). Cambridge, UK: Polity Press.

Braestrup, P. (1978). *Big story: How the American press and television reported and interpreted the crisis of Tet 1968 in Vietnam and Washington.* Garden City, NY: Anchor Press.

Buchanan, L., & Yourish, K. (2019, March 23). The characters and the issues. *The New York Times,* A14.

Carlsen, A., Salam, M., & Miller, C.C. (2018, October 24). How #MeToo realigned the corridors of power. *The New York Times,* A1, A14, A15.

Christensen, C. (2016). WikiLeaks and "indirect" media reform. In D. Freedman, J.A. Obar, C. Martens & R.W. McChesney (Eds.), *Strategies for media reform: International perspectives* (pp. 58–71). New York: Fordham Univeristy Press.

Coddington, M. (2015). The wall becomes a curtain: Revisiting journalism's news-business boundary. In M. Carlson & S.C. Lewis (Eds.), *Boundaries of journalism: Professionalism, practices and participation* (pp. 67–82). New York: Routledge.

Condit, C.M. (1994). Hegemony in a mass-mediated society: Concordance about reproductive technologies. *Critical Studies in Mass Communication, 11,* 205–230.

Corner, J. (2003). Debate: The model in question. A response to Klaehn on Herman and Chomsky. *European Journal of Communication, 18,* 367–375.

Cranberg, G., Bezanson, R., & Soloski, J. (2001). *Taking stock: Journalism and the publicly traded newspaper company.* Ames, IA: Iowa State University Press.

Dance, G.J.X., LaForgia, M., & Confessore, N. (2018, December 19). Facebook offered users privacy wall, then let tech giants around it. *The New York Times,* A1, A22, A23.

Dearing, J.W., & Rogers, E.M. (1992). AIDS and the media agenda. In T. Edgar, M.A. Fitzpatrick & V.S. Freimuth (Eds.), *AIDS: A communication perspective* (pp. 173–194). Hillsdale, NJ: Erlbaum Associates.

Denby, D. (2019, February 8). Nothing sacred. *The New Yorker,* 62–67.

Di Salvo, P., & Negro, G. (2016). Framing Edward Snowden: A comparative analysis of four newspapers in China, United Kingdom and United States. *Journalism*, *17*, 805–822.

Eisinger, J. (2014, April 30). Why only one top banker went to jail for the financial crisis. *The New York Times Magazine*. Online: www.nytimes.com/2014/05/04/ magazine/only-one-top-bank… (Accessed: October 1, 2018).

Entman, R.M. (2004). *Projections of power: Framing news, public opinion, and U.S. foreign policy*. Chicago, IL: University of Chicago Press.

Entman, R.M. (2017, September 20). Email to author.

Entman, R.M., & Page, B.I. (1994). The news before the storm: The Iraq war debate and the limits to media independence. In W.L. Bennett & D.L. Paletz (Eds.), *Taken by storm: The media, public opinion, and U.S. foreign policy in the Gulf War* (pp. 82–101). Chicago, IL: University of Chicago Press.

Entman, R.M., & Usher, N. (2018). Framing in a fractured democracy: Impacts of digital technology on ideology, power and cascading network activation. *Journal of Communication*, *68*, 298–308.

Evans, M.R. (2002). Hegemony and discourse: Negotiating cultural relationships through media production. *Journalism*, *3*, 309–329.

Faludi, S. (2017, December 31). The patriarchy isn't going anywhere. *The New York Times* (*Sunday Review*), *1*, 3.

Farrow, R. (2017, October 10). From aggressive overtures to sexual assault: Harvey Weinstein's accusers tell their stories. *The New Yorker*. Online: www .newyorker.com/news/news-desk/from-aggressive=over. (Accessed: October 23, 2018).

Fenton, N. (2019). (Dis)trust. *Journalism*, *20*, 36–39.

Frenkel, S. (2018, October 12). Made in U.S.: Untruths infest social media. *The New York Times*, A1, A12.

Gitlin, T. (1980). *The whole world is watching: Mass media in the making and unmaking of the New Left*. Berkeley, CA: University of California Press.

Goldman, S.K., & Mutz, D.C. (2014). *The Obama effect: How the 2008 campaign changed white racial attitudes*. New York: Russell Sage Foundation.

Goss, B.M. (2009). "The Left-Media's stranglehold": Flak and accuracy in media reports (2007–8). *Journalism Studies*, *10*, 455–473.

Gramsci, A. (1971). *Selections from the prison notebooks of Antonio Gramsci* (Ed. & Trans., Q. Hoare & G. Smith). New York: International Publishers.

Hallin, D.C. (1986). *The "uncensored war": The media and Vietnam*. New York: Oxford University Press.

Hallin, D.C., & Gitlin, T. (1994). The Gulf War as popular culture and television drama. In W.L. Bennett & D.L. Paletz (Eds.), *Taken by storm: The media, public opinion, and U.S. foreign policy in the Gulf War* (pp. 149–163). Chicago, IL: University of Chicago Press.

Hallin, D.C., & Mancini, P. (2004). *Comparing media systems: Three models of media and politics*. New York: Cambridge University Press.

Handley, R.L. (2010). Cascading activation: Bush's "war on terrorism" and the Israeli-Palestinian conflict. *Journalism*, *11*, 445–461.

Hayes, D., & Guardino, M. (2010). Whose views made the news? Media coverage and the march to war in Iraq. *Political Communication*, *27*, 59–87.

Herman, E.S., & Chomsky, N. (2002). *Manufacturing consent: The political economy of the mass media* (2nd ed.). New York: Pantheon.

Herring, E., & Robinson, P. (2003). Too polemical or too critical? Chomsky on the study of the news media and US foreign policy. *Review of International Studies, 29*, 553–568.

Hertog, J.K., & McLeod, D.M. (2001). A multiperspectival approach to framing analysis: A field guide. In S.D. Reese, O.H. Gandy, Jr. & A.E. Grant (Eds.), *Framing public life: Perspectives on media and our understanding of the social world* (pp. 139–161). Mahwah, NJ: Lawrence Erlbaum Associates.

Hutcheson, J., Domke, D., Billeaudeaux, A., & Garland, P. (2004). U.S. national identity, political elites, and a patriotic press following September 11. *Political Communication, 21*, 27–50.

Iyengar, S., & Simon, A. (1994). News coverage of the Gulf crisis and public opinion: A study of agenda-setting, priming, and framing. In W.L. Bennett & D. L. Paletz (Eds.), *Taken by storm: The media, public opinion, and U.S. foreign policy in the Gulf War* (pp. 167–185). Chicago, IL: University of Chicago Press.

Jones, T.M., & Sheets, P. (2009). Torture in the eye of the beholder: Social identity, news coverage, and Abu Ghraib. *Political Communication, 26*, 278–295.

Kantor, J., & Twohey, M. (2017, October 5). Harvey Weinstein paid off sexual harassment accusers for decades. *The New York Times*. Online: https://www.nytimes.com/2017/10/05/us/harvey-weinstein-harassment-allega tions.html. (Accessed: August 5, 2019).

Karim, K.H. (2011). Covering Muslims: Journalism as cultural practice. In B. Zelizer & S. Allan (Eds.), *Journalism after September 11* (2nd ed., pp. 131–146). New York: Routledge.

Kellner, D. (1993). The crisis in the Gulf and the lack of critical media discourse. In B.S. Greenberg & W. Gantz (Eds.), *Desert Storm and the mass media* (pp. 37–47). Cresskill, NJ: Hampton Press.

Kinsella, J. (1988). *Covering the plague: AIDS and the American media*. New Brunswick, NJ: Rutgers University Press.

Kitch, C. (2011). "Our duty to history": Newsmagazines and the national voice. In B. Zelizer & S. Allan (Eds.), *Journalism after September 11* (2nd ed., pp. 113–130). New York: Routledge.

Klaehn, J. (2002). A critical review and assessment of Herman and Chomsky's "Propaganda Model". *European Journal of Communication, 17*, 147–182.

Kolhatkar, S. (2018, October 22). Breaking the news. *The New Yorker*, 30–31, 34, 36–40, 42.

Kumar, D. (2006). Media, war, and propaganda: Strategies of information management during the 2003 Iraq war. *Communication and Critical/Cultural Studies, 3*, 48–69.

Kuypers, J.A. (2006). *Bush's war: Media bias and justifications for war in a terrorist age*. Lanham, MD: Rowman & Littlefield.

Lang, G.E., & Lang, K. (1983). *The battle for public opinion: The president, the press, and the polls during Watergate*. New York: Columbia University Press.

Lang, K., & Lang, G.E. (2004). Noam Chomsky and the manufacture of consent for the American foreign policy. *Political Communication, 21*, 93–101.

Leff, L. (2005). *Buried by the Times: The Holocaust and America's most important newspaper*. New York: Cambridge University Press.

Leland, J. (2016, January 31). They're mad and sure their guy is the one to lead the fight. *The New York Times, 1*, 21.

Lipstadt, D.E. (1986). *Beyond belief: The American press and the coming of the Holocaust 1933–1945*. New York: Free Press.

Lipton, E., & Creswell, J. (2016, June 5). Panama Papers show how rich United States clients hid millions abroad. *The New York Times*. Online: www .nytimes.com/2016/06/06/us/panama-papers.html. (Accessed: October 10, 2018).

MacKinnon, C.A. (2018, February 5). #MeToo and law's limitations. *The New York Times*, A19.

Macy, B. (2018). *Dopesick: Dealers, doctors, and the drug company that addicted America*. New York: Little, Brown and Company.

Manheim, J.B. (1994). Strategic public diplomacy: Managing Kuwait's image during the Gulf conflict. In W.L. Bennett & D.L. Paletz (Eds.), *Taken by storm: The media, public opinion, and U.S. foreign policy in the Gulf War* (pp. 131–148). Chicago, IL: University of Chicago Press.

Manjoo, F. (2017, October 25). Can Washington stop Big Tech companies? Don't bet on it. *The New York Times*. Online: www.nytimes.com/2017/10/25/technol ogy/regulating-tech-... (Accessed: September 30, 2018).

Manjoo, F. (2018, June 12). How net neutrality actually ended long before this week. *The New York Times*. Online: www.nytimes.com/2018/06/11/technology/ how-net-neutralit... (Accessed: September 30, 2018).

Manning, P. (2013). Financial journalism, news sources and the banking crisis. *Journalism, 14*, 173–189.

McChesney, R.W. (1999). *Rich media, poor democracy: Communication politics in dubious times*. Urbana, IL: University of Illinois Press.

McChesney, R.W. (2011). September 11 and the structural limitations of US journalism. In B. Zelizer & S. Allan (Eds.), *Journalism after September 11* (2nd ed., pp. 104–112). New York: Routledge.

McChesney, R.W. (2013). *Digital disconnect: How capitalism is turning the Internet against democracy*. New York: The New Press.

McCombs, M. (2004). *Setting the agenda: The mass media and public opinion*. Cambridge, UK: Polity Press.

McLeod, D.M., & Shah, D.V. (2015). *News frames and national security: Covering Big Brother*. New York: Cambridge University Press.

McManus, J.H. (2009). The commercialization of news. In K. Wahl-Jorgensen & T. Hanitzsch (Eds.), *The handbook of journalism studies* (pp. 218–233). New York: Routledge.

Morgenson, G., & Rosner, J. (2011). *Reckless endangerment: How outsized ambi- tion, greed, and corruption led to economic Armageddon*. New York: Times Books.

Mullen, A. (2009). The propaganda model after 20 years: Interview with Edward S. Herman & Noam Chomsky. *Westminster Papers in Communication and Culture, 6*(2), 12–22.

Mullen, A., & Klaehn, J. (2010). The Herman-Chomsky propaganda model: A critical approach to analyzing mass media behavior. *Sociology Compass, 4* (4), 215–229.

Myrdal, G. (1944). *An American dilemma: The Negro problem and modern democ- racy*. New York: Harper & Brothers.

Nacos, B.L., & Torres-Reyna, O. (2003). Framing Muslim-Americans before and after 9/11. In P. Norris, M. Kern & M. Just (Eds.), *Framing terrorism: The news media, the government and the public* (pp. 133–157). New York: Routledge.

Nechushtai, E. (2018). Could digital platforms capture the media through infrastructure? *Journalism, 19*, 1043–1058.

Nisbet, M.C. (2010). Knowledge into action: Framing the debates over climate change and poverty. In P. D'Angelo & J.A. Kuypers (Eds.), *Doing news framing analysis: Empirical and theoretical perspectives* (pp. 43–83). New York: Routledge.

Patterson, T.E. (1993). *Out of order.* New York: Knopf.

Perloff, R.M. (2000). The press and lynchings of African Americans. *Journal of Black Studies, 30*, 315–330.

Perloff, R.M. (2018). *The dynamics of political communication: Media and politics in a digital age* (2nd ed.). New York: Routledge.

Public attitudes toward the war in Iraq: 2003–2008. (2008, March 19). *Pew Research Center.* Online: www.pewresearch.org/2008/03/19/public-attitudes-toward-the-war... (Accessed: October 8, 2018).

Reese, S.D. (1990). The news paradigm and the ideology of objectivity: A socialist at *The Wall Street Journal. Critical Studies in Mass Communication, 7*, 390–409.

Reese, S.D. (2008). Theorizing a globalized journalism. In M. Löffelholz & D. Weaver (Eds.), *Global journalism research: Theories, methods, findings, future* (pp. 240–252). Hoboken, NJ: John Wiley & Sons.

Reese, S.D., & Lewis, S.C. (2009). Framing the war on terror: The internalization of policy in the US press. *Journalism, 10*, 777–797.

Roberts, G., & Klibanoff, H. (2006). *The race beat: The press, the civil rights struggle, and the awakening of a nation.*

Robinson, M.J. (1976). Public affairs television and the growth of political malaise: The case of "The Selling of the Pentagon". *American Political Science Review, 70*, 409–432.

Schiffrin, A. (2011). The U.S. press and the financial crisis. In A. Schiffrin (Ed.), *Bad news: How America's business press missed the story of the century* (pp. 1–21). New York: The New Press.

Schiffrin, A. (2018). Introduction to special issue on media capture. *Journalism, 19*, 1033–1042.

Shoemaker, P.J., & Reese, S.D. (2014). *Mediating the message in the 21st century: A media sociology perspective* (3rd ed.). New York: Routledge.

Shoemaker, P.J., & Vos, T.P. (2009). *Gatekeeping theory.* New York: Routledge.

Siapera, E. (2013). Platform infomediation and journalism. *Culture Machine, 14*, 1–28.

Soley, L.C., & Craig, R.L. (1992). Advertising pressures on newspapers: A survey. *Journal of Advertising, 21*(4), 1–10.

Soloski, J. (2019). The murky ownership of the journalistic enterprise. *Journalism, 20*, 159–162.

Sorkin, A.R. (2018, September 10). From Trump to trade, the financial crisis still resonates 10 years later. *The New York Times.* Online: www.nytimes.com/2018/09/10/business/dealbook/financial-... (Accessed: October 1, 2018).

Speer, I. (2017). Reframing the Iraq War: Official sources, dramatic events, and changes in media framing. *Journal of Communication, 67*, 282–302.

Starkman, D. (2014). *The watchdog that didn't bark: The financial crisis and the disappearance of investigative reporting.* New York: Columbia University Press.

Steiner, L. (2009). Gender in the newsroom. In K. Wahl-Jorgensen & T. Hanitzsch (Eds.), *The handbook of journalism studies* (pp. 116–129). Thousand Oaks, CA: Sage.

Usher, N. (2013). Ignored, uninterested, and the blame game: How *The New York Times*, Marketplace, and TheStreet distanced themselves from preventing the 2007 2009 financial crisis. *Journalism*, *14*, 190 207.

Wahl-Jorgensen, K., Bennett, L., & Taylor, G. (2017). The normalization of surveillance and the invisibility of digital citizenship: Media debates after the Snowden revelations. *International Journal of Communication*, *11*, 740–762.

Waisbord, S. (2011). Journalism, risk, and patriotism. In B. Zelizer & S. Allan (Eds.), *Journalism after September 11* (2nd ed., pp. 273–291). New York: Routledge.

Wakabayashi, D., & Benner, K. (2018). How Google has protected its elite men. *The New York Times*, A1, A16.

Williams, R. (1977). *Marxism and literature*. Oxford, UK: Oxford University Press.

Woodall, A. (2018). Media capture in the era of megaleaks. *Journalism*, *19*, 1182–1195.

Wyman, D.S. (1984). *The abandonment of the Jews: America and the Holocaust*. New York: Pantheon Books.

Zelizer, B., & Allan, S. (2011). Introduction: When trauma shapes the news. In B. Zelizer & S. Allan (Eds.), *Journalism after September 11* (2nd ed., pp. 1–31). New York: Routledge.

Zernike, K., & Steel, E. (2018, September 30). Fight over Kavanaugh shows the power, and limits, of #MeToo. *The New York Times*, *1*, 25.

11 Epilogue

Newspaper death watch. Print apocalypse. Journalism in crisis.

These are among the memes that have circulated in recent years to describe the economic and technological challenges that threaten the fabric of journalism. This book has discussed them all, from tremors of social media eroding journalism's authority to the plunging drops in newspaper circulation, as alternative funding mechanisms flounder. News, a Jeffersonian cradle of democracy, is under siege from political leaders, who undercut the critical hold-their-feet-to-the-fire role of news with dangerous remonstrations that the best of journalism is fabricated and un-American. With social media awash in fake news that undermines the credibility of hard-working journalists, the public skeptical of the news business, news outlets themselves playing to the lowest common denominator to capture ratings, and media conglomerates manipulating the system to control economic markets, there are reasons to wonder about the viability of news and the larger journalistic project.

And yet journalism has always been in crisis, fearing the worst, as illustrated by the colonial newspaper in Pennsylvania that blanketed its pages in black borders in the wake of the British imposition of the Stamp Act, anticipating the demise of print. "Journalists have always been a hysterical lot," van Tuyll (2010) observes (p. 483), confronting disruptive innovations (Prenger & Deuze, 2017). Today is no different. Naturally, there are different views on the nature of, and just what constitutes, the contemporary crisis in news (Alexander, Breese, & Luengo, 2016). Is the crisis economic, ideological, rooted in a failure to sufficiently involve the public, or a multifaceted problem that differs, as a function of the media outlet (Waisbord, 2017)? Even so, there is consensus that technological and financial changes have transformed news, imperiling its mission. Journalism, scholars are wont to say, has lost its once-cohesive purpose and no longer controls the borders of the field (Ryfe, 2012).

Are there reasons for hope? Some believe there are, welcoming the decline in journalistic authority, which has privileged journalists over citizens for so many years, and heralding the growth of citizen journalism, with the multitude of web-based projects that give thoughtful individuals an ability to disseminate their stories across online media (Allan, 2013; Wahl-Jorgensen, 2017). "Worries about the past are fueling much innovation in the future of news," Ryfe (2012) observes (p. 184).

Journalism, scholars note with a nod to existentialism, is not static, but in a state of "becoming," as rigid boundaries bend, journalistic practices diversify, and storytelling moves to ever-more entrepreneurial platforms outside the space of traditional news (Deuze & Witschge, 2017; Singer, 2017). Complicating this heady optimism are darker trends of recent years with which you are all too familiar: dissemination of fabricated, digitally altered reports by extremist groups; proliferation of so-called news outlets that traffic not in news, in either the traditional or participatory/citizen journalism sense, but in ideologically biased accounts; algorithms that promote articles that reinforce, rather than broaden, citizens' worldviews; and concerns that informational, interpretive, and investigatory news has been trimmed, sliced, and eviscerated, replaced by listicles, clickbait, and lowest-common-denominator reports that shortchange the American public.

And yet, a silver lining remains. In this complex public space, in which conventional, participatory, and bogus sites coexist, there is increased recognition on the part of journalists, scholars, and devotees of the public square that news remains a vital resource and must develop new economic and technological resources if it is to survive. Ideas are burgeoning, and they mix private with public sector, offering new ways to tell stories. Ending our exploration of news on an optimistic note, one glimpses innovative funding models that recruit money for investigative reporting from foundations, rich donors, state government, and, ironically, even the classified advertising-decimating Craigslist, all concerned with the future of journalism (Bowles, 2018a; Brennen, 2009; Rojas, 2018).

In other cases, a nonprofit enterprise guided by an AmeriCorps model has given fellowships for reporting in smaller, journalism-starved locales; start-ups are affording readers more control over content, including an online civic commons project with software that neatly organizes discussions by topic. Other models feature collaborations among university, ethnic media, and community activists, as well as conventional journalists themselves, to develop proactive, constructive, solutions-oriented stories to pressing problems (Bowles, 2018b; Hermans & Gyldensted, 2019; McIntyre, 2019; Peiser, 2018a; Ryfe, 2012; Wenzel et al., 2018; Zelizer, 2017)

Innovative story-telling strategies have harnessed online comics and gaming simulations, such as the simulation in a newspaper series on cell phone-distracted driving, where users navigated an online car through highway toll booths, texting at the same time to illustrate texting-while-driving dangers in ways print could not (Delkic, 2018; Usher, 2014). Another story used crowdsourcing, gathering recollections from teachers on how they struggle with deteriorating conditions in schools and

publishing teachers' own photographs and stories, fact-checked by reporters (Van Syckle, 2018). Updating public and citizen journalism, news
outlets have collaborated with an online journalism site that gathers
information in response to citizens' questions, while also partnering
with community volunteers to examine how thoroughly Ohio police
departments followed up rape kit results, calling on volunteers to gain
and verify information (Dissell, 2018). Technologies can enhance the
traditional watchdog function, as use of data science, algorithms, and
computational techniques promise insights into secretive elite practices,
like campaign finance violations, as well as identifying false social media
claims perpetrated by political elites, documenting fake video images,
and adjudicating different factual accounts of violent protests (Hamilton, 2016; Russell, 2019).

Infused by new technologies, as well as new financial models – spanning private foundation-funded outlets, entrepreneurial platforms,
financed by crowdfunding, and nonprofit newsrooms – innovations
promise hopeful change (Ferrier & Mays, 2018; Singer, 2017). Let's not
forget podcasts, which have more than tripled of late, as news organizations spanning the *Guardian*, Vox, and Axios are linking up with mobile
device-connected listeners, combining professionalism with profit (Peiser,
2018b). Far from dying on the journalistic vine, innovative journalists
are launching new platforms that discuss solutions to community problems, such as the Solutions Journalism Network and The Constructive
Institute, or explore broad issues and urban problems overlooked by
conventional media, exemplified by News Deeply and CityLab.

With new models, questions emerge, including, on the economic front,
whether non-private sector funders, like foundations and state government, will seek to control news output, how effectively new interactive
techniques tell complex stories, whether innovative platforms offering
solutions discuss their pitfalls as well as possibilities, if solutions-oriented
articles evaluate the merit of different solutions, and the degree to which
innovative citizen journalism projects are more likely to occur in upscale
communities than in less affluent neighborhoods that need them more.

Conventional journalism continues apace in the new milieu, explaining
how migrants cope with unbearable quandaries, exposing corrupt corridors in the government, and offering diverse frameworks on social
problems, while at the same time raising a panoply of questions, discussed throughout this book, about the ability of news to comprehensively cover issues in the wake of organizational, economic, and
ideological pressures. Through it all, the edgy social media environment
is testing journalism, raising concerns about whether reliable, credible
news can find a viewing audience on new technological devices. Scholars
emphasize that journalism must rise to the challenge, affirm its mission,
and strive to be relevant to the public, remaining resilient in the face of
commercial strain and political pressures (Wasserman, 2019).

Journalism is in flux, as it frequently is. The fundamental verities – verification, along with interpretive, watchdog, and democratic dialogue functions – continue, of course. However, blurred boundaries, novel news-gathering techniques, and readers' restiveness coexist and collide. Will news survive? If history is any guide, and it usually is, the answer is, Yes. Young people still want to be journalists. The number of students majoring in journalism has risen, partly as a result of anger at national leaders' contempt for the press (Anderson, 2018). Journalism, as noted earlier, cognizant that it must adapt to survive, is nothing if not inventive, with thoughtful blogs, new strategies to involve audiences in public service investigative articles, and innovative methods to employ verification to corroborate users' online posts (Schudson, 2016; Singer, 2019).

News, Marshall (2011) notes, "will endure for a few simple reasons. People are curious about the world around then. They want to make sure no one is taking advantage of them. They like a good story. And they want to know the truth" (p. 216).

Truth is the centerpiece of journalism. It remains the province of journalists, broadly defined, to stand for truth and call out falsehoods that emerge in the cacophonous, ethically challenged public sphere. Journalism is changing, but remains important, vital to the future of the democratic project, increasingly fragile but of central import to society and a robust public life.

References

Alexander, J.C., Breese, E.B., & Luengo, M. (Eds.) (2016). *The crisis of journalism reconsidered: Democratic culture, professional codes, digital future.* New York: Cambridge University Press.

Allan, S. (2013). *Citizen witnessing.* New York: Polity Press.

Anderson, N. (2018, September 16). A Trump effect at journalism schools? Colleges see a surge in admissions. *The Washington Post.* Online: www.washingtonpost.com/local/education/a-trump-effect-at. (Acccessed: November 23, 2018).

Bowles, N. (2018a, September 24). A news site dedicated to peering at Big Tech and its surprise effects. *The New York Times*, B4.

Bowles, N. (2018b, April 16). A new way newsrooms can get help. *The New York Times*, B1, B3.

Brennen, B. (2009). The future of journalism. *Journalism, 10*, 300–302.

Delkic, M. (2018, May 29). More than words can say. *The New York Times*, A2.

Deuze, M., & Witschge, T. (2017). What journalism becomes. In C. Peters & M. Broersma (Eds.), *Rethinking journalism again: Societal role and public relevance in a digital age* (pp. 115–130). New York: Routledge.

Dissell, R. (2018, October 21). Follow-up to rape kit tests is uneven. *The Plain Dealer*, A1, A12-A13.

Ferrier, M., & Mays, E. (Eds.) (2018). *Media innovation and entrepreneurship.* Online: https://press.rebus.community/media-innovation-and-entrepreneurship/. (Accessed: February 15, 2019).

Hamilton, J.T. (2016). *Democracy's detectives: The economics of investigative journalism.* Cambridge, MA: Harvard University Press.

Hermans, L., & Gyldensted, C. (2019). Elements of constructive journalism: Characteristics, practical application and audience valuation. *Journalism, 20,* 535–551.

Marshall, J. (2011). *Watergate's legacy and the press: The investigative impulse.* Evanston, IL: Northwestern University Press.

McIntyre, K. (2019). Solutions journalism. *Journalism Practice, 13,* 16–34.

Peiser, J. (2018a, June 18). *Denver Post* defectors and blockchain start-up team up in news outlet. *The New York Times,* B4.

Peiser, J. (2018b, December 10). Podcasts are getting newsier: Here are 8 that are worth a listen. *The New York Times,* B4.

Prenger, M., & Deuze, M. (2017). A history of innovation and entrepreneurialism in journalism. In P.J. Boczkowski & C.W. Anderson (Eds.), *Remaking the news: Essays on the future of journalism scholarship in the digital age* (pp. 235–250). Cambridge, MA: The MIT Press.

Rojas, R. (2018, July 31). State wants to pay journalists to cover schools and potholes. *The New York Times,* A1, A20.

Russell, A. (2019). "This time it's different": Covering threats to journalism and the eroding public sphere. *Journalism, 20,* 32–35.

Ryfe, D.M. (2012). *Can journalism survive? An inside look at American newsrooms.* Cambridge, UK: Polity Press.

Schudson, M. (2016). The crisis in news: Can you whistle a happy tune? In J. C. Alexander, E.B. Breese & M. Luengo (Eds.), *The crisis of journalism reconsidered: Democratic culture, professional codes, digital future* (pp. 98–115). New York: Cambridge University Press.

Singer, J.B. (2017). The journalist as entrepreneur. In C. Peters & M. Broersma (Eds.), *Rethinking journalism again: Societal role and public relevance in a digital age* (pp. 131–145). New York: Routledge.

Singer, J.B. (2019). Habits of practice, habits of thought. *Journalism, 20,* 135–139.

Usher, N. (2014). *Making news at The New York Times.* Ann Arbor, MI: University of Michigan Press.

Van Syckle, K. (2018, July 20). "The power of the crowd." *The New York Times,* A2.

van Tuyll, D.R. (2010). The past is prologue, or how nineteenth-century journalism might just save twenty-first-century newspapers. *Journalism Studies, 11,* 477–486.

Wahl-Jorgensen, K. (2017). Is there a "postmodern turn" in journalism? In C. Peters & M. Broersma (Eds.), *Rethinking journalism again: Societal role and public relevance in a digital age* (pp. 97–111). New York: Routledge.

Waisbord, S. (2017). Afterword: Crisis? What crisis? In C. Peters & M. Broersma (Eds.), *Rethinking journalism again: Societal role and public relevance in a digital age* (pp. 205–215). New York: Routledge.

Wasserman, H. (2019). Relevance, resistance, resilience: Journalism's challenges in a global world. *Journalism, 20,* 229–232.

Wenzel, A., Gerson, D., Moreno, E., Son, M., & Morrison Hawkins, B. (2018). Engaging stigmatized communities through solutions journalism: Residents of South Los Angeles respond. *Journalism, 19,* 649–667.

Zelizer, B. (2017). *What journalism could be.* Cambridge, UK: Polity Press.

Index

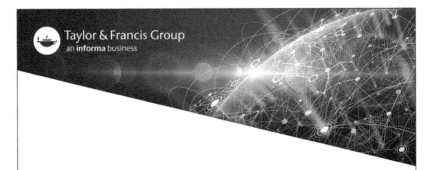